# Public Sphere and Experience

## *Toward an Analysis of the*

## *Bourgeois and Proletarian*

## *Public Sphere*

Oskar Negt and Alexander Kluge

Foreword by Miriam Hansen

Translated by Peter Labanyi, Jamie Owen Daniel, and
Assenka Oksiloff

VERSO

London • New York

This edition first published by Verso 2016
First published in English by the University of Minnesota Press 1993
First published as *Öffentlichkeit und Erfahrung: Zur Organisationsanalyse
von bürgerlicher und prôletarishcer öffentlichkeit*
© Suhrkamp Verlag, Frankfurt 1972

3 5 7 9 10 8 6 4 2

**Verso**
UK: 6 Meard Street, London W1F 0EG
US: 20 Jay Street, Suite 1010, Brooklyn, NY 11201
versobooks.com

Verso is the imprint of New Left Books

ISBN-13: 978-1-78478-241-2
eISBN-13: 978-1-78478-243-6 (US)
eISBN-13: 978-1-78478-242-9 (UK)

**British Library Cataloguing in Publication Data**
A catalogue record for this book is available from the British Library

**The Hardcover Edition Has Been Catalogued by the Library of Congress As Follows:**

Negt, Oskar.
[öffentlichkeit und Erfahrung.   English]
    Public sphere and experience   :   toward an analysis of the bourgeois and
proletarian publica phere  /  Oskar Negt and Alexander Kluge   :   foreword by Miriam
    Hansen:   ;   translated by Peter Labanyi, Jamie Daniel, and Assenka Oksiloff.
            p.   cm. – (Theory and history of literature   ;   v. 85)
                Includes bibliographical references and index.
                    ISBN 0-8166-2031-8 (alk. paper)
    1. Mass media – Social aspects.   2. Public relations and politics.   3. Social
        classes. I. Kluge, Alexander, 1932–   .   II. Title.   III. Series.
                    HM258.N4313   1993
                        302.23 – dc20
                                                93-910
                                                CIP

Printed in the US by Maple Press

# Contents

# Foreword
*Miriam Hansen*

> *The public sphere is the site where struggles are decided by other*
> *means than war.*

Alexander Kluge

The belated English-language publication of German debates on the public sphere
is itself an example of the vicissitudes of the "public" in a postmodern age.[1] What
determines which theories enter the field of intellectual discourse, as a specialized
public sphere within a larger field of cultural "publicity"? How do certain concepts gain wider currency and when, at which juncture of academic paradigm
shifts, cultural politics, and publishing trends? To what extent can a conceptual
framework developed with regard to European formations of publicity be transferred to an American context? When Jürgen Habermas's influential *Habil*-thesis,

---

1. The German term *Öffentlichkeit* encompasses a variety of meanings that elude its English rendering as "public sphere." Like the latter, it implies to a spatial concept, the social sites or arenas where
meanings are articulated, distributed, and negotiated, as well as the collective body constituted by and
in this process, "the public." But *Öffentlichkeit* also denotes an ideational substance or criterion—
"*glasnost*" or openness (which has the same root in German, "*offen*")—that is produced both within
these sites and in larger, deterritorialized contexts; the English word "publicity" grasps this sense only
in its historically alienated form. In the dialectical tension between these two senses, Negt and Kluge
develop their concept of *Öffentlichkeit* as the "general horizon of social experience." See Peter
Labanyi, translator's note, "*The Public Sphere and Experience*: Selections," *October* 46 (Fall 1988):
60. For discussions and readings that helped shape this Foreword, I wish to thank the members of the
Mass Culture Workshop and the Committee on Critical Practice, University of Chicago, especially
Lauren Berlant, William Brown, Michael Geyer, Thomas Holt, Arthur Knight, Loren Kruger, and
Moishe Postone.

*The Structural Transformation of the Public Sphere* (1962), was published in English close to three decades later, critics mused over its "simultaneous relevance and anachronism."[2] Now that Negt and Kluge's study, *Public Sphere and Experience*, appears in translation twenty years after its initial publication in 1972, its temporal, political, and geocultural coordinates are just as much in question, if not more so.

How dated is it? How German is it? Instead of adjudicating upon the book's relative anachronism or contemporaneity, I will try to encircle the question of its current relevance through the back door of its historicity, its pivotal relation to the German seventies. Undoubtedly, the particular imbrication of *Public Sphere and Experience* with the historical moment will transport the reader through a time warp, with the added twist of cross-cultural comparison. But the book's historicity not only creates nostalgic or anachronistic effects (depending on where you were and how old you were at that time); it also suggests indirect routes of relevance to issues of the 1990s.

What may ensure the book more than a merely archeological interest is the unusual mixture of discourses, questions, and perspectives it mobilizes in pursuit of its subject. This is to some extent due to the different backgrounds of its authors, not only because they come from different academic disciplines and cultural professions but also because each individually had already strayed from the narrow paths of disciplinary and professional discourses. Oskar Negt, trained as a sociologist, had written an influential study on working-class culture, *Social Phantasy and Exemplary Learning: On the Theory and Practice of Worker's Education* (1966). Alexander Kluge, known in this country primarily as a filmmaker and promoter of independent German cinema, got his doctoral degree in law with a minor in religious music. By the time *Public Sphere and Experience* appeared, he had completed four feature films and several shorts, had published two volumes of stories, and was deeply involved in political battles over the Federal Film Subsidy Law. What brought them together was the context of the Frankfurt School—Negt was an assistant to Habermas, Kluge a friend and disciple of Adorno—and debates in the wake of the student movement about the relation between Critical Theory and social practice. If Negt's focus was on the problem of political organization and the role of culture and education in fostering working-class consciousness, Kluge's work revolved around the problem of an alternative film and media culture and the political and economic conditions that made such a culture both necessary and possible. Their concerns overlapped in the question of how social experience is articulated and becomes relevant—in other words, by which mechanisms and media, in whose interest, and to what effect a "social horizon of experience" is constituted. For Negt and Kluge, this question

---

2. Dana Polan, "The Public's Fear, or Media as Monster in Habermas, Negt, and Kluge," *Social Text* 25/26 (1990): 260.

was at the core of, if not synonymous with, the problem of the public sphere. More precisely, it challenged the very possibility of defining the "public" (and attendant divisions of public and private) in any singular, foundational, and ahistorical manner.

In a number of ways, Negt and Kluge's project has an affinity with recent debates in the United States. To be sure, nothing is new about the concept of the public sphere as such. There is a vast literature on the topic in American political and social thought, ranging from John Dewey, Walter Lippmann, C. Wright Mills, and Hannah Arendt through Jean Elshtain and Richard Sennett. Since the end of the 1980s, however, the term "public" has cropped up with a new urgency and concurrently in different disciplines and contexts—history, cinema and television studies, art criticism, feminist, gay and lesbian, postcolonial, and subaltern perspectives, to mention only a few. The term is now proliferating in titles of books, articles, and college courses. The Center for Transnational Cultural Studies (University of Pennsylvania) began in 1988 to publish its biannual bulletin under the title *Public Culture*. In 1990, the journal *Social Text* devoted a special issue (no. 25/26) to the "Phantom Public Sphere," containing critiques of Habermas as well as sections from Negt and Kluge's book. By alluding in their subtitle to Walter Lippmann's polemic of 1925, *The Phantom Public*, the editors signaled their attempt to bridge the American discourse on the public sphere with the German debate, whose reception had been limited by and large to more specialized journals like *New German Critique*.[3]

What distinguishes this recent concern with the category of the public from traditional approaches is a greater degree of disciplinary promiscuity, prompted in turn by a more direct engagement with contemporary political issues and social developments. These seem to fall into, roughly, three overlapping areas of contestation: (1) gender and sexuality, specifically, struggles over reproduction, childrearing, and the regulation of forms of sexual expression and intimacy; (2) race and ethnicity, specifically, the backlash against civil rights, the increase of ethnic-racial violence, separatism and nationalism, the question of identity politics; and (3) cutting across all these areas, the ineluctibly changed and changing relations of representation and reception, marked, on one level, by the accelerated globalization of the media of private and electronic consumption and, on another, by national controversies surrounding federal funding for the arts and the question of multiculturalism in the humanities.

In all these issues something is at stake that is neither wholly social nor wholly political but, rather, involves the dimension of the public. This dimension, how-

---

3. See, for instance, Jürgen Habermas, "The Public Sphere: An Encyclopedia Article" (1964), *New German Critique* 3 (Fall 1974): 49–55; Eberhard Knödler-Bunte, "The Proletarian Public Sphere and Political Organization," *New German Critique* 4 (Winter 1975): 51–75; also see Peter Uwe Hohendahl, *The Institution of Criticism* (Ithaca: Cornell University Press, 1982), chap. 7.

ever, can no longer be confined to the space of "public opinion" or to any other normative sense of the term; rather, it presents itself today in disparate locations and diverse, contradictory constellations. What does it mean, for instance, when antiabortion activists adopt tactics of resistance developed in the civil rights movement and the protests against the Vietnam War, that is, of oppositional groups that aimed to disrupt operations on the local level so as to tap the larger public sphere of nationwide television and press? What does it mean when feminists against pornography resort to censorship legislation, one of the oldest weapons from the bourgeois public sphere's arsenal of exclusions and disavowals? How does the growing homophobia in all sectors of public life accord with the assimilation of gay images by the fashion and life-style industry? Can the experience thus extracted be reappropriated, both by gay and lesbian subcultures and toward a general critique of norms of sexual identity and polarity? How do African-Americans negotiate the multiple rifts between their diasporic cultural heritages, white appropriations of them (in music, fashion, language), and a dominant media culture that still renders them stereotyped or marginal, barring them from anything but exceptional, spectacularized authorship, self-representation, and power? How can such cultural "hybridity" be mobilized in the political fight for social and economic equality?[4]

If these and similar questions are perceived today as part of the problematic of the public, it is itself a measure of major changes in the constitution of the public sphere, in the very fabric and parameters of experiential horizons. By a logic that is key to Negt and Kluge's concerns, the global unification of the public sphere through electronic media and transnational networks of production and consumption goes hand in hand with a diversification of appeals and constituencies, as the media strive to get an ever more "direct" grasp on the "raw material" of people's experience. This structural diversification, however, does not automatically translate into a "new cultural politics of difference" (Cornel West). On the contrary, it provokes powerful campaigns and mechanisms to prevent such a politics from making a difference that would go beyond subcultural networks or the masscultural moment, that would transform traditional institutions of culture and general education. The current "culture wars" over federal funding for art projects and exhibits, over humanities curricula and the status of the Western canon, are but one instance of such efforts, a reaction to the growing manifestation of diversity on American college campuses and other sectors of public life.

---

4. Cornel West, "The New Cultural Politics of Difference," in Russell Ferguson, Martha Gever, Trinh T. Minh-ha, Cornel West, eds., *Out There: Marginalization and Contemporary Cultures* (New York: New Museum of Contemporary Art; Cambridge, London: MIT Press, 1990): 19–36; 29. In this context, it is not insignificant that, ever since the early sixties, African-Americans have been attending movies—predominantly mainstream movies, but for the most part consumed in neighborhood theaters—more frequently than any other group; according to the *New York Times* (17 July 1991, B1), they currently constitute 25% of the audience (as opposed to 12% of the population).

The neoconservative attempts to restore an ostensibly value-free hierarchy of cultural values (that never existed to begin with) are a real threat, especially in a period of restrictive funding and budget cuts, and need to be fought vigorously and imaginatively. This, however, requires reformulating the issues from a wider perspective of structural changes in the public sphere, involving media and constituencies outside the traditional domains of literary culture. Compared, for instance, to the publicity machines of TV evangelism and the right-to-life movement, the intellectual battles conducted in such journals as *Commentary, The New Criterion, The New Republic, The New York Review of Books,* or, respectively, *The Nation* and *The Village Voice* appear like rearguard skirmishes in the public sphere of middlebrow journalism. This is not to dismiss the fight, say, over how art and literature—and which arts and literatures—get taught as irrelevant or anachronistic. The point is rather to recognize how the institutions of art and literature, including criticism and theory, have long since been recontextualized by other media of expression, representation, and reception. These media have in no way obviated the occupation with art and literature; but they irrevocably, as Walter Benjamin was among the first to observe, put into question claims to cultural centrality made in the name of art and literature, challenging their normative function for the constitution of the public sphere.

The new types of publicity that have been proliferating over the past decade or two, especially with the electronic media, not only urge us to rethink, once again, the function, scope, and mode of intellectual activity; they also force us to redefine the spatial, territorial, and geopolitical parameters of the public sphere. Traditional approaches tended to assume a public sphere delineated by national boundaries, even if the public was defined as a matrix capable of negotiating cosmopolitan diversity.[5] The restructuring and expansion of the communications industries on a transnational, global scale more than ever highlights the quotation marks around the terms of national culture and national identity. Indeed, the accelerated process of transnationalization makes it difficult to ground a concept of the public in any territorial entity, be it local, regional, or national.

In this process of deterritorialization, we witness the emergence of new, highly ambivalent forms of particularity and universality, specifically a redefinition of the local in relation to changing global structures.[6] On the one hand, the local is being reinvented as idiom and spectacle, masking the complexity of transnational financial, political, and cultural economies. Global issues are transmuted, in television newscasts and the press, into suburban and parochial terms: the world

---

5. See, for instance, Richard Sennett, *The Fall of Public Man: On the Social Psychology of Capitalism* (1974; New York: Vintage, 1978), chap. 3.

6. Arjun Appadurai, "Disjuncture and Difference in the Global Cultural Economy," *Theory, Culture & Society* (SAGE) 7.1–2 (1990): 295–310; 306f.; Mike Featherstone's introduction and other articles in this special issue on global culture. Also see Cynthia Schneider and Brian Wallis, *Global Television* (New York: Wedge Press; Cambridge: MIT Press, 1988).

seems to be governed from a golf course in Maine. On the other hand, the flow of commodities, technologies, and populations, of information, images, and narratives, of life-styles, means of expression, and modes of representation has also enriched the arsenal of alternative public spheres that continue to emerge and organize on the local level (e.g., Paper Tiger, Deep Dish Television and Edge, Pacifica Radio, the Chinese student movement, women's video production groups in Brazil).

At the same time, the global is fetishized in dominant publicity as a pseudo-public sphere, the "new world order" that means the defeat of communism instead of the beginning of a global politics of civil rights and ecology. This pseudo-public sphere thrives on the twin genres of inter/national spectacle (the Persian Gulf war, the events in Tiananmen Square, the demise of the Soviet Union) and the universal human interest story, a particular specialty of CNN. In the measure that televisual dramaturgies of global synthesis and transparency are being perfected, the "context of living" (Negt and Kluge's term "*Lebenszusammenhang*") of large populations in the United States, not to mention the rest of the world, appears increasingly disjointed, fragmented, and irrelevant. It is not that mass unemployment, pauperization, brutalization of social relations, pollution, the collapse of urban infrastructures, health care, and education systems are simply ignored or suppressed. But to the extent that these realities do come into the purview of mainstream publicity, they are represented in such a way that they appear separate and unrelated, rarely delegitimizing the master narratives of national identity and international leadership.

## The Seventies: Decade of Disjunction

Negt and Kluge could not foresee these developments when they were writing *Public Sphere and Experience* in the 1970s, nor would they have described them from the same vantage point. They were writing in a country in which the twin fixations on a problematic literary culture and on a problematic national identity continued—and continue—to preoccupy public life. In this context, however, Negt and Kluge provided a conceptual framework that galvanized political and critical reorientations closer to the concerns of the present. Specifically, these include the formation of the women's movement and the "new social movements," as well as significant developments in media theory and media practice.

From the perspective of the 1990s, the German seventies appear less like a decade that ostensibly encapsulates a particular "spirit" or epochal essence (such as "the twenties," or "the sixties") than a period of transition, a watershed between larger historical currents. The seventies began with the disintegration of the student movement, with the death of Theodor W. Adorno in 1969, with the election of the Federal Republic's first social-democratic chancellor, Willy Brandt, the same year; they reached one kind of ending in the "German Autumn" of 1977, with the kidnapping of a prominent industrialist, Hanns-Martin Schleyer, and the deaths of leading terrorists of the first generation, and another with the election of chancellor Helmut Kohl in 1982. The student movement had pushed at the limits of the bourgeois public sphere, challenging artificial divisions between academic freedom and citizenship and crystallizing a critical, oppositional force outside parliamentary and party politics (the so-called APO). By the early 1970s, that critical forum, itself in many ways still predicated on principles of bourgeois revolutionary publicity, was proliferating into a variety of causes and strategies, such as successive anti-imperialist campaigns, Marxist-Leninist party building and *Betriebsarbeit* (organizing of factory workers by joining their ranks), the regrouping of the antinuclear movement, the emerging women's movement and the struggle over the abortion law, the squatter movement and opposition to real estate speculation, the turn to oral history and histories of everyday life, the discovery of the political in the personal, rural communes, food coops, and consciousness-raising groups—activities that were obviously parallel to, if not patterned on, similar formations in the United States.[7]

In this situation, Negt and Kluge's book seemed to fulfill two major functions. For one thing, it offered an alternative to orthodox Marxist and Communist strategies and thereby absolved leftist intellectuals from having to engage in forms of organization that amounted to self-denial and nostalgic misreadings of contemporary social and cultural realities. For another, while mounting a radical critique of the dominant public sphere, Negt and Kluge maintained an emphatic notion of publicness derived from the systematic negation—whether by political exclusion or economic and ideological appropriation—of large realms of social experience by the former. By grounding their notion of a counterpublic (*Gegenöffentlichkeit*) in a more comprehensive "context of living," they offered a conceptual framework through which a number of diverse movements could identify and generalize their concerns. It is therefore no coincidence, Heide Schlüpmann observes, that *Public Sphere and Experience* came to figure "as a theoretical umbrella under which a left disintegrating into individuals, into ecological, peace, and women's movements, could once more imagine itself unified"—even if, as in the case of

---

7. On the German 1970s see, for instance, Michael Rutschky, *Erfahrungshunger: Ein Essay über die siebziger Jahre* (Frankfurt: Fischer, 1982), and Hanns-Josef Ortheil, *Köder, Beute und Schatten: Suchbewegungen* (Frankfurt: Fischer, 1985). On the "new social movements" in West Germany, see Karl-Werner Brand, *Aufbruch in eine andere Gesellschaft: Neue soziale Bewegungen in der Bundesrepublik* (Frankfurt, New York: Campus, 1984), and Brand, ed., *Neue soziale Bewegungen in Westeuropa und den USA im internationalen Vergleich* (Frankfurt, New York: Campus, 1985); Roland Roth and Dieter Rucht, eds., *Neue soziale Bewegungen in der Bundesrepublik* (Frankfurt, New York: Campus, 1987); Margit Mayer, "Social Movement Research and Social Movement Practice: The U.S. Pattern," in D. Rucht, ed., *Research on Social Movement: The State of the Art in Western Europe and the USA* (Frankfurt: Campus; Boulder, Colo.: Westview, 1991): 47–120.

the women's movement, that unity was largely deceptive and in many ways inhibiting.[8]

To someone reading the text independently of this context, it may seem odd that Negt and Kluge's book would have had such an effect. Proportionally, topics relating to the causes of the 1970s take up much less space than more traditional Marxist concerns (though, of course, the critique of the "ideology of the camp" and other comments on the historical failure of the labor movement clearly point beyond those concerns). Considering that the "new social movements" challenged the very centrality of the working class—and the validity of "productionist" definitions of class—for leftist politics, *Public Sphere and Experience* gives little attention to nonlabor issues or constituencies that might project an alternative organization of the public sphere. There is the section on "the public sphere of children" in the appendix, there are occasional references to the environment and war, and there are the controversial footnotes on a specifically "female productive force."[9] If the book nonetheless provided a rallying point for a whole spectrum of groups and movements, it did so not necessarily because it would have spoken to any particular cause or causes, but because it allowed these groups to think of their work as at once oppositional and public: to organize on the basis of specific and concrete interests yet in tandem with other marginalized groups and with a view to changing society as a whole. It may be that the epithet "proletarian" in Negt and Kluge's conceptualization of a counterpublic sphere was a slightly quaint, nostalgic effort to assert the continuity of Marxist thought. Yet it may also be that their self-conscious revival of an "anachronistic" concept allowed them to theorize something qualitively new under the mask of the old, to register major changes in the public sphere that were barely visible on the horizon.

What made the term "*Gegenöffentlichkeit*" such a powerful keyword during the German seventies was that it linked the notion of a critical and oppositional public sphere with another keyword of the decade—"*Erfahrung*" (experience). This term requires some translation, since it has different historical and theoretical resonances from its English and American counterpart, at least in contemporary colloquial usage. To begin with, *Erfahrung* does not have as much of an empiricist connotation as "experience," which links it to "expert" and "experiment" and tends to assume a basically unmediated, stable relationship between subject and object. The German root of "*fahren*" (to ride, to travel), by contrast, conveys a sense of mobility, of journeying, wandering, or cruising, implying both a temporal dimension, that is, duration, habit, repetition, and return, and a degree of risk to

8. Heide Schlüpmann, "Femininity as Productive Force: Kluge and Critical Theory," *New German Critique* 49 (special issue on Alexander Kluge) (Winter 1990): 69–78; 70.

9. See chapter 1, n. 35, chapter 6, n. 4; commentary 18, note 5. Also see Kluge, *Gelegenheitsarbeit einer Sklavin: Zur realistischen Methode* (Frankfurt: Suhrkamp, 1975): 223–41, and Negt and Kluge, *Geschichte und Eigensinn* (Frankfurt: Zweitausendeins, 1981): 309–40: "Der Anteil von der Frauenarbeit an der Menschenproduktion."

*Erfahrung*
*Erlebnis*

the experiencing subject (which is also present, though submerged, in the Latin root *periri* that links "experience" with "peril" and "perish"). These connotations distinguish *Erfahrung* from the more neutral, singular occurrence of *Erlebnis* (event, adventure), a meaning contained in the English term "experience." The distinction between *Erfahrung* and *Erlebnis* was, of course, crucial to Walter Benjamin, and it is this tradition, a theory of experience suggested, with different emphases, in the writings of Benjamin, Kracauer, and Adorno, that Negt and Kluge assume and resume in their book.[10]

Without going into the philosophical differences, one can trace a particular concern with the concept of experience in these writers—that is, Critical Theory of the 1920s and 1930s, including, for instance, Ernst Bloch—specifically, an attempt to grasp the changing nature of experience in modernity within a widely interpreted Marxist framework. While indebted to directions in *Lebensphilosophie* (especially Simmel, but also Bergson) and phenomenology, Critical Theory sought its answers more systematically on the borders of philosophy—by questioning the parameters of philosophy as a discourse and discipline and moving freely across the areas of history, sociology, and, in Adorno's case, aesthetic theory.[11] What seems significant about this concern with *Erfahrung*, especially in the writings of Benjamin and Kracauer (which were being rediscovered in the 1970s), is that the concept oscillates between an emphatic and an empirical pole: on the one hand, it refers to the capacities of having and reflecting upon experience, of seeing connections and relations, of juggling reality and fantasy, of remembering the past and imagining a different future; on the other, it entails the historical disintegration and transformation of these very capacities with the onslaught of industrialization, urbanization, and a modern culture of consumption. With a dialectical twist, then, experience in the emphatic sense comes to include the ability to register and negotiate the effects of historical fragmentation and loss, of rupture and change.

Accordingly, *Erfahrung* is seen as the matrix that mediates individual perception and social horizons of meaning, including the collective experience of alien-

10. On the distinction between *Erfahrung* and *Erlebnis*, see Benjamin, "On Some Motifs in Baudelaire" (1939), *Illuminations,* ed. and intr. Hannah Arendt (New York: Schocken, 1969): 163 and passim. Benjamin's interest in the self-destabilizing connotation of *Erfahrung* comes across, among other things, in the following quotation from Kafka: "I have experience . . . and I am not joking when I say that it is a seasickness on dry land" (*Illuminations* 130). Surely, the translation, in *Social Text* (25/26 [1990]: 24) of *Erfahrung* as "practical knowledge" misses the point.

11. See, for instance, Walter Benjamin, "Program of the Coming Philosophy" (1917), trans. Mark Ritter, *Philosophical Forum* 15.1–2 (Fall-Winter 1983–84): 41–51; Siegfried Kracauer, "Der Detektiv-Roman: Ein philosophischer Traktat" (1922–25), *Schriften* 1 (Frankfurt: Suhrkamp, 1971): 103-204; "Die Wartenden" (1922), *Schriften* 5.1 (Frankfurt: Suhrkamp, 1990): 160-70; Theodor W. Adorno, "Die Aktualität der Philosophie" (1931), *Gesammelte Schriften* 1 (Frankfurt: Suhrkamp, 1973): 325–44; "Erfahrungsgehalt" ("Drei Studien zu Hegel"), *Gesammelte Schriften* 5 (Frankfurt: Suhrkamp, 1970): 295–325.

ation, isolation, and privatization. As is well known, the relation of individual and collective experience was a major point of controversy between Adorno and Benjamin, as between the former and Kracauer.[12] It is no coincidence that these controversies erupted around the issue of mass culture, the vortex of social experience in the twentieth century. For Adorno, notably, any existing collectivity— under the homogenizing force of monopoly capitalism and fascism alike—could not be but false; truth was buried in nonidentity, to be grasped only in the paradoxical autonomy of modern(ist) art. Adorno knew well that the esoteric status of autonomous art was part and parcel of the capitalist logic that had produced its other half, the "culture industry"; as Andreas Huyssen put it, that any theory of modern culture had to recognize both high art and mass culture as "engaged in a compulsive *pas de deux*."[13] Adorno's concept of experience, however, remained predicated on the former, on the ruptured *promesse de bonheur* of autonomous works of art.

The problem is not simply that this aesthetic norm gave Adorno's concept of experience an individualistic and elitist bias—Benjamin and Kracauer were in many ways just as individualistic—but that it tended to arrest the dialectic of the emphatic and the empirical aspects of *Erfahrung* at one of the darkest moments in history. By pinning the conditions of the possibility of experience on the division between high and low art, Adorno not only hypostasized the difference between critical subjectivity and the subject of mass manipulation; he also denied the empirical possibility that new forms—and other kinds—of experience, new modes of expression, self-reflection, and intersubjectivity might emerge from the same cultural technologies that were destroying the old. In other words, he occluded the very dimensions of *Erfahrung* that Negt and Kluge were to stress in their attempt to reconceptualize the public from the perspective of experience: openness, inclusiveness, multiplicity, heterogeneity, unpredictability, conflict, contradiction, difference.

But to play Negt and Kluge against Adorno (and thus make their dedication of the book to him look like a curious gesture of disavowal) would be just as simplistic, and ahistorical to boot. At the end of the sixties, Adorno's notion of experience still held an enormous moral and political authority. It did so because it epitomized the catastrophe of German-Jewish history, a historical rupture that

12. See Adorno's response to Benjamin's Artwork Essay in "On the Fetish-Character in Music and the Regression of Listening" (1938), in Andrew Arato and Eike Gebhardt, *The Essential Frankfurt School Reader* (New York: Urizen, 1978): 299; Adorno's correspondence with Benjamin on the Artwork Essay and Benjamin's work on Baudelaire and the Paris Arcades (1935-38), trans. Harry Zohn, in Ernst Bloch et al., *Aesthetics and Politics* (London: Verso, 1980): 110–41; Adorno's letter to Kracauer, 25 July 1930, and Kracauer's response, 2 August 1930, Kracauer papers, Deutsches Literaturarchiv, Marbach a.N.

13. Andreas Huyssen, *After the Great Divide: Modernism, Mass Culture, Postmodernism* (Bloomington: Indiana University Press, 1986): 24.

continued to be very much present and unresolved. The decade was characterized, Michael Rutschky asserts, by the persistence of the "structure" of Adorno's central experience: "the essence [*Inbegriff*] of experience is horror"—"the horror that the object threatens to annihilate the subject without leaving a trace: whoever gets involved, whoever compromises, will be destroyed. . . . Life is not alive, no experience is that with reality."[14] Adorno's return from exile was of more than just symbolic significance: he had come to represent a traumatic absence—that of German-Jewish culture—even though that sense of "nonidentity" remained largely unacknowledged, encoded in the projects of negative dialectics, aesthetic theory, and dissenting sociology. Thus the "structure" of Adorno's experience was not merely a generalized perception of "horror"; it was the insistence on a fundamental *Zusammenhang* (relation, connection, context), the persistence of the past in the present that maintained the imperative to engage the legacy of mass annihilation across generational boundaries.

In the decade following Adorno's death (1969), however, the historical trajectory that had lent his experience, and the concept of experience based upon it, authority (at least in intellectual circles and the critical media) was no longer a binding force. By the end of the 1970s, the term *Erfahrung* had disintegrated into a variety of meanings: something that could be desired, privately owned, and consumed (as in the title of Rutschky's essay, "hunger for experience"); something that could be invoked to justify unreflected behavior ("*das ist halt meine Erfahrung* [that's my experience, period]"); something that could be cultivated and fetishized (as in the aesthetics of New Sensibility, e.g., Handke, Wenders); and, in a more complicated way, something that could be collectively reinvented (as in the public rituals of memory and mourning that began to mushroom, from *Holocaust* to *Heimat*, as working "through" the past became part of the quest for a "new" national identity).[15]

*Public Sphere and Experience* no doubt played a significant role in the dissemination of the term "*Erfahrung*" during the German seventies, for better or for worse. The book managed to turn an esoteric concept into a keyword for new cultural practices, such as nonacademic research projects on everyday life in the History Workshops, the revival of the gay and lesbian movement, or environmentalist and antinuclear campaigns (leading to the formation of the Green party). Indeed, the book helped bring into view kinds of experience that it itself had left unanalyzed, differences that eluded its heterosexual and ethnocentric lens. Suffice it here to evoke the experience of Turks or other diasporic groups who lack even the public status in the narrow sense that comes with citizenship, and who are

14. Rutschky, *Erfahrungshunger* 65, 64.

15. Michael Geyer and Miriam Hansen, "German-Jewish Memory and National Consciousness," in Geoffrey Hartman, ed., *Shapes of Memory: The Holocaust and Modern Memory*, forthcoming (Oxford: Basil Blackwell, 1993).

forced daily to negotiate multiple and conflicting horizons—kinship ties and values, industrial work discipline, the promises of life-style and consumer culture and, not least, the context of discrimination and violence of an increasingly xenophobic society.[16]

Finally, Negt and Kluge's book opened up the discussion of the material conditions of experience onto an arena that had previously figured only as an abstract term: the media of mass and consumer culture, in particular the so-called New Media. Critical Theory had registered and reflected upon the impact of the mass media early on; indeed, the debate on their social, political, and historical significance was a distinctive feature of Critical Theory from the 1920s through the 1940s. Its postwar successors, however, did little to develop this debate further, let alone to explore new developments in mass and consumer culture—developments that, after all, crucially affected the constitution and conceptualization of the public sphere.

In the context of the Frankfurt School (the members of the Institute for Social Research who had returned from exile and their disciples), the approach to mass culture that prevailed through the end of the 1960s was, by and large, that of the "Culture Industry," formulated by Horkheimer and Adorno in the historicophilosophical framework of *Dialectic of Enlightenment* (1944; first published 1947). Adorno had reiterated the thesis of "total manipulation and delusion" in his 1963 essay, "Culture Industry Reconsidered," and had extended his indictment to the administrative cultural order of the Federal Republic. Under the law of monopoly capitalism, the argument went, all cultural products were smitten with sameness, geared to the single purpose of reproducing the spectator/listener as consumer; any differentiation only advanced an ever greater homogenization and standardization, and any attempt to make a difference was doomed to be assimilated and thus to serve the validation of the system as a whole. Taken literally, that vision preempted the very idea of an alternative media practice on both aesthetic and sociological grounds, because of the media's technological basis and because of their imbrication with mass consumption. Yet Adorno himself went on to modify this absolutist stance in the last few years of his life. Among other things, he wrote an essay in support of "Young German cinema" and also resumed his earlier interest in film music—both, as I have suggested elsewhere, under the influence of Alexander Kluge.[17]

Habermas, in his 1962 study on the public sphere, basically remained within

---

16. Russell A. Berman, Azade Seyhan, and Arlene Akiko Teraoka, eds., *Special Issue on Minorities in German Culture, New German Critique* 46 (Winter 1989); Czarina Wilpert, "From Guestworkers to Immigrants (Migrant Workers and their Families in the FRG)," *New Community* 11.1/2 (1983): 137–42; "Migration and Ethnicity in a Non-Immigration Country: Foreigners in a United Germany," *New Community* 18.1 (October 1991): 49–62.

17. Adorno, "Transparencies on Film" (1966), trans. Thomas Y. Levin, *New German Critique* 24-25 (Fall/Winter 1981–82): 199–205; Hansen, "Introduction," ibid., 186–98. Shortly before his death in

*Acts of individuated reception, however uniform in mode*

the paradigm of the Culture Industry, at least with his account of the "disintegration" of the public sphere following the eighteenth century. A major factor in this disintegration was the shift from cultural *Räsonnement* to cultural consumption. Industrially produced and designed for mass consumption, culture could no longer function as the matrix of publicity in Habermas's sense, that is, as a discourse mediating between a subjectivity rooted in the intimate sphere (the bourgeois family) and the intersubjectivity of a self-constituting public sphere. Like Horkheimer and Adorno, Habermas does not blame the commodification of art as such; on the contrary, the rise of a capitalist market is the very condition of the notion of aesthetic autonomy, the assertion of culture as a domain separate from and above private economic interest. The point is that under advanced capitalism cultural artifacts are not just *also* commodities, resisting that status on the level of form, but are, in Adorno's words, "commodities through and through."[18] In the measure that the laws of the market pervaded and, in fact, came to generate cultural activity, Habermas contends, "the web of public communication unravelled into acts of individuated reception, however uniform in mode."[19] These acts of reception may take place under "public conditions," that is, as a mass event, but because they short-circuit the sphere of intimacy with "de-literarized," industrially and socially determined forms of publicity, they add up to nothing but a "pseudo-public sphere." *Pseudo-public sphere*

The Culture Industry paradigm also persisted, in a simplified version, in attitudes toward mass culture among the New Left. While the thesis of total manipulation was occasionally supplemented with Marcuse's notion of "repressive tolerance," the focus of opposition was primarily on the print media, notably the papers owned by Axel Springer. With Springer, the problem had found a personification, a political enemy who had perverted the principles of critical publicity. (It is no coincidence that one of the more successful projects of *Gegenöffentlichkeit* that evolved from the 1970s is the daily newspaper, *TAZ* [Berlin], which is sold by subscription and on newsstands, even in the provinces, and gets quoted on national television.)[20] Toward the electronic media, however, leftist intellectuals

1969, Adorno authorized the republication (or, rather, the first complete publication of the original German text) of *Composing for the Films* (New York: Oxford University Press, 1947), which he had coauthored with Hanns Eisler but then disavowed in the wake of McCarthyite attacks on Eisler's brother Gerhard. In the preface to the 1969 edition, Adorno expresses the hope to resume his interest in film music in another collaboration—this time with Alexander Kluge (repr. in *Gesammelte Schriften* 15 (Frankfurt: Suhrkamp, 1976): 144–46.

18. Adorno, "Culture Industry Revisited" (1963), trans. Anson G. Rabinbach, *New German Critique* 6 (Fall 1975): 13.

19. Habermas, *The Structural Transformation of the Public Sphere*, trans. Thomas Burger, with the assistance of Fredrick Lawrence (Cambridge: MIT Press, 1989): 161.

20. On *TAZ* and the alternative press in the context of West German counterpublic activity, see Karl-Heinz Stamm, *Alternative Öffentlichkeit: Aktionen, Interaktion und Erfahrungsproduktion* (Frankfurt, New York: Campus, 1988): 71–98, 139–46, 243–59.

maintained an almost Luddite hostility, a bourgeois fear of contamination with mass society; as a result, Hans Magnus Enzensberger charged in his programmatic essay, "Constituents of a Theory of the Media" (1970), a crucial area of cultural practice remained untheorized and uncontested.[21]

Enzensberger's essay marked a turn in new-leftist discourse on the media that was, in part at least, a return to Brecht and Benjamin. With its call for an alternative media practice, the essay anticipates key concerns of *Public Sphere and Experience*. Enzensberger restores to the media a critical ambivalence (reminiscent of Benjamin's assumption of the "double-edgedness" of the phenomena of consumer culture), insisting that their ideological practice and their mobilizing, utopian potential are dynamically interrelated. Against the thesis of total delusion and manipulation Enzensberger maintains that the success of the electronic media depends not so much on an insidious "sleight of hand" but on the "elemental power of deep social needs that come through even in the present depraved form of these media."[22] This power can be reappropriated by the masses, Enzensberger argues, because the homogenizing, depoliticizing use of the media in advanced capitalism does not essentially inhere in the technical structures of the apparatus. On the contrary, the electronic media in particular do not posit any fundamental opposition between sender and recipient. Hence, Enzensberger argues, borrowing from Brecht's radio theory, the media "have to be transformed from an apparatus of distribution into an apparatus of communication."[23] On the level of political practice, this "refunctioning of the apparatus" would require an active, aggressive production of publicity on the part of the masses, with the goal of reappropriating the representation of their experience. On the level of mass culture theory, Enzensberger's invocation of the Brechtian apothegm put into question more traditional Marxist (Lukácsian) oppositions between production and consumption, creation and reception. With his emphasis on the dynamics of appropriation and reappropriation, he shifted the discussion of masscultural reception from terms like disintegration, isolation, and manipulation to a framework allowing for the possibility of historically new and potentially democratic formations of publicity that emerged with the very media of consumption.

---

21. Hans Magnus Enzensberger, "Baukasten zu einer Theorie der Medien," *Kursbuch* 20 (March 1970): 159–86, trans. Stuart Hood, "Constituents of a Theory of the Media," in *Critical Essays* (New York: Continuum, 1982): 46—76.

22. Enzensberger, "Constituents" 60.

23. Enzensberger, "Constituents" 49 (trans. modified). Brecht's contributions to radio theory are reprinted in *Gesammelte Werke* 18 (Frankfurt: Suhrkamp, 1967): 117–34; excerpts trans. in: John Willett, ed., *Brecht on Theatre: 1918–1932* (New York: Hill & Wang, 1964): 51–53. Loren Kruger points out that Brecht's endorsement of the reversibility of the apparatus did not necessarily imply a techno-optimistic celebration of radio's emancipatory potential but that, on the contrary, the public, interactive dimension of radio was immediately subordinated to a Leninist, didactic-authoritarian conception of political art ("Radio Fatzer: Brecht, Müller and Broadcasting the 'Asozialen,'" lecture, MLA, 1990).

But neither the cultural-conservative hostility toward mass culture nor the techno-optimistic revival of Brecht and Benjamin were adequate to the changes brewing on the horizon of the German and European media landscape. These changes were somewhat delayed in the Federal Republic because of a longstanding tradition of state-sponsored culture. When in 1962 the signatories of the Oberhausen manifesto announced that "Papa's Kino" was dead, its efforts to foster a "Young" German cinema were directed primarily toward instituting a federal subsidy system for first films and establishing state-supported schools and programs in filmmaking. The enemy in this struggle was a monster with two heads: the moribund domestic industry (marked by certain continuities with the Third Reich in terms of stars, directors, and genres) and the American major companies that effectively controlled the West German market through monopolistic practices of distribution and exhibition (e.g., ownership of theater chains). The year of the Oberhausen manifesto, however, was also the year of the installation of "Telstar," a satellite that linked West German television to a global network of electronic publicity, thus allowing its patrons to participate in worldwide spectacles such as the Tokyo (1964) and Rome (1968) Olympics.[24]

The constitutionally guaranteed "public" status of West German television inhibited the full-scale economic exploitation of satellite and cable technology for at least two more decades. Although dependent on the market in many ways (the most obvious being the programming of American television series and feature films), public television continued to function as a protectionist niche for cultural productions that would otherwise not have been able to compete with commercial enterprises.[25] With the 1974 and 1979 amendments to the Film Subsidy Law, the Television Framework Agreement, television became one of the most important funding sources and exhibition outlets for independent filmmakers, whether commercially more established directors like Fassbinder, Schlöndorff, and Von Trotta or avant-gardists such as Ottinger and Schroeter. At the same time, though it no doubt enabled several outstanding films to come into existence, the institutionalization of television coproductions perpetuated the split between commercial cinema and the so-called authors' film (*Autorenfilm*)—and with it the basic problem of how to make films that resist commercial pressures and are still capable of speaking to a wider audience.

In this situation, Kluge played a remarkable role. On the one hand, he was a

---

24. Eric Rentschler, *West German Film in the Course of Time* (Bedford Hills, N.Y.: Redgrave, 1984), chap. 2; Thomas Elsaesser, *New German Cinema: A History* (New Brunswick, N.J.: Rutgers University Press, 1989), chap. 1; Siegfried Zielinski, *Audiovisionen: Kino und Fernsehen als Zwischenspiele in der Geschichte* (Reinbek bei Hamburg: Rowohlt, 1989), chap. 3; 206.

25. Richard Collins and Vincent Porter, *WDR and the Arbeiterfilm: Fassbinder, Ziewer and Others* (London: British Film Institute, 1981); Martin Blaney, "The Relation between the Film Industry and Television in the Federal Republic of Germany 1950–1985," doctoral dissertation, University of Bath, 1988.

major force in forging the legal and institutional framework for an independent film culture, from Oberhausen through the founding of the film academy at Ulm to the various revisions of the Film Subsidy Bill (his version of the "long march through the institutions"). On the other, he early on excoriated an authors' cinema that would naively assume the state-sponsored free space of the traditional arts and would exhaust itself in the production of isolated, esoteric works. Despite his adamant critique of the commercial media, Kluge insisted that the market, with its professed goal of catering to as many people as possible, still provided a better model for engaging the viewer's imagination than the bureaucratically protected enclaves of high culture.[26]

Together with Negt, Kluge elaborated this position in terms of the structural mechanisms of the public sphere, pinpointing the mutually paralyzing cohabitation of bourgeois and industrial forms of publicity. Thus, they analyze the organization of West German television as a bad compromise between the bourgeois public sphere (represented by agencies of the state, parties, churches, and institutions of high culture) and industrial forms of publicity: saddled with the ballast of "balanced programming," public television promotes, among other things, an inbuilt lack of time almost as bad as that of commercial broadcasting, yet without the latter's bid for the viewers' experience. The urgency of Negt and Kluge's critique derived from the fact that this compromise was more than ever threatened by developments from within the market, in particular the emergence of the so-called New Media—videotape and laser disc, cable and satellite broadcasting, new computer and telephone technologies—and their oligopolistic integration in transnational corporations (such as Bertelsmann and Berlusconi) that made Springer look like a minor feudal overlord. It is part of the historical significance of *Public Sphere and Experience* that its authors discerned the gravity of these developments as early as 1972, a good decade before critical intellectuals and cultural conservatives alike teamed up to decry the "industrialization of consciousness."[27] A general awareness of that process only set in when the Christian-Democratic administration, in response to massive lobbying efforts, loosened the constitutional restriction on private ownership of broadcasting stations and admitted private television channels. These satellite

26. Kluge, in Michael Dost, Florian Hopf, Alexander Kluge, *Filmwirtschaft in der BRD und in Europa: Götterdämmerung in Raten* (Munich: Hanser, 1973): 76–77 and passim. See also Miriam Hansen, "Cooperative Auteur Cinema and Oppositional Public Sphere: Alexander Kluge's Contribution to *Germany in Autumn,*" *New German Critique* 24–25 (Fall/Winter 1981–82): 36–56.

27. Klaus von Bismarck, Günter Gaus, Alexander Kluge, Ferdinand Sieger, *Industrialisierung des Bewußtseins: Eine kritische Auseinandersetzung mit den "neuen" Medien* (Munich, Zurich: Piper, 1985). See also Kraft Wetzel, ed., *Neue Medien kontra Filmkultur?* (Berlin: Spiess, 1987); Kay Hoffmann, *Am Ende Video—Video am Ende? Aspekte der Elektronisierung der Spielfilmindustrie* (Berlin: Bohn, 1990).

and cable-based channels are available for an additional fee ("pay TV") and air a considerably larger portion of entertainment programs than the public channels, including porn shows and violent action thrillers, as well as depoliticized, "soft" news programs such as CNN.

It is also significant that Kluge, first and more or less alone among German filmmakers, has been producing a weekly show for two of these commercial channels since 1985. In conjunction with a critical news magazine produced by *Der Spiegel*, Kluge's show, *Ten to Eleven*, features conversations with writers, actors, and directors, montage essays on particular topics, such as the archeology of advertising, nuclear fallout, cinema, the circus, and the guillotine, or his ingenious rereadings of famous opera plots.[28] How does this tally with Kluge's role as a champion of independent cinema and state sponsorship of film culture? The chapters, in *Public Sphere and Experience*, on the problematic status of public television may suggest an answer. Given its bureaucratic structure and generalized "will to program," public television, in Negt and Kluge's analysis, is much less capable of establishing even the semblance of communicative reciprocity that the privately owned, market-based media to some extent depend upon. As a kind of subversive mimesis, therefore, the critique of private television has to take the form of "counterproductions," programs that at once learn from and compete with the enemy at the most advanced technical and economic level.

But *Public Sphere and Experience* itself is still a book, not a film or a video. Nor does it push against the limits of that format in the manner of Negt and Kluge's subsequent collaboration, *Geschichte und Eigensinn* (History and Obstinacy/Autonomy, 1981). This 1,283-page book, which Fredric Jameson calls "something of a theoretical film," juxtaposes a vast variety of texts—economic history and statistics, fairy tales, comparative studies of warfare, disquisitions on physics, engineering, and psychoanalysis, domestic labor, animal and infant locomotion, a conversation with Wilhelm Reich, anecdotes about Marx and Kant—set off through contrasting typefaces, frames and blocks of white print on black and interacting with a vast variety of images, diagrams, lab photographs, film posters and film stills, popular and scientific illustrations, and much more.[29] A similar degree of discursive and graphic heterogeneity can be found in Kluge's films as well as his later volumes of stories and film "scripts"

28. Margaret Morse, "Ten to Eleven: Television by Alexander Kluge," *1989 American Film Institute Video Festival* (Los Angeles: The American Film Institute, 1989): 50–53; Miriam Hansen, "Reinventing the Nickelodeon: Notes on Kluge and Early Cinema," *October* 46 (Fall 1988): 178–98; Stuart Liebman, "On New German Cinema, Art, Enlightenment, and the Public Sphere: An Interview with Alexander Kluge," ibid., 23–59; 30ff.; Yvonne Rainer and Ernest Larsen, "'We Are Demolition Artists': An Interview with Alexander Kluge," *The Independent* (June 1989): 18–25; Gertrud Koch, "Alexander Kluge's Phantom of the Opera," *New German Critique* 49 (Winter 1990): 79–88.

29. Fredric Jameson, "On Negt and Kluge," *October* 46 (1988): 151f.

(such as *Die Patriotin* and *Die Macht der Gefühle*).[30] Compared to such textual promiscuity, *Public Sphere and Experience* "clearly suffers under the constraints of classical discursive form," as Jameson observes. This does not mean, however, that the book can be read as a unified theoretical work. What militates against such a reading is not only the proliferation of "excursus" and "commentaries" in the appendix but, most importantly, the polyphonic relation between text and notes, which are often, though not always, distinguished by the voices of the two collaborators. At times the notes may read like one of Kluge's idiosyncratic stories or exempla (for instance, notes 17 and 18 of chapter 5, or note 19, chapter 6); at times they will spin off from an argument in the text and develop it in another direction (note 19, chapter 1). Although the notes appear in smaller type, they do not always submit to an academic hierarchy of text and apparatus. Rather, they respond to the text from various speaking positions, multiplying perspectives on the argument at hand. Thus, they invite the reader to add his or her own examples, to raise questions that leave the text behind.

## Questions for the Nineties

In the remainder of this Foreword, I will sketch out some theoretical perspectives in Negt and Kluge's book that provide a trajectory from the changes imminent in the 1970s to questions that pose themselves with greater clarity and urgency in the 1990s.

Any reading of *Public Sphere and Experience* will have to take into account Habermas's *Structural Transformation of the Public Sphere*, a book that Negt and Kluge both assume and revise. Habermas's contribution to the debate rests primarily on two points: (1) his attempt to reconstruct the public sphere as a fundamentally *historical* category, linked to the formation of bourgeois society under liberal capitalism; and (2) his delineation of the public as a *fourth* term, distinct from the state, the marketplace, and the intimate sphere of the family.

The distinction between the public (the condition of democratic politics) and the social (the domains of family and economy) had been emphasized by other theorists, notably Hannah Arendt, who developed both the distinction and its breakdown in relation to the Greek polis.[31] Habermas's historical grounding of

---

30. See, for instance, Kluge, *Neue Geschichten, Hefte 1–18: "Unheimlichkeit der Zeit"* (Frankfurt: Suhrkamp, 1977), selections translated by Joyce Rheuban in *October* 46 (Fall 1988): 103–16; *Die Patriotin: Texte/Bilder 1–6* (Frankfurt: Zweitausendeins, 1979); *Die Macht der Gefühle* (Frankfurt: Zweitausendeins, 1984). Also see "Kluge on Opera, Film, and Feelings," trans. Sara S. Poor and Miriam Hansen, *New German Critique* 49 (Winter 1990): 89–138, and Negt and Kluge, "Happiness and the Work of Relationality" (from *Geschichte und Eigensinn*), trans. Sara S. Poor, *Polygraph* 2/3 (1989): 186–92.

31. Hannah Arendt, *The Human Condition* (Chicago: University of Chicago Press, 1958), chap. 2. As Nancy Fraser points out, Habermas's more precise distinction of the public from, on the one hand,

the public sphere in the eighteenth century permits him to elaborate more concretely the dynamics that link the emancipation of the public as a distinct sphere to the very spheres of intimacy and property relations that were bracketed off as "private." Rooted in the sphere of familial intimacy, the subjectivity that subtended the bourgeois public sphere was articulated through the symbolic matrix of culture, especially writing, reading, and literary criticism—activities that challenged the interpretive monopoly of church and state authorities. The institutions of this reading public (salons, coffeehouses, book clubs, and the press) prepared the ground for a political public sphere, a forum of discursive interaction that was ostensibly open and accessible to all, where private citizens could discuss matters of public interest freely, rationally, and as equals. The bracketing of social and economic status, however, not only masked the persistence of power and interest; it also entailed the idealization of the nuclear family, as the source of a private autonomy whose economic origin and contingency were denied. The conflation of *bourgeois* and *homme*, of property owner/patriarch and human being, provided the bourgeois public sphere with a unity, albeit a fictive one. With the disintegration of that unity, Habermas concludes, the idea of humanity upon which it was founded collapsed into the ideology that naturalized the subjectivity of a particular class as "generally human."

As Habermas himself points out, his concept of the public sphere oscillates between an empirical and a normative pole: even as its historical, bourgeois foundations are disintegrating, the *idea* of the public, though never fully realized, continues to provide an objective standard for political critique.[32] Here is where Negt and Kluge mark their departure from Habermas's model. Specifically, they question the relation of idea and ideology in his conception of the public sphere, that is, his attempt to rescue an Enlightenment ideal from and, as it were, against its historical realization. The contradictions of the bourgeois public sphere, Negt and Kluge object, do not just erupt with its disintegration and decline; rather, they inhere in the very constitution of that public sphere. Whether in Kant's critical philosophy or in political practice, they argue, the bourgeois public sphere is founded on an abstract principle of generality, deployed in the fight against any and all particularity. In its abstractness, this principle of generality (the bracketing of social status and special interest) is no more human or democratic—and no less violent—than the universalizing tendency of the liberal-capitalist market that it presumes to set aside. Thus, from its inception, the bourgeois public's claim to represent a general will functions as a powerful mechanism of exclusion: the ex-

the sphere of the state and, on the other, that of the marketplace and paid employment is especially important in view of feminist discussions that tend to conflate these terms and use the term "public" "to refer to everything outside the domestic or familial sphere"; see Fraser, "Rethinking the Public Sphere: A Contribution to the Critique of Actually Existing Democracy," *Social Text* 25/26 (1990): 57.

32. Habermas, *Structural Transformation* 36, 160–61; Hohendahl, *Institution of Criticism* 246.

clusion of substantial social groups, such as workers, women, servants, as well as vital social issues, such as the material conditions of production and reproduction, including sexuality and childrearing—the exclusion of any difference that cannot be assimilated, rationalized, and subsumed.

The charge that Habermas idealizes the liberal public sphere has been leveled in recent years from a variety of positions. Feminist historians and theorists in particular have elaborated on the exclusionary nature of that public sphere with regard to women. Although Habermas notes a gender asymmetry between the—predominantly female—reading public and the political public, he fails to see, Joan Landes argues in her study on the French Revolution, that the gendering of the bourgeois public sphere was central to its foundation. Not only was one of its founding acts the suppression of an active female and feminist public sphere, that of the prerevolutionary *salonnières*, but the masculinization of public life also involved a restriction of women's activities to the domestic space and a concomitant alignment of the familial sphere with a new discourse of an idealized femininity.[33] Moreover, by accepting, albeit critically, the bourgeois public sphere's claim to represent *the* public in general, Habermas excludes from view any concurrent and competing formations of publicity. As historians such as Mary Ryan and Geoff Eley have elaborated for American and, respectively, European contexts, there arose, in Nancy Fraser's words, "virtually contemporaneous with the bourgeois public sphere . . . a host of competing counterpublics, including nationalist publics, popular peasant publics, elite women's publics, and working class publics." In other words, the contestation of the bourgeois public sphere's claim to unity and singularity did not just begin, as Habermas implies, in the second half of the nineteenth century.[34]

Although Negt and Kluge acutely discern the exclusionary mechanisms of the liberal-bourgeois public sphere, they share the gender blindness of Habermas's model; worse perhaps, by grounding their notion of a specifically "female productive force" in the needs-oriented relation between mother and child, they end up reinscribing the idealization of female subjectivity as maternal and familial—which Habermas at least recognized and analyzed as a historical and ideological construction. Nonetheless, I think that *Public Sphere and Experience* still offers a conceptual framework that could contribute to the current debate, in particular questions raised from feminist, gay/lesbian, diasporic, and subaltern perspectives. I see the book's theoretical challenge linked to the fact that Negt and Kluge set out

33. Joan Landes, *Women and the Public Sphere in the Age of the French Revolution* (Ithaca: Cornell University Press, 1988); for Habermas on women's role in the public sphere, see *Structural Transformation* 32–33, 47–48, 56.

34. Fraser, "Rethinking the Public Sphere" 61; Mary P. Ryan, *Women in Public: Between Banners and Ballots, 1825–1880* (Baltimore, London: Johns Hopkins University Press, 1990); Geoff Eley, "Nations, Publics, and Political Cultures: Placing Habermas in the Nineteenth Century," in *Habermas and the Public Sphere*, ed. Craig Calhoun (Cambridge: MIT Press, 1992).

radically to reconceptualize the very notion of the public from the perspective of the present, that is, proceeding from a situation dominated by industrially produced, electronically mediated forms of publicity. This perspective allows them to conceive of the public sphere as (1) an unstable mixture of different types of publicity, corresponding to different stages of economic, technical, and political organization; (2) a site of discursive contestation for and among multiple, diverse, and unequal constituencies; (3) a potentially unpredictable process due to overlaps and conjunctures between different types of publicity and diverse publics; and (4) a category containing a more comprehensive dimension for translating among diverse publics that is grounded in material structures, rather than abstract ideals, of universality.

In contrast with Habermas, Negt and Kluge insist on the need to understand postliberal, postliterary public formations in terms other than those of disintegration and decline (the Culture Industry approach). Moreover, they assert that it is impossible to define or describe *Öffentlichkeit* in the singular, as if it had any homogeneous substance. Rather, it can only be grasped as an accumulation or "aggregation of phenomena that have quite different characteristics and origins." They attempt to analyze this aggregation of phenomena by distinguishing, for heuristic purposes, three different *types* of public life—which, however, cannot be grasped in purity or isolation from each other but only in their mutual imbrication, in specific overlaps, cohabitations, and contradictions. Thus, in addition to the "classical," liberal-bourgeois model, they discern two other modes of organizing social experience—the "public spheres of production" (*Produktionsöffentlichkeiten*) and the "proletarian public sphere," prefigured in alternative and counterpublics.

The most ambivalent term among these is that of the "public spheres of production," especially in their late-capitalist, industrial incarnation. These forms of publicity differ from the liberal-bourgeois model in that they no longer pretend to a separate sphere above the marketplace but are an "immediate expression" of the process of production. They include a variety of contexts, ranging from "factory communities" and corporate public relations, through spaces of commerce and consumption, to the privately owned media of the "consciousness industry." Lacking political legitimation of their own, the branches of industrial-commercial publicity, especially the mass media, enter into alliances with the disintegrating classical public sphere, epitomized by the institutions of parliamentary representation and the state. Just as these institutions depend upon the former for a more comprehensive horizon—what would Senate hearings be without live coverage?—industrial-commercial publicity has tended to graft itself onto the remnants of a bourgeois public sphere for cultural respectability and legitimacy (e.g., the gentrification strategies of the American film industry, and other national cinemas, from about 1907 on).[35] These alliances usually work to reproduce dominant

---

35. Strategies of adorning the cinema with the trappings of high art and bourgeois culture (literary

ideology and, above all, to simulate the fictive coherence and transparency of a public sphere that is not one. But even as they adapt and reproduce the exclusionary mechanisms of the bourgeois prototype, the industrial-commercial public spheres depend, for economic reasons, upon a maximum of inclusion; hence they harbor the contradiction between immediate market interests and pressures of legitimation—a contradiction that cuts across and takes the place of the traditional opposition of public and private.

What makes this contradiction politically significant is a third element in the makeup of industrial-commercial publicity, the fact that the object of appropriation is the very "life context" of its consumers. Founded with the explicit purpose of making a profit, these public spheres voraciously absorb, as their "raw material," areas of human life previously bracketed from representation—if only to appropriate, commodify, and desubstantiate that material. Likewise, they often cater to social constituencies that had not been considered before as a public—if only to integrate them into the community of consumers. Thus, in their structural dynamic, Negt and Kluge contend, industrial-commercial forms of publicity bring into view a substantially different function of the public sphere: that of a "horizon of experience," a discourse grounded in the context of everyday life, in material, psychic, and social (re-)production.

While Habermas's notion of public life is predicated on formal conditions of communication (free association, equal participation, deliberation, polite argument), Negt and Kluge emphasize questions of constituency, concrete needs, interests, conflicts, protest, and power. Without using the Gramscian term, they describe mechanisms of exclusion and silencing as hegemonic principles and, conversely, formulate the contestation of those principles from the position of the subaltern.[36] While Habermas and, for that matter, theorists of "civil society" such as Charles Taylor, see the political function of the public sphere primarily in its

adaptations, historical epics, casting of stage celebrities, gentrification of exhibition venues) had a twofold purpose: (1) to avert the threat of censorship and antifilm campaigns and claim "public" status, that is, First Amendment protection; and (2) to attract better-paying, middle-class audiences. See Miriam Hansen, *Babel and Babylon: Spectatorship in American Silent Film* (Cambridge, Mass.: Harvard University Press, 1991): 63ff.

36. I am using the term "subaltern" here in the broad sense of Gramsci's *Prison Notebooks* (1947) rather than the more specific, postcolonial and poststructuralist inflection the term has acquired in the writings of Gayatri Chakravorty Spivak and the project of Subaltern Studies; see Spivak's by now classic essay, "Can the Subaltern Speak? Speculations on Widow Sacrifice," *Wedge* 7/8 (1985), rev. repr. in Cary Nelson and Lawrence Grossberg, *Marxism and the Interpretation of Culture* (London: Macmillan, 1988): 271–313; Edward Said's "Foreword" and Spivak's "Introduction" to *Selected Subaltern Studies*, ed. Ranajit Guha and Spivak (New York: Oxford University Press, 1988): v–x, 3–32. The shift to the conditions of subaltern representation and "speaking" no doubt has a parallel in Negt and Kluge's concern with the alienation, destruction, and fragmentation of the "proletarian" horizon of experience, including language, but their insistence on the dialectics of production seems incompatible with the linguistic skepticism that informs Spivak's theory.

ability to challenge, "determine or inflect the course of state policy," Negt and Kluge de-emphasize that function and extend the notion of politics to all social sites of production and reproduction.[37] Or, rather, they reverse the angle on the question of political efficacy to focus on the material conditions of its possibility—the structures that control what can be said and how and what cannot be said, which and whose experience is considered relevant and which irrelevant. The conflicts over those structures take place at diverse levels (local, national, global) and on many different fronts (workplace, party and union politics, education, family, sexual intimacy, associational life, consumption, media, individual consciousness); the issue for Negt and Kluge is in each case whether and to what extent experience is dis/organized from "above"—by the exclusionary standards of high culture or in the interest of property—or from "below," by the experiencing subjects themselves, on the basis of their context of living.[38]

The utopia of such a self-determined public sphere, which is ultimately a radical form of democracy, involves not just the empowerment of constituencies hitherto excluded from the space of public opinion, but also a different principle of organization, a different concept of public life. As a "counterconcept" to both bourgeois and industrial-commercial variants of publicity, Negt and Kluge develop the notion of a "proletarian" public sphere. As they note themselves, this term seems anachronistic. It is worth remembering, however, that in Marxian philosophy the proletariat, though predicated on the working class as the historical subject of alienated labor and living, is not an empirical category. It is a category of negation in both a critical and a utopian sense, referring to the fragmentation of human labor and existence and its dialectical opposite, the practical negation of existing conditions in their totality. While Negt and Kluge go out of their way to distinguish the proletarian public sphere from the sectarian and bureaucratized publics of party and labor organizations, they claim that rudimentary and ephemeral instances of the proletarian public sphere have already emerged in the past (their examples include English Chartism, Italian Maximalism, and certain moments in the October Revolution)—in the fissures, overlaps, and interstices of nonlinear historical processes.[39] But even if such vestiges did not exist, they con-

37. Charles Taylor, "Modes of Civil Society," *Public Culture* 3.1 (Fall 1990): 98. Negt and Kluge's shift in focus to the conditions of politics in the contexts of everyday life, typical of much of 1970s leftist theory in West Germany, does run the risk of losing sight of the State, as the agency that at once wields power and tries to make it invisible, and with it the political struggle bent on changing state policy—except, of course, in conflicts over public television and film subsidy.

38. The perspectival switch between the view from "above" and the view from "below" is a structuring principle in Kluge's story on the air raid of his hometown, "Der Luftangriff auf Halberstadt am 8. April 1945," *Neue Geschichten* 33–106; also see *Die Patriotin* 151 and passim.

39. Negt and Kluge's concept of history is indebted to the critique of historicism, progress, and linearity in writers like Bloch and Benjamin; in substance, their notion of a proletarian public sphere converges with English and American directions in social history, the tradition of history from the bottom up associated with the work of E. P. Thompson, Raymond Williams, and Herbert Gutman.

tend, the concept of a proletarian public sphere could be constructed, discursively, from its systematic negation, that is, from hegemonic efforts to suppress, fragment, delegitimize, or assimilate any public formation that suggests an alternative, autonomous organization of experience.

In that sense, the basic configuration of proletarian experience persists—into the present and for a wide range of subordinate groups. It persists in the negation of existing contexts of living on the part of the dominant public sphere, the alliance of classical-bourgeois and industrial-commercial publicity. While the latter subsumes large chunks of these life contexts in the interest of capitalist valorization, it rejects them qua context or *Zusammenhang*; it destroys, in Jameson's translation, their "relationality." From the perspective of the dominant pseudosynthesis, the life contexts of subordinate groups seem fragmented and disjointed, even if they appear momentarily synthesized in the media dramaturgy of the human-interest story or social reportage (as, for instance, by representing the individual fate, class, and environment of urban blacks as an "integral" narrative but one that only confirms their status as "other"). From the perspective of the experiencing subjects, however, these life contexts, to whatever degree appropriated and/or "othered" by dominant publicity, still constitute a *Zusammenhang*, a horizon of a different kind, which in turn makes dominant publicity look incoherent and arbitrary. This configuration is not just a duck-rabbit pattern of "inauthentic," dominant publicity and a repressed, "real" life context. Rather, it involves the dialectical interplay of three distinct elements: the experience of re/production under capitalist, that is, alienated conditions; the systematic blockage of that experience as a horizon in its own right, that is, the separation of the experiencing subjects from the networks of public expression and representation; and, as a response to that blockage, resistances and imaginative strategies grounded in the experience of alienated production—protest energies, psychic balancing acts, a penchant for personalization, individual and collective fantasy, and creative reappropriations.

This generalized notion of a "proletarian" public sphere is associated with, and to some extent hinges upon, a greatly expanded notion of production, indeed, as Jameson points out, a "most unseasonable foregrounding of the category of production itself." But, Jameson adds, Negt and Kluge understand production "in a very different way from fashionable and metaphorical, often cultural uses of [the] term in the Althusserian and post-Althusserian period."[40] For them, the notion of production is inseparable from the historical constitution of labor power, a topic they explore at great length in *Geschichte und Eigensinn*. On the one hand, labor power can be thought of only in conjunction with the historical process of "sepa-

---

40. Jameson, "On Negt and Kluge" 158. Christopher Pavsek, "Alexander Kluge and Postmodernism or Realism and the Public Sphere," unpublished ms., offers an interesting comparison between Negt and Kluge's expanded concept of production and similar notions in the work of Ernesto Laclau and Chantal Mouffe.

ration" (*Trennung*) (primitive accumulation, division of labor, commodification, reification, alienation); on the other, labor power contains and reproduces capacities and energies that exceed its realization in/as a commodity—resistance to separation, *Eigensinn* (stubbornness, self-will), self-regulation, cooperation, skills, and feelings in excess of capitalist valorization.[41] The later book not only traces the effects of capitalist production on the human body and senses, but also extends the model of labor power to a whole range of physiological, sexual, social, and national relations.

Similarly, *Public Sphere and Experience* assumes a comprehensive notion of "social production," in which the material production of commodities is but one particular formation, one that under capitalism, however, has dominated all other areas of social production. These include processes of socialization, language, libidinal structures, and the creation of intimacy, experience (as well as experience in generating the conditions for experience), structures of social interaction, and publicity—in short, the production of life contexts that can never be totally subsumed to the valorization interest and that produce, along with the commodity context, contradictions and mass doubt that delegitimize that very context.

Negt and Kluge's notion of production still contains an—equally unseasonable—utopian perspective, patterned on the Marxian axiom that social wealth is created, and can therefore be reappropriated, by the producing subjects.[42] In this regard, they also differ from current tendencies in Cultural Studies that focus on activities of consumption, at the expense of a critique of production, and tend to celebrate "the popular" as a site of resistance.[43] To be sure, Negt and Kluge's notion of the production of life contexts crucially includes practices of consumption, of masscultural reception and interpretation. In Kluge's concept of cinema, for instance, every spectator is already the producer of the film on screen, supplying labor of emotion, fantasy, experience to the media, which both assimilate and negate that productivity, usurping the role of producer.[44] Because of the ambiguous, unstable, and contradictory makeup of industrial-commercial publicity, this spectatorial initiative can be reclaimed, at particular junctures, in collective, subcultural formations of reception (crystallizing, for instance, around particular stars, genres, or modes of exhibition); the point, however, is to change the relations of production.

---

41. Oskar Negt and Alexander Kluge, *Geschichte und Eigensinn* (Frankfurt: Zweitausendeins, 1981), Part I.

42. This axiom is elaborated, as an at once epistemological and political problem, in Max Horkheimer's influential essay, "Traditional and Critical Theory" (1937), trans. Matthew J. O'Connell, *Critical Theory* (New York: Continuum, 1986): 188-243.

43. See, for example, John Fiske, *Reading the Popular* (Boston: Unwin Hyman, 1989), chap. 2: "Shopping for Pleasure."

44. Kluge, "On Film and the Public Sphere," trans. Thomas Y. Levin and Miriam Hansen, *New German Critique* 24–25 (Fall/Winter 1981–82): 206–20.

The fact that Negt and Kluge consider reception as a potential activity of reappropriation does not make them lose sight of the question of who controls the means of production or who benefits from the current organization of the pleasures and pressures of consumption. The possibility that they could be organized differently, in the interest of the producing/experiencing subjects rather than profit, provides a standard of critique for prevailing products and practices. This critique, in Negt and Kluge's view, cannot be limited to the ivory tower, but most effectively will take the form of "counterproductions," of an alternative media practice that intervenes in the contemporary public sphere (e.g., Paper Tiger, Edge, or Kluge's own media activities).

In the 1990s, Negt and Kluge's emphasis on production may appear less timely than the object or stake of an alternative politics of production, summarized in the book's closing sentence: "Proletarian public sphere is the name for a social, collective process of production that has as its object the human senses in their interrelatedness." This principle of *Zusammenhang* or "relationality" differs fundamentally from the spurious claims of combined bourgeois and industrial-commercial publicity to represent a coherent whole, from national subject to the "new world order." As Jameson points out, Negt and Kluge's principle of relationality no longer presumes a traditional Marxist-Hegelian notion of totality (though I think there is still a good deal of early Marx in their emphasis on an integral context of living). But, in a social order in which experience itself is irrevocably fragmented, what is at stake is the very possibility of making connections—between traditionally segregated domains of public and private, politics and everyday life, reality and fantasy, production and desire, between diverse and competing partial publics. Hence the insistence, on Kluge's part, on an aesthetics of montage in film and media practice, as a "morphology of relations" (*Formenwelt des Zusammenhangs*) that encourages the viewer to draw his or her own connections across generic divisions of fiction and documentary, of disparate realms and registers of experience.[45] In Jameson's words, "this act of relating will be, as a whole range of contemporary thought testifies, a punctual and discontinuous one, a provisional exchange of energies, a spark struck across boundaries of separation."[46]

However, since these boundaries are continuously shifting and being redrawn, Negt and Kluge might reply to Jameson, it is crucial that the work of relationality be more than a series of momentary sparks, that it include, above all, the capacity for remembering, an essential dimension of *Erfahrung* in the emphatic, Benjaminian sense. For Benjamin, the ability to gauge the distance between past and present was synonymous with the ability to imagine a different future, even though he knew well that both were declining rapidly. For Negt and Kluge, "the

---

45. Ibid., p. 206; on Kluge's concept of montage, see M. Hansen, "Alexander Kluge, Cinema and the Public Sphere: The Construction Site of Counter-History," *Discourse* 6 (Fall 1983): 53–74; 61–63.

46. Jameson, "On Negt and Kluge" 170.

assault of the present on the rest of time" (Kluge) is a key problem of the public sphere because it erodes the temporal matrix of the horizon of experience, the possibility of collective memory, which is the precondition for any counterhegemonic politics. How can experience, including that of organization, resistance and defeat, be remembered and transmitted over generations? How can individual and collective learning cycles interact under the regime of an industrial-capitalist temporality that divides life into a mere succession of valorizable chunks of time and fragmented leftovers? How do people make sense of the arbitrarily intersecting parameters of everyday life, individual life story, and history?[47]

In subsequent writings, both in *Geschichte und Eigensinn* and in separately authored publications, Negt and Kluge seem to have abandoned the epithet "proletarian" in conjunction with the public sphere. Kluge in particular has shifted his argument in the direction of an emphatic notion of public life reminiscent of Habermas and Richard Sennett, a vision of direct participation, openness, and self-reflexivity grounded in face-to-face relations, the territorial unity of urban space.[48] At the same time, he knows all too well that no local counterpublic can emerge today outside or independently of existing industrial-commercial, especially electronic, publicity. The latter is, quite evidently, deterritorialized, comprising transnational networks of distribution and consumption such as pop music and video, food and fashion industries, communications and information technologies. These deterritorialized forms of publicity are increasingly transacted in private, in networks of individual consumption: "commodities and industries now realize themselves in human beings. That is the battle line."[49] Since the local and the global have become irreversibly entwined in people's experience, the category of the local itself needs to be reconceptualized, beyond a nostalgic restoration of urban space, if it is to have any significance for an alternative or counterpublic sphere.

Inasmuch as Negt and Kluge's notion of a counterpublic is grounded in multi-

---

47. Kluge elaborates on the disjunctures of life stories and history in a number of films; see, for instance, the sequence entitled "The Relationship of a Love Story to History" in *The Patriot* (1979), in which a mirror shot of a couple, the man in uniform, is accompanied by the voice-over: "Rome, August 1939. Fred Tacke and his wife Hildegard, nee Gartman. This is their first trip together . . . September: he has to join his regiment . . . In 1953 Tacke returns from Russian captivity. Now they are expected to resume the love story of August 1939" (*Patriot* 109–12). Also see "The Assault of the Present on the Rest of Time" (1985), excerpts, trans. Tamara Evans and Stuart Liebman, *New German Critique* 49 (Winter 1990): 11–22.

48. For Kluge's Habermasian turn, see "On Film and the Public Sphere" 211–13; "Die Macht der Bewußtseinsindustrie und das Schicksal unserer Öffentlichkeit," in Bismarck et al., *Industrialisierung* 51–129; 59, 72–73 and passim; Kluge, ed., *Bestandsaufnahme: Utopie Film* (Frankfurt: Zweitausendeins, 1983): 49–50. For a critical view of territorial notions of the contemporary urban public sphere, see Vito Acconci, "Public Space in a Private Time," *Critical Inquiry* 16 (Summer 1990): 900–918.

49. Kluge, in Liebman, "Interview" 40.

ple and mediated contexts of production and consumption, it also differs from reinscriptions of the local with meanings surrounding the notion of "community." This distinction is particularly important in light of recent efforts to resuscitate the category of the community as a site of resistance, whether as a suppressed narrative for postcolonial politics or as a framing agenda for identity politics.[50] The ideal of community refers to a model of association patterned on family and kinship relations, on an affective language of love and loyalty, on assumptions of authenticity, homogeneity, and continuity, of inclusion and exclusion, identity and otherness. The notion of a counterpublic, by contrast, refers to a specifically modern phenomenon, contemporaneous with, and responding to, bourgeois and industrial-capitalist publicity. It offers forms of solidarity and reciprocity that are grounded in a collective experience of marginalization and expropriation, but these forms are inevitably experienced as mediated, no longer rooted in face-to-face relations, and subject to discursive conflict and negotiation. No doubt, the language of community provides a powerful matrix of identification and thus may function as a mobilizing force for transformative politics (e.g., in the African-American community and, in different ways, the gay/lesbian/queer movement). The counterpublic status and effectiveness of such language, however, depends upon two factors: (1) the extent to which it knows itself as rhetoric, as a trope of impossible authenticity, reinventing the promise of community through synthetic and syncretistic images; and (2) the extent to which it admits difference and differentiation within its own borders, is capable of accepting multiply determined sexual-social identities and identifications. The admission of discursive struggle into the process of subordinate groups, after all, is the condition of the possibility for different counterpublics to overlap and form alliances.

Once the public sphere is defined as a horizon for the organization of social experience, it follows that there are multiple and competing counterpublics, each marked by specific terms of exclusion (class, race, gender, sexual preference) in relation to dominant publicity, yet each understanding itself as a nucleus for an alternative organization of society. Negt and Kluge do not elaborate on the question of a plural counterpublic—perhaps because, compared to American conditions, the (West) German critical public of the seventies still seemed relatively homogeneous—although the great diversity of examples in the appendices clearly registers a sense of dispersal. It is only when they abandon the notion of the "proletarian" public sphere in the following decade that they explicitly address, in *Geschichte und Eigensinn*, the emergence of a wealth of dispersed activities that

50. For the distinction between the idea of "community" and a notion of the public grounded in the concept of civil society, see Partha Chatterjee, "A Response to Taylor's 'Modes of Civil Society,'" *Public Culture* 3.1 (Fall 1990): 119–32. For a critique of the concept of community, see Iris Marion Young, "The Ideal of Community and the Politics of Difference," in *Feminism and Postmodernism*, ed. Linda J. Nicholson (New York: Routledge, 1989): 300-323. Negt and Kluge touch on the idea of community, "*Gemeinschaft*," in chapter 2.

can no longer be subsumed under a common, generalizable concept of a single counterpublic.[51]

As developments in this country have shown, the "proliferation of subaltern counterpublics" (Nancy Fraser) does not necessarily lead to a multiplication of forces. Unless powerful efforts at alliances are made—and such efforts have been made, successfully, especially in the areas of ecology and health care—the oppositional energy of individual groups and subcultures is more often neutralized in the marketplace of multicultural pluralism or polarized in a reductive competition of victimizations (e.g., the splitting within the African-American community and between the latter and the women's movement over the Clarence Thomas confirmation hearings). Apart from the hegemonic interest in preventing counterpublic alliances, the structural problem that arises with the proliferation of counterpublics is, of course, one of translation, of communicating across a widening arena of discursive contestation. Discussing possible relations among multiple, competing publics in a hypothetical egalitarian, multicultural society, Fraser speaks of the need for "an additional, more comprehensive arena in which members of different, more limited publics talk across lines of cultural diversity." Thus, it may not be enough that individuals participate in more than one public; there may be "many different publics, including at least one public in which participants can deliberate as peers across lines of difference about policy that concerns them all."[52]

The need for a more comprehensive public appears evident; the alternative is ethnic-racial separatism and violence, religious crusades, civil war. The problem is that such a comprehensive horizon already exists—in the structures of the dominant public sphere, the violent pseudosynthesis of power, profit, and meaning—even though this horizon is becoming increasingly invisible, retreating into the functional. Therefore, it seems questionable whether a counterpublic horizon of translation can be constructed in the abstract, as an "additional" dimension, and how this could be done without once again resorting to the idealist universalism of the liberal-bourgeois public sphere, which after all sanctioned both formal and informal mechanisms of exclusion and subordination. The answer Negt and Kluge might offer is at once simple and daunting, and may indeed be the utopian core of their notion of a "proletarian" public sphere: that the universal structures for an inclusive, counterhegemonic public sphere have to be sought, not on the intellectual plane, but in the ongoing transformation of existing contexts of production and consumption, in the material dynamics of expropriation and reappropriation, of differentiation and globalization.

---

51. *Geschichte und Eigensinn* 484f. Explicitly questioned by Stuart Liebman, Kluge acknowledges the emergence of a plural counterpublic but then goes on to dismiss it as a "'Babylonian' phase," as a chaotic precondition for "building a public sphere anew" ("Interview" 44).

52. Fraser, "Rethinking the Public Sphere" 69–70.

*So good*

As long as a hypothetical egalitarian, multicultural society does not exist—it may not happen in our lifetime and it may look quite different from what we imagine—we have to confront the fact that not all counterpublics are equal or proceed from the same conditions of subalternity. Moreover, not every partial public is oppositional, and the boundaries between the two may be sliding or relative. We cannot speak of a proliferation of subaltern counterpublics unless we confront the proliferation of partial publics at large. Over the past decade or two, there has been a veritable explosion of partial publics, from the multimedia publicity crystallizing around traditional sports, through TV evangelism and pro-life organizations, to computer bulletin boards, video jukebox circuits, and telephone sex. What such partial publics have in common is that they operate through industrial-commercial venues; that they are usually not constructed on an identitarian model; that they organize vast constituencies (in the case of some electronic churches, whole social subsystems); but that their activities tend to remain more or less (in the case of sports, certainly less) hidden from public view, that is, from anyone who is not directly paying for and participating in them. This compartmentalization of issues and constituencies may be one of the markers, tentatively, that distinguish partial publics from counterpublics.

Whenever partial publics do come into the purview of a more general media public (broadcast news programs, national press), it is usually as a result of particular combinations, conjunctures, or collisions with other types of publicity. This seems to be the case, for instance, when the antiabortion movement tries to influence state and federal policy by resorting to the rhetoric and militant tactics of the 1960s counterpublics, while recycling elements of traditional religious and bourgeois ideology. At the same time, both organizational form and ideological focus of the antiabortion movement speak to some very real needs—such as ethical and emotional problems too long neglected by feminist and liberal publics—and thus succeed in binding massive psychosexual, social, and political energies. In quite a different way, such needs and energies come into public view in the state's attempt to regulate telephone sex, an electronically based partial public that mushroomed overnight and inevitably collided with even the most minimal understanding of communication as a public good and responsibility and attendant standards of bourgeois sexual morality.

But there is also the possibility that partial publics link up, at particular junctures, with otherwise separate or competing counterpublics and thereby create a window for a larger oppositional publicity. When basketball player Magic Johnson used his resignation upon having tested HIV positive to advocate safe sex he did more than put his star status in the service of a political cause; he made a connection, albeit a highly personalized one, between the industrial-commercial public sphere of sports, its local reappropriation within the African-American community, and the counterpublic struggle surrounding AIDS. While the latter is by now organized on an international scale, it continues to be marginalized

*Contiguity*

domestically as a "special interest," to be denied public status with reference to its roots in gay subculture. Johnson's gesture not only made public a concern that the neoconservative lobby has been trying to delegitimize as private; it also, if only temporarily, opened up a discursive arena, in both mainstream publicity and within the African-American community, in which sexual practices could be discussed and negotiated, rather than merely sensationalized or rendered taboo. Not least, it provided a way to return sex education to schools from which it had disappeared under Reagan.[53]

These examples illustrate two interrelated points that are key to Negt and Kluge's theory. One, the question of what constitutes a counterpublic cannot be answered in any singular, foundational manner but is a matter of relationality, of conjunctural shifts and alliances, of making connections with other publics and other types of publicity. It is the task of theory, Negt and Kluge assert in *Geschichte und Eigensinn*, to identify points of contiguity (*Berührungsstellen*), of overlap, among diverse and disparate counterpublic projects, just as it is the task of media professionals to carry information from one place of society to another, to establish lines of communication blocked or ignored by dominant publicity.[54] But it is also important to identify such points of contiguity with partial publics, in particular issues and areas in which they might transcend their limited agendas. Likewise, we need an analysis of the conjunctural dynamics of classical-liberal bodies of public representation, such as parliaments, which on their own hardly command more than administrative authority. Senate hearings and courtroom trials become public events because of live broadcasting, which increasingly adapts the style of daytime soap operas; this bricolage of formats and genres in turn complicates the script of the conflicts transacted and tends to make their outcome less predictable. A world-historical example of this conjunctural dynamic could be seen operating in the Soviet Union (and other countries of the former Soviet bloc), as a major factor advancing the demise of the party state: it was the conjuncture of popular protest, opposition within the party, and televisual coverage that created *glasnost* or "open"-ness (the root of the German word *Öffentlichkeit*).

Hence, and this is the second point, the debate on what constitutes a counterpublic has to take into account the irrevocably composite, hybrid makeup of any public sphere in postbourgeois, postliterary, and postcolonial societies. This composite quality is an effect both of the material—economic, technical—imbrication of distinct types of publicity and, concomitantly, of the coexistence of multiple,

53. I do not mean to privilege Johnson's intervention as a single cause nor to idealize the results; it had the effect it did in the context of other powerful, if relatively less "popular," efforts to forge a linkage between African-American and gay causes and challenge the assumptions of sexual/racial identity underlying the prevailing divisions and exclusions; I am thinking here in particular of the films *Tongues Untied* (1989, Marlon Riggs) and *Paris Is Burning* (1990, Jennie Livingston), both sponsored by PBS, and subject to controversies over public funding and access.

54. *Geschichte und Eigensinn* 484; Kluge, "On Film and the Public Sphere" 211–12.

*a process not a site*

interacting, and competing horizons of experience on the level of individual consciousness. We, as intellectuals, may or may not watch television or listen to talk radio, heavy metal, or rap; and we may associate counterpublic practices with writing, discussions, demonstrations, T-shirts, and bumper stickers. But none of these practices exist outside or independent of larger, more anonymous, electronically mediated forms of publicity, whether on the level of production, circulation, or reception.

It is one of the major advantages of Negt and Kluge's approach that they recognize the irrevocably mediated and syncretistic quality of modern or postmodern publicity, whether dominant or oppositional. They do not stake their utopia of a proletarian public sphere on the model of face-to-face relations—even though they insist on the necessity of such relations for the ecology of human consciousness. But neither do they celebrate the global proliferation of electronic media in the spirit of McLuhan. Rather, Negt and Kluge see the media of industrial-commercial publicity, in their most negative implications, as an inescapable horizon, and as the most advanced site of struggle over the organization of everyday experience which contextualizes all other sites.

Finally, for Negt and Kluge the public sphere is not so much a site as a process, and the possibility of change hinges on mobilizing the different temporal markers inscribed in different types of publicity. The cohabitation of uneven organizational structures of publicity contains a potential for instability, for accidental collisions and opportunities, for unpredictable conjunctures and aleatory developments—conditions under which alternative formations, collective interests, may gain a momentum of their own. A key source of instability is the dependence of industrial-commercial public spheres on other forms of public life: on the disintegrating institutions of bourgeois publicity for purposes of legitimation; on popular traditions or subaltern memory for experiential substance. These alliances not only tend to be precarious in themselves, because of conflicting vectors of interest; they also are subject to an accelerated pressure of modernization—hence they disintegrate almost as fast as they are formed, leaving mass-mediated shells of experience to be recycled and reappropriated.[55]

The seams and overlays between different types of publicity, conflicts between short-term economic interests and longstanding ideological norms, bricolages of deterritorialized media and participatory interaction—such hybrid, impure forms provide the blueprints from which counterpublics can and do emerge, the conditions under which industrially mediated experience can be reclaimed for the artic-

---

55. The utopian investment in the accelerated obsolescence of the modern commodity world echoes Benjamin's approach to mass and consumer culture in the nineteenth century, elaborated in his unfinished work on the Paris Arcades; see *Das Passagen-Werk,* ed. Rolf Tiedemann (Frankfurt: Suhrkamp, 1983), vol. 2: 1045 and passim; also see Benjamin, "Surrealism: The Last Snapshot of the European Intelligentsia" (1929), *Reflections,* trans. Edmund Jephcott (New York: Harcourt Brace Jovanovich, 1978): 181.

ulation of concrete needs and contradictions, for discursive struggles over sub-jectivity, meaning, and representation. Whether the margin of unpredictability, disjunction, and improvisation has increased with the 1980s turn to a post-Fordist economy of cultural diversification, or whether it is rendered irrelevant by the concomitant move toward ever-greater privatization, remains a crucial, and open question. As can be inferred from Negt and Kluge's critique of (West German) "public" television, the answers—and there will be surely more than one—can only be ambivalent, depending on the particular cultural and political constella-tion. One thing, however, seems clear: a cultural politics of counterpublicity can be founded neither on abstract ideals of universality nor on essentialist, identitari-an notions of community. Rather, it has to begin with understanding the complex dynamics of existing public spheres, their imbrication of global and local parame-ters, their syncretistic, unstable makeup, their particular modes of dis/organizing social and collective experience—gaps and overlaps that can be used for agency, solidarity, and the fashioning of a common future.

Chicago, December 1991

"mobilizing the different temporal markers inscribed in different types of publicity"

"cohabitation of uneven organizational structures of publicity"

# Introduction: On New Public Spheres

It has now been forty-eight years since we got together to write this book. Since then the public spheres of the seventies, which were the starting point for Habermas's *Structural Transformation of the Public Sphere* and our book, have changed shape massively. This is also true of the "counter–public spheres," which are of particular interest to us. And it is also the case with the category of the "proletarian context."

Meeting in Vienna last year we resumed our collaboration. We turned our attention to the latest developments, including the Internet as an imposing modern public sphere. We came to the conclusion, however, that the fundamental elements and forces, the antagonisms, had not changed across recent decades within the framework of such concepts as "experience," "public sphere" and "alienation." Alienation from individual productive forces and human resistance in the face of this alienation—both so relevant to the constitution of autonomous public spheres and thus of enlightenment and emancipation—have been displaced from what were once compact zones of industry to various parts of the globe, and driven ever further into the innermost realm of the individual. The dangers emanating from these developments are immeasurably greater than they were in 1972, but the counterforces are also manifest.

The consciousness industry and the gravitational conditions radiating from the stock market and the economy that we sketched out in Chapters 4 and 5, for example, have long since passed through the stage of "multimediality." The European media oligopolies we attacked now find that they are hopelessly defending themselves against innovations from Silicon Valley. Structures founded on contradiction end up spinning like a carrousel. Societal battles and characteristics are relocated to the innermost realm of the individual or else they emerge—in the other, objectified realm—as petrified structures of wealth and poverty stretching across entire continents. It is thus the case that the questions and search items underpinning our book—probing the constitution of experience and its expression within an autonomous public sphere—are merely *radicalized*. Radical questioning is proof of a larger "root system" (*radical* comes from the Latin *radix*, the root).

Neither of us believes that the human community, our *subjectivity*, as ancient as evolution itself, can be vanquished or desiccated, even when in many parts of the world we see the collapse of classical public spheres, and where intact public and counter–public spheres are in danger of being eclipsed by the media and advertising. Some of these tendencies are certainly extremely dangerous because market forces have learnt in the meantime to plunder the "interior décor of intimate thought," the libidinous forces necessary to the formation of the emancipated individual, the workshops of the ego, and to appropriate systematically the individual's potential desires, hopes and capacity for work. To adopt the conceptual framework of Marx: spiritual forces that hitherto had only been formally appropriated by capital have now undergone "real subsumption" on a grand scale. This is, however, in our opinion, precisely the point at which a countermovement can begin to take shape. It is a characteristic of libidinous forces that they learn from the experience of exploitation. Above all, they prove to be allergic to any form of heteronomy. They are by nature rebels.

In lieu of more and longer words, a short story (written after our meeting in Vienna):

### Sirens in the Age of Mechanical Reproduction

They stem from the spirit of the so-called commodity fetish, the tiny fragments of soul embedded within the commodity. They cannot be seen. In no way do they obey the advertising people, editors or start-ups that would like to employ them to stimulate the consumer's desire to buy things. Seductresses cannot themselves be seduced. They laugh at the dilettantes who try.

Yet the *commodity and service sector* is itself no fool. It is fuelled by millions of ideals. They pulverize particles of soul just as the wind crushes stone to form the sand of the Nefud. In a rock pan of this kind—if one may venture to call phantasy a rock—one finds the *sand of second nature*. Grains of desire, magnets. They draw fire from our hearts. They are the new sirens. They come into being spontaneously. No mere technology can beget them. As such they are "mechanically non-reproducible." Yet they belong to the age of mechanical reproduction. Amid the storm of modernity these seductresses fashion from the splinters of longing that are within us, yet beyond our control, a world *beside* the world.

Emancipation presupposes the acquisition of experience. For people to attain this with self-assurance they require not the media but an autonomous public sphere they have themselves produced. It is this that our book is about.

*Oskar Negt and Alexander Kluge, 2016*

# Chapter 1
# The Public Sphere as the Organization of Collective Experience

At the heart of our investigation lies the use-value of the public sphere. To what extent can the working class utilize this sphere? Which interests do ruling classes pursue by means of it? Every form of the public sphere must be examined in light of these questions.

It is difficult to determine the use-value of the public sphere because it is a historical concept of extraordinary fluidity. "The use of the terms 'public' and 'public sphere' reveals a diversity of competing meanings. These derive from different historical phases and, when applied simultaneously to the conditions of an industrially advanced society and the welfare state, amount to an opaque combination."[1]

To begin with, there is a limiting factor underlying the usage of the term. Public sphere is understood as the "epochally defining category" (Habermas) of the bourgeois public sphere. This definition, in turn, is derived from the **distributional network** of the public sphere. The latter thus appears as something invariable; the **form in which the public sphere manifests itself** conceals the actual social **structure of production** and, above all, the history of the development of its institutions.

Amid these restrictions, "public sphere" as a frame of reference fluctuates confusingly. The public sphere denotes specific **institutions**, agencies, practices (e.g., those connected with law enforcement, the press, public opinion, the public, public

---

1. Jürgen Habermas, *Strukturwandel der Öffentlichkeit*, 4th ed. (Neuwied and Berlin: 1969): 11. This book is a prerequisite to our discussions here, particularly those that pertain to the emergence of the context of the bourgeois public sphere.

sphere work, streets, and public squares); however, it is also a general social **horizon of experience** in which everything that is actually or ostensibly relevant for all members of society is integrated. Understood in this sense, the public sphere is a matter for a handful of professionals (e.g., politicians, editors, union officials) on the one hand, but, on the other, it is something that concerns everyone and that realizes itself only in people's minds, in a dimension of their consciousness.[2] In its fusion with the constellation of material interests in our "postbourgeois" society, the public sphere fluctuates between denoting a facade of legitimation that is capable of being deployed in diverse ways and denoting a mechanism for controlling the perception of what is revelant for society. In both of these aspects of its identity, the bourgeois public sphere shows itself to be illusory; it cannot, however, be equated with this illusion. As long as the contradiction between the growing socialization of human beings and the attenuated forms of their private life persists, the public sphere is simultaneously a genuine articulation of a fundamental social need. It is the only form of expression that links the members of society to one another by integrating their developing social characteristics.[3]

This ambiguity cannot be eliminated by definitions alone. These would not result in the actual "utilization of the public sphere" by the masses that are organized within it. **The ambiguity has its roots in the internal structure and his-**

---

2. In social practice there is repeated alternation between both uses of the concept of "public sphere." Something that is a purely private matter will be considered public simply because it belongs within the parameters of a public institution, or because it has been provided with the official seal of approval of a public authority. Something that is labeled a private matter, such as early childhood education, can in reality be a matter of great public interest.

3. In "On the Jewish Question," Marx analyzes the nineteenth-century state. According to Marx, "the political suppression of private property does not abolish private property; it actually presupposes its existence" (*The Marx-Engels Reader*, ed. Robert C. Tucker, trans. T. B. Bottomore [New York: W. W. Norton, 1972]: 31). Precisely because of the fact that it has declared differences of birth, social standing, and education to be nonpolitical, it does not sublate (*aufheben*) them as such, but rather confirms them as the materially existing elements upon which it itself is founded. The problem is not that it sublates these differences, but rather that it positions itself negatively toward them: this is the way it acknowledges them. What is accomplished here is a kind of doubling of society into, as Marx puts it, "a double existence—celestial and terrestrial. [Man] lives in the *political community*, where he regards himself as a *communal being*, and in *civil society*, where he acts simply as a private individual. . . . The political state, in relation to civil society, is just as spiritual as is heaven in relation to earth" (p. 32). For the nineteenth-century state, the public sphere corresponds to this heaven of ideas. This concept of public sphere is ambivalent. On the one hand, it tends to cling to the parallel of the state and bourgeois society; it claims its validity from the authority of the state. On the other hand, it tends to distinguish itself from the state as a sort of "authority of control and conscience." In this, it is able to bring together, on a synthetic level, the socialized characteristics of humanity that are accumulated in the private realm and within the process of alienated labor. The "public sphere" in this sense can be distinguished as much from the socialized process of labor as it can from private life and the state. The ambivalence of "public sphere" as a concept makes it impossible to determine objectively what is really of public interest; it is not a matter of a material level, but rather of one that is constructed.

torical function of this public sphere.[4] It is, however, possible to exclude from the outset *one* incorrect use of the concept: the swaying back and forth between an interpretation of the intellectual content (or, for that matter, of the actual fundamental need for public, social organization) and the reality of the bourgeois sphere. The decaying forms of the bourgeois public sphere can neither be salvaged nor interpreted through reference to the emphatic concept of a public sphere of the early bourgeoisie. The need that the masses have to orient themselves according to a public horizon of experience does nothing to reform the public sphere as a mere system of norms when this need is not genuinely articulated within this system. The alternation between an idealizing and a critical view of the public sphere does not lead to a dialectical, but rather to an ambivalent outcome: one moment the public sphere appears as something that can be utilized, the next as something that cannot. What needs to be done, rather, is to investigate the ideal history of the public sphere together with the history of its decay in order to highlight their identical mechanisms.

## The Concept of Experience and the Public Sphere

The public sphere possesses use-value when social experience organizes itself within it.[5] In the practices of a bourgeois mode of life and production, experience and organization have no specific relationship to the totality of society. These concepts are primarily used in a *technical* manner. The most important fundamental decisions about modes of organization and the constitution of experience *antedate* the establishment of the bourgeois mode of production. "What we call private is so only insofar as it is public. It has been public and must remain public in order that it can be, whether for a moment or for several

---

4. See also the more precise definition of the fundamental mechanisms of the bourgeois public sphere to be found in later sections of this book, such as chapters 2 and 6, and chapter 1, the section titled "The Processing of Social Experience by the New Public Spheres of Production."

5. This concept will be used initially in a general sense, and then more narrowly defined as the book proceeds. The organization of social experience can be undertaken on behalf of a specific dominant interest, or for the purpose of emancipation. For example, scholars or scientists can be interested in a worldwide exchange of their scholarly experience, which has as its object the domination of nature within forms of the scholarly, scientific public sphere, and therefore organize it, specifically and autonomously. A collective experience that is limited in this way will as a rule tend not to be concentrated into a political collective will that encompasses the whole of society. Another example is the interest of the dominant classes in linking the actual social and collective experience of the majority of the population to the illusion of a public sphere and a supposed political collective will and in this way organizing the suspension of this experience. While the use-value characteristics of many industrial products such as tables or bicycles are the same for almost everyone, determination of the use-value characteristics of the public sphere is fundamentally dependent on class interests, on the specific relationship between a particular interest that is linked to a specific public sphere and the whole of society.

thousand years, private."[6] "In order to be able to isolate capital as something private, one must be able to control wealth as something public, since raw materials and tools, money, and workers are in reality part of the public sphere. One can act in the market as an individual, one can buy it up, for instance, precisely because it is a social fact."[7]

The interdependent relationship between that which is private and the public sphere also applies to the way in which language, modes of social intercourse, and the public context come into being socially and publicly. Precisely because the important decisions regarding the horizon and the precise definitions of the organization of experience have been made in advance, it is possible to exert control in a purely technical manner.[8] In addition, bourgeois society's awareness of its own experience and the organization of that experience is almost consistently **analogous to genuinely existing commodity production**.

The value abstraction (above all the division of concrete and abstract labor) that underlies commodity production and has the world in its grip provides the model and can be recognized in the generalizations of state and public activities, in the law. Although anarchistic commodity production is motivated by private interest, in other words by the opposite of the collective will of society, it develops universally binding patterns. **These patterns are mistaken for and interpreted as products of the collective will, as if the actual relationships, which have only been acquired retroactively, were based upon this will.**

The structures of this bourgeois tradition also determine the way of life and production practices of the present, whose classes and individuals are themselves no longer citizens in the traditional sense. Today's middle classes, those sectors of the working class influenced by the bourgeois way of life such as students, the technical brainpower, all successors of the educated and petty-bourgeois class of

---

6. Ferruccio Rossi-Landi, "Kapital und Privateigentum in der Sprache," in *Ästhetik und Kommunikation* 7 (1972): 44.

7. Ibid.

8. The actual interaction between experience, its organization, and the horizon of the public sphere is also dialectical for bourgeois relations of production and does *not* function technically. This is not immediately apparent within the framework of everyday consciousness because the historical production of experience, organization, and public sphere disappears into its resulting product, the public sphere that determines the present. The apparatus of distribution of this public sphere, from which experience is in turn derived, can thus be experienced. This distributive public sphere is, however, now as before really determined by its *structure of production* as the overdetermining factor; this is based not simply on previous production, but rather is constantly reproduced anew from the everyday experience of the people who are subsumed beneath it. If one understands the essential context, production is that which overdetermines the public sphere. However, it appears not only to be separate from this context of production, but also as something exceptional vis-à-vis this production, as an independent sphere. In reality, though, the material context is such that the production of the public sphere precedes that of commodities, just as the production of spheres of circulation and distribution within the framework of commodity production is also a prerequisite of production, but the *production of this separation* is no longer apparent in the separation.

the nineteenth century, are repeating the individual elements of these models of organization and experience under late-capitalist conditions. The purely technical application of these models within the context of a mastery over nature and of the social network is no more elementary than it was in the bourgeois epoch. Perhaps the possibility of a purely technical functioning rests upon a high level of learning processes, of the socialization required by these learning processes, and of those decisions that are made in advance within a social and public context but are experienced subjectively as second nature. **The actual dialectical character of all of these preconditions only becomes clear if one goes back to this prehistory.**

In the classical theory of the bourgeoisie, this multilayeredness is reflected in the opposition between the concept of experience derived from the Humean tradition[9] and the critique of that concept in Hegelian philosophy. "The dialectical movement, which consciousness performs on itself, both on its knowledge as well as on its object, in so far as the new, true object emerges for consciousness from this movement, is in fact what is known as experience."[10] This dialectic concept of experience indicates the real workings of bourgeois society and any other society and its experience, regardless of whether the empirical subjects of this society are aware of the dialectic or not. In what follows, the concept of organized social experience derives from Hegel's definitions, which underlie the work of Marx as well. This is not to say that the concepts of experience and organized experience (in the sense of the dialectical social mediation of this experience) play only a subsidiary role in orthodox Marxist vocabulary.

---

9. The concept of the experience of empiricism, of receptivity, of the recognition of the given, of "merely contemplative materialism," attempts to dispose of the subject as a distorting intermediary. Thus this concept of experience seems to satisfy the claim of a heightened objectivity of knowledge. A second level of the concept of experience in bourgeois philosophy must be differentiated from this, one that is linked to the concept of the production of experience. In Kant, the only object of experience is that which is a product of the subject; this subject itself produces the rules and laws for the coherence of the phenomenal world. It experiences only that which it has itself already produced. For only in this way is it possible to create an experiential context that is separate from mere imagination. This experiential context is the functioning of the subject, which is, however, able to function only when it has an opposite, a block (Adorno), a thing-in-itself (*Ding an sich*), against which it must labor and which cannot be sublated in the functional mechanism of experience produced by this subject. One could say that the material production of the subject never allows itself to be completely appropriated. Everything that is real experience, that can be verified and repeated by other reasoning subjects, is the expression of a process of production that is founded not on isolated individuals, but rather characterizes the activity of a collective social total subject (*Gesamtsubjekt*) into which all activities that have to do with the encounter with internal and external nature are drawn. Experience is in a strict sense simultaneously a process of production and the reception of social contracts pertaining to the phenomenal manifestations of objects or their conformity to laws.

10. G. W. F. Hegel, *The Phenomenology of Mind*, trans. J. B. Baillie (New York and Evanston: Harper, 1967): 142. See also Theodor W. Adorno, "Erfahrungsgehalt," in *Drei Studien zur Hegel*: *Gesammelte Schriften*, vol. 5 (Frankfurt am Main: Suhrkamp, 1971): 295-325.

An individual worker—regardless of which section of the working class he belongs to and of how far his concrete labor differs from that of other sections—has "his own experiences."[11] **The horizon of these experiences is the unity of the proletarian context of living [*Lebenszusammenhang*].**[12] This context embraces both the ladder of production of this worker's commodity and use-value characteristics (socialization, the psychic structure of the individual, school, the acquisition of professional knowledge, leisure, mass media) as well as an element inseparable from this, namely, his induction into the production process. It is via this unified context, which he "experiences" publicly and privately, that he absorbs "society as a whole," the totality of the context of mystification.[13] He would have to be a philosopher to understand how his experience is produced, an experience that is at once preorganized and unorganized and simultaneously molds and merely accompanies his empirical life. He is prevented from understanding what is taking place through him because the media whereby experience is constituted (that is, language, psychic organization, the forms of social interaction, and the public sphere) all participate in the mystificatory context of commodity fetishism. Even if he did understand what was happening, he would still have no experience, but at least he would be able to analyze why he had none. Not even philosophers could produce social experience on an individual level. Before the worker registers this lack, he encounters a concept of experience derived from the natural sciences, which, in that narrow sector of social practice whose object is domination over nature, has a real function and suggestive power. He will take this scientific body of experience, which is not socially but rather technically programmed, as the form per se in which experience is secured. This will lead him to "understand" that there is nothing he can do with "experience," that he cannot alter his fate with its help. It is an issue for his superiors in the workplace and for specialists.

Nothing in this situation would change even if this worker is promoted in the company hierarchy or if he is elected to positions in the union or in public office. This public sphere (e.g., the vantage point of the executive committee of a political party or of the heads of a trade union) lies, without a doubt, far outside the proletarian context of living; it provides new, largely technical experience, which relates to the functioning of individual social forces. It is possible for the worker to have new individual experiences here; however, none of the barriers of his libidinal structure, of language, of socially recognized modes of intercourse are torn down. He has increasingly distanced himself from the production process,

---

11. On the differentiation of industrial labor, see Horst Kern and Michael Schumann, *Industriearbeit und Arbeiterbewußtsein*, Part I (Frankfurt am Main: 1970), as well as the bibliographical citations therein.

12. Reimut Reiche, *Proletarischer Lebenszusammenhang*, manuscript (Frankfurt am Main: 1971), and *Die proletarische Familie* (Frankfurt am Main: 1971).

13. On the concept of the context of mystification, see Adorno, "Erfahrungsgehalt."

yet neither alone nor with the aid of the organization at his disposal is he able to set in motion to a sufficient degree new production processes, whose object is, for instance, the production of social relationships between people. What is more, after a while he comes to the conclusion that he is dragging around inside himself the proletarian context of living, **within which both his experiences and the blocking of this experience are bound**. Thus prepared, he encounters a universal fact of the labor movement experience: as soon as the worker participates in the bourgeois public sphere, once he has won elections, taken up union initiatives, he is confronted by a dilemma. He can make only "private" use of a public sphere that has disintegrated into a mere intermediary sphere. The public sphere operates according to this rule of private use, not according to the rules whereby the experiences and class interests of workers are organized. The interests of workers appear in the bourgeois public sphere as nothing more than a gigantic, cumulative "private interest," not as a collective mode of production for qualitatively new forms of public sphere and public consciousness. To the extent that the interests of the working class are no longer formulated and represented as genuine and autonomous interests vis-à-vis the bourgeois public sphere, betrayal by individual representatives of the labor movement ceases to be an individual problem. It is not a question of an individual's strength of character. **In wanting to use the mechanisms of the bourgeois public sphere for their cause, such representatives become, objectively, traitors to the cause that they are representing.**

One arrives at a different result only if one resorts to a fiction: if the collective worker existed as a real, thinking subject, the situation would present itself differently.[14] It is true that initially the situation would be the same: the proletarian context of living, the tools and media of the process of social transformation, experience itself—all of these would be an alienated context for the collective

---

14. The category of the macroworker is central to the question of the organization of the working class. While the macrocapitalist also actually has organized himself in the form of an object context, of an "enormous collection of commodities," the proletariat as a context of subjects has until now been unorganized and is mutually brought together only via the capitalist process of labor and exploitation in accordance with rules that are alien to it. The category of the macroworker is nonetheless not one that is utopian. Even the capitalist principle of organization, that of exchange, proceeds initially only from one *organizing principle*: the capitalists' quite solid belief in the universal exchangeability of their commodities, even if they, for instance, from the fifteenth through the nineteenth centuries, collide empirically with a society in which prebourgeois, nonexchangeable relations of property and rank determine the image of society. Similarly, it is possible to derive the organizing idea of an associative network of immediate producers from the initially alienatedly produced socialization of labor and cooperative contact, that is, the purely objectively produced bringing together of the workers that anticipates the macroworker as the actual organizing subject of history. The fact that the question of organization discussed by the left proceeds from party-line thinking and not this actual question of organization does not alter it at all. The macroworker would be nothing other than the council system (*Rätesystem*) that is carried out universally and internationally in production plants and in life processes.

worker, which he could not confront without separating himself from his own real life. Even this hypothetical subject, the collective worker, would be exposed to the suggestive power of the scientific method and its particular concept of experience. This form of experience would flatter the macrosubject since the latter feigns an immediacy of experience, **an experience of the subject** to the object. These apparent advantages, along with the "objective dimension within the collective worker as subject," would lead the subject to this undialectical understanding of experience. This applies, however, only to the initial situation. Every method, even an intentionally undialectical one that further organizes the experiences of the social producer-subject, would—through the totality of the production process that is integrated in the subject—broaden the concept of experience as production, **experience in the production of experience**. This social experience, which is in the process of organizing itself, recognizes the limitations of commodity production and makes the context of living itself the object of production. This production tends toward a public form of expression that bases the dialectical subject-object relationship not upon the impotent opposition of thinking individual and social totality but on the subject character of organized social experience. It is evident that organization is no longer to be understood here in a technical sense but dialectically, as the production of the form of the content of experiences themselves.[15]

---

15. The concept of production here does not describe a mere analogy to the production of material goods; rather, it is meant as the comprehensive concept of social production toward which the material production of goods is conducted as one particular formation (*Ausformung*). Whenever Marx speaks of "communism as the production of forms of social intercourse themselves," he is referring to this general concept of social production. Production is socially necessitated activity. Its necessity is materialized in, among other things, the fact that its form of production is oriented toward the most advanced level of societilization. Among the prerequisites for bourgeois society, commodity production is so much in the foreground that it conceals this general concept of production that also encompasses the production of modes of living. Correspondingly, Marx uses the concept of production narrowly in the sense of commodity production within the context of the political and economic analyses of this commodity-producing society. The difference between productive and nonproductive labor here results from the narrow context of commodity production. On the other hand, in societies that find themselves in a process of transformation—in which, therefore, alongside the dominant commodity relations, mass doubt and a lack of legitimation repeatedly interrupt the stringency of the commodity context—there result mixed forms that cannot be interpreted with only the narrow analytic production concept of commodity production, but that are also linked to a new, overlying concept of production. Here it becomes obvious that a concept of production was at the base of social production all along (but concealed by the absolute dominance of commodity production), a concept that had as its object the production of agents of socialization, of language, of the construction of the drive structure, the production of experience, of collective entities and public spheres—in other words, the production of life contexts. This concept of production is oriented toward the production of social wealth and the appropriation of this production by the producers themselves. The alternative to commodity-producing society can be apprehended through it.

## The Concept of the Public Sphere in Classical Bourgeois Theory

The concept of the public sphere is originally one of the revolutionary rallying cries of the bourgeoisie.[16] It comes as a surprise when Kant ascribes to the public sphere the status of a transcendental principle, indeed that of the mediation between politics and ethics.[17] The public sphere is, according to Kant, a principle of the legal framework of society and simultaneously a method of enlightenment; it is the only medium within which the politics of the revolutionary bourgeoisie can articulate itself. The emphasis of this principle of the public sphere becomes apparent through what is accepted along with it: secret societies are, for instance, generally unsuited to take part in true politics. "The injustice of rebellion becomes clear as a result of the fact that the latter's maxim would, if one *publicly committed* oneself to the rebellion, render its own goals impossible. One would therefore necessarily have to conceal these goals. This would, however, not be necessary from the point of view of the ruler. He can freely proclaim that he will punish every rebellion with the death of the ringleaders, even if the latter believe that he has himself been the first to transgress the law."[18] When the head of state declares publicly that he will punish every rebellion with death, this does not contradict his own intentions to uphold the authority of the state by every means. In other words, one has to accept the fact that the state is in occupation of the public sphere and the rebel is not, for this is the only way that legitimate discussion and communication between citizens can be maintained.

The statement "that reason alone has authority," and that this reason is the product of a collaborative, communicative, intellectual exertion on the part of those members of society who are qualified for this task has been a cardinal point of emancipatory bourgeois political thought since Descartes. When I think, I ascribe my capacity for thought not to my isolated existence but to my connection with all others who think, with the community of rational individuals, such as mathematicians, astronomers, natural scientists, logicians. "I think, therefore I am" could therefore also be formulated as: "**I am**, precisely because I am able to disregard the fact that I am an isolated individual."

The medium of the public sphere, which performs this task of collective mediation, is based on the model of the republic of scholars; the public, made up of private individuals making use of their reason, also behaves as though it were composed of scholars. "What I understand by the public use of one's own reason is, however, that use which someone makes of it as a scholar before the entire

16. For a discussion of this concept, see Habermas, *Strukturwandel der Öffentlichkeit*, pp. 102ff., esp. 117ff.

17. Immanuel Kant, *Werke*, vol. 6, ed. Wilhelm Weischedel (Frankfurt am Main: 1964): 244. See also Habermas, *Strukturwandel der Öffentlichkeit*, pp. 117ff.

18. Kant, *Werke*, vol. 6, p. 246.

public of the world of leaders.[19] The pathos with which Kant stresses the moral code, the abstract character of civil laws, the rigid imperative of all rules that determine human conduct, is a reflex of the fact that bourgeois commodity production is in the process of development. **The inner violence of these principles, including the principle of the public sphere, is rooted in the fact that the main struggle must be waged against all particularities. Everything that resists the universalizing tendency of commodity production must be sacrificed to the general, to the principle. This is the source of the compulsive way in which criteria such as definitions, subsumptions, and categorizations are used to circumscribe the public sphere. In this way, Kant excludes from politics and the public sphere all those sections of the population that do not participate in bourgeois politics because they cannot afford to.**

The construction of the public sphere derives its entire substance from the existence of owners of private property. At the same time, the public sphere cannot base itself on the empirically arbitrary characteristics of these property owners; Kant is thus forced, if he is to establish universally valid rules of public communication, to negate this material base on which the public sphere rests. What he retains is, to be sure, something general; but it is an abstract general, which lacks all the concrete elements of the bourgeois that would constitute a living public sphere. In a word: he can constitute bourgeois publicity neither *with* the empirical bourgeois-subject nor *without* it. The interest of critical philosophy is to draw boundaries. Such boundary concepts are, for instance, the thing-in-itself, dignity, and the public sphere as a medium for bringing about "unanimity of politics and ethics." **These concepts indicate perspectives on an unfolding of the human species that sets itself against empirically given capitalist commodity production.**[20]

---

19. Ibid., p. 171. See as well Habermas, *Strukturwandel der Öffentlichkeit*, p. 120. It is the duty of the public sphere as an end in itself to determine a *closed society*, within which peace agreements are possible on the basis of reason. This experience of safeguarding the peace that Kant attempts to formulate on a political level with the a priori principle of public sphere is also viewed by Kant as the principal purpose of his entire theoretical philosophy.

Here as well it is to a great extent a matter of excluding all elements of knowledge that might disrupt order and the peace: "The *culture* of human reason, [in order that] it no longer serve merely as speculation to prevent mistakes, but extend knowledge, does not detract from its value, but instead grants it dignity and prestige through the censorship office, which insures general order and harmony, indeed the very well-being of the common scholarly person, and prevents this being's gallant and fruitful labors from being deterred from their main goal, which is the general happiness" (Kant, *Werke*, vol. 2, pp. 708ff.)

20. See Habermas, *Strukturwandel der Öffentlichkeit*, esp. p. 124. In order to do this Kant must—with considerable violence of thought—exclude *one substantial group of humanity after the other* as inadequate to this "true politics": children, women, store clerks, day laborers, "even the hairdresser." Even the private uses of reason that man can practice "in a specific civil post or government office that has been entrusted to him" are nonpublic and unsuitable for politics. The goal of this true bourgeois

## The Classical Bourgeois Public Sphere—in Practice

In the eighteenth and nineteenth centuries, the bourgeois public sphere did not, in reality, develop at the level at which Kant conceived of it. The bourgeois property owners—the raw material of the Kantian construct—were not interested in the formation of public experience. Their knowledge of the market is private. In relation to the state and the public sphere, their prime interest is in the possible countereffects of this public sphere on their private interests. What was strictly an end in itself for Kant was merely a means for the real bourgeois society. The public sphere widened the perspective on appropriation for whole groups of capitalists: they attempt to acquire contracts to supply the army, to float public loans; they want to become involved in public works, to appropriate state authority so as to strengthen and protect property interests, to secure advantageous positions in world trade by means of gunboat diplomacy and tariffs, to win state protection for colonial exploitation. For the ruling class, this framework of the public sphere was in any case not the real horizon of their social experience and formation of opinion, but merely a subsidiary aspect. "Having experience" within this public sphere means to have dominant knowledge—a specialized knowledge of how to exploit this public sphere properly. This knowledge includes the capacity to cloak the immediate fractionalized interests of capital in the form of an imagined sovereignty, a feigned collective will.

Whereas Kant, as a philosopher, reflects upon the relationship between bourgeois and public sphere and distances the latter from bourgeois reality to arrive at a principle of experiencing the world, the practical bourgeois takes the opposite course. Although the sale of his goods may entail contact with the world, the production of these goods rests on local experience. If the practical bourgeois had been capable of having real experience of the world, things would not have ended with historical catastrophes. From the subjective point of view, these catastrophes have their roots not least of all in an altogether faulty evaluation of the interplay of forces and constellations of profit and loss on an international scale.[21] The identifi-

politics is a republicanism and eternal condition of peace that represents the opposite of actual relations in the economic struggle among the established members of bourgeois society. There is no empirical experience that fulfills this concept of public sphere; it is intended as the intercourse that takes place among lovers of truth. It is important to note that in the intellectual tradition of the bourgeois domination of nature, the interest in a legal synopsis of "appeasement" in the sense of domination and pacification is the foundation of *formalism*, of the intellectual show of force vis-à-vis the object, and of the *mechanism of exclusion*. This tendency lies at the base of the production mechanism of the bourgeois public sphere as a whole. The *reversal* of this would mean precisely an understanding of conflict and the organizing of the experience that results from it as the integration mechanism of a public sphere that would encompass, sublate (*aufheben*), and in no case exclude all members of society. This would correspond not only to a different attitude toward the concept of public sphere, but also to a mode of production that would not ruinously exploit nature and humanity.

21. A mass slaughter like Verdun must appear to the practical bourgeois as a terrible error: billions

cation or linking of private and general interests cannot, however, be allowed to go so far that demands are made on the bourgeois that entail the sacrifice of his private interests. In such a case, he sees himself forced to withdraw his interests, which constitute the raw material of his public policy, from the public sphere. If he does not do this, if he himself takes seriously the identification of his private interests with the general interest, he becomes a representative of the general interest and fails as a bourgeois. He loses the material basis, but also the confidence of that sector of capital which, along with the general representation of his interests, sees theirs represented as well. This context lays bare structural relationships between private capitalist interests and the public sphere, which is portrayed as the world.

The dead end in which the bourgeois individual finds himself if he wants to participate in the public sphere and in its global character is apparent as well by the way this individual relies on the delegation of global interests. "The man of the world," knowledge of the world, global citizenship, the concept of the "world" as such that is associated with the bourgeois public sphere—all of these terms indicate situations that exclude, on principle, the narrow horizon of experience of the bourgeois's factory. In order to be able to play a real part within a global context, the bourgeois needs adventurers, traveling salesmen, aristocrats, people undertaking grand tours, who are able to depict this world for him. He must retain Junkers for himself if he wants to pursue realpolitik on a global scale. The fact that his own experience, which is in any case produced in a restricted framework, reappears in the public sphere only to a limited extent, while bourgeois society's political and economic thrust embraces the whole world, lends bourgeois politics an inherent tendency for catastrophe.[22]

## The Processing of Social Experience by the New Public Spheres of Production

The traditional public sphere, whose characteristic weakness rests on the mechanism of exclusion between public and private spheres, is today overlaid by *indus-*

blown to bits with no purpose, and the labor power of millions of people blindly obliterated. The long-term interests of the involved bourgeoisies of England, France, and Germany also suffer in equal measure from the results of such a "bloodletting." But the path (*Weg*) that leads away from catastrophe is one that is closed off to the experience and perception of the practical bourgeois.

22. Marx analyzed these fundamentals of classical bourgeois politics in *The Eighteenth Brumaire of Louis Bonaparte.* The historical substructure of the bourgeois public sphere also determines all later, postbourgeois public spheres; in them, this desperate classical storehouse of experience enters into a liaison with powerful worldwide constellations of interests such as colonialism, imperialism, economic and monetary associations, the policies of the blocs and military alliances. Although external appearances would seem to contradict this, the difference between the actual scope of experience and the practical range of political or military intervention into the world is also characteristic of the "strong" public spheres of fascism and national socialism.

*trialized public spheres of production*, which tend to incorporate private realms, in particular the production process and the context of living.[23] These new forms *seem* to people to be no less public than the traditional bourgeois public sphere. **Here and in what follows we only understand the public sphere as an aggregate of phenomena that have completely diverse characteristics and origins. The public sphere has no homogeneous substance whatsoever.** It always consists only of numerous elements that give the impression of belonging together but are in reality joined only outwardly. Thus, the classical public sphere is originally rooted in the bourgeois context of living, yet separates itself from the latter and the production process. By contrast, the new public spheres of production are a **direct expression of the sphere of production.**

---

23. On the concept of industrialized public spheres of production (one can use the singular only insofar as one is clear about the fact that this overdetermining "public sphere" is an accumulation of numerous individual public spheres that are as manifold and differentiated with respect to one another as the subdivisions of the capitalistic process of production itself):

1. *The public sphere of production has its nucleus in the sensual presence of the public sphere that emanates from the objective production process—of society, just as it is.* Included here are the organizational structure of production overall as well as "industry as the open book of human psychology" (Marx), that is, in what has been internalized by human beings and the external world—the spatiality of bank and insurance complexes, urban centers, and industrial zones as well as processes of labor, learning, and living, in addition to work plants. Because of the fact that the overpowering objectivity of this production context becomes its own ideology, the doubling of society at the outset into a "celestial and a terrestrial" life, the bifurcation into a political communal being and a private one (see footnote 3 above, this chapter): the rest of the earth itself counts as an intellectual heaven. Only within this public/nonpublic totality do the contradictions engender new doublings and mechanisms of exclusion.

2. *The consciousness industry* (see chapters 3, 4, and 5) *as well as the context of consumption and advertising* (see chapter 6, "The Transformation of Commodities into Fantasy Values")—that is, production and distribution that are applied to the sphere of secondary exploitation (see chapter 6, "Primary and Secondary Exploitation")—overlap and are linked to the primary public sphere of production.

3. *The public-sphere labor of conglomerates and that of social institutions* (interest groups, political parties, the state) form an abstraction of individual public spheres of production and enter into the public sphere of production as an additional overlying element (see chapter 2, "The Public Sphere as an Illusory Synthesis of the Totality of Society").

Within this *total complex* of industrial public spheres of production, traditional labor organizations or labor relations laws—even individual components of protest movements—form an integrated ornament from the perspective of emancipation, *even if, from the perspective of nonemancipation, they are real and effective partial forces* (cf. the discussion of the labor relations laws below). The ways and means with which the public sphere of production overdetermines the political public sphere in the classical sense (seasonal elections, professional politics) can make one aware, if one thinks about it, of how self-evident a threatened collapse of a great economic unit such as Krupp or the Ruhr Valley coal works (which are private enterprises) becomes a matter of public concern and forces an intervention by the state. It would, for example, be inconceivable that, in the course of the Bundestag elections, a decision could be made to evacuate the Ruhrgebiet, while one could imagine that a demolition and rebuilding of entire industrial zones—as a result of EEC developments, for example—could take place on the basis of real shifts in the public sphere of production. Since interaction occurs between all of the elements of this organic whole, it can happen that in atypical cases political decisions as well exert a

1. The classical public sphere of newspapers, chancellories, parliaments, clubs, parties, associations rests on a quasi-artisanal mode of production.[24] By comparison, the industrialized public sphere of computers, the mass media, the media cartel, the combined public relations and legal departments of conglomerates and interest groups, and, finally, reality itself as a public sphere transformed by production, represent a superior and more highly organized level of production.[25]

2. The ideology production of the public spheres of production, which permeates the classical public sphere and the social horizon of experience, embraces not only the pure interests of capital—as articulated via the large interest groups of industry—but also the interests of the workers in the production process to the extent that they are absorbed by the context of capital [*Kapitalzusammenhang*]. This represents a complex connection between production interests, life interests, and needs for legitimation. In light of this, the production public sphere is obliged—because it is an expression of an overarching production apparatus on the one hand, and because of the life interests that have become part of it on the other—to solve its contradiction no longer solely according to the reflexes of capital. **Instead of the mechanism of exclusion characteristic of the classical public sphere, what characterizes the public sphere of production, which is linked with the classical one, is the oscillation between exclusion and intensified incorporation: actual relations that cannot be legitimated become the victims of a deliberately manufactured nonpublic sphere; power relations in the production process that are not in themselves capable of being legitimated are injected with the generalized interests that have become legitimate and are thereby presented within a context of legitimation. The differentiation between public and private is replaced by the contradiction between the pressure exerted by production interests and the need for legitimation.** The

dominating effect; as a rule, however, this dominance is triggered here as well by real infrastructural forces (*Basiskräfte*) such as the mass doubt that is currently produced in the sphere of production (cf. the example of the popular referendum in Norway against joining the EEC).

The anticipatory form of the public sphere of production in early capitalism was the concurrence of housing settlements and social-service facilities with the factory complex, as was the case, for example, for Krupp. Today, a plant develops alongside the plants of individual concerns in a more comprehensive sense that embraces the totality of social production. The social contract that could only be feigned by the revolutionary bourgeoisie is produced positively within the industrial spheres of production as the internalization of the objective impression of the social order. This totalization of the public sphere has a dual effect: the making public of the social totality and the countertendency as well, the most extreme efforts to avoid this publication in the interest of upholding private property.

24. Kurt Tucholsky characterizes this fundamental situation when he lists the following as the necessary elements for founding a political party during the Weimar Republic: one chairperson, one telephone, and one typewriter.

25. The encounter between these differing levels of public sphere will take place as in the following example: a public prosecutor and a clerical secretary will come up against thirty lawyers and sixty public-relations experts from a chemical conglomerate if they attempt to uncover an incident of environmental pollution.

context of capital is thereby enriched and becomes capable of expansion; at the same time, however, the spectrum of possible capitalist solutions to contradictions is narrowed. The result is a type of transformation-society that is dominated by conditions specific to capital.[26] **Relative to the classical public sphere, the public sphere of production thus seems to possess no mechanism of exclusion that dislodges it from its foundation of interests and weakens it. Relative to the social horizon of experience, however, the aggregated and intermeshed classical and production public spheres reiterate identical mechanisms.**

3. If the demands of the classical public sphere coincide with those of the public sphere of production, the former as a rule gives way. **The mere ideality of the bourgeois public sphere is confronted here by the compact materiality of the new public spheres of production.** Even within the latter, those demands that regularly prevail are the ones with the most direct connection to the profit interest or those that are capable of amassing a greater context of living within themselves. The seams holding the various public spheres of production together are characterized by fissures and a wealth of contradictions. These include the intersection between the private consciousness industry and public-service television; between mass media and the press on the one hand, and the public-sphere activities of corporations on the other; between the state public sphere and monopolies of opinion; between the public sphere of trade unions and that of management, and so on. Papering over these fissures is the task of a special branch of public-sphere activity. This is necessary because there is no equilibrium among the public spheres of production, but rather a struggle to subsume one beneath the others.[27]

4. It is the function of this cumulative public sphere to bring about agreement, order, and legitimation. It is, however, subordinated to the primacy of the power

---

26. The aporias that result from this are in part new, in part continuations of aporias of the classical bourgeois public sphere at a higher level of organization. Constitutive for the claim to domination of any public sphere is its ability to legitimate: the order that is grounded in law. A real writing of the history of bourgeois society would nonetheless have to own up to the fact that its history was the history of violence, just as this violence is always produced anew in the process of production. Once the public sphere accumulates legitimations, it becomes stronger as a public sphere, but must also separate itself from production interests that cannot be legitimated—it becomes increasingly unsuitable as a public sphere of production. If, on the other hand, it introduces more substantive interests into its public-sphere context, it also grows stronger, it becomes "binding" for more powerful components of society. But if it in this way makes public its own existence, which is precisely the contradictory structure of the production process, it also tendentially sublates its own foundations, and endangers the validity of private property.

27. The public-service structure of a public sphere of production such as that of television, for example, hereby indicates nothing about its actual capacity for implementation. On the one hand, a higher level of public-service, "ideal," statutory intention effects a separation from the characteristic profit interests that predominate in society. This separation has a weakening effect. On the other hand, public-service television also indirectly binds profit interests to its suppliers and itself responds to a particular type of value abstraction: it makes "legitimation profits."

relations that determine the sphere of production. **For this reason, the work of legitimation within this public sphere can be carried out and overseen only distributively, and it can itself be changed only superficially since its real history is taking place nonpublicly in the domain of production. As in the classical bourgeois public sphere, albeit for different reasons, the structure of production of the public sphere, and the nonpublic experience that is linked to it, separates itself from its mere image manifested in the apparatus of distribution, in the public sphere as finished product, which is experienced publicly.**

5. This is in no way altered by the fact that the state, as a summation of the classical public sphere, itself influences a significant part of the private sector by its interventions. On the contrary, the same rules apply to the state's contribution to the public sphere of production.

6. Any change in the structure, any movement within the public sphere's system of legitimation, opens the possibility for a formal subsumption of sections of society under the control of other sections. The fact that this is how the public sphere operates in reality—its utilization by private interests, which have of course enriched themselves with the interests of those engaged in the domain of production and have thereby become imperative—makes it difficult **to incorporate coherently critical experience into the public sphere**.

7. If the function of the public sphere were wholly transparent, if it corresponded to the early bourgeois ideal of publicity, then it could not continue to operate in this form. **This is why all the substations of this public sphere are organized as arcane realms.** The keyword "confidential" prevents the transfer of social experience from one domain into another. This mechanism of exclusion is admittedly more subtle than that of the classical bourgeoisie, but no less effective.

8. The bourgeois public sphere's network of norms is under occupation by massive production interests to such a degree that it becomes an arsenal that can be deployed by private elements.[28]

---

28. Here one can speak of a network of norms in the sense that norms are released from their original historical context. In this formally substanceless form, they are seized upon by the strongest of capital interests and often turned precisely against claims that hold to the original historical content of these norms. Thus, for instance, the constitutional right to *freedom of the press*, which is supposed to defend an independently critical press founded on a plurality of opinions against the absolute state, is now understood by the Springer conglomerate in such a way that it protects precisely the very production of interests of this conglomerate that destroy the plurality of opinion. The exploitation of the historically developed context of public norms described here can already be found in the classical public sphere, but it is accentuated in the phase of the public sphere of production. Then, as now, the system of publicly sanctioned norms appears for profit interests as a second nature that expects its exploitation. The norms cast off products to be exploited just as trees cast off fruits. The more abstract the level, the more fruitful and the less transparent it is. On the abstract level of *world economy*, the norms of the world currency system are in the foreground. The strongest of capital interests—that of American capital—participates here in the so-called special withdrawal rights of the world currency

9. Reiterated in the amalgamation of classical public sphere and the new public sphere of production is **the rejection of the proletarian context of living as it exists**. This context is acknowledged to the extent that it plays a part, in a domesticated form, in the realization of valorization [*Verwertung*] interests. In the process, the latter's form of expression modifies itself; the valorization interest accommodates itself to real needs, but must simultaneously model all real needs so that it can slot them into its abstract system. Everyday experience is confronted with a confusing picture: the context of living clearly becomes part of production and the public sphere; at the same time, it is excluded because it is not recognized in its concrete totality as an autonomous whole.

10. Marx says that for the nineteenth-century proletariat, the abstraction from everything that is human, even from the **semblance** of the latter, has been achieved in practice. The old and new public spheres of bourgeois society can respond only with palliatives; **they provide, without any real change in the class situation, the semblance of the human as a separate product.** This is the foundation of the culture industry's pauperism, which destroys experience.[29] In

---

fund, while these same norms are unusable for developing countries. Every regulation of the *European Common Market* contains in the same sense standards that form the structures of entire branches to conform in the interests of the great apparatuses of production. On the national level, there are determinations of security, supervision, and censure that were originally set up to protect a common interest, but that nonetheless are reinterpreted in connection with the interests of the conglomerates into mechanisms for eliminating the competition. Thus it will be possible, for example, to supersede Volkswagen competition on the U.S. market after 1975 with the help of safety regulations for automobile production.

The most consequential exploitation of the public standard is the so-called *syndicate contract* that was the typical form of economic organization during the Third Reich. Within this system, the structuring of the economic branches that was adequate to the interests of the conglomerates was realized in that statutory, state-mediated institutions were created by means of which the redistribution of economic means and skeleton-law contractions of production and distribution were carried out. Such syndicates would come up against the prohibition of cartels in the private sphere, but they are still possible in statutory form. An example of this can be found in *the first federal legislation in the area of media policy,* the so-called Film Subsidy Law. In this case, certain commercial film interests took advantage of the distribution of jurisdiction in the legislation between the federation and the individual states to the effect that the unified cultural-economic medium of film was to be abstractly supported economically, since the federal government has jurisdiction only for the economic aspects of film. The result is the so-called tearjerker cartel, a law that benefits only certain conglomerate-financed films, while it excludes independent productions as being merely of cultural interest. In the Film Subsidies Board that was set up by the Film Subsidy Law, representatives of the Bundestag, the churches, and of television collaborate with certain factions of the film industry so that a combination of public and private power developed that is completely impossible to monitor. Characteristic here is the confusion of the relationships of responsibility: as presidents of this body, Bundestag members become representatives of economic interests, thereby subject to the legal control of the ministries that they in turn control as members of Parliament. Such legalized nonsense would not have been possible in the classical public sphere, but it has become standard practice, especially in supranational organizations.

29. Cf. Jürgen Habermas, "Die Dialektik der Rationalisierung. Vom Pauperismus in Produktion

the programming and consciousness industry, but also in the public practice of other spheres of production whereby power is unfolded and ideology produced, **the consciousness of the worker** becomes the raw material and the site where these public spheres realize themselves. This does not alter the overall context of class struggles, but augments them with a higher, more opaque level. The situation is thus altered insofar as those parts of the context of living that had not hitherto been directly valorized by the interests of capital are now likewise preorganized by society. The proletarian context of living is thus split into two halves. One is reabsorbed into the new public spheres of production and participates in the process of industrialization; the other is disqualified in relation to the framework established by systems of production and the public sphere of production that determine society. The proletarian context of living does not as such lose its experiential value; however, the experience bound up in it is rendered "incomprehensible" in terms of social communication: ultimately, it becomes a private experience. As a result, those domains that relate to human activities that are not directly necessary for the production process and the substructure of legitimation are subjected to an organized impoverishment. At the same time, public-sphere activity, ideology production, and the "management" of everyday life—the latter in particular, in the form of pluralistically balanced leisure and consciousness programs—appropriate **as raw material human beings' desire for a meaningful life, as well as parts of their consciousness,** in order to erect an industrialized facade of programming and legitimation. Genuine experience is torn into two parts that are, in class terms, opposed to one another.

## The Life-Historical Construction of Experience— The Differing Time Scales of Learning Processes

Experiences have a specific temporal rhythm that cannot be altered at will if they are to succeed. It is not, for instance, possible to transfer that dominant temporal rhythm that governs **direct actions** onto the **development of theory** or the **learning processes of early childhood**. This by no means suggests that these temporal rhythms can be completely isolated from one another; on the contrary, **the dialectical unity of these various temporal structures is a precondition for the concept of social experience as production.** These different rhythms are determined by the manner in which individuals and objects are experienced; at the same time, they exist prior to these experiences. One can speak here of a primacy of the object, for objective conditions necessitate quite specific rhythms of experience.

Advanced capitalist commodity production knows only *one* concept of time: this determines the abstractly quantifying measure for the production of value and

und Konsum," in *Merkur* VIII (1954): 701ff., reprinted in *Arbeit, Erkenntnis, Fortschritt* (Amsterdam:1970): 7ff.

surplus value as an aggregate of units of time. Socially necessary time, which the manufacture of a product requires; overtime, which is done within a specific period; leisure time as the residual part of the day, which, however, is marked by behavior carried over from the domain of production—all of these concepts of time have equal status. This concept is derived from the working day familiar to every worker, even if he knows nothing at all about the highly ingenious modern methods of measuring time. This concept of time is based on the logic of commodity production itself. As Adorno has tried to show, the latter runs in potentially sporadic cycles in which time loses its directionality and is basically timeless. This dominant concept of time is that of "universal exchange, of the equal values of equations that work out and have nothing left over; everything historical would, however, be a residue. Exchange is, as the revocation of one act by another, by the logic of its execution, itself timeless, even if it takes place in time: just as ratio, by virtue of the purity of its form, eliminates time from itself in the operations of mathematics. Concrete time too disappears from industrial production. The latter runs, rather, in identical, sporadic, and potentially simultaneous cycles. With the movement from feudal traditionalism to radical bourgeois rationality, remembrance, time, and memory are ultimately eliminated from developing bourgeois society as an irrational mortgage, in the wake of the growing rationalization of industrial production methods, which, along with other rudiments of the artisanal mode of production, also reduce categories such as the length of apprenticeship, the model of qualitative, stored experience, which is scarcely required anymore."[30]

This time, which tears apart and fragments the real context of living, is experienced as "life," as second nature. This is probably the only level on which a worker can directly experience the inversions linked with commodity fetishism: **the experience of his life as a mere succession of units of time capable of being valorized by capital, along with a residue that cannot be valorized, or only with difficulty.**

Since the result of this is the objective appearance that all productive activities operate within this industrial time scheme, there is a tendency to transpose the latter onto all other areas of social life. This is evident in the mass media's programming according to time slots and in the division of educational processes into hour-long lessons, as well as school and college years of study. The industrial time scheme also overlays the early phase of the production of labor power as a commodity within the family: the mother-child bond, whose real, preindustrial structure, which rests on human relations between the child and its primary objects, is overlaid by compartmentalizing mechanisms, as when the child is

---

30. Theodor W. Adorno, "Über Statik und Dynamik als soziologische Kategorien," in Max Horkheimer and Theodor W. Adorno, *Sociologica II. Reden und Vorträge* (Frankfurt am Main: Suhrkamp, 1962): 234.

trained to satisfy its needs (e.g., hunger, thirst, toilet training) at predetermined times. It is a fundamental feature of the principle of self-regulation, which is associated with antiauthoritarian education, that the child from the very beginning of his life develops a "timetable" that corresponds to his own needs and to his stage of development as a person. Here in particular it becomes apparent that the transposition of the production scheme of the working day onto a layer of primary socialization is not justified by the object itself but corresponds to extraneous motives, namely the inculcation of work discipline.[31] However, this creates a contradiction, which the capitalist system is unable to resolve: **the methods of disciplining and of extraneous motivation employed in the interests of production equip labor power in a way that is increasingly less in demand with regard to the interests of the most advanced forms of capital.**

The logic of capital drives it to attempt to appropriate the full productivity of labor. Modern capitalism cannot afford not to develop certain qualities of labor power in the first place, or to lay them off as incapable of valorization. It is therefore compelled to endeavor to bring preschool and school socialization under social control while recognizing the specific life rhythm of the genesis and maintenance of labor power and freeing it from the abstract time scheme of commodity production. Modern capitalism cannot achieve this by means of its alliance with the institutions of a conservative educational system. It is evident that capitalism is dependent, in this case, upon the social forces and individuals who alone possess the necessary expertise in sublimatory education: educators, scholars, and parents, who constitute the progressive and anticapitalist groups,[32]

This reorientation within the valorization interest reactivates preindustrial modes of production. Preindustrial, because the production of human labor power in its preindustrial structures has hitherto been only formally subsumed by capital. Both **childrearing** and **academic knowledge** are transformed whenever the educational system and the socialization of labor power as commodity are in the process of being remodeled. Both spheres represent forms of production that are atypical of the workings of capital; both, unlike the process of industrial production, are determined by different time scales: that of dead labor, which is

---

31. In the tradition of pedagogy there has also always been, from Pestalozzi to Makarenko, a countermovement in opposition to this schematism. Today the interests of advanced capitalism are bound to the rationalization of the area of education with pedagogic trends that take into account the child's context of needs even in school (preschool education, all-day schooling, curriculum research, and the revision of the education program in accordance with the findings of this research).

32. Gunnar Heinsohn, *Vorschulerziehung heute. Eine soziologische Untersuchung der Ursachen, systemverändernden Möglichkeiten und Verwirklichungsschwierigkeiten von Reformbestrebungen in der Vorschulerziehung des kapitalistischen Deutschland* (Frankfurt: 1971); Jürgen Habermas, "Thesen zur Theorie der Sozialisation," in *Arbeit, Erkenntnis, Fortschritt: Aufsätze 1954–1970* (Amsterdam: 1970): 376–429.

articulated in quantifying time, and that of living labor, which is articulated in qualitative, historical time.

## Primary Socialization as the Cultivation of the Capacity for Experience

**Living labor power can neither be generated nor sustained without detours, without a qualitative intensification of biographical stages of development (maturity, "killing time," free time during which one can lose onself, regression and relaxation, remembrance, passivity, etc.).** What Rousseau says of childrearing is generally true of this living rhythm, which cannot be industrialized: **what matters is not gaining time, but losing it.** In this sense, qualitative time has no knowledge of the notion of linear progress. But it would be wrong to assume that these qualitative rhythms would have no firm structures or could not be organized on a social scale unless they followed the dictates of the valorization context. Nevertheless, the organizational structures—which have as their object the relations between human beings, and between human beings and their ideas or their own prehistory—are concealed by the reified abstractions of the valorization structure and thereby prevented from fully unfolding.

In the primary socialization of the child, the goal of which is the cultivation of the capacity for learning and gaining experience, the time scale of commodity production faces particular difficulties. **Early socialization** in the nuclear family has a dual character. Horkheimer describes upbringing in the bourgeois family as, on the one hand, the preservation of a residue of life that lies in opposition to the work process, and, on the other hand, the establishment of labor power as a commodity for the capitalist valorization process.[33] In the successful mother-child relationship, the rudiments of a preindustrial mode of production based on the satisfaction of human needs by real use-values have been preserved. The early relations between mother and child, insofar as they are satisfactory, cannot be reduced to relations of exchange, even if they are surrounded by exchange abstraction.

In highly industrialized societies today, this family socialization is anything but uniform. The focus of research has been above all on differences in childrearing that run according to class. Even within each individual social stratum, however (for example, in the middle class), a plurality of different and in part contradictory styles of childrearing is evident.[34] This anarchic diversity is a consequence of the private character of childrearing. In this private form, it is precise-

---

33. Cf. Max Horkheimer, "Allgemeiner Teil," in *Autorität und Familie* (Paris: 1936).

34. See above all Peter Brückner, *Zur Sozialpsychologie des Spätkapitalismus* (Frankfurt: 1972). With extreme sensitivity, Brückner has analyzed the inner contradictions of the socialization process as it extends into forms of subliminal violence and child abuse and designated it as a formal expression of pervading transsocietal contradictions.

ly the emancipatory elements associated with the specific mode of production of early socialization that are incapable of any impact on society. This applies both to the awareness that it is by the self-regulated steering of libidinal drives and the recognition of infantile sexuality alone that the productivity of human cognitive capacity is activated, as well as the knowledge that security is the fundamental prerequisite for an undisturbed relation to objects on the part of children. The realization of these insights in a mode of childrearing practiced as a private and for the most part isolated, presocial form must appear accidental given society's basic interest in the development of these capacities in future workers. Added to this is the fact that the terrorizing context of the nuclear family[35] repeatedly gives rise to blockages in the child's subject-object relationship, even in the face of emancipatory awareness. In childrearing, especially in primary socialization, there is a type of emancipatory minimum, which, if not attained, can lead to serious disturbances.[36]

## The Fate of the Cognitive Drives[37]: Experience through Production of Knowledge[38]

Social experience is both dependent upon and a product of the structure of the cognitive drives. However, no complex of drives is made of such fragmentary elements or is so specific to the survival of the species as the cognitive drive. When Wilhelm Reich says that "love, work, and knowledge are the wellsprings of our life; they should also rule it"; when Habermas speaks of "knowledge and human

---

35. On the concept of the context of terror, see footnote 49.

36. In the forms of interaction that define the successful mother-child relationship, a mode of production is maintained that can be considered the residue of a matriarchal mode of production. It is incorrect to attribute it solely to hormonal processes, to a "maternal instinct" in merely biological terms. It is much more the case here that a female means of production that is aimed at the satisfaction of needs ("handling the child in accordance with its capacities, satisfying its needs at any cost") is vindicated in opposition to the patriarchal and capitalistic world surrounding it. This mode of production is absolutely superior to the mechanisms of that world, but is isolated from the degree of socialization of overall social communication. The superiority of this mode of production legitimates women's claim to emancipation: it makes use, however oppressed and deformed, of experiences within a superior mode of production, if only it is able to grasp society in its entirety.

37. This does not mean that there are primary cognitive drives. Rather, it would appear that labor and knowledge develop as partial concepts of labor—with the generic development of the organization of the cerebral cortex—as an inhibition of the impulses of primary exploitative behavior. This specific inhibition of a drive makes possible for the first time the rudiments of collective behavior, of society, upon whose foundation human labor as a cooperative confrontation of nature becomes possible.

38. [The German term *"Wissenschaft"* has a broad meaning that includes both scholarly pursuits (e.g., academic work) and scientific research. As it is used here, it refers to these activities in general as they exist in various institutionalized forms. "Production of knowledge" is intended to convey this broader notion of *Wissenschaft. —Trans.*]

interests," the connections that are formed here between work, knowledge, power, and the historical organization of the foundations of our drives presuppose the entire evolution of human society.

Within the context of this book, we are concerned not with investigating the complex intermeshing of these individual elements, but rather with arriving at a relatively simple differentiation, which is possible at a more highly organized level of the productive forces. The difference lies between, on the one hand, a cognitive capacity that, irrespective of its composition and socialization, is guided by the need to change the lives of human beings and is held by all oppressed people, and, on the other, a type of knowledge that has constituted itself within the structure of domination and with a view to its professional survival, and thus develops itself as a specialized productive force at supplementary levels of production. The relationship between the knowledge institutionalized in the role of the researcher and its libidinal foundation is thus clearly distinct from that between the mental acitivity of a member of an oppressed class and his household, which is structured by a libidinal economy. Our terms for this specific relationship between libidinal economy and knowledge, for the **varying social and economic ground for knowledge**, is the cognitive drive.

A researcher or theoretician who is not engaged within the framework of large-scale research gives the impression that his work is like that of the artisan; he appears to be an individual thinker "working in isolation and freedom." Research circles in the natural sciences are different only in that they practice individualism as a group. On closer scrutiny, however, another picture emerges. This requires an understanding of the specific theoretical work process: insofar as this involves thought, it entails an activity of exploration that has been retracted into the mind and carries only a weak libidinal charge (S. Freud). The prerequisite for this work process is a conscious or unconscious collective and cooperative working together. The exploratory activity that constitutes thinking is a discussion carried out not only in the imagination, but on a social scale—otherwise, this form of thinking would be unsuccessful. Numerous chains of research experiments are based on the communicative context of the respective developing, specialized field; without the basis of cooperation, these experiments would be nothing but a blind groping in the dark.

All of these work processes constitute a separation, at a high level, of individual elements of the concept of work that underlies the social totality. The specialization and instrumentalization to which the sensibility of the theoretical and scientific thinker is subject creates an arsenal of tools that—from the standpoint of the fundamental qualities of human labor—are totally unnatural.[39] They demand

---

39. It is no coincidence that, in the popular imagination, the activities of scientists take on misanthropic characteristics. Scientists appear as Dr. Mabuse, Prof. Frankenstein, Dr. Jekyll, the scientist Dr. Strangelove in the Stanley Kubrick film, and so on.

exceptional exertions and activate individual faculties, while other human qualities and interests apparently remain dormant. The high degree of instrumentalization of individual elements is only possible through a simultaneously forced and
restricted linkage with the libidinal infrastructure, which directs cognition and
controls perception. At the same time, specialized knowledge, which has been
developed through bourgeois production relations, must demand something of the
structure of the human being that he or she cannot perform: the *how* of ideas and
invention and the *motive* of curiosity and cognition must be produced according to
the laws of a character that is defined by a libidinal economy and an economy of
drives. By contrast, the *tools*—such as logic, the objective, scientific system of
rules, the way in which an experiment is set up—consist of extremely reified,
"hard" matter, which by its nature goes against the laws according to which living
labor functions. The tools used by the rationalistic disciplines negate the mimetic
foundation that is necessary for them to operate.[40]

This hazardous mode of production is repeatedly driven to extremes by the
competitiveness and commodification within the research arena.[41] But theory
too, which tries to keep itself free from the constraints imposed by production
and which, on the contrary, aims to enlist the consciousness of its specific labor
power against the commodity nexus, is subject to similar pressures to achieve
results because it approaches its object, which can be grasped only as a totality,
solely by means of a drastic division into instrumental conceptual precision on
the one hand, and the most intense activation of its motives on the other.[42] The

---

40. Horkheimer and Adorno examined the fundamental concepts of this contradiction in *Dialectic
of Enlightenment*, even though they did not specifically apply their findings toward the interpretation
of scientific labor.

41. Whenever he conducts research, the scholar must exclude from his research findings the basis
in fantasy that moves him; he must dilute and domesticate the reasons for which he has become active
as a scholar. If he mobilizes this foundation for his activities, he must also curb these rational mechanisms of exclusion, and thus mitigate the rigidity of his intellectual approach. A merely unstable connection between drive-base and labor emerges. The intellectual labor that emerges as if in a hothouse
thus possesses a particular structure of production whose individual components and bonds are
extremely weak and sensitive. This organizational structure therefore seeks the contact of competitive
and commodity relations because of the strong potential for concurrence they contain.

42. Here theory finds itself confronting a dilemma: it distances itself from its object whenever it
wants to approach it, since it to the same extent exceeds the concurrence that is still possible between
its own nature (by means of which even the mimetic connection to the other facets of society proceeds)
and its own objectification within the scholarly labor process. I have only notions, I can only make
observations, if I am bound to my own nature and thus to history and society. But this connection is
realized in the individual, who exists in no congruent relationship to a social objective that can only be
grasped as a whole. A production process such as one that is stringently theoretical tears the researcher
apart to a certain extent. Or, to use a different image: this mode of production can only be realized
along a narrow range of possibilities. To express this through the image of Odysseus as it is used in
*Dialectic of Enlightenment* (excursus 1, "Odysseus, or Myth and Enlightenment"): while Odysseus
has himself bound to the mast so that he can listen to the sirens, he must displace and almost forget the

material base of the cognitive activity of science or theory that has, through the division of labor, been abstracted from the production process, is to be found primarily in the libidinal state of affairs. This is one whereby the sexual interest, as the motor of curiosity and of the cognitive drive, is thwarted in its attempts at satisfaction already in the earliest stages of socialization and is required, via a series of subsequent educational and socialization processes in schooling and academic study, to make repeated efforts at sublimation. In this respect, scientific and theoretical activity is the form of human labor that is still most fully based upon the pleasure principle. Worn down by constant use, the reality principle underlying the production of knowledge, which is more highly structured than the reality principle of everday life and of healthy human understanding, continually changes its form; its material base nevertheless remains the pleasure principle.

**We are dealing here with a cognitive pressure that is different from the one that is objectively exerted on the worker by his social situation and the proletarian context of living. In comparison to the objective need of the worker, who must use knowledge to break through the barriers of his context of living, the cognitive pressure exerted upon the scientist or scholar seems almost artificial; it is the cultural product of a deferment of real satisfaction that is based on a variety of fictions.**[43] **To put it simply, the scientist or scholar is capable of subjectively placing behind his cognitive activity a sense of necessity that is not directly rooted in his economic situation. The worker is, under the conditions of his socialization, unable subjectively to form an image of the objective cognitive pressure that his context of living exerts upon him or to convert it into cognitive activity.** If he attempts to understand his situation by means of his imagination, for instance with the aid of fantasy, the defense mechanisms of the pleasure principle, which is tied to fantasy, distort the real image of society. The worker will not be stirred

---

purpose of his journey, which is to return home from his adventures. If he were instead, however, to bind himself tightly to his wish to return home, he would not even notice the sirens. In order to circumvent this dilemma, he would not be allowed to stop up the ears of his companions with wax and stash them in the ship's hull. He would have to bind himself to these companions, rather than organizing the trip home and observing the sirens as an individual. Only in a social form, with an alternatively configured collective practice of theory, can the extreme labor process of theory and scholarship be adequately linked to the productive labor that defines the whole of society. The avant-garde character of successful theoretical and scholarly labor is precisely the reason why the contradictions of its mode of production cannot be sublated within the present period of transformation of this scholarship.

43. Briefly: the proletarian needs to organize his experience in order to change the conditions of his life. The researcher organizes his scholarly experience so as to maintain his standard of living. This economic reason apparently has the effect such that a multitude of highly gifted scholars are creative only early on in their careers, and then live off of their early creativity as tenured professors who merely repeat themselves.

to action on the basis of this distorted, and in part even harmonized, picture of the world.

Traditional research activity, as a pressurized process that takes place under extreme and unnatural circumstances, has a tendency, on account of these characteristics, to decline to the level of ordinary work. This fact is noticeable in the way that universities and all schools of thought and theories have developed. Society, in particular the ruling classes, has the most need for the supreme achievements of scientific and theoretical knowledge; for this reason, it handles this specialized productive force with particular care. Neither normal industrial discipline, which governs all the rest of society, nor social and state regulations are imposed. It is here, rather than in sundry juridical issues, that the concept of university autonomy has a real chance. The university possesses autonomy not because it is a place of teaching and education, but on account of the precarious achievements of theory and research, of which, as all economists who study the educational system have confirmed, only the apex of the pyramid—roughly ten percent of total investment—is useful or profitable to society. Society also reacts to the scarcity and particular needs of the spheres of knowledge production by offering them privileges and bribes, such as economic incentives, and thus linking the production of knowledge to the ruling interests. It is only by means of such incentives that it seems possible to have control over the production of knowledge. These external economic incentives, however, are in no way coordinated with the cognitive process's real, material foundation in the libidinal sphere. This is why they are not in a position to harness knowledge production to the interests of society as a whole. Accordingly, the system of material incentives for scientists and scholars in socialist societies is no more successful than in the West: in both instances, the real material foundation for cognitive activity is different from that to which the material incentives relate. Society's funding of knowledge production merely acts as a second, additional incentive alongside the real impetus for cognitive activity.

A production of knowledge that is directed in such a way can only compile specialized knowledge and cannot organize the experience of society as a whole. The modes of expression of this specialized knowledge, as well as its content, can thus not be adopted by the majority of the population. This does not have to do with the extreme limits of academic speech or with the "backwardness of the experience of the people"; the very coexistence of the proletarian production of experience and that of scientific and scholarly knowledge is based on their diverse material foundations. This is why attempts by researchers and theoreticians to move in an emancipatory direction, while retaining their structure of production and the abstractly constructed edifice of cognitive enterprises, must continue to end in failure.

## The Appropriation of Mediated Experience
## within the Learning Rhythms of Immediate Experience[44]

People's immediate experience does not unfold as a mere appropriation and accumulation of knowledge; when it is successful, experience does not represent a process of appropriation alone, for a person is appropriated by objects in the same way in which he appropriates them.[45] This immediate experience has a complex structure; it is shaped by the predominance of the object world, which, throughout the entire life cycle, confronts it as a concrete reality, the labor process, relations of production, and social totality—in other words, as the world. This same objective context of living determines immediate experience in the form of the libidinal economy, lifelong fantasy production, the psychic structure of the individual personality, and the molding by family, upbringing, and one's own learning processes—this is the subjective side of immediate experience. **The experience derived from dealing with the learning rhythms of this type of experience is the site where motivation, practical actions, and mental activity converge. Only to the extent that workers can have experiences of their own behavior and consciousness are they in a position to develop their own forms of experience.[46]** It

---

44. The designations "mediated" and "immediate" experience sound comparatively bland when measured against known concepts within the Marxist tradition. However, the difference between them comprises a whole stepladder of different types of learning processes. Immediate experience moves first of all on what Mao Tse-tung calls the level of sensual knowledge, the level of sensations and impressions. (See Mao Tse-tung, "Über die Praxis" [Berlin: 1968]: 10.) However, it refers just as much to all higher levels upon which class consciousness is formed. The key to the capacity to form immediate experience obviously lies in a sort of learning process that has little to do with the mere inclusion of working knowledge, of learning in the narrower sense. Rather, this ability to learn, to construct immediate experience, is formed in earliest childhood. This capacity is transformed into the ever-broader steps of a long-term learning process that alters the structure and framework of experience, in addition to the innumerable short-term learning processes that accumulate knowledge. This rhythm of learning, which determines the organizational structure of experience, is not arbitrary— something that can be changed through resolutions, for instance—but a collective social product. Within it are programmed the contents of possible experience, the temporal fount within which experience is constituted, as well as the interrelationship between experience and practice.

45. Immediate experience appears as accumulated knowledge. In this respect it forms an immense accumulation of commodities because the immediate present interest in the process of accumulating handed-down experience cannot be sufficiently recognized, even if the original production of mediated experience was almost pure use-value production. This is the domain of the tradition of rational thought. The "totality of society" seems comprehensible on the path toward this immediate experience since this experience distances itself from the resistance to reality that is latent in subjective experience (*Erleben*). *It is evident, however, that mediated experience exerts an effect on all practical activity and immediate knowledge and perceptions, but that it can be the organizer and regulator of experiential interests only to a limited extent. Mediated experience is for the most part practical only if it is relevant within the rhythm of learning of immediate experience.*

46. The version of traditional humanism that displaces the formation of experience back onto the individual personality brings the real movement of experience to a standstill. Certainly, this movement

is of no use to the workers that these experiences have been formulated on a scholarly and scientific level by, for instance, Hegel and Marx. In such a theoretical formulation, in other words as mediated experience, workers can appropriate experience only when they have already organized some of it themselves. This is the meaning of Marx's assertion that it is not sufficient that the thought presses toward reality, but reality must press toward the thought, as well as his assertion that the liberation of the workers can only be the task of the workers themselves. They must recapitulate, in the forms of their own specific mode of expression and experience, the highly differentiated process of organization of social experience that is accumulated in the handful of successful forms of social theory. In our view, this is possible only within the framework of a proletarian public sphere: in other words, the autonomous, collective organization of the experience specific to workers.[47]

The interplay between immediate and mediated experience is echoed, at the level of the organization of these experiences, in the relationship between the empirical public sphere of workers and the overall category of the proletarian public sphere. The latter is not developing within the present context of the empirical public sphere of workers; the existing empirical sphere organizes the proletarian public sphere in a way that is indicative of the tendency to sublate experience, which is blocked in the proletarian context of living, by relating it to the totality of society.

The reality of the working class is made up of quite heterogeneous elements: a series of behavioral patterns, intentions, fantastic inversions of reality, wishes, and hopes, which, in their isolated state, do not in and of themselves form an organized context of experience. **However, they do not remain isolated, but form combinations that can be fitted into the frame of reference of bourgeois society.**

## The Blocking of Social Experience in the Proletarian Context of Living

The proletarian context of living is, as a specific form of reality, multidimensional. This multidimensionality is repeated in the constellation of different experiences of time. The division into that which is present, past, and future can never be completely objectively determined. For this reason, an assessment of the form

can only be remembered, transformed, or castrated through the minds of human beings. But its production and organization is a cooperative social process that can only be understood once the fiction of individual knowledge has been abandoned.

47. Contrary to this, the experience that is present in the workers cannot be defined as that which appears as *conscious experience*. Herein lies the difference between the findings of sociological studies of, for example, worker satisfaction, and the real state of consciousness that usually is not incorporated into the workers' responses. For example, a worker who is used as a "floater" at constantly

of reality of the proletarian past must necessarily take on a different shape from that of the past of a bourgeois individual, for it is only through such an assessment that **the forms of the present and of the future** are also grasped, which are not distinct from those of the proletarian past and future. The form of a worker's reality can never—in either past, present, or future—be defined in purely individualistic terms; those elements of individualism that can be found are synthetic. Although the worker seems to have a personal history, this is precisely what is unreal, what is not his reality but rather an adapted one. It is therefore wrong to contrast the **unreality of proletarian fantasy** to the **reality of the bourgeoisie**. These are two distinct levels that have nothing in common as far as their specific experience (and especially their concept of reality) is concerned apart from the fact that they are parts of a reality that, as a site of a ruin, makes possible two completely different modes of building.

For the overwhelming majority of workers, the place where they spend the greater part of their waking hours is marked by strictly delineated and limited room for movement. They are not capable of perceiving the compartmentalized space within the factory as a totality. Whereas other groups, such as foremen, clerical workers, to say nothing of members of the board or security personnel, are virtually obliged to gain an overview, the productive activity of the worker is harnessed to individual components of the factory's overall machinery. This constitutes one blocking element, which in and of itself prevents the experiencing of the external factory setting as a whole. The machinery, which confronts the worker only in fragments, takes on the form of a mystified objectivity precisely because it is not perceived as a totality. It is a small step from this limited experiential base to the mystification of commodities and capital, which is experienced as a blind mechanism. The actual level of cooperation in which production is carried out lies in sharp contrast to this.[48]

---

differing workstations during operation declares, on one particular day during which he has been expected to accomplish extremely difficult, exclusively physical labor under especially hot conditions, that he is "satisfied" with his job. It is obviously impossible for him, in responding to the situation that burdens him psychically and physically, to thereby confess that he is also still consciously reinforcing this situation; he must compensate in his consciousness for the alienation that originates in his job situation. On another day, the same worker is occupied with a less strenuous task, but finds himself at odds with one of the supervisors—he expresses vehement dissatisfaction with his job. This dissatisfaction is related not only to the present moment but to all other previous activities that come to his mind as well. This worker takes an active part in a strike movement and is very vocal in the labor struggle. During a period of calm on the job, he feels resigned, he no longer reflects his own interests in his responses, and so on. All of these different reactions, which can and cannot be expressed in words, form his consciousness and exert an influence on his behavior. Günther Hörmann of the *Institut für Filmgestaltung* in Ulm has devoted particular attention to this problem in his long-term film study of skilled laborers.

48. See in particular Konrad Frielinghaus, "Belegschaftskooperation. Belegschaftskooperation und gewerkschaftliche Betriebspolitik," in *Heidelberger Blätter* 14–16 (November 1969–April 1970: 112ff., 160ff.

In the factory, life interests and the interests of capital are opposed to one another; these give rise to specific conflicts and are not capable of being totally organized by management. The complete suppression of informal contacts between factory employees would result in a lowering of productivity levels. This has been known for at least as long as studies, which have been going on for over a decade, have been conducted in the Western Electric Company in Chicago (the Hawthorne study). Individual groups of workers, such as repair and relief workers, create links between isolated work teams. In certain advanced and specialized apparatuses of production, particularly in the chemical industry, as well as in the quasi-structural form of cooperation within the factory, interdependencies are formed that directly link individual workers with one another. The system of bonuses for suggested improvements and inventions sporadically stimulates interest in the factory as a totality. All of these mechanisms, which are unifying and potentially lead to cooperation, remain unorganized, however. In their isolated state, it is impossible to assemble these mechanisms according to the emancipatory interests of the workers.

Marx has described the Ten Hours Bill as the victory of a principle, namely of the political economy of labor over that of capital. The practical effect of the bill was to increase that portion of the individual worker's time that remained after he left the factory premises. Free time was necessary not merely for the regeneration of labor power but also for meetings and other political activities by the workers. However, this free time is not structured by an autonomous public sphere but by the terrifying structure of the modern nuclear family.[49] The proletarian family, which is characterized by the irreconcilable conflict between the utopia of use-value and value abstraction, is determined by particularly rigid behavioral norms. Any emancipatory experience that does arise within this environment is immediately consumed again.

A constrictive atmosphere within the production process and the family leads, up until a certain age, to attempts at escape; these attempts take place, however, inside prison walls. In this way, a subject discovers the limiting factors confronting any emancipatory or evasive action that is merely individual or restricted to isolated gestures.

All of these experiences are summed up in the "lifelong principle." By means

---

49. On the concept of the context of terror, see Reimut Reiche, "Was heißt: proletarische Familie?," photocopied manuscript (Frankfurt: 1971): 2ff., esp. 7ff.: "Needs are satisfied within the family, but, to an equal degree, needs are also introduced or awakened into it that cannot be realized within it. . . . This is the permanent terrorizing function of the family: it is meant to so disable human beings in terms of their life history that they are at the disposal of wage labor . . . and then to reinforce this availability on a daily basis in that all needs that extend beyond it are repeatedly mutilated." It is Reiche's claims that "*all* families in capitalist society are modeled on the prototype of the bourgeois family. This family type itself, however, no longer exists."

of the firm expectation, which has become "second nature," that the position of dependency in the work process and the narrowness of the context of living can never be changed, a block directed against the interest in experience as such becomes consolidated.

If it were nonetheless possible to connect the separately developed experiences of these different stages of the life cycle, a further intervention into the proletarian structure of experience would take place, one that applies to almost all individuals subsumed under bourgeois society: **the destruction of the identity of the experience acquired during the course of a lifetime**. This experience is compartmentalized into that of children, of school-age adolescents, and of adults who are in the production process. Each of these cycles of experience is sealed off from the others. To a certain extent, the experience of school negates and uproots experiences that the child has made in the family. For adults, school is, in turn, a trauma, but regression into childlike behavior is, on the other hand, prohibited. In this way, the experience that is actually accumulated during the entire life process cannot be grasped as something continuous.

All of the instances mentioned above constitute the initial situation encountered by the disqualification of the proletarian experience, which is not integrated by the valorization interest of the new public spheres of production. This deprives any initiatives, as fragmentary as they may be, of their relation to reality. What one is allowed to feel, express, communicate as a realistic person is molded by the modes of interaction in the factory, in everday life, and above all, transmitted by the mass media. That which is negated by this superstructure of experience would need to have an incredibly strong nature or a childlike self-confidence in order to sustain itself against the social pressure amid which the worker is confronted by the public sphere, in whose production he has himself unconsciously and collectively been involved.

This disqualification has, as far as the overall experience of the labor movement is concerned, a further historical dimension. This history of the defeats of the labor movement—along with the ideology production of some one hundred years of restoration politics, which has, as in the case of National Socialism, partially assimilated working-class experience—creates a mechanism of repression. For this reason, it is not only overt terror tactics against the labor movement that cripple the articulation of the proletariat's understanding of itself.

To this overall system of blockages of experiences in the proletarian context of living—blockages that must be eliminated together, as a whole system—is added another serious obstacle, which throughout the history of the labor movement has repeatedly ruled out a spontaneous crossing of experiential boundaries, especially for those workers who are organized. Each historically delimited form of a proletarian public sphere has hitherto tended to situate itself in terms of a historical totality of the labor movement and to thereby impair the development of more sophisticated and comprehensive forms of the proletarian public sphere. This is particularly true of certain typical forms of workers' parties. To the extent that early, still rudimentary forms of working-class organizations see their prime task as building external fronts, organizing self-defensive actions, fashioning an awareness of the identity of labor movement and party, they are all the more inclined to establish the organization of the proletariat public sphere in opposition to capitalist society. The result in this case is the mechanism of thinking in terms of "camps."[50]

The category of the proletarian public sphere would need to be developed even if it did not correspond empirically to the lived experience of the working class. But there are, in fact, elements in the consciousness of workers that are in themselves geared toward such a proletarian public sphere. To this extent, the latter is a category of reality that finds expression in different degrees of development in the labor movement. One can also define the reality of this sphere negatively, in terms of the endeavors of the ruling class to extinguish attempts at constituting a proletarian public sphere and to appropriate for itself the material on which this sphere is based—in other words, the proletarian context of living. The mechanisms used in this process are isolation, division, repression, the establishment of taboos, and assimilation. Methods range from the persecution of socialists, the "Strength through Joy" movement, the Nuremburg rallies, the ideology of industrial partnership, to the harnessing of real interests to the products of the entertainment industry—we are dealing here with a whole arsenal of influences spanning a historical period of one hundred and fifty years.

The proletarian public sphere is thus an index of the degree of emancipation of the working class at any given moment; it has as many faces as there are levels of development within the working class. The proletarian public sphere is not, like the bourgeois and the public spheres of production that overlie it, characterized by identical mechanisms. Rather, the forms of expression that determine it would be without a doubt different at the end of their development from what they were in the initial stages of the blocked context of living.[51]

## The Workings of Fantasy as a Form of Production of Authentic Experience

Throughout history, living labor has, along with the surplus value extracted from it, carried on its own production—within fantasy. The characteristics of this activ-

50. See commentary 3, entitled *The Ideology of the Camp: The Public Sphere of the Working Class as a Society within Society*.

*The organization of the party is based on the fiction that it is a definitive form of proletarian public sphere, between the society as a whole and concrete proletarian experience; it interrupts the potential for developing new forms of experience and proletarian public sphere.* Certain imputative mechanisms of orthodox Marxism and the utilization of Marxism as a science of legitimation have the same effect. See also commentaries 12 and 13.

51. See also commentaries 3, 19, and 20, as well as chapter 2 of this book. Proletarian public

ity are multilayered and have developed as a necessary compensation for the experience of the alienated labor process. The unbearable real situation experienced by the worker leads to the creation of a defense mechanism that shields the ego from the shock effects of an alienated reality.[52] Since living dialectical experience would not be able to tolerate this reality, the oppressive component of reality forces its way into fantasy. Within the libidinal economy of fantasy, the nightmarish quality of this component disappears. In seeking to transform the experience bound up in fantasy into collective practical emancipation, it does not suffice to simply utilize the products of fantasy. Rather, the relation of dependency between fantasy and the experience of an alienated reality must be determined theoretically. Only in this way can the experiences that are bound up in the fantasy structure be translated back into reality. **In its unsublated form, as a mere libidinal counterweight to unbearable, alienated relations, fantasy is itself merely an expression of this alienation. Its contents are therefore inverted consciousness. Yet by virtue of its mode of production, fantasy constitutes an unconscious practical critique of alienation.**[53]

---

sphere is in this sense *not* identical as a category with the empirical public sphere of workers—it is an operative process within this working-class public sphere, which has at the same time bourgeois structures. The proletarian public sphere and the underlying concept of organized social experience here are in a broad sense what is referred to within the Marxist tradition as *class consciousness* and *class struggle. These latter concepts, however, characterize the results, not the mediation and conditions of emergence and the concrete context of their individual elements.* It would be impossible to deduce these conditions of emergence and the concrete context of their mediation from the results.

52. See, for example, Anna Freud, *Das Ich und die Abwehrmechanismen*, 6th ed. (Munich: 1971): 137: "The reaction formation serves as a protection against the return of the repressed from within, while fantasy, on the other hand, serves as a protection of denial against the shocks of the outside world."

53. In this context, the following passage from Marx can be interpreted more literally than is usually possible: "Then we shall confront the world not as doctrinaires with a new principle: 'Here is the truth, bow down before it!' We develop new principles to the world out of its own principles. We do not say to the world: 'Stop fighting; your struggle is of no account. We want to shout the true slogan of the struggle at you.' We only show the world what it is fighting for, and consciousness is something that the world *must* acquire, like it or not. The reform of consciousness consists *only* in enabling the world to clarify its consciousness, in waking it from its dream about itself, in *explaining* to it the meaning of its own actions. Our whole task can consist only in putting religious and political questions into self-conscious human form—as is also the case in Feuerbach's criticism of religion. Our motto must therefore be: Reform of consciousness not through dogmas, but through analyzing the mystical consciousness, the consciousness which is unclear to itself, whether it appears in religious or political form. Then it will transpire that the world has long been dreaming of something that it can acquire if only it becomes conscious of it. It will transpire that it is not a matter of drawing a great dividing line between past and future, but of carrying out the thoughts of the past. And finally, it will transpire that mankind begins no *new* work, but consciously accomplishes its old work" (letter from Marx to Ruge, "For a Ruthless Criticism of Everything Existing," *Marx-Engels Reader*: 9–10).

This is in no sense a matter of a point in a text that has not yet been permeated by a materialist method and that speaks of the "dream" only for purposes of comparison. Rather, it is a question of a movement that materializes within individual consciousness but that does not yet assume the *form* of

Without a doubt these workings of fantasy, which are supposedly useless within the framework of valorization, have until now been suppressed on a vast scale; human beings are expected to be realistic. But it is precisely at the very sites of this suppression that it is impossible for bourgeois society to assimilate entirely the contents of proletarian consciousness and imagination or to simply subsume them under the valorization interest. The suppression of fantasy is the condition of its freer existence in present society. One can prohibit the activity of fantasy, the spinning of a web around reality, as something unrealistic; but if one does this, it becomes difficult to influence the direction and mode of production of fantasy. The subliminal activity of consciousness has been neglected until now by bourgeois interests and by the bourgeois public sphere, and thus represents a partly autonomous, proletarian mode of experience. The existence of this subliminal activity is presently in danger because it is precisely the workings of fantasy that constitute the raw material and the medium for the expansion of the consciousness industry.

The capacity of fantasy to organize people's individual experiences is concealed by the structures of consciousness, the screens capturing our attention, and the stereotypes molded by the culture industry, as well as by the apparent substantiality of everyday experience in its bourgeois definition. The quantifying time of the production process, which is composed of nothing but linear units of time linked functionally with one another, is generally hostile to fantasy. But it is precisely this linear time that is helpless vis-à-vis the specific temporal mechanism, the "date-mark" (Freud) of fantasy.

The workings of fantasy are in an oblique relation to valorized time. Its specific movement, as described by Freud, fuses within each moment immediate present impressions, past wishes, and future wish fulfillment.[54] Beneath the opposition of pleasure principle and reality principle, fantasy will display in all people the same mechanism, which attempts to associate present, past, and future. This mechanism is in and of itself not class-specific. However, the fantasy material that is converted by means of these associations, and in particular the degree of

---

consciousness. Empirically, this is expressed in the flow of associations that accompanies the lifelong labor process, but also in the historical sedimentations of this flow of consciousness in the form of cultural products and ways of life.

54. Freud describes this by way of an example. It is surely no coincidence that he takes it from the labor process, even though the essay is about creative writers: "Let us take the case of a poor orphan boy to whom you have given the address of some employer where he may perhaps find a job. On the way there he may indulge in a day-dream appropriate to the situation from which it arises. The content of his phantasy will perhaps be something like this. He is given a job, finds favour with his new employer, makes himself indispensable in the business, is taken into his employer's family, marries the charming young daughter of the house, and then himself becomes a director of the business, first as his employer's partner and then as his successor" (Sigmund Freud, "Writers and Day-dreaming," in *The Standard Edition of the Complete Psychological Works of Sigmund Freud*, vol. 9, trans. James Strachey [London: Hogarth, 1959]: 148).

distortion of these fantasies under the pressure of a social reality principle and under the influence of the fragmentation of lived time, would be entirely dependent upon one's position within the production process. This position would also determine whether the fantasy material is expressed in a stunted or in a fully developed form.

It is important to recognize that fantasy relates to a concrete situation in a threefold sense: **the concrete situation in which a wish develops; the concrete situation of the current impression that has been processed; and the concretely imagined situation of wish fulfillment.** It is precisely these situations, however, that are "damaged" ones in the proletarian context of living. In the real life cycle, they appear fragmented, mixed up with other moments, transposed back and forth without regard for the fantasy harnessed to them. Fantasy is not truly chaotic; rather, it manifests itself in this way in situations that do not take its specific mode of production into account. This mode, moreover, remains reactive: it is linked to reality and therefore reproduces the distorted concreteness of this reality.

**Whereas standard language and instrumental rationality do not cross the boundary between the bourgeois and proletarian public spheres, colloquial language and the workings of fantasy are exposed to the conflict between these two forms (understood as the expression and comprehension of life). The boundary between the bourgeois and proletarian public spheres, between the bourgeois and proletarian articulation of the circumstances of everyday life, does not exist as a spatial, temporal, logical, or concrete threshold (one that could, for instance, be secured by an act of translation). The proletarian public sphere negates the bourgeois one because it dissolves, partially destroys, and partially assimilates the latter's elements. In serving its opposing interests, the bourgeois public sphere does the same to every form of the proletarian, which is not supported by the powers opposing it and thus cannot protect itself from attack. A coexistence is impossible. It is true that centers for the articulation of proletarian interests can confront corresponding bourgeois centers in one and the same society; but when they come into contact, their interaction reveals itself as unreal. The workings of fantasy, which are drawn away from this conflict, take on that distorted form that has until now made impossible the conceptualization of science, education, and aesthetic production as organizing forms of the fantasy of the masses. Conversely, it has been impossible to incorporate fantasy, as it manifests itself in the masses, into emancipatory forms of consciousness appropriate to the level of industrial production. In this way, one of the raw materials of class consciousness, the faculty of imagination as the sensual-fantastic, remains cut off from overall social relations and situated in a lower level of production, that of individuals or of merely random cooperation. The higher levels of production, in turn, exclude this raw material. At the same time,**

**industry, in particular the consciousness and programming industry, attempts to develop techniques to reintroduce fantasy in a domesticated form.**

Insofar as fantasy follows its own mode of production, one that is not structured by the valorization process, it is threatened by a specific danger. Fantasy has a tendency to distance itself from the alienated labor process and to translate itself into timeless and ahistorical forms of production that "do not and cannot exist." Thus, fantasy would prevent the worker from advocating for his interests in reality. This danger is not, however, as great as it may appear from the bolstered standpoint of the critical-rationalist tradition of thought. As fantasies move farther away from the reality of the production process, the impulse that drives them on becomes less sensitive. Thus, all escapist forms of fantasy production tend, once they have reached a certain distance from reality, to turn around and face up to real situations. They establish themselves at a level definitively separated from the production process *only if* they are deliberately organized and confined there by a valorization interest.[55]

The term fantasy, as it is used commonly in indicating dissociation, is a product of the bourgeoisie. Accordingly, the word does not denote an underlying, unified productive force, which represents a specific work process with laws of movement specific to it. On the contrary, this productive force is from the outset schematized according to alien principles, those of the capitalist process of valorization. Through this process, what is subsequently called fantasy is created by dissociation and confinement.[56] That which, from the standpoint of valorization,

---

55. This can be a valorization interest or an interest in legitimation profits. "Legitimation profits" are the money that allows for subsumption under particular relations of power. This can mean legitimation based on a claim to orthodoxy, but also, for example, entertainment or news values that are meant to justify subsumption under a news industry. The bourgeois novel, of which Lukács wrote that it must be gulped down rather than read, also produces—at least in part—the sort of context within which fantasy to a great extent moves alongside reality and not within it. It is absurd for Lukács to require that precisely this quality of the "hermetic" work of art be introduced into socialist realism.

56. The *internment* of fantasy takes place on two levels: components of its power are absorbed as a bonding adhesive for reinforcing alienated labor and life relations, that is, of culture. Ultimately, as is the case in assembly-line or hard manual labor, for example, it consists almost exclusively of the internalized power to perceive the consequences—real or imagined loss of love, punishment, isolation, and so on—that one might face if one were to simply run away from forced relations. Here fantasy is transformed into discipline, "realism," apathy. Other elements of the same capacity for fantasy that appear to be free-floating wander aimlessly through the past, present, and future, but, for their part, because of their own libidinously controlled laws of motion, seek to avoid coming into contact with alienated contemporaneity, and with the bourgeois reality principle. They are barricaded away into the ghettos of the arts, dreaming, and "delicate feelings."

Within this bifurcation, the "realistic" and "unrealistic" powers of fantasy develop need structures and capacities that are set in opposition to each other. Their opposition cannot be relinked into a unified productive force by means of simple addition. Their linkage into a real working intellectual productive force presupposes the reactualization of the whole prehistory of this bifurcated capacity for fantasy.

appears particularly difficult to control—the residue of unfulfilled wishes, ideas, of the brain's own laws of movement, which are both unprocessed and resist incorporation into the bourgeois scheme—is depicted as fantasy, as the vagabond, the unemployed member of the intellectual faculties. **In reality, this fantasy is a specific means of production engaged in a process that is not visible to the valorization interest of capital: the transformation of the relations of human beings to one another and to nature, and the reappropriation of the historically marked dead labor of human beings.**[57] Fantasy is thus not a particular substance (as when one says "so-and-so has a lot of imagination"), but the organizer of mediation. It is the specific work process whereby libidinal structure, consciousness, and the outside world are connected with one another. An obstacle is erected for any emancipatory practice when this productive force of the brain is divided up to such a degree that it cannot obey its own laws of operation. This means that an important tool is lost for the self-emancipation of the workers, the precondition of which is an analysis in the social and historical sense. This latter process is analogous to the principle of the reappropriation of the repressed as developed by Freud for the *individual* life history of human beings.[58]

That which Freud has developed from individuals, who do not as a rule have a concrete connection with the labor process, into the form of a dialogue situation between patient and therapist, is a segment of a collective social production that has been isolated to the history of one individual. The possibility to actually work through repressions and fixations of individual stages of development would only exist if the production process, of which these fixations are the result, were itself the object of collective transformation. Discourse and recollective, reflexive, and hence purely linguistic activities are not the typical forms for mastering past conflicts through reactualization. The concept of communication as the linear con-

---

57. In contrast to the use of "fantasy" in bourgeois language, Freud thus also correctly speaks of dream-*work* (*Traumarbeit*), mourning-*work* (*Trauerarbeit*), the *work* of the capacity to fantasize, and so on. However, these are still only partial aspects of the total productive force of fantasy, which would be able to develop as a whole only if its own laws of movement were to enter into the reality principle, in opposition to which it exhausts itself, and thus forms a new reality principle.

58. For Freud it is a question of the reappropriation of the individual life history and its conflicts. The mode of analysis for accomplishing this is language. For the emancipation of social classes, the readaptation of the dead labor that is bound up with the specific history of human beings, the mode of analysis is on the contrary not verbal language, but rather a language in the wider sense that includes all mimetic, cultural, and social relationships as means of expression. Here a linguistic analysis is only a partial aspect. The most important means of expression for a self-analysis on the part of the masses would, instead, be labor. But as a result of the bifurcation of the productive force of fantasy, it is among other things not understood as an agent for communication between the past, the present, and the desire for one's own identity in the future, but rather is able to operate only in the real context of the alienated labor process. If the process of social revolution is not understood in the form of state intervention, but instead as a specific labor and production process, it becomes clear what political significance is possessed by the productive force that is at the base of fantasy. Without its organization, the process of social change cannot be undertaken by the producers of social wealth.

nections made by people in the present is too limited; rather, one must take into account the real process of human communication, which is mediated by past, present, and future. The interest of workers in not being cut off from their own histories is situated within this experience of the full, historically articulated concept of human labor. This is why they cannot come to terms with the ahistorical, quantifying time and with the ahistorical present and future of the bourgeois concept of work, which has been evolved out of commodity production.

**Again and again in the history of the labor movement, workers have made demands with regard to the public sphere that workers' organizations are incapable of fully satisfying. One can say of these needs that either they develop in the direction of a proletarian public sphere or they become—even independently of the bourgeois public sphere—an instrument for the suppression of the working class.**

## Solidarity That Can Be Grasped with the Senses

The need for mass demonstrations, for physical closeness, is an expression of the level of socialization, cooperation, solidarity, and mutual protection that has been attained within the production process. This too can develop in either a reactionary or an emancipatory direction.

Wilhelm Reich has discussed the working class's changing needs for self-expression, using those workers who marched in Hitler's SA as an example.[59] This need for physical closeness is, to begin with, an inversion of the actual isolation of individuals at work. Such an inversion confirms the existence of human relationships within a situation governed by abstract and alienated competitiveness.[60] Added to this is the oldest experience of workers: concentration within the workplace. They do not band together of themselves for they have already been banded together by the production process. This relates to another experience of the workers' struggle: Marx notes that the barricades always had more moral than military significance; they safeguard one's own solidarity and demoralize the

59. See Wilhelm Reich, "Was ist Klassenbewußtsein?" in *Massenpsychologie des Faschismus* (1934; pirated edition Frankfurt am Main: 1967).

60. The industrial discipline of the process of production is legitimated with the statement that human relationships constitute society. This is the opposite of actual relationships between human beings in a society that produces commodities. Workers attempt, in their need for a solidarity that can be sensually grasped, to redeem this claim of society for themselves. This stance is prepared by socialization within the family and the humanist tradition. which is a precondition of education and the mass media. Throughout the history of the labor movement, the need for sensually graspable solidarity has more often led the working class into the nets of dominant interests than liberated them from them. The stability of comradely relationships during both world wars, for example, is an indication of the fact that a portion of this need can even be satisfied in senseless wars. This need was also exploited emphatically by National Socialism.

forces of the enemy. For people who as a rule do not carry weapons, only physical massing can achieve anything against the military, the police, or security guards in the workplace.

At the same time, the need for a solidarity that can be grasped with the senses is a response to the invisibility of the real enemy. The police and immediate superiors in the labor process are not the real antitheses to workers who could win their identity not in the struggle against these advance guards but only against private property. **Massing together serves as a mutual confirmation of their own reality, for who else but the other workers can confirm that their struggle is not a mere illusion, if even the destruction of the factories does not do away with the relations of production and with the workers' state of dependency? It is only in this reaffirmed reality that an atmosphere of collective revolt comes about, that the workers begin to talk, make suggestions, and become active.** If such a revolutionary mood is not present, this same need is expressed in the shape of powerful loyalty toward the organizations of the working class, even if the individual recognizes that his immediate interests are no longer represented. This is why, in the case of wildcat strikes and mass demonstrations, the vehement criticism of established working-class organizations is never completely serious. As soon as these organizations give their attention to even a part of the demands made by the base, the workers will once again fight on their behalf.

The need for physical, direct mass communication is frustrated in every aspect of our society, both in the nonpublic structure of the public sphere of the factory and in the structure of the mass media.[61] The bourgeois public sphere, which confronts the worker in the form of his own organizations, confirms his inability to express himself in an autonomous manner.[62] The organization of workers in clandestine, nonpublic, vanguard groups is more or less the opposite of the fundamental need that has been described here.

---

61. Cultural criticism and television humanism advise the worker to not simply spontaneously follow his need for a solidarity that can be sensually perceived. He is supposed to learn to differentiate, critically and as an enlightened individual, between the mass movements he follows, and riotous mobs that he should in no case follow. This mere alleviation of his need means for the worker a withdrawal of reality (*Realitätsentzug*). As an individual, he can avoid mistakes only by doing absolutely nothing.

62. That this situation is a product of oppression, of the limitation of the individual's objectively available potential in the sense of his socially produced potential, is evidenced especially clearly in the example of the politicization of the nuclear research center in Saclay. The technical cadre of this center had not been the least bit politicized before May 1968. Indeed, in its initial stages, there had been specific mechanisms put in place to protect against politicization, a protection mechanism that was supported in part by the established unions. But at the moment in which it was no longer a question of numbers and investments, but rather of the meaning (*Sinn*) of production itself, a political interest was spontaneously awakened, especially in those who had previously not taken part in any gatherings or union activities. See *Pesquet, Räte in Saclay*, p. 55.

## The Desire for the Simplification
## of Social Circumstances—Personalization

The workers' need for social orientation is often described as a split conscious-ness. This sociological view does not, however, enable the various components of the underlying need to be distinguished from the forms of the bourgeois public sphere that overlay them. What underlies this need is the impulse toward direct, immediate experience, because "the world is after all human, in other words, our own world." This is overlaid by an attempt to understand the surrounding world in terms of generalities and recognizable commodity relations. If workers do not have their own forms for expressing their interests, they will, as a rule, fall back on the stereotypes that society offers them. This is also true in terms of the divi-sion of the world according to friend/foe relationships. There is, however, also a real impulse underlying this: **the attempt to grasp circumstances as they really are.** Yet this impulse is contradictory as well, for although it does indicate the cor-rect path for understanding reality, this path is negotiated by means of oversimpli-fications; in other words, by means of an unrealistic, ideological picture of the world.[63] When it takes on such a form, this need corresponds with the products offered by the consciousness industry, for instance the weekly tabloids. In other situations that are not dominated by the bourgeois public sphere, such as wildcat strikes, the same need leads to feelings of partisanship and militancy. In this case, we are not dealing with ingrained stereotypes; for although the emancipatory potential of these qualities has no effect in controlled situations, it does in "wild-cat" situations. At present such revolutionary climates are the exception. A real-ization of this need is not possible in such conflicts, however, which as a rule are of only short duration. It is only possible in learning processes in which the regressive desire for simplification can be separated from the underlying emanci-

---

63. This double significance, additionally complicated by the fact that stereotypes are superim-posed over one's own autonomous activity, affects the whole of the social behavior of the worker. Thus, for example, the "buying of rounds" in a pub was originally a form of sales pressure that was used by the breweries by way of the proprietor on the workers. The increased consumption of beer is the condition under which the workers are allowed to come together and have a roof over their heads in a pub. The fulfillment of the condition linked up to it is not an autonomous activity; it does not corre-spond to their interests. This is not expressed in their behavior, that is, their increased consumption of beer, but rather in the *form* of their behavior, in the fact that they link an acknowledgment of mutual solidarity with this increase in consumption. This process is camouflaged by the "buying of rounds." The total "rounds bought" cancel each other out in turn, that is, there is simply more beer consumed. This form is one of their own invention, while the forced consumption of beer has been determined from without.

This situation is replicated in sports events. Here as a rule workers view the stereotype of the achievement-oriented society to which they themselves are subjected during the labor process. They value alienated and one-dimensional physical skill, the professionalism of the soccer players, and so forth. These forms of public behavior are rarely proletarian, even if they represent solid habits on the part of the workers that they certainly would not allow themselves to be simply talked out of.

patory need to understand reality and, armed with organized experience, collectively to improve the situation of the working class.

Strategies for overcoming this blockage can be found, above all, in the intelligentsia's method of work. Differentiation, complexity, interaction, totality, and so forth, as conceived by the great theoreticians of the labor movement, are the conceptual emancipatory forms of the intelligentsia, not of the working class. As cognitive tools of the intelligentsia, these forms are not simply superior because they generally produce more highly qualified individuals through middle-class socialization and through the division of manual and mental labor that is so typical of the intelligentsia. However, the very quality that distinguishes intellectuals—their artificially forced capacity for abstraction—is a tool for grasping alienated social realities. The intelligentsia produces abstract cross sections of society in a manner that is faulty in many respects. This mode of production reveals that the separation of knowledge and collective human interests, the hothouse method by which qualities of the intelligentsia have been cultivated, in particular during the course of bourgeois development, is itself a phenomenon of alienation. This is expressed in academic language that reproduces the experience of the intelligentsia but excludes that of the working class. Moreover, the abstracting work of intellectuals simplifies in a way that does not correspond to the interests of workers. The type of labor performed by the intelligentsia is thus not helpful in a direct way. It would only be helpful if it were collectively transformed and rebuilt within the experiential context of the working class. The workers' need for a simplified picture of society often manifests itself together with the **desire for personalization.**[64] It is wrong to dismiss this need as a "personality cult" or as an obsession with authority. The abstract, critical approach, which, for instance, television producers expect even of workers, minimizes both the workers' need and the possibility of organizing experience through the fulfillment of this need. It is conceivable that theory and mediated experience can be conveyed to nontheoreticians only when expressed through a person, through his very behavior, gestures, and personal integrity. It must be possible to directly emulate immediate experience rather than to accept it merely as an idea or a logical result.

---

64. Apparently the relationships of workers toward objects are in no way dichotomous in the way their relationships to people or organizations are dichotomous. In the case of the arrangement of machines or approaches to other complex objects, there in no way emerges an absolute desire for simplification. Indeed, as regards technical objects, there frequently emerges what amounts to a desire for increased complexity. Motorcycles and cars are additionally equipped with "all the extras" in order to differentiate them as much as possible. This is due not only to the influence of advertising. Rather, it can be assumed that the desire for simplification does not correspond at all to any originary need, but is rather solely a reflection of a present defensive experience on the part of the workers with the bourgeois public sphere. This is not to say that the experience of objectified reality itself is in any respect one that is *lived (erlebt)* in a simplified way. It is simply abbreviated in the course of its being reproduced within a situation that is not suited to expression.

The mechanism whereby desires and hopes become attached to specific people is, however, effective only if an individual is able to establish a trusting relationship with these people. This is mirrored in the individual's relationship to organizations and parties. Loyalty to leaders is founded on the leaders' integrity. This loyalty extends to cases where workers no longer have an overview of the situation or where they would decide differently than their leaders do. Loyalty, however, always presupposes reciprocity. It is preserved because the leaders appear to be loyal as well.[65]

Other forms of expression—banners in demonstrations, pictures, slogans, songs, bands, and so on—in which the experience of the collective struggles of the labor movement is generally made manifest, play a comparable role in promoting identification.[66] These aids to identification serve to express a common ego-ideal. The opposite to this would be the invocation of the superego that predominates among most of the charismatic figures of the bourgeoisie. This mechanism of experience enables one to differentiate between, among other things, the

---

65. This need for loyalty does not appear in this form in any bourgeois social strata. Whenever bourgeois leaders are no longer needed, are unsuccessful, or die, they are forgotten. In the history of the workers' movement, however, the desire for relationships of mutual trust has repeatedly proven to be the most powerful means of organization. One example among many is the mass trust that was placed in the labor leader Largo Caballero during the Spanish Civil War. This union secretary and agitator of the leftist wing of the Spanish Socialist Party, born into a working-class family in Madrid in 1869, had originally been an exponent of reformism. He vehemently opposed joining the Comintern and wanted to lead the Spanish workers toward the state. He became a government advisor under Primo de Rivera and labor minister in the Azaña cabinet. He then collided with the ministerial bureaucracy, which openly sabotaged his instructions. On the basis of his experience in government he concluded that reformism was leading the labor movement into a dead end. In 1934 he came to the conclusion that "It is impossible to realize even a fraction of socialism within the framework of bourgeois democracy." During the revolution he became head of the republican government that was elected by the unions and that succeeded in defending Madrid and in driving out the Italian expeditionary forces. The Spanish workers evidently realized their potential for action in the outwardly unlikely person of this head of government. The turning point in the Civil War was the fall of Largo Caballero. This view corresponds to the evaluations of historians whose findings cannot be undermined by the claim that they exaggerate the significance of personality in history.

The opposite was the case in the government of Negrín. Juan Lopez Negrín overthrew Caballero by means of intrigue. He was the exponent of the state finance administration. His dynastic power lay in the tariff troops he had newly assembled. He attempted to improve the Spanish position internationally, tightened up internal organization, and centralized; he also received substantial shipments of arms from the Soviet Union, and for a time possessed objectively richer sources of aid than had Caballero, and yet he was only the bankruptcy trustee of the Spanish Revolution. He lost the Civil War not because he was weaker militarily, but because there was no point at which he won, or even attempted to win, the support of the masses. See also the interpretations of Pierre Broué and Émile Témime, *Revolution und Krieg in Spanien. Geschichte des spanischen Bürgerkriegs* (Frankfurt: 1968), as well as the sources cited therein.

66. On the other hand, for example, it is hard to see what might bind workers as experience in a performance of Schumann's "Rhineland Symphony" or of labor songs by three professional singers in evening gowns, if these entertainments appear as the highlights of a union congress.

bourgeois and the proletarian element in working-class demonstrations and events. Whereas the proletarian use of these symbols or of identification with working-class leaders serves to develop an ego-ideal, these same symbols and mechanisms of identification can be enlisted for opposite ends: for the stabilization of a superego marked by its authoritarian and repressive aspect. **This is why, in the case of demonstrative identifications, especially identification with public figures (e.g., Mao, Lenin, Guevara, Luxemburg, Liebknecht), what counts is strictly the identity of the experiential content. Only if the collective experience expressed by these individuals has a concrete and communicable historical connection with the autonomous experience of the demonstrators is it possible to differentiate between ego-ideal and authoritarian superego fixation.** The former case involves an appropriation of history and an enrichment of experiences whereby reifications are potentially broken up. In the latter, real experiences are concealed by a supplementary layer of reification. It is basically a borderline case when left-wing groups identify with individuals such as Che Guevara, Castro, Ho Chi Minh, and Mao, who, because of the revolutions that they stand for, represent quite different concrete experiences for the masses than for European intellectuals, whose thoughts and actions are motivated by different factors. This is not to say that one should renounce internationalism. On the contrary, it is precisely the intelligentsia's mode of production, which enables one to perceive complexity, differentiation, and interrelationships, that insists upon concrete and differentiated definition of one's relations to the revolutionary experiences of other countries. Only such differentiation, together with the recognition that experiential contexts cannot be transposed from one country to another, could give rise to an internationalism that would have to be taken seriously.

## The "Materialist Instinct"

The masses live with experiences of violence, oppression, exploitation, and, in the broader sense of the term, alienation. They possess material, sensual evidence of the restriction of possibilities in their lives, of their freedom of movement. Accordingly, the resistance to this restriction has a sensual credibility: "This is a threat to us as human beings." This level of concrete experience applies just as well to workers as to peasants or intellectuals. These groups may all be radically different in terms of their weapons, their mode of discipline, and the obstacles that arise from their specific forms of socialization; but they are not different in the way they react spontaneously to the situation.

The concrete experience of the lack of freedom is the important factor here. When Hobbes describes freedom as a human being's actual physical sphere of movement, he captures precisely the masses' material mode of experience. The extent of a person's freedom in prison is measured by how much he is able to move. His thoughts may offer him consolation, but they do not give him one extra yard of freedom. Schiller's line, "man is created free, is free, even if he were born in chains," is absolutely incomprehensible to the masses in relation to their own experience. All it does is express the radical division between intellectual and physical labor.

Why can this "materialist instinct" not be permanently suppressed by the dominant forces, not even by the authority of bourgeois culture? Why is it that the materialist instinct is spontaneously triggered among the masses? Each ruling class manufactures sensually palpable products of a better life. It manufactures needs within the masses that it cannot satisfy. The palaces were assuredly not built for the masses, but these masses measure their needs by them. This is articulated in its most uncensored form in fairy tales.

Modern capitalism necessarily produces, in answering to its own valorization interest, ideas and needs whose satisfaction on a mass scale could bring about its own destruction. By thus nourishing the materialist instinct, it accumulates the conditions (and does not abandon them to a spontaneity coming, as it were, from nature) that lead to an explosion. The explosive points are varied; they may occur when the system relaxes its constraints, or when additional repression occurs.

**Experiences become commodities to the extent that they can be reduced to a common denominator. All experiences of the proletariat are specific. They can be generalized, but they cannot be reduced to such a general level—to, for instance, criteria, legitimations, or hierarchies of revolutionary behavior. These experiences are produced as qualitative moments. It is difficult to work through proletarian experience because it lacks the commensurability of commodity relations. It changes with each situation.**

Two directions can be distinguished in the revolutions familiar to us, which, under certain circumstances, meet in one and the same revolutionary action. We are familiar with the "virtue" of Robespierre, the "new socialist human being," revolutionary formal and logical consistency, centralizing thought, thinking in terms of systems, and economic calculation. All of these hierarchies may, in separate contexts, admit to a "radicalism," but this does not make them revolutionary. They can be every bit as restricted as the commodities producer's horizon of experience. They split up the revolutionary process into essential and inessential, into what is of value to the revolution and what is useless, into active subjects (the avant-garde) and objects of education and administration. In this respect they are all in fact following the logic of a value abstraction.

The human relationships that are produced by this process take on the character of dead products. Such results of revolutionary activity are "*entirely new*" and strive for *changed circumstances* in the sense that they sever the connection between the living experience of the masses and their living labor. "Radical" components of this kind are, in the Marxist sense, sensual-supersensual things. Whenever one identifies them in the context of proletarian revolution, they are the revolution's bourgeois element. They are mystifications of authentic revolutionary experience. This authentic experience organizes itself at the outset of each movement through positions, through platforms that are formulated in a revolutionary way. In simple, clearly defined political situations, revolutionary slogans (e.g., "All power to the soviets," "Peace," "All land to the peasants") are so closely linked with immediate experience that if a "more radical" position is superimposed, *it would immediately be recognized as unrealistic.* This does not apply to the types of complex situations that generally exist in highly industrialized capitalist countries. If "more radical" positions are superimposed on positions that represent real experience, there is a tendency to substitute these "radical" positions for revolutionary experience itself as experience that has already been discussed and associated with the revolutionary hierarchy of values. It is difficult, in this socialized form, to correct matters through immediate experience. First, experience produces the radical positions, and then the radical positions produce experience—a dramatized, processed form of experience. Real experience, which is constantly forming itself anew, runs alongside but is unrelated to this processed experience. The enemy can pick it up off the streets and organize it for his own ends. This is one of the mechanisms of the Thermidor.

Radicalism is not a form of experience. Once the foundation of real experience has been abandoned, a hierarchy of radicalism rises above it. This can be surpassed, it would appear, only by further radicalism.[67] A mystical constellation is formed that can be overcome only by doing away with the inverted relation between the two levels of radicalism—in other words, by going back to experience itself. When Marx says that being radical means nothing more than getting hold of things by their roots, and that the root of a human being is the human being, it becomes clear that radicalism in analysis and struggle can only be intensified downward. It is a bourgeois reflex to process it upward, toward ideas, platforms, and authorities. The only reliable means of penetrating this veil is the "materialist instinct" of the masses. In fact, this instinct acts like an emergency brake in bringing the entire train to a halt, as is proved in the case of all counterrevolutions.

## Language Barriers

All bourgeois forms of the public sphere presuppose special training, both linguistic and mimetic. In public court proceedings, in dealings with officials, it is expected of all parties involved that they be concise and present their interests with forms of expression fitting to the official business at hand (for instance, that they be "objective," "pertaining to the petition," etc.) Speeches given in meetings are shaped by a precise knowledge of the situation and of the audience's expecta-

---

67. Karl Kraus describes this process with the comment: "We have once again risen to a higher level. There is only one disadvantage in this—there are none that are higher."

tions. As a rule, they must be grammatically correct. A public appearance on television is especially complicated. A second element enters the scene in this case: the speaker finds himself in a position determined by the recording equipment and the program, not by his own speech.

The unsettling point for the layperson in any one of the public spheres is the **economy of speech** specific to it. In the worker's form of expression, the connection between two different experiences is not secured through pure logic. The worker proceeds to portray an aspect of the situation; by doing so, he establishes his emotional stance and probes for the position to take on the issue while he is talking. This is an attempt at orientation, a rudimentary form of self-reflection, and an offer to those around him to comment and to cooperate during the speech. Within the context of the bourgeois public sphere, above all in school and on television, this attempt is seen as a digression and is immediately rejected.

It is a well-known fact that "high German" is effectively used, above all, in school, as a mechanism for selection. Performance in school is measured according to the degree that one masters this language. If the child "passes the test" in this area, he moves up a grade, and his chances for upward social mobility can be preprogrammed. This is one of the most important exclusionary mechanisms of the bourgeois public sphere that confronts working-class children. They are subject to this mechanism without being able to comprehend it. For them, language is less an instrument of cognition and thought than a means for communication within their own social class. The socialization effect of this language is more important than the individualization effect of the "elaborated code" to which middle-class children are accustomed. The colloquial forms of the "restricted code," as they are generally used by working-class children, correspond to the symbolic representations of objective reality and interpersonal relationships within which these children's entire experience of socialization is expressed. They are dependent upon using these "internal means of production" if they are supposed to have experiences and extend these into a "picture of the world." They are separated from these "internal means of production" if they have to learn what is, for them, a "new" language—the standard language, whose relationship to symbols and psychic representation is not and cannot be taught in school. It is, precisely, compensatory education, when implemented successfully, that makes it possible for them to function in the communication network of school and university. It is hardly possible to imagine a more effective exclusionary mechanism than the one mobilized by the bourgeois public sphere in separating the real producers of experience from their own means of production. One fails to understand the relationship of the bourgeois public sphere to the concept of experience if one regards this mechanism merely as an instrument of class rule. This would mean that sections of the ruling class could decide, on the basis of shifting constellations of interests, to exclude, either partially or completely, their own interests so as to ensure their subsequent survival by taking into account and deliberately incorporating the interests of the overwhelming majority of the population. On the contrary, the bourgeois public sphere's mechanisms for excluding and destroying experience are situated in those very areas where it believes it is operating according to "idealistic" and "humanistic" principles.[68]

When a worker is in control in a concrete situation, he does not orient statements and thoughts according to previous statements, nor by an abstract intellectual content, a so-called message; he gains, rather, a sense for the objects on an associative level. We are dealing with an elemental form of expression that grasps the activity of the brain in a different way than logical and grammatical discourse or the dramaturgical construction of speech. This elementary form of expression is only slightly removed from the libidinal control of the processes of thought and perception and, in particular, does not distance itself from the concrete situation to which speech relates. Sociologists say that the worker has a tactile relationship to language and a need for confirmation through objects and other people. It is obvious that the ground is literally pulled out from under him if he loses the ability to confirm his sentences through objects that can be experienced, through the situa-

---

68. This complex context has recently been worked out with increased clarity. In our context here, we can only refer to the more recent attempts by Habermas, Oevermann, Lorenzer, Wygotski, Du Bois-Reymond, and so on. See also the synopsis of the status of these discussions in Joachim Rossbroich, "Probleme einer kritischen Theorie und Praxis der Spracherziehung," in *Ästhetik und Kommunikation* 7 (1972): 59ff; Eike Brechstein, "Die Sozialisation des Arbeiterkindes in Familie und Schule," 75ff., as well as the bibliographical literature cited therein. Also, Johannes Siegrist, *Das Consensus-Modell*, Soziologische Gegenwartsfragen, Neue Folge no. 32 (Stuttgart: 1970), with an extensive bibliography. Basil Bernstein, by the way, also refers to the language of the working class as "public language." *It is in fact a matter of a language that is excluded from the public sphere under the terms of bourgeois institutions, a language that tends, on the basis of this exclusion, to sublate* (aufheben) *its experiential content that has no public validity via an autonomous organization.* Empirically, this tendency corresponds to the precise opposite—the linguistic conservatism of the working classes. The requirements of teachers and the special training of the bourgeois public sphere are perceived as attacks on the self-understanding and the affective security of workers and working-class children. They are responded to with an intensified withdrawal and self-restriction to one's own class experience and the colloquial idiom. Viewed from this position, the "social topoi" of the limited linguistic codes exert a restrictive, retrograde effect on all of the mass media and the communicative structure of the public sphere. Since the educational system, the mass media, and the expressive context of the intelligentsia do not really organize the linguistically apprehended experience of workers, but merely reduce it, the language that is actually spoken by the oppressed majority of the population itself hinders the deployment of the systems of their oppressors. See also chapter 3 on the public sphere of public-service organized television stations.

Ferruccio Rossi-Landi (*Ästhetik und Kommunikation* 7 [1972]) has examined linguistic production and private property within the three dimensions of (1) control of the codes and the forms of codification, (2) control of channels of communication and of the forms developed for news circulation, as well as (3) the control of forms of decoding and interpretation. The production of language, as the production of conditions and of a total context *and* as the use of this language, appears here as the most effective particular power relation of the public-sphere context and of the bourgeois form of communication determined by capitalist production.

tion, or through his addressee. This is the case when he attends a labor-relations board meeting or when he testifies in court: here, the worker is expected to talk abstractly about the very same things that, in their real context, he can describe exactly. What Basil Bernstein has termed "circular conversation" should thus be understood as, among other things, an attempt to construct a situation for allowing one to speak freely in cases where the situation cannot be constructed or where one is conscious of its underlying fragmentary nature.

Economy of thought and an abstract flexibility—in other words, the ability to talk abstractly about all situations—are, as demanded by the ruling public sphere, the value abstractions of speech. They dominate the standard language of communication, but they are by no means characteristic of language as such.[69] This is made especially obvious by the many rules that allegedly work toward a tighter economy of speech: avoid repeated words, be sparing with metaphors, use complete sentences, observe correct spelling, and so forth. The constrictive and oppressive nature of these rules is already clear to children. The entire system of rules bound up with standard language results, moreover, in a crude distortion of experiences because it does not articulate essential elements of the production sphere and of everyday life (among other things, the whole of sexuality). Insofar as it does express experiences, it stands in an oblique relation to the real organization of perceptions, associations, and feelings. This is important because the unfolding of immediate experiences requires their public expression and exchange.

Since roughly the 1960s, a whole branch of research focusing on the subject of language barriers has developed. These studies examine linguistic codes: in other words, the symbolic transformations of the social relationships that for their part control interaction (Bernstein). The initial practical goal was to make visible a problem of class division, one that results in the one-sided selection procedures of educational institutions and that has gone unnoticed by working-class organizations. This practice has now largely disappeared and an academic industry of projects and posts has developed whose interest in language barriers evidently lies in the fact that these barriers exist. In following the underlying impulse of the

---

69. Rossi-Landi (Ästhetik und Kommunikation 7 [1972]) differentiates language as an already-produced social system that represents dead labor from the living labor of human beings who labor against this linguistic system and produce mutual understanding from out of this machinery. Thus they are subject to the particular power relation that language represents whenever particular groups and classes of society control the production and distribution of language, the channeling of information, and the situations within which speaking takes place. See in this context the exercise machinery of the dead languages (Ancient Greek, Latin), upon which the coming generation of the dominant class overexerts itself at the more prestigious schools, without these languages offering it any resistance, as is the case with a colloquial language that is permeated by reality. Here they learn to control in a disciplined way their own living linguistic labor. The consequence of this is that they later find themselves able to deal abstractly with linguistic material. They learn to move linguistically and maintain control independently of the concrete situation. It is precisely in this that the educational value of Latin for the development of dominant knowledge can be located.

social sciences, most investigations are performed according to quite generalizing methods.

Bernstein himself looks for general and, whenever possible, measurable criteria of differention in establishing an opposition between restricted code and elaborated code. This presupposes that there is such a thing as one general working-class linguistic capacity in which generalizable stereotypes keep recurring. Such a presupposition does not take sufficient account of the extent to which this linguistic capacity is, within every concrete situation, dependent upon a social dimension (which, within an extended time frame, appears to be invariable). What has yet to be clarified is the relationship between linguistic capacity and action in a given situation. It should be assumed that the former expands to the degree that the latter is possible. It is also evident that when the worker is in control of a situation, he will develop a wealth of linguistic references appropriate to the circumstances.[70]

## The So-called Public Sphere of the Factory

The bourgeois public sphere has the tendency to separate immediate political impulses from their realization, speech from action.[71] Numerous measures are

---

70. An all-inclusive critique of the entire sociolinguistic appendage can be found in W. Girnus, H. Lethen, F. Rothe, *Von der kritischen zur historisch-materialistischen Literaturwissenschaft. Vier Aufsätze* (Berlin: 1971): 19ff. The authors endorse the position that the empirical findings of bourgeois social research (p. 25) cannot be gathered simply through conducting "poles." Such a "poling" would also not provide the grounds for any theoretician to accept the findings of bourgeois social research, since these could be legitimated with experience if need be. Contrary to this, we hold fast to our contention that, within deep-seated stereotypes of working-class language, a hidden potential of the working-class consciousness, the assets of the experience of a struggling class, are contained. Any political effort that forgoes engaging these energies and experience would certainly be condemned to failure. Here we can speak of deep-seated stereotypes only insofar as they remain stereotypes in situations that are governed by the bourgeois public sphere or nonpublic situations, as well as in the case of the total futility of an activity.

In situations in which behavioral consequences are also apparent, the usual stereotypes prove to be ciphers of real experience. What workers are actually unable to do is distance themselves abstractly from the situation by means of linguistic expression, as does the dominant form of knowledge. That they are unable to do this, that they do not simply exercise control over situations but rather experience them as concrete, can be understood as proletarian and political behavior and interpreted merely as a disadvantage vis-à-vis the mechanisms of the bourgeois public sphere to which workers remain exposed. The analysis of the experience that is reduced to the so-called stereotypes of working-class language cannot be examined solely with the methodology of social research. Rather, such an analysis must be oriented toward a self-organization of this experience. In this respect, the charge made by the authors on p. 25 misses the mark. At the same time, however, a counterattempt must be made to refer back to experience that affects qualitative observation, using scholarly methods that are appropriate to the late-capitalist level of production.

71. Regarding the interests thus pursued that determine the entire history of the bourgeois public sphere, see chapter 2.

taken in ensuring this separation. Workers are, for instance, told to completely exhaust a legal avenue that is impractical for them; in order to enforce rights or to call strikes, formalities and procedures are necessary, which managements enforce as well. In the United States, in the case of a strike decision that "concerns national interests," it is possible to order a cooling-off period of up to sixty days. But in all general forms of the bourgeois public sphere, in particular the conventional public meeting at which a series of speakers deliver monologues expressing the general will while the audience is restricted to one or two responses, the shaping of political will cannot be translated into autonomous activity. This applies also to the distinct lack of topicality of celebrations such as those organized by workers' organizations for May 1 or other occasions. It is interesting in this context that May 1 is almost always celebrated outside of the factory, although it would seem fitting to link the public sphere of streets, squares, and auditoriums with the public sphere of factories on this day at least.[72]

All these are still forms of the public sphere. However, the so-called **public sphere of the factory** can no longer be portrayed as "public." It constitutes an **arcane realm**, which is protected by factory security, law-enforcement measures, and alleged legal institutions. This lies in sharp contrast to the fact that the labor taking place in factories rests on cooperation and social interrelations and spans the greater part of the lifetime of employees and the organized labor force; it also lies in contrast to the overwhelming influence that the domain of production exerts on the public sphere. These circumstances are recognized only in the shape of the public sphere labor of the factory, which is itself manufactured on a nonpublic basis. The shielding of the domain of production from the public sphere is thereby not limited to privatized heavy industry but determines, in a similar manner, the organizing codes of the program and consciousness industries and of the state itself, whose product is, after all, the public sphere itself.

The nonpublic character of the most important part of capitalist social practice cannot be traced back to a publicly made decision, in the manner that one can say that private property, the market, and the subsumption of labor power under capital were never a secret in their developmental phases. The power relation associated with the classical institutions of the bourgeois legal and economic order was in absolute accord with a historically and publicly developed collective will. The fact that it could be discussed, and therefore potentially criticized, was a condition for its genesis.

It is necessary to confront this classical constitutional situation with the narrowness and casuistry of industrial-relations regulations. The focus here is upon legally regulated and constituted factories, which basically, however, do not have any constitution, if constitution is understood as the establishment of rights that

---

72. There are few exceptions to the evidence described here. One example for an "active" demonstration is the proclamation made by I. G. Metall during the last week of the 1971 strike in Stuttgart.

can be exercised. It is a sign of the stunted awareness of the public sphere that this cynical state of affairs is simply allocated to the guarantee of socially responsible private-property ownership, a guarantee that exists solely on a constitutional level. It is instructive to look at the relevant norms of labor law, which discuss the only institution within the factory where workers meet as a body (except in the case of a strike): the **industrial-relations boards**.[73]

Arthur Nikisch, *Arbeitsrecht*, vol. 3: *Betriebsverfassungsrecht*, 2d edition (Tübingen: 1966), p. 217:

"Industrial-relations meetings are nonpublic. . . . Admission may, accordingly, be granted only to persons who are entitled to participate . . . , others will not be granted admission, even if they belong to the same factory as those mentioned in paragraph 4 II of the Law on Industrial Relations. Above all, people who do not belong to the factory are not permitted entry, nor, therefore, are representatives of the press. Exceptions cannot be made, not even with the agreement of all participants. The chairman of the meeting is responsible for the observance of this rule. If he fails to do so, he is in breach of his legal obligations and, under certain circumstances, to such a degree that he can be dismissed from the works committee."

p. 226:

"Certainly, it is unpleasant for an employer to bear the costs of an industrial-relations meeting at which party politics or union propaganda are illegally pursued, but he is not entirely defenseless against this. If he attends the meeting, he

---

73. The following quotes are taken from the standard handbook of labor laws. They represent the average, that is, the dominant opinion. Nonetheless, cases that were decided by the courts are the source for these examples. The relationship of the labor and management constitutional law to the public sphere also finds expression in the fact that, in the subject index to this nearly 2,000-page handbook, "public sphere" is referred to exactly twice, and then in a nonspecific context (such as, for example, "public service").

The revised version of the Labor Relations Law of 15 January 1972, *Bundesgesetzblatt* I, p. 13, paragraph 45, contains a broadening of the thematic range of the Labor Relations Law (published in Beck's Textausgaben, *Betriebsverfassungsgesetz*, 22d ed., [Munich: 1972]: 47). Paragraph 44 of the Labor Relations Law of 1952 reads: "It [the Labor Relations Board] may only hear cases that concern the factory or its employees." Paragraph 45 of the 1972 Labor Relations Law reads: "The labor-relations board and departmental board hear cases, including those involving tariff policies, social policy, and the economy, that immediately affect the factory or its employees; the principles of paragraph 74, section 2 are applicable." Paragraph 74, section 2 reads: "Measures taken in a labor dispute between employer and works committee members are not permitted: labor disputes between parties subject to tariff are not affected by this. Employer and works committee members must refrain from activities through which the continuation of operations or the peace of the factory are affected."

It is questionable whether this modification of the wording of the law, as indicated in the examples provided in the text, will change the practice of the labor-relations boards, which is determined by legal decisions and by everyday practice in the workplace. The amended Labor Relations Law cites

can, unless the chairman intervenes, prohibit the speaker from continuing and, if necessary, expel him, in accordance with his legal status as proprietor. He can institute proceedings against the guilty chairman of the industrial-relations board according to paragraph 23 of the Law on Industrial Relations and bar the union representative from entering the premises, if the latter's presence is a matter for complaint."[74]

These excerpts from case law highlight the tendency to remove the factory from the public social process and to establish it as a kind of private enclave of power.[75]

It is remarkable how strongly the nonpublic character of the factory is reminiscent of the nonpublic organization of the eighteenth-century state. The system of relations within the factory is, as manifested among other places in the industrial-

---

compromises formulated by the workers' unions and management. These formulations describe a status quo that is identical to the one appearing in the excerpts of legal decisions cited in the text. [Several additional quotes appearing in the German edition have been omitted.—*Trans.*]

74. For additional material on labor-relations law, see Wilhelm Herschel, "Die Beratungsgegenstände der Betriebsversammlung," in *Der Betrieb* (1962): 1110, 1142; Gerhard Höhne, "Der Beratungsgegenstand der Betriebsversammlung," in *Betriebsberater* (1953): 770; Olaf Radke, "Über die Grenzen der Diskussionsfreiheit in der Betriebsversammlung," in *Arbeit und Recht* (1957): 129; J. Wagner, "Die Betriebsversammlung, insbesonders ihre Zuständigkeit," in *Der Betrieb* (1954): 976.

75. Legal institutions such as, for example, domestic rights or the right to regulated and practiced commercial enterprise also correspond to this tendency. Rudolf Wiethölter has shown in a brilliant analysis in *Kritische Justiz* 1 (1970) that the so-called *right to regulated and practiced commercial enterprise*, which is supposed to render impossible any influence of a third party on plant operations and thus any public influence, has been founded on a causal chain of legal decisions and commentary, of which one is plagiarized from the next and all of them together can be attributed back to a misunderstood juridical structure of the Reich's Court that never handed down a decision on this question.

Just as questionable is the establishment and jurisdiction of domestic rights. It is entirely questionable whether a plant in which socialized labor takes place and which in a material sense represents the most important form of public sphere of the workers who belong to it (and fulfills an interest of the company in unifying the workers within the plant) can again be made into an area for private domination from the perspective of landed or factory-owned property. Our method of analysis here does not proceed from an assessment of the opinion that is dominant in legal scholarship and the administration of justice, but rather refers to the social problem at its base. In accordance with the entire tradition of the public order of bourgeois society, the order of private rights guarantees *private property*; this social order, however, does not recognize any property in relationships between people, in people themselves, or in groups of people. There is also a limit at such points for compromise decisions on the part of lawmakers in the areas of labor and labor-relations law. If legal regulations are developed, on the basis of which power relations similar to those governing property are carried over to people and their relationships toward one another—and the capitalist sphere of production tends toward precisely this—a fundamental premise of the social contract is thus violated. *For it is not at all a matter of law in the strict sense, but rather of power that expresses itself in the form of justice.* The background for this problem shapes a question that also cannot be answered in terms of legality. The shielding of the public sphere contains a principled negation of society and thus the foundation for law in general. Within this framework, a law that exerts an effect from without on factories structured in this way can only be imagined.

relations meeting, **absolutist**.[76] In this case, the bourgeois public sphere returns, in distorted form, to its starting point. In its treatment of the factory as public sphere, capitalist society retrospectively denies the whole thrust of the bourgeois concept of the public sphere and of publicity.

---

76. From this perspective, the language used by the left to discuss the contradiction between autocratic works organization and the political, democratic construction of the whole of society is decidedly flattering, measured against factual conditions.

# Chapter 2
# On the Dialectic between the Bourgeois and the Proletarian Public Sphere

The mechanism at work in the production and reproduction of the bourgeois public sphere can be described only after examining the interest that the bourgeois has in the public sphere, **insofar as it is an interest in a character mask**, in the personification of capital. This interest can be outlined as follows:

1. The bourgeois mode of production must publicly install itself as a social order. This is a **constitutive public sphere**.[1] It cannot significantly be held in check by any separation of powers or procedural rules during the political implementation of the bourgeois order. In the nonpublic manufacturing phase of the bourgeois mode of production, extraeconomic power (in, for instance, primitive accumulation) allies itself with economic power relations. In a similar fashion, the constitutive public sphere sweeps aside as merely private all obstacles, privileges, special rights, atavisms, and peculiarities that stand in the way of the public establishment of this order. This mode of producing the public sphere characterizes not only the early phase of bourgeois rule but is repeated at each new stage in which the contradictions of the capitalist mode of production are no longer capable of

---

1. Here and in the following we refer to cross sections within which contradictory primary interests and the functions that appear within the context of reality *not in elemental forms*, but rather in *complex combinations*, can be distinguished from one another. The concept of an absolute constitution within constitutional doctrine refers to this aspect of the public sphere, which we designate the constitutional public sphere; see Carl Schmitt, *Verfassungslehre*, 4th ed. (Berlin: 1965): 3ff. See also p. 20ff. of the same text vis-à-vis the corresponding distinction in its treatment of a positive concept of constitution: "This act constitutes the form and content of the political unity, the continuance of which is presupposed."

being resolved within the framework of the old political order. The contradictions are then reworked into a new political order, which, rather than resolving them, makes use of these contradictions by transposing them and changing them back into extraeconomic political power relations—**a process that goes against the historical current.**[2]

The constitutive public sphere is distinct from both feudal absolutism on the one hand, and living labor on the other, albeit in different historical phases. What we are dealing with here is a material concept of the public sphere, of real politics and power for which this public framework is necessary.[3]

2. **The public sphere as the organizational form of the "dictatorship of the bourgeoisie."** This is that network of norms, legitimations, delimitations, procedural rules, and separation of powers that prevents the political public sphere, once established, from making decisions that disturb or nullify the order of bourgeois production. It is the organized obstacle to the material public sphere and politics—**the opposite of the constitutive public sphere.**[4]

The external signs of this aspect of the bourgeois public sphere, as expressed in constitutional law, are its formalization, its demonstrability, its stability, and the fact that it is difficult to amend. The mechanism of division with regard to the substantive will of society extends, however, from politics right into the structures of the psyche. This mechanism is just as preorganized within the real basis of this public sphere, in other words in the productive sector, as it is in language, culture, life-styles, and forms of communication. **Its inherent tendency is to separate the producers of use-values and social experience, in other words the bearers of the collective will, from the tools with which this collective will can be created.**[5] **Its goal is to prevent the political public sphere from existing.**

---

2. The consequence of this exploitative relationship toward history is, as a rule, war or revolution, and most often both. A truly emancipated society would have to recognize *crimes against history* alongside *war crimes* and *genocide* (which are, of course, interconnected with this praxis of establishing new orders).

3. A characteristic example of the constitutional public sphere described here is the dominance of the Convention during the French Revolution. This form of public sphere has also determined every new phase of bourgeois politics (see, for example, the concentrated political violence of the coming to power of Napoleon III, the installation of the French Republic of 1871 to 1875, Mussolini's seizure of power, and the "national uprising" in Germany in 1933).

4. The concept of a relative constitution in constitutional doctrine corresponds to this concept; see Carl Schmitt, *Verfassungslehre,* pp. 11ff. See also the interaction between the absolute and relative concepts of constitution within the *positive concept of constitution,* pp. 20ff. There the concepts of constitutional doctrine have narrower parameters than the differentiation used here, which refers to the public sphere as a whole. On the concept of the "dictatorship of the bourgeoisie," see A. Gurland, *Marxismus und Diktatur* (Leipzig: 1930), esp. "Klassenherrschaft und Diktatur, juristischer oder soziologischer Diktaturbegriff?" pp. 66ff. In our context, the designations "sociological" and "nonpublic" (*nicht staatsrechtlich*) are not used.

5. See chapter 1 of this book. The context of social experience is determined by *all* of the aspects of bourgeois public sphere characterized here. The effects, however, are entirely different, depending

3. **The public sphere as the illusory synthesis of the totality of society.** This must compensate for what in the constitutive public sphere appears as merely the power of social subgroups and what in the "dictatorship of the bourgeoisie" is the negation of all public spheres and sociality.[6] This aspect of the public sphere has to manufacture the appearance of a collective will, of a meaningful context that embraces the entire world, along with the illusion of participation on the part of all members of society. It is *one* of the foundations of social discipline. Without it, neither the established order nor the protective block of inhibiting procedures could be sustained. Added to these interests of the bourgeois as character mask, which determine both the classical public sphere and the new public spheres of production (and the combination of the two in practice), there is also:

4. **The public sphere as a form for expressing use-values as they are determined by the bourgeoisie.** The real human beings constituted within the bourgeois and "postbourgeois" public sphere have, during all phases of the construction and decay of this public sphere, engaged in the production of use-value. They possess human needs and have worked at manufacturing human relationships, modes of social intercourse, and intellectual edifices. In pitting themselves against the character mask without being able to assert their dominance, these people have pursued a permanent **idealistic revolutionizing** of the public context as a whole, which goes hand in hand with the production of the public sphere as such.[7]

In real historical processes, as they present themselves to the investigations of historians, all four syntheses of the contradictory individual impulses of the bourgeois public sphere are interconnected. Despite the confusing nature of the public sphere as a concept, they **appear as a unity**. This overall process is to be grasped by analogy with commodity production. **In the public sphere as a product, its**

---

on which of these aspects such effects result from. There are from time to time various alliances of these aspects that exert an influence on the production of social experience, particularly in the different historical phases of the movement of construction and disintegration. Each of these aspects has a different history of construction and disintegration. This is not apparent in the context or in the method of presentation of the traditional writing of history.

6. See section 3 below, "The Public Sphere as an Illusory Synthesis of the Totality of Society."

7. Marx and Engels repeatedly elaborated the useful characteristics of the bourgeois public sphere. See Karl Marx and Friedrich Engels, *Pressefreiheit und Zensur*, edited and with an introduction by Iring Fetscher (Frankfurt: 1969), esp. pp. 94 1ff., 146ff., 175, 200ff., 227ff., 232ff. See also our comments below in commentary 15, "Friedrich Engels on the Party Press and the Public Sphere." The student protest movement attempted to take up this self-claim of the bourgeois public sphere in the same way. The fact that violations of the forms and practices of the bourgeois public sphere are met with considerable resistance on the part of many workers can also be explained by the fact that the workers rightfully fear the loss of the rudimentary use characteristics of this public sphere, which at least mediate the rudiments of a social context. It is important to not allow oneself to be seduced into an ambivalent approach by these emancipatory auxiliary phenomena of the bourgeois public sphere. But neither can one simply "radically" ignore them.

**process of production disappears.** It is therefore not surprising that, once the bourgeois public sphere has achieved what it is meant to, it tends once again toward privatization. The market, property, and the subsumption of labor power under capital **develop publicly.** The activity of the bourgeois is no secret. Everyone can see what he is doing. "Everyone has the opportunity to emulate him." This opportunity is even suggested. Once this bourgeois mode of production has been attained, it falls back into the sphere from which it emerges: starting out from the productive sector (from the material base of the public sphere), **arcane realms,** exclusive and particular power relations, repeatedly come into being. These realms have the tendency to incorporate the totality of the context of living.[8]

It is only the unfolding of the dialectic immanent within the public sphere that enables one to determine the concrete relationships between private and public with more precision. **The two are not externally related to one another, but rather produce their respective opposite from within themselves.**

### The Proletarian Public Sphere as a Historical Counterconcept to the Bourgeois Public Sphere

In the bourgeois class, the interests of individuals are organized and implemented in both private and public forms. By contrast, the interests of workers can, since they are unrealized, be organized only if they enter into a context of living, in other words into a proletarian public sphere. Only then do they have the chance to develop as interests, instead of remaining mere possibilities.

Since these interests can be realized as social ones only through the needle's eye of the valorization of labor power as a commodity, they are initially merely the objects of other interests. If they are then directly suppressed, in other words if they are not socially valorized, they survive as living labor power, as raw material. As extraeconomic interests, they exist—precisely in the forbidden zones of fantasy beneath the surface of taboos—as stereotypes of a proletarian context of living that is organized in a merely rudimentary form. As such, they cannot be suppressed further, nor can they be assimilated. **In this respect, they have two characteristics: in their defensive attitude toward society, their conservatism, and their subcultural character, they are once again mere objects; but they are, at the same time, the block of real life that goes against the valorization interest.** As long as capital is dependent on living labor as a source of wealth, this element of the proletarian context of living cannot be extinguished through repression.

This state of affairs represents the initial phase of the constitution of the prole-

---

8. See chapter 1, as well as chapter 5.

tarian public sphere, namely, at every stage of historical development. Where attempts are made to fit this block into the interests of capital, for instance by the subsumption of the context of living under the programming and consciousness industry or the new public spheres of production, the accompanying process of oppression and exclusion produces the substance, appropriately differentiated, of a newly emergent block. Lenin's belief that there is no situation without some solution is grounded in this block of proletarian life interests. It is no contradiction that, initially, at the level of social mediation depicted, no concrete solutions present themselves. Capital cannot destroy this block, and the proletariat cannot take hold of society from within it.

In reality, this founding phase of the proletarian public sphere is only rarely encountered in this pure form. It is concealed by more highly organized levels of the proletarian public sphere.[9] Two aspects of this higher level of organization have been of primary import in the history of the labor movement. It is necessary to distinguish them, since all forms of the proletarian public sphere are the qualitative expression of the proletarian context of living and therefore tend—by contrast with the costume character of the rapidly changing bourgeois public spheres—to exclude more developed forms.

## The Assimilation of Elements of the Proletarian Context of Living into the Integrative Mechanism of the Bourgeois Public Sphere

This includes the integration of the energies of the labor movement into forms of organization that are modeled on the bourgeois public spheres. In all such cases, workers are as a rule separated from the psychic and institutional tools with which they could adapt the bourgeois public sphere to their interests or create specific forms of their own public sphere. In this sense the empirical working-class public sphere often appears as a variant of the bourgeois public sphere.

If workers try to overcome the particularity of their interests by seeking to take hold of the apparent totality of bourgeois production, of the bourgeois world, they fall victim to a deception.

For they are trying to sublate their proletarian context of living with the aid of something that is its exact opposite. They overlook the fact that the former is produced precisely by this opposition. One cannot sublate the conditions of proletarian life without sublating those of the bourgeoisie, any more than one can sublate wage labor without at the same time sublating capital.

That which is unrealistic in the labor movement's repeated historical attempts to constitute its interests without the sublation of the bourgeois social context,

---

9. On the other hand, it would not be concealed by the pure form of bourgeois public sphere. It is precisely the result of exclusion and oppression, that is, precisely the *other* of this bourgeois public sphere.

separate from this context, is not, however, palpable in concrete situations. These efforts are expressed above all in the adoption of ideals. "The ideals of the labor movement should be achieved." Man, progress, the right to work—ideas take the place of a real emancipatory movement.[10]

In those areas of society where this hybrid of proletarian interests and universal, ubiquitous bourgeois norms of organization develops, it is no longer possible to speak simply of a bourgeois public sphere. It is decaying in these areas, but it still exists in this decayed state. The type of proletarian public sphere that has developed by using bourgeois organizational forms not only binds together real proletarian interests and experiences but concentrates them into a specific stage of a proletarian public sphere. This sphere distinguishes itself from the bourgeois in its external forms—the workers' association, the working-class housing estate, and the trade union.

At this level, proletarian interests participate in the movement of society. Insofar as they do, this is not a mere semblance but real participation. Not only can the apologists of the existing system point to this fact, but the workers themselves rightly see some of their demands thereby fulfilled while regarding others as promises for the future, as granted in principle. This assumption is not a total delusion. Their interests have in reality been incorporated into the social context of living—as they will also be in the future programming and consciousness industry—but they are incorporated as merely objective interests, as the satisfaction of reified needs. The integration begins with the fact that their marriages are modeled on the bourgeois family; that they employ the language and culture of bourgeois society; that they have to frequent institutions or organizations—generally centralized ones—to maintain this status quo. This results in an aporia: they are unable to abandon this manifestation of the proletarian public sphere that restricts them to a passive standpoint, for if they did they would have to cut themselves off from their experiences and interests that have been organized by it and have taken on its forms. But neither are they able, on the other hand, to maintain this state of affairs. They remain blind to the laws of the movement of capital and the whole historical process if they simply try to maintain the status quo defensively—even if defense appears to be their strength. At the least sign of crisis or of

---

10. An analysis of the process at the base of this is complicated because labor power is, on the one hand, merely an object as the object of relations of production, while, on the other, it is simultaneously a subject in that it is living labor. *Its subject quality becomes an object by way of its being subsumed beneath the power relations of the bourgeois public sphere.* Precisely in that the workers "consider themselves human" at this stage—without their social situation having changed—they have been overcome by exchange via the degree of reality in their actions and their social organization. Within this state of mystification, they are unable to recognize that they are the object of an organizational context that is foreign to them, and over which they exercise no control. They experience this situation in the form of personal conflict with the immediate representatives of the relevant public-sphere apparatus.

a change in the status quo—for instance, through additional political repression—this state of affairs, which has been accepted as stable, works to the disadvantage of the workers. They become the object of redistribution or the mere raw material in the process of social exploitation.[11]

## The Self-Organization of Working-Class Interests in a Proletarian Public Sphere That Establishes Itself as a Separate Camp in Opposition to Capitalist Society

Self-defensive reactions have been characteristic of the labor movement since the historic defeat of the English labor movement in the middle of the nineteenth century.[12] At this stage of organization, the workers define their own identity through resistance against their bourgeois enemy. In the process, they maintain themselves as a concrete particular. The unsublated proletarian context of living is at the heart of the development of their identity. The capacity of labor power as a commodity to "speak" and to develop consciousness—in other words, to develop itself into a subject—is lost, because the pressure, which existing bourgeois society as a whole exerts on the proletarian camp adjacent to it, makes workers politically into objects to the same degree that they are the objects of the relations of production in the economic sphere.

The bourgeois public sphere confronts the individual worker as a relation of capital; it confronts **the whole of the working class, however, primarily as a state monopoly of power, as an extraeconomic power relation**. Correspondingly, the working-class party organizes itself as a political party, in other words, as an extraeconomic counterforce. This level of conflict and class struggle is, however, a derived one.

In this situation, the actual strengths of the working class are ineffective. **The worker's real struggle is waged between his abstract, general bourgeois characteristics and his concrete, specific, proletarian ones. He has, however, to organize himself in the proletarian party as an individual among other individuals: the fiction must be upheld that he is, as a whole, a proletarian individual, or else he belongs in the enemy camp.** He is mainly defined by the fact that he could spontaneously develop an awareness of his own commodity

---

11. See also the section in the commentaries on Austro-Marxism below. This form of proletarian public sphere has been unable to maintain itself in the face of an ordinary crisis within the context of capitalism; it has been able to muster almost no resistance to state empires and fascism. In this situation, workers are not merely the result and object of the capitalist process—it is only their leftover object qualities that are organized, through which they are again linked via short circuit with capital interests. These object qualities are what are left behind as a remainder by exploitative interests. In this context, political interests as well still possess characteristics of freedom.

12. See, in the commentary section, commentary 1, the sections on the camp mentality, the Italian labor movement in 1919–20, and the German Communist party during the 1920s.

character. As the representative of counterforce against the preexisting power of bourgeois society, he has to bracket out this process. He must present himself in the guise of the defender of human rights, of a finished product. In reality, he is confined within an extremely restricted horizon; in his imagination, however, he defends this "human existence" like a bastion. **He has to reify himself and turn himself into an instrument so that he can fight the enemy. He does not develop conditions necessary for life, but rather combative skills, which are oriented toward the enemy. If the enemy wins, he has at his disposal norms and modes of behavior with which he fills the space that he has gained for himself. If the worker or his organization wins, he must first of all develop a new mode of production and a new way of life. This is when the actual work first begins.** Before this, he has to fight for something that he cannot yet know in any detail. The most important obstacle in this situation is **that the relationship of the emancipatory movement of the proletariat to the totality of society—in other words, the real historical mission—appears, from the vantage point of its own camp, to be blocked.** The worker is unable to conceive of the totality of society without finding himself in the bourgeois camp. He has to choose between his own present identity and his historical capacity as a proletarian, revolutionary force that sublates the totality of society in a new mode of production.

Within this form of the proletarian public sphere as **the working-class's defense organization**, the proletarian characteristics of individuals are, in their reified form, combined to constitute proletarian characters. At this historical stage of the proletarian public sphere, its prime function is to protect individuals from the direct influence of bourgeois interests and ideologies. This stage is, however, not sufficiently rooted in the production process itself for it to be able to revolutionize production. It possesses no modes of production to break through the barriers of family, education, and the inhibition of the development of proletarian experience. It can attempt to unite awareness of this problem, as it is generated elsewhere, only theoretically, in other words, at the level of mediations. The conditions for producing an awareness within the organization are different from those necessary for individuals in reality. **The stronger these organizations seem to be compared with the classical bourgeois public sphere, the less capable they are of holding their line of defense against a fascist mass movement or a capitalist mode of production that is able to organize wide sections of the proletarian context of living, albeit only in the form of mass deception.**

Nevertheless, important individual interests and experiences of the working class are associated with this false mode of organization. The workers cannot separate themselves from their mass organizations without also losing this anchored component of their interests and experiences. It is thus of no help if isolated, theoretically aware individuals or groups set themselves apart from the mass party or the trade-union organizations. The masses could follow these individuals only if they give up elements of their existing identification. Taking part in an individual group's theoretically formulated—and possibly correct—experience is not enough to make them do so.[13]

The result of this process is a state of affairs in which the workers no longer have faith in their own experience; yet, precisely because they embody labor power as a commodity, it is they who would be in a position to develop consciousness. Instead, the fact that they are always right is ascribed to the party. The latter can, however, develop only as much experience as has previously been introduced into it by real human beings. The opposite illusion is conveyed through the bourgeois public sphere: in this sphere, we see the workings of a collective security system, the sedimented consciousness of the bourgeoisie; yet individuals imagine that it is they who determine the movement of society. In the party organization of the camp, no individual still believes that he is in a position to produce spontaneous experience. However, the organization, which in no sense grasps the totality of proletarian experience any more than it embraces the overall context of social production, is considered the center of truth, the subject. This specific construction of a particular stage of the proletarian public sphere is effective primarily against any superior form of this sphere. The development of such a superior form is consistently opposed and impeded.

If the working class successfully organizes itself as a separate camp within bourgeois society, the potential is reduced for a proletarian public sphere that embraces the totality of society. If the organization of the proletarian context of living is not geared toward such a public sphere, this camp becomes subject to a curious dialectic: although its intention is to insulate itself from all forms of the bourgeois context of living, to immunize individuals against the latter, it uncon-

---

13. One of the decisive reasons for the failure of groups of advanced intellectuals who splinter off from mass organizations lies in the difference between the mode of production for the experience of the intelligentsia and that of the workers. If the intelligentsia is in a position to very rapidly construct for itself new contexts for communication, even on the basis of its connections with groups in other countries, through reading books, or through communication among groups of bourgeois intellectuals, and so on, the experiential context of the worker is so closely linked to the organization to which he has hitherto belonged that only a very narrow margin of movement remains open for him to win new friends, change his location, and in general replace the old context for communication. If he follows these advanced groups with which he is possibly in complete agreement politically, he will be forced to give up the ways of living he is accustomed to. In any case, the sacrifice he must make in the event of any break away from the parent organization is considerably greater than that to be made by the intellectual. In general, it has also been proven that such splinter groups lose their base very quickly. In most cases, the workers return to their customary organization in time for the next election (this was, for example, the fate of the PSIUP in West Germany, and probably that of the Manifesto groups, the intellectual splinter groups within the French PSU, the fate of the KPO, the "Leninbund," etc.). Something completely different is occurring if, for example, the Russian Social Democracy is divided or if the USPD splits away from the SPD on the question of the public peace policy. In these cases, it is the parent organization that accomplishes the separation.

sciously reproduces the mechanisms of the bourgeois public sphere: exclusion, pseudopublicity, dictatorship of procedural rules. It is permeated with value abstractions. This, above all, shows how remote the camp mentality of many communist organizations is from the Leninist conception of the party.

## Decaying Forms of the Bourgeois Public Sphere

In what follows, not all aspects of the decaying bourgeois public sphere will be analyzed. Our account will restrict itself to the most important contradictions, which come into play at each fissure that provides an opening for the proletarian public sphere. This applies above all to the **public power monopoly** and the production of the public sphere as an **illusory synthesis of society as a whole**.

The absolutist state, which, as a framework of security and order, is neccesary to the bourgeois mode of production, was an artificial, historical construct. It was the synthesis of many particularities, which, in various European countries in different ways, had been brought under authoritarian rule. Absolutist rule was based on the principle of the "patriarchal government of society in the manner of a country estate." This was, in almost every respect, the opposite of the principle of the social contract, according to which the revolutionary bourgeoisie interpreted the historical state edifice. Neither in those countries in which a bourgeois revolution took place, nor in those where monarchy and cameralistics, acting as trustees, concluded deals on behalf of the bourgeoisie, was this contradiction resolved. Like the concept of the public sphere, the concept of the state therefore possesses an extraordinary breadth.[14] In some instances, the state appears in the guise of the positive interventionist welfare state of the cameralists, of the absolute power of the monarch, or that of committees of public safety; in others, it appears as the negative defensive state, as a constitutional state. The change from offensive to defensive state activity cannot be explained solely in terms of the growth or decline of bourgeois and feudal interests. Rather, both social interests express themselves at different times in this change in state power. Franz Neumann has this fact in mind when, in a critique of the "liberal nightwatchman's state of the nineteenth century," he says that the bourgeois state has always been as strong as the ruling class felt was necessary. The changing nature of the bourgeois state is echoed at every stage of the development of the state in the eighteenth, nineteenth, and twentieth centuries, and it is not specific to absolutism.[15]

_____

14. See chapter 1.

15. In his introduction to Leon Trotsky's _Wie wird der Nationalsozialismus geschlagen?_ ed. Helmut Dahmer (Frankfurt: 1971), Ernest Mandel refers vis-à-vis Trotsky's theory of fascism to the characteristic loss of memory of bourgeois ideology, which attributes to bourgeois societies a stronger sense of democratization than to those of previous centuries, as well as an inclination toward parliamentary and constitutional government. He makes note of the fact that the essential forms of the state

## 1. Contradictions of the State's Power Monopoly

The state of the eighteenth, nineteenth, and twentieth centuries is an accumulation of historical compromises. Alongside the state as treasury, as judiciary, and as the administration of sovereignty—whose common goal is to exist as rational forms of state power—there stands, unrelated, authoritarian rule, of which Jellinek says: "One can speak of authoritarian government to the extent that the power proper to the state or to other bearers of public authority is confirmed in government. The authoritarian element lies in the supremacy of public authority over the individual. This supremacy is, to begin with, only an image. It can be grasped legally if one considers the means whereby authoritarian government carries out its goals. These means are, however, . . . that administrative act which has the greater effectiveness, one that, in extreme cases, is coupled with overwhelming physical force. The greater effectiveness of the administrative act consists, however, in its relative lack of sensitivity toward its own imperfections."[16]

Exercise of the power monopoly becomes increasingly specialized within the state system as a whole. Army and police, special agents and organizations become the exclusive holders of this monopoly. This specialization is the product of the conflict between precapitalist elements, which are regarded as alien by the bourgeois public sphere, and the interest of the bourgeoisie to subsume the state under its class and its rationalizing tendency, which strives to universalize the relations of production and of social intercourse.

Bourgeois sociologists such as Comte have, in the aftermath of the French Revolution, tried to prove the inherent irreconcilability of the industrial and military spirit. For them the military, including the purely public police, is a relic of an antiquated feudal order. At the same time, the bourgeoisie recognized that peaceful commodity production and exchange require the protection of the private legal order through force. This is why bourgeois interests, which were in conflict with the precapitalist forms of the power monopoly, could not, in their ambivalence, unequivocally assert themselves. **Even in cases where bourgeois interests were powerful enough to assert themselves, prebourgeois instruments of power were maintained. Bourgeois interests attempt to enlist these forces, especially the army, police, a network of informants, and a censorship system, in a limited and instrumental way. These bodies, however, operate according to their own, in part noncapitalist, norms. This is the most important definition of the bourgeois state: in its content it is**

in Western Europe since the first industrial revolution have oscillated between aristocratic monarchy, plebiscite Caesarism, a conservative parliamentarianism with voting rights for ten percent and occasionally less than five percent of the population, and unmediated autocracy.

16. Walter Jellinek, *Verwaltungsrecht* (Bad Homburg, Berlin, Zurich: 1966): 21.

**merely an echo of production interests, but in its forms it possesses a specific substance—the independent existence of its own executive organs.**[17]

Precisely because the bourgeoisie does not develop these instruments of power through its own mode of production, it is unable to monitor the use of force by the state with any precision. It enlists the army, the police, and the judiciary for its own interests, but it cannot reduce or redirect these instruments as quickly as its own interests are satisfied or changed. The bourgeoisie has repeatedly attempted to resolve the following contradiction: whereas it defines the content of threats of force, it has to entrust the form in which force is implemented to extraneous specialists (such as officer corps, police agents, diplomats, or the aristocracy). This has been attempted by introducing general conscription, the idea of the militia and national guard, and by demanding that world politics should be public, that cabinet politics be abolished. Some of these (e.g., militia, national guard) were fundamental to the success of bourgeois revolutions, for instance those of 1848 in Germany and France. Nevertheless, the idea of the citizens' army was unable to assert itself against the dead weight of professional armies on the Continent. On the contrary, since the end of the nineteenth century, professional armies have existed in the external form of conscript armies.[18]

---

17. The police authorities, for instance, behave toward capital like professional members of an organization that is mediated autonomously within itself and that does not understand itself as a profit-making endeavor. On the *ambiguity of the police apparatus*, refer to the following: Erhard Denninger, *Polizei in der freiheitlichen Demokratie* (Frankfurt: 1968); B. Drews and G. Wacke, *Allgemeines Polizeirecht—Ordnungsrecht—der Länder und des Bundes*, 7th ed., (1961); Karl Friedrich Friauf, "Polizei- und Ordnungsrecht," in *Besonderes Verwaltungsrecht*, ed. Ingo von Münch, 2d ed., (Bad Homburg, Berlin, Zurich: 1970). On *interaction within the monopoly on power*, see Fritz von Calker, *Das Recht des Militärs zum administrativen Waffengebrauch* (1888); Endres, *Der militärische Waffengebrauch* (1903); Romen Rissom, *Waffengebrauch und Festnahmerecht des Militärs* (1914); R. Liebmann, *Die polizeilichen Aufgaben der deutschen Wehrmacht* (1926); Janisch, "Militär und Polizei," in *Die Polizei*, vol. 23 (1926): 327ff.; Fry, "Militärhoheit und Polizeihoheit," in *Die Polizei*, vol. 24 (1927): 41f. Within the history of the German police, two mutually exclusive trends compete with each other. The logic of Paragraph 10 II 17 of the Prussian General Common Law of 1794 restricted the police to the status of *defending against danger*. At the same time, individual legislation and the *concept of the police* that carried over from the absolutist state and that *was oriented toward welfare work* punctuated the practice of these fundamental liberal principles. Thus Fr. J. Stahl assigns to the police generally the task of "maintaining the common good" in *Die Philosophie des Rechts*, vol. 2, Part Two, 5th ed. (1878): 587ff. The police are said to be "the truly constant political vocation. Constant development, challenge, and improvement" are said to be "its character." The opposite tendency, which limits the police to the role of defending against danger, is introduced in the Kreuzberg Decision of the Prussian Superior Court of 14 June 1882 (in *Rechtssprechung des Preußischen Oberverwaltungsgerichts*, vol. 9: 353ff.). This liberal development was superseded during National Socialism by an excessive employment of police. The police in the Federal Republic bear the traces of each of these historical epochs. Its rookies are trained like a military unit, while at the same time its catalogue of duties is defined constitutionally for normal police service. The different agendas come together in one and the same police authority, and there actuate a state of *continuous crisis*.

18. It is only in the Anglo-Saxon countries that these relationships are different. Here capital inter-

The instrumentalization of state power, together with the inability of bourgeois interests to control the forms and methods of this power, characterizes, above all, the state during the era of imperialism. There can be no doubt that capital is not prepared to pay for its exports of capital and the expansion of its spheres of power over new sources of raw materials through world wars. Bourgeois politics was, however, never able to maintain this position in the face of the mechanisms controlling the power monopoly. On the contrary, precisely on account of the First World War, new constellations, which realigned themselves in the network of contradictions characterizing the 1920s and 1930s, grew out of the interests of the monopolies. National Socialism presents us with a complex and rich collection of these contradictory elements. It is "both the realization and the negation of the tendencies inherent in monopoly capitalism toward the totalitarian organization, according to its interest, of the whole of social life."[19] **In this case, capital instrumentalizes a mass movement whose only apparent goal is the mobilization, once again, of the power monopoly against the interests of the working class; at the same time, however, capital itself becomes an instrument of this movement.** Capital is not just extensively expropriated in its political representation; it can no longer determine the direction that expansion will take—which inflations, which wars must be reckoned with, to what extent capital will be destroyed.[20]

The constellation of contradictions characterizing state power cannot be explained at the present stage of development if one restricts one's analysis to the state. The latter has been joined by social monopolies of indirect power. These indirect relations of power—regardless of whether they are organized publicly, through legal channels, or privately, and whether they are organizations of social services or of public opinion—work together in excercising state monopoly

---

ests that emerged with greater autonomy have also been able to industrialize the military. Thus, for example, the reduction of the British Army after the war of liberation (1813–15) is impressive. The U.S. armies of World War II were also built up and dismantled in accordance with industrial standards. In the interim, however, the situation in the United States has obviously changed. The budgeted hierarchy of the Pentagon indicates something like a refeudalization at an advanced industrial level. The reasons for this, however, do not lie in the fact that American society has instituted legal tools that are structured differently historically. Rather, it has occurred because they have lost control over the legal instruments they themselves have produced. See section 2 below on "The State's Power Monopoly and the Theory of Delegation."

19. Ernest Mandel, Introduction to Trotsky's *Wie wird der Nationalsozialismus geschlagen?*: 8.

20. This relationship of mutual instrumentalization is repeated within the National Socialist movement itself, which indeed implemented the masses instrumentally, but also had to partially make itself available as an instrument to these masses, and which used history as an instrument for exercising domination while at the same time becoming merely the reacting object of the history that has been set in motion. See also the permanent necessity of building up and then eliminating instruments of power, such as the liquidation of the SA leadership in 1934, the gradual liquidation of the *Reichswehr* leadership, etc. See also in this context Franz Neumann, *Behemoth: The Structure and Practice of National Socialism 1933–1944* (New York: 1966).

power. It may be said that the individual public spheres that represent the domain of production, and thereby represent the interests of capital *and* of workers, are the most important of these factors. They provide the framework in which state power can be exercised; on the other hand, they orient themselves, in turn, according to their limited relation of authority within the framework established by the state in the exercise of its power monopoly.[21]

It is evident that the way in which state power functions cannot be grasped by the formulations of *The Communist Manifesto*: "The executive of the modern state is but a committee for managing the common affairs of the whole bourgeoisie";[22] "political power, properly so called, is merely the organized power of one class for oppressing another."[23] An analysis that ascribes to the state power monopoly— above and beyond its constellation of contradictions—the role of a social power, as the theory of state monopoly capitalism attempts to do, is equally inadequate. The state is not an independent power, but rather a specific level of the contradictions of society—a level at which society can undergo specific metamorphoses in a manner historically determined by the state. This becomes clear as soon as one thinks not only of nation-states but of supranational organizations, economic communities, and military alliances, whereby elements of state power are safeguarded on an international scale. At these specific levels of contradiction, in which economic and extraeconomic power relations can be fused into a great network, different conditions apply to the assertion of social interests and conflicts; they develop in a different aggregate, but they are the same powers. This applies also when individual social powers, such as almost all proletarian ones, can realize themselves only with difficulty under the conditions set by the state, while other powers, such as those of the apparatuses or production, can be organized quite successfully. **The state is not an independent power but merely a battlefield. In order, among other things, to legitimate the power monopoly, it must declare itself independent, a *pouvoir neutre*. In other words, it must lay claim to the power monopoly while at the same time being unable, on its own, to make use of it. This contradiction is expressed in the fact that, in modern society, the state's direct**

---

21. The interdependence of these structures of mediated force and of the monopoly on force cannot be properly understood only through the example of phenomena like the Springer conglomerate. What is at issue here is not merely a tendency toward abuse, as is made possible for Springer as an individualist through his private capital assets, but rather the intelligent use of violent means that is programmed into the social context. Strauß and Springer distort, on the basis of their particular practice of brutality, the proper perspective on the genuinely determinate context of power.

22. Karl Marx and Frederick Engels, *The Communist Manifesto*, trans. Samuel Moore, ed. and intro. A. J. P. Taylor (London: Penguin, 1967): 82.

23. Ibid., p. 105. See also Ralph Miliband, *Marx und der Staat,* "Internationale marxistische Diskussion 15" (Berlin: Merve, 1971): 11ff. Miliband criticizes the stereotypical reliance on these formulations. He refers to the numerous places in Marx in which the functional methodology of the state is defined more specifically. Thus Marx mentions in *The Eighteenth Brumaire of Louis Bonaparte* that the "executive power subordinates the parliament to itself, and the state subordinates society."

**power monopoly is regarded as atavistic. Public authority is supposed to delegate its material power to intermediaries.**[24] This delegation compensates for the permanent loss of legitimacy (because the state is not what it makes itself out to be); it is, at the same time, however, the expression of interests that appropriate sections of the state for themselves. The processes of delegation, or the nondeployment or counterproductive deployment of individual direct instruments of rule, are not instigated by the state at its abstract level nor directly by ruling interests; rather, these processes strike at the core of the executive instruments, whereby the latter begin to transform themselves accordingly and seek a change of function.[25] None of these mechanisms are new. They have been visible since the 1920s at the very latest.

One should not underestimate the ambivalence of the interest of the ruling class in the public sphere's power monopoly (since this monopoly came into being to protect trade routes against gangs of thieves). As long as it is fully in operation, it prevents certain predatory forms of accumulation; it also prevents, amid certain constellations of the weakness of the ruling interest, the use of direct force against the enemies of the ruling class. This is why the ruling elite in the Weimar Republic repeatedly bypassed the power monopoly (e.g., the illegal Schwarze Reichswehr). Today as well, there is pressure to add—alongside the state power monopoly that exists in the form of factory security and the measures taken against industrial espionage—a second security system that is apparently supposed to lack the limited and contradictory character of the public power monopoly. The Third Reich too saw its greatest successes in the shape of mediated state control. The concentration camps were not backed by the state's authority, nor was the largest corporation forming public opinion, Cautio GmbH, which dominated the cinema and sections of the press, directly under state control. Up to the final phase of the war, the organization of armaments production was not under immediate control—irrespective of how far state rule actually extended. The economy was institutionalized in the form of syndicates and consisted, at its base, of private companies. These were organized on a semisovereign basis into interest groups and trade associations, with the inclusion of party officials, and were coordinated by the central ministry. It would be wrong to deduce from the fact that direct coercive measures were liberally applied in the Third Reich that this force was necessary to maintain rule, in particular the rule of private economic interests.[26]

---

24. See section 2 below, "The State's Power Monopoly and the Theory of Delegation."

25. Thus, for instance, an army that cannot have as its goal engagement in a worldwide context must provide some sort of justification for its training activity. This tendency must be suppressed through supervision. The result of this is the production of yet more new tendencies that attempt to elude supervision, and so on—*a mechanism that could make an army inclined to seek out its own domestic policy missions.*

26. See Neumann, *Behemoth.*

In late capitalism, dismantling structures of direct public power, and decentralizing and dispersing the state power monopoly, is a way of maintaining a system that corresponds to the contradictions of its social order—this is the only means whereby the preservation of the late-capitalist system can assume a flexible and accommodating shape. In the process, contradictions that arise within the economic sphere are transferred into the political domain.[27] On the other hand, the system of rule cannot do without a reliable domination of the instruments of power. However expedient it may be to delegate the state's instruments of power, the legitimation of all mechanisms of rule and coercion—including indirect ones—depends on the fact that power ultimately remains under lock and key, that the system is safeguarded against civil war. The function of the monopoly rests in the neutralization of power rather than in its direct enlistment. If direct coercion is employed, this is a sign of a borderline case, a conflict, in which the normal, indirect controls of society were not effective. In each of these cases the power monopoly must face an irresolvable dilemma: if force is necessary, legitimation is reduced; if, on the other hand, it is not needed, there is a danger that the threat of force will lose its effectiveness. A consequence of this is the growing weakness and uncertainty of the traditional instruments of power with which sections of capital are once again linked (e.g., armaments production/the military; monopoly of opinion/the police), whose economic weight renders a political solution of these conflicts impossible.

## 2. The State's Power Monopoly and the Theory of Delegation

The delegating of power takes on, among others, the following forms: in the area of information it is evident in the television networks' monopoly over broadcasting. This has its origins in the almost total loss of legitimacy that the state radio network suffered under National Socialism. In the legal system, it is evident in the

---

27. To put it more simply, the monopoly on power is legitimated primarily through the mere fact that it actually functions. Within this context, one should keep in mind the concept of the monopoly on the legitimate use of power in Max Weber's sociology of the state. Weber's concept of legitimation is dependent on a readiness to follow that neither results from the historical character and historical necessity of the state, nor is linked implicitly with the demand, which can still be found in Kant, that humankind be led out of its natural state. In Kant, the state is the instrument of power that is supposed to liberate the human being from his evil natural characteristics—this coincides completely with the thought of Frederick II, who spoke of the "*maudite race.*" Weber also uses the concept not in the sense that the state is seen as a historically legitimated form for the use of power that contributes to the civilizing of humanity (as is the case in Hegel, for example), and that is therefore historically justified. The state in Max Weber has the monopoly on the legitimate use of force for the simple reason that the masses of the population indicate a willingness to follow, and no single social group is at hand that could muster any resistance to this state monopoly. Here the "legitimate use of force" means simply the inability of society to resist this force. (See Max Weber, *Wirtschaft und Gesellschaft, Grundriß der verstehenden Soziologie,* vol. 1 [Cologne, Berlin: 1964]: 22ff.)

practice of arbitration and the "contractual freedom of contract of general trading conditions" in which the de facto power relations of the industrial giants assert themselves against the principle of the exchange of equivalents. In the area of **armed force**, factory security and the private detectives of department stores and insurance companies are the most prominent examples of delegation. On the other hand, the interventions of the Springer press, of "crime-watch" television programs, and of taxi drivers in combating real or alleged crimes can be of far greater significance. In these cases, executive functions are exercised privately— although admittedly with the stipulation that the state keeps out of the way of such private appropriations of its authority and reveals itself to be inwardly divided in its reactions, while in other cases adamantly rejecting any encroachments on its monopoly.

**Whereas the state looks for effective ways of preventing the participation of left-wing groups in the educational system, it reveals itself to be "liberal" toward the privatization of infrastructures of the educational and scientific sphere by the consciousness industry, by private research, by correspondence courses that undercut the educational system, as well as by a private educational sector that is not even geared to public interests. The state here displays the tendency to delegate the monopoly of education, which is one component of its overall power monopoly, in a piecemeal manner.**

An analysis of the contradictory development of the state's monopoly within highly organized capitalist industrial societies should set out from the basic fact that these societies lack legitimacy on a structural level. An immediate result of this is that a linear development of state power, in the sense that the state attracts more and more potential for power to itself, is out of the question. Such an approach brackets out, however, that domain that includes tax sovereignty, the redistribution of subsidies, and social services. Our focus is upon those instruments of the state that are linked with the traditional instruments of its power monopoly: police, army, education, and state security. **In these contexts, the contradictory nature of the power monopoly reveals itself in the fact that two types of impulses are at work: there is an oscillation between increasing centralization, the accumulation of instruments of power on the one hand, and, on the other, state-sanctioned decentralization, the delegation of such instruments to other social realms.**

The production interest can appropriate elements of state authority only if it dislodges the norms from their concrete anchors. A cultural sovereignty that is anchored in eleven federal provinces provides resistance to the interest of capital in socializing and privatizing the infrastructures of the educational sector. Law enforcement that is organized on a municipal or regional basis is not as easy to subsume, either formally or substantively, as when it is centralized. The effect of this tendency is a centralization of the state's power monopoly. Added to this is the fact that, in highly industrialized societies, the power relations that characterize production can be exercised only by being closely tied to the context of legitimation. The capitalist process of production creates not only the relations of production, its specific valorization interest, but also widespread doubt among people that these relations can be legitimated. The desire for legitimation leads, likewise, to a tendency toward centralization, to the increasing authority of the state, because it is absolutely necessary.

The same circumstances lead to a permanent erosion of state authority. **If the state exercises its power monopoly on the basis of the network of social contradictions, it loses legitimacy in direct proportion to the degree that it exercises this power. This mechanism makes delegation absolutely necessary. The tendency toward decentralization is a feature of the accumulated public spheres of production.**[28]

The principle of delegation does not stem from Stein's reforms of the Prussian administration or from the notion of delegation referring to the autonomy of universities in the early nineteenth century. It is not based on a substantive, integral state that, in its sovereignty and autonomy, confers statelike authority in accordance with self-determination. The practice of "indirect rule," as developed in the school of English colonial administration, seeks to integrate those interests that are capable of being integrated. The types of delegation (understood in this sense) that have occurred primarily since the 1920s are, by contrast, decaying forms of an integration that is no longer succeeding on a state or an economic level. If the state contracts out such delegations today, it does so in a covert manner; in the 1920s it did it openly. The Weimar Republic clearly had a model for state structure. In the Third Reich, the state does not change its form, but merely its function. The state disintegrates into ruling "in-groups," which occupy sectors of the state and turn parts of these sectors into separate institutions. For instance, the Reichstag and the groups working with it operated virtually alongside the "custodians of the constitution"—the president and the forces surrounding him.

On the other hand, the individual sectors of capital constituted by the different branches of industry are no longer in a position to reach a consensus regarding their integration into an overall economic process or their place within the political framework of the state—much in the same way that, in the Wilhelmine Empire, landed property and heavy industry were caught up to some extent in an antagonistic relationship. New industries, such as the rapidly expanding chemical industry, develop almost completely separately from that of iron and coal, while the remaining branches, in all their diversity, organize themselves in a quasi-syndicate form based upon their specific and anarchic partial interests. Both in the Weimar Republic and in the Third Reich, these partial structures could secure public authority and a partialized power monopoly by forming coalitions with any

28. Cf. chapter 1, "The Processing of Social Experience by the New Public Spheres of Production."

group that had a share in state power. This procedure takes on a different form today. For instance, the interests of individual economic sectors are formally combined, and the executive and legislative branches cannot simply be kept separate by the interest of an individual sector. This is the case because these particular interests have already sufficiently cultivated their connections with both executive and legislature and, without altering their partial character, are able to respect the outward forms of our constitution. The Leber plan is an especially striking example of this. In this case, a specific branch of industry worked together with the appropriate members of parliament and their advisors to reduce truck traffic on the roads and to coordinate public and private forms of transportation.[29]

This tendency, which manifests itself here on a broader social level, was apparent in the 1920s at the level of the individual firm. Fritz Croner, in his book about white-collar workers, was the first to develop the theory of delegation. His theory suggests that the legally and capitalistically defined framework of production is unsuitable—in light of increased productive forces and increased difficulties in exploitation—for organizing the overall process of capitalist production according to the criteria established by private enterprise. What was defined with reference to state authority as a decaying form is apparent here in the context of the private entrepreneur. He is no longer both the figure of authority in the factory and the representative of the principle of production itself; instead, he delegates functions, which are sanctioned by the authority of the private property holder, to employees of his firm and to the apparatuses of valorization. These workers and apparatuses organize, on a practical level, the production and valorization process according to the demands made by the delegated authority of the private capitalist.[30]

---

29. The Film Subsidy Law provides a further example, the so-called tear-jerker cartel of December 1967. The Film Subsidies Board that was established as a result of this law, which distributed a high subvention to films that would show a good profit at the box office, was covered up in the Bundestag by a series of representatives, such as Wolfram Dorn and Joachim Raffert, who were in personal union the presidents of this economic organization and parliamentary representatives, and who practically transformed, like Hypnos or mouthpieces, the prescribed phrasing of the economic groups that represented the Film Subsidies Board into parliamentary majority opinions. They were destined to fail because of this conflict of interest, but actually lost their posts only once it had been proven that they had accepted money from a farmers' organization.

30. This delegation clearly leads just as little to a regime of the managers as the delegation of the state monopoly on power to social authorities leads to the dissolution of the state. According to Burnham, management establishes itself as an autonomous class that wrests control of the mode of production from the owners and exercises domination over the companies. This description is one-sided, however. On the one hand, there is delegation, but on the other, economic substance flows toward the possessors of capital, and continues the primary tendency of the conglomerates to construct ever-higher forms of concentration. Similarly, new responsibilities constantly accrue toward the state monopoly on power in which the substance of social conflicts that cannot be resolved economically are represented. Conversely, responsibilities wander away from the state through delegation. Within this formal reversal, the original contradictions and social forces are as little affected as anarchistic commodity production and the movement toward concentration are opposites—the one develops the other from out of itself.

The issues surrounding the delegation of authority should be carefully analyzed, for they expose decisive contradictions in the dominant mode of production. The importance of these contradictions becomes clear when one compares the present situation with the crises surrounding feudalism and the monarchy in the eighteenth century, and the attempts to solve this crisis by delegating power to a responsible civil service. In Germany this process clearly led to the survival of the monarchy, although precisely here (compare the crisis of the state from 1807 to 1848) the feudal mode of production and form of government had become obsolete. In France, by contrast, the breakdown of the system and the manner by which delegation (cf. the fall of finance minister Necker) exposed the processes of decay led to the Revolution.

## 3. The Public Sphere as an Illusory Synthesis of the Totality of Society

The initial need for a public sphere as a sphere for representation seems to have originated in the ruling feudal class's need to repeatedly imprint its authority, to assist in the internalization of terror. The leopards, camels, and elephants that accompanied the army of Frederick II of Hohenstaufen to Germany, and helped to crush his sons' rebellion in a "nonviolent" manner, served this need, as did the rituals of tribal chieftains or the festivities of Louis XIV. These forms of the public sphere have a demonstrative as well as a "mnemonic" and "fascinating" function. They are supposed to mediate between the libido, the life cycle, and the power structure. They are the cement holding the diffuse totality together in the centrifugal system of the feudal order. Mature bourgeois society takes over these forms for expressing authority, and alters their function to some extent. Since bourgeois society in Central Europe has never completely cast off feudalistic structures but has adapted itself to them or coexists with them symbiotically, it has always incorporated an archaic element that enters into the representation of society as a whole, in particular into the nationalist tradition (e.g., military parades, the institution of the Hohenzollern monarchy, the stereotype of the officer). In reality, bourgeois society does not need the public sphere to formulate its synthesis of society. Competition and the law determining value create a centripetal tendency that holds the social totality together, even if it isolates individuals.[31]

The bourgeoisie's increasing lack of interest in representative festivals and manifestations of the public sphere can be quite accurately traced in history. This is expressed to begin with in the ever more insipid character of public ceremonies, even when they are arranged by hereditary ruling houses. Compare the contrived

---

31. Marx and Engels, "The Holy Family," in *Marx-Engels Werke*, vol. 2, p. 128: "Only political superstition can still imagine that bourgeois life must be held together by the state; in reality, it is the state that is held together by bourgeois life."

character of the ceremonies for the opening of the Suez Canal; the threadbare quality of the representative appearances of Louis Bonaparte and his circle, as described by Marx; the improvised nature of the proclamation of the German Empire in the Hall of Mirrors at Versailles; the self-portrait of the bourgeois public sphere in the architecture of the period between 1880 and 1914, and so on. What is expressed throughout is the fact that vital interests do not find their way into public representation.[32] This is also the source of a critical distancing from public pomp. "Be what you are, don't put on airs" is, in Germany, the motto of both the educated property-owning bourgeoisie and of the agrarian-bourgeois-Prussian ethos. During the republic that succeeded the Wilhelmine Empire, there were only a few instances of grand public representation. Of primary importance were the funerals (especially Ebert's) and the memorial days, perhaps also May 1, for serving the articulation of the public sphere. The Federal Republic, too, has been lacking in this respect. A grand display was occasioned only by the funeral of Adenauer. Another reason for the absence of interest in a representative public sphere is its increasing lack of legitimacy. **Each form of this public sphere represents, as it were, a parade of legitimations. Once legitimacy has been called into question by the mere display of the weapons of the bourgeoisie (the military parade)—even though the bourgeois mode of production can legitimate only ongoing social production, not its own private appropriation—the loss of legitimacy becomes a permanent feature. If the representative public sphere were a living reality, this sphere would become a site for the production of social critique, because the inadequacy of legitimations would be clear to everybody. It is no accident that conflicts between the student movement of the 1960s and the state often broke out at public ceremonies.**

The bourgeoisie's lack of interest in a substantive, living public sphere coincides with a significant need for a public sphere that should represent a synthesis of the totality of society. This is the need for identity, for the representation of society as a totality, as "community."[33] Such a synthesis cannot, however, exist in a class society, and has until now never existed within bourgeois society. One can

32. In his book *Die verspätete Nation*, Hellmuth Plessner has interpreted the bourgeois architecture before and after the turn of the century (and above all that of the *Gründerjahre*) as an expression of a feeling of power on the part of the bourgeoisie that felt politically powerless, but wanted nonetheless to express its real power. Impressive examples of representative decor from the latter half of the nineteenth century can be seen in Hans-Jürgen Syberberg's film, *Ludwig II.*

33. In an unpublished manuscript, Rudolf Sinz points to the fact that a need for emancipation underlay the bourgeois revolutions, and especially the French Revolution, a need that was related to the unchecked emergence of the whole human being into all of his characteristics as a member of the human species; here one can impute the idea of an explosionlike extension of all qualities in all directions, as is expressed in the characteristic extravagance of earlier bourgeois political goals. Actually, however, this emancipation was bound up within the narrow confines of the principle of competition. The whole of the human being's general and rich need for development had to pass through the eye of

thus speak in this case only of an illusory public sphere. What is striking about this sphere is that the oppressed classes orient themselves according to it as well. Thus the word "illusion" does not denote something impotent that could be eliminated by direct demystification; on the contrary, this illusion has a material core.

## The Material Core of the Illusion

Why do the oppressed classes stubbornly participate in a public sphere that excludes their most vital interests? Evidently, this stems from the contradictory relation between a **totally socialized context**—which is governed by manifold forms of division of labor, interdependence, and cooperation—and the private **forms of appropriation and of life**. The libidinal economy of individuals is not completely exhausted in the everyday expression of isolated existence and the labor process. There thus develops in the masses a surplus interest that enables those groups that associate power with the public sphere to repeatedly reactivate (especially when the existing power relations are endangered) symbols of community and of general welfare, confirmations of their own reality.

Every class society produces collective ideologies. It is a commonplace that this is how the ruling interests within society assert themselves. Consequently, theory must not only concern itself exclusively with this fact, but also ascertain the **forms and agencies** through which such ideology production operates. Under the immediate impact of the collapse of the labor movement in the face of National Socialism, theorists such as Horkheimer, Wilhelm Reich, and Franz Neumann

---

this needle. Herein lies the mechanism for the fact that capitalism has succeeded, on an almost epochal scale, in mobilizing the negative capacities of human beings for social production.

See Robert Musil, "The German as Symptom," in *Precision and Soul: Essays and Addresses*, trans. and eds. Burton Pike and David S. Luft (Chicago: University of Chicago Press, 1990): 150–92. Musil refers above all to the fact that unequivocality, clarity in the formation of concepts, and positivism are simultaneously linked with violence toward things and people, and that the capitalist mode of production sustains itself on this combination of qualities. Emancipation took place, therefore, via narrowly specialized qualities and left the overall structure of the human forces that are historically attributable to the species unexpressed. The undeveloped potential forces that remain diffuse can only be expressed in the form of idealistic movements within a society that is determined by commodity exchange. There thus remains a desire for an identity and "unity" that has not been mediated by competition, intellectualization, and exploitative interests, a desire for "release." The idea of the civil war after 1813, the idealism of the movement of 1848, the blind effort of 1914, the mass recognition of all of these patterns of behavior immediately after 1933—all of these are forms of expression of the experience that emancipation failed without being able to sublate the desire for it. The workers repeatedly took part in the "idealism" delineated here in great numbers in, for example, 1914, 1933, and during the reconstruction after 1945. The mobility of the labor process, the fact of being thrown out of one's own life cycle, surely engenders the desire to try to convince oneself of a continuous life context. See, in chapter 1, the section on "The Workings of Fantasy as a Form of Production of Social Experience." The lifetime that is actually rent asunder is accompanied by a flow of associations, governed by an economy of drives, into the mind that dreams of historical continuity, of "community."

examined, both empirically and theoretically, the question of the agencies of social-ization.[34] In its early stages, the student movement focused on this problem as well.

The public sphere, in its spatialized, pseudohistorical continuity, would not be able to constitute such an effective core of stabilizing ideology if its image were not linked with two other factors, which to a large degree mold subject-object relationships: *the effects of the alienated labor process* on wish projections and the *aftereffects of early socialization within the family.*

1. The fragmentation of human beings in the **labor process**, their isolation by competition, and the breaking up of their lives into mere quantities of work and leisure time require an ideological libidinal compensation. There develops a need for harmony.

2. The **family** has a dual character: on the one hand, life is protected from the world of work and, on the other, the libidinal structure is erected whereby individ-uals become capable of being exploited. Out of this tension grows the desire for closeness, family solidarity, and security, for a renewed encounter with familial relationships in reality. This yearning encloses the whole world in a framework in which originally learned familial relationships, love and hate toward the primal objects, are recapitulated. This *form* of ideology has not become any weaker today because the family is less significant in comparison with the labor process. Nor does the fact of the diminishing authority of the father lead to any change here; on the contrary, this level of primary socialization becomes all the more diffuse. It is, moreover, overlaid by the many compensatory functions that the family has taken over today.

**At times of relative social calm, the socialization aspects of work and fam-ily are predominant; in periods of historical transition, crises, prewar situa-tions, the illusory public sphere becomes decisive for the actions of individuals. In this sphere, the need for ideology—which is synthetically unit-ed through the process of production and the family—joins together, in a murky but incredibly effective manner, with everything that presents itself within the context of culture: education, national symbols, ethnocentric worldview, xenophobia, and bourgeois utopia.**[35] The truce between the ruling elite and organized labor in 1914, the adherence of the masses to the majority Social Democrats in 1918, the idea of the National Assembly in 1919, the rein-statement of national continuity with the election of Hindenburg, Hindenburg's welcoming of Hitler in the Garrison Church at Potsdam in 1933, and all the repre-

---

34. See *Studien über Autoritat und Familie*, ed. Max Horkheimer (Paris: 1936), esp. "Allgemeiner Teil," reprinted in Horkheimer, *Kritische Theorie*, vol. 1: pp. 277ff.; Wilhelm Reich, *The Mass Psychology of Fascism*, trans. Vincent R. Carfagno (New York: Simon & Schuster, 1970); Franz Neumann, *Angst und Politik* (Tübingen: 1954).

35. It is striking that any activation of the public sphere as a synthesis of illusion encompassing the whole of society is linked, especially during times of crisis or in wartime situations, with a rise in the notion of consensus, be it that of the bourgeoisie or that of factory personnel.

sentatives of the old illusory public sphere that collapsed in 1918—these are all examples of the masses' intense willingness to invest their hopes and to entrust their needs.[36] After 1945 the institutions of the public sphere disintegrated again in Germany—a more comprehensive disintegration can scarcely be conceived. There was an immediate shift of energies toward the family as the form of social self-sufficiency in an emergency, as well as toward the production process: the factories had to be rebuilt. The process is reminiscent of what we refer to as "occupational therapy." The reason for this collective behavior lies in the interaction between bourgeois culture and the bourgeois mode of production, both of which continue to remain in force even if they have declined in their original bourgeois form. It appears that—in a manner analogous to the circulatory system—as soon as one system collapses, the *socialization determinants* of those systems that have remained intact are strengthened. Thus it is evident that destroying the illusion of the public sphere merely leads to a search for new ways of expressing the need for spatial continuity and identity.[37]

## The Reversal of the Functions of Power and Illusion

Certain new developments of the public apparatus of power are not readily apparent for the sole reason that they develop at a more advanced stage of the overall capitalist context. On the other hand, the backward, though still effective, forms of power—such as the Greek colonels, direct military campaigns, police raids, threatening gestures by the organs of the state, for example, the judiciary branch—draw attention to themselves. This prevents one from recognizing that these phenomena are not typical of the present period. What characterizes this age, rather, is the fact that the developed power monopoly finds itself prevented, at vital points, from putting its threatening gestures into action. The same applies to internal force. Its effectiveness against groups, minorities, and individuals is incontestable. Nevertheless, attempts to eliminate contradic-

---

36. Cf. the great attention devoted to this question in Levi's critique of the March action of 1921 (Levi, "Unser Weg. Wider den Putschismus," in *Zwischen Spartakus und Sozialdemokratie* (Frankfurt: 1969): 48ff. The vehement reserve expressed by Rosa Luxemburg toward the national question does not in the least contradict this; rather, it is an indication of how dangerous Rosa Luxemburg believed this pseudopublic category to be.

37. This interaction is also evident in, for example, the case of longer strikes. To the extent that the coercive behavioral determinants escape the process of production, the pressure to reestablish the normal situation that is appropriate to its function seems to be increased, not only by the mass media, but also by the workingmen's wives. See Reimut Reiche, *"Was heißt: proletarische Familie?"* (Frankfurt: 1971). The wives have to see to it that there is something to eat. They are not relieved of this responsibility by the temporary breakdown of production. Either it succeeds in creating a new life context in which everyone can contribute his own distinctive characteristics and where everything is infused with a new meaning, or prevailing forces proliferate in the direction of the old bourgeois situation in which, at least, everyone thinks he knows his place.

tions by threats and direct force have, in almost every case, proven futile in the long run. A system can maintain itself on a foundation of pure force only when the opposition is so weak that the mere appearance of a threat is sufficient. Even in such cases, one must ask whether it is not other, material causes that bring about stabilization, while open force merely accompanies this process. Imperialistic threats directed inward can therefore be described as just as illusory as those directed outward.

On the other hand, the production of illusion, of words, ideologies, structures of public consciousness, contains a real potential for violence. The violence of present social relations is reproduced in the systems of press monopoly, the mass media, and the illusory public sphere. In the process, cause and effect are reversed. Because this violence articulates itself via the internalized power relations that have been socially produced within individuals, there develops an illusory responsibility for crimes, an illusory individualism of the individual criminal. It is therefore no accident that the mentally retarded and social outsiders appear to be the perpetrators of violence; their deeds are prepared by a social production process that disappears in the violent act. The actual use of force is, for instance, concealed behind the basic right of the freedom to express an opinion.[38] Amid the present level of aggressive tendencies and prejudices brought about by oppression, a considerable degree of self-control is required to resist the permanent invitations to violence, which are always a by-product of the fabrication of illusion.

National Socialism was, among other things, an attempt to solve contradictions that were economically insoluble on a capitalist basis by a comprehensive activation of extraeconomic force. The new public spheres of production and their specific forms of expression in the programming and consciousness industry tend to carry out a comparable redistribution of power with economic methods; these spheres thereby transpose contradictions from sectors of society where these contradictions cannot be resolved to other sectors where they apparently can be. It is incorrect to describe this wholly different, but in no sense less violent or (so far as its results are concerned) less effective, mechanism as fascistic. Rather, this is a case where the production of social illusion and the production of social force merge into one another in such a way that each produces its opposite.

38. In the legal opinion that Ernst Forsthoff handed down in 1968 in favor of Axel Springer's publishing house, the public-access guarantees of the Basic Law are interpreted in such a way that they become simply a means for justifying an almost arbitrary actualization of the power of the private press as opposed to practically any public control. The legal arguments here are for the most part arguments that accommodate the employer; they do not correspond to interpretations that prevail in jurisprudence. This opinion is recommended for all readers of this book, because it reflects the cynical legal reinforcement of the open brutality of the press as it corresponds to the point of view of certain powerful social groups. See Ernst Forsthoff, *Der Verfassungsschutz der Zeitungspresse*, Planungsstudien 3, ed. J. H. Kaiser (Frankfurt am Main, 1969).

## The Superstructure of Society Lags Behind the Development of the Productive Forces; the Illusory Public Sphere Is Ahead of Them

It has often been demonstrated how law, ethics, philosophy, and culture all lag behind the development of the productive forces. However, the public sphere as an illusory synthesis of the totality of society has the tendency to modernize itself more rapidly than the actual tempo of historical development.[39] In this respect, the public sphere is bound to a rule: it must sustain the claim that it represents the totality of society. On account of its mechanisms of exclusion, it cannot, however, fulfill this claim. It disintegrates rapidly because at no time does it possess the substance it purports to have.[40] The public sphere must overcome this disintegration through permanent variation. One of its specific forms of expression is thus the attempt to reach out into the future, the long-term program, the replacement of its present by the anticipation of its future.

Herein lies the weakness of a cultural critique that is intent on nailing down the illusion of this public sphere. While critiques of individual manifestations of the existing public sphere are still being performed and disseminated, the public sphere has already changed its identity. Precisely because it does not fulfill its own claims, it is able to permanently modify the form of its influence, its appearance, and the temporal situation to which it refers. Substantive critique, on the other hand, by virtue of its own claims, holds on to the object; it stands there empty-handed when the criticized object slips out of its grasp.

**A counterpublic sphere that is based on ideas and discourses with progressive content cannot develop effective weapons against the combined elements of illusion, the public sphere, and public power. In this situation, the compensations that the classical bourgeois public sphere possessed, as compared with the public power relations, become increasingly ineffective. The only antidotes to the production of the illusory public sphere are the counter-**

---

39. One could compare this to the ready use of political campaigns, agendas, state events, special reports, and historical moments during the Third Reich. Only by incorporating a perspective on the future could National Socialism maintain the contradictory context of its "movement." The compulsion thereby necessitated to accelerate the movement of history—to push the contradictions forward into the future, since their resolution is violently prevented in the present—was not merely an illusory movement, although it initially set only an illusion in motion; rather, it had direct consequences in new plans for expansion, strategic trends, declarations of war, that were subsequently in part very difficult to motivate from the position of various interests. These were not the result of historical movement; rather, they resulted from the fact that no historical movement had occurred. Real interests are a matter for the future, and a multiplicity of delusions and projections that are ordinarily a matter of the future shape the present.

40. The more quickly it disintegrates, the less it is able to be a horizon of experience. Viewed from this practical and performative perspective, a public sphere is characteristically either stimulating or hindering. Without this specific perspective, the concept of any public sphere is necessarily ambivalent; as an idea it appears to be useful, but there is no way of putting it into practical use.

products of a proletarian public sphere:[41] idea against idea, product against product, production sector against production sector. It is impossible to grasp in any other way the permanently changing forms that social power takes on in its fluctuations between capitalist production, illusory public sphere, and public power monopoly. It is not the gods, but rather the real social circumstances, that practice metamorphosis. It is against this background that the following chapters—using the public-service programming industry, the private-media cartel, and the new public spheres of production as examples—set out to describe the interweaving of power relations, which, only by working together, produce the fragile equilibrium that is supposed to pass for the public sphere.

## The Proletarian Public Sphere and
## the Social Production of Use-Value

There is at present no socialist society in which commodity categories have already become obsolete. The actual status of commodity production is therefore especially important, because it is the basis and the index of the perversion and blurring of the social awareness of the masses. So long as commodity production exists (even as a subordinate mode), the social whole is permeated by value abstractions that rest on the separation of concrete and abstract labor. Never-

---

41. Here there are also dangerous inherent laws to the proletarian public sphere that will require precise theoretical inquiry. The proletarian public sphere is itself a matter of the future, but at the same time it is the only opportunity available for putting historical ground under one's feet and for structuring experience in historical temporal sequences. *Only on this solid basis of real mass experience does the proletarian public sphere have the weight it needs to be able to bring the movements of the bourgeois illusory public sphere, which are scurrying in every direction, to a halt.* It itself, however, has the tendency to construct illusory public spheres as soon as it is not firmly anchored in the experiences of the masses and in history. To the extent to which it must itself claim to embody the entirety of proletarian interests, it will attempt to balance this contradiction through a hurried, that is, a premature fulfillment. Specific practice is necessary to keep this mechanism under control. Here it is a prerequisite that the intellectual dissonance required to simultaneously implement proletarian interests against dominant interests *and* acknowledge the incompleteness of proletarian interests be sustained. No way of living or drive-economic system for gratification has thus far existed that sufficiently meets this requirement. It is therefore a characteristic of almost all emancipatory movements that establish themselves within the periphery of the labor movement that they reproduce bourgeois mechanisms precisely in their utopian tendencies. But these must suffer defeat in the face of bourgeois combinations that have been more comprehensively organized socially. This tendency is less effective at the center of the labor movement. It is precisely the inhibiting factors of the proletarian context of blockading, of the conservatism of the labor movement, that hold it secure in the present historical period in which forces of production are actually moving. Besides, social cooperation almost never continues to take place within the mechanism of premature acceleration, because the velocity of the movement of the various groups and factions, and so forth (their constant change of position) does not permit long-term synchronization and adaptation of work practices and interests. On the contrary, this form of movement is a gold mine for competitive relations.

theless, a social system cannot choose either to do away with or to tolerate (albeit only in parts of the economy) commodity production. This production always emerges from a specific, long-term stage of the productive forces. Its disappearance is not the result of directives or measures of the planning authorities, but, like the withering away of the state as a political force, the result of a prolonged process of the transformation of the whole of society. It is only in this way that the stage described by Marx is reached in which labor has become the paramount need of life: from each according to his abilities, to each according to his needs. It is only at such a stage that a wealth of different individualities, that something approaching an individual, can develop.

The withering away of the relations of production does not mean that they simply disappear as virulent forces within history. They can develop anew with every social regression to earlier stages of production. **Rather, this withering away is a stage of social wealth itself, of the socialization of interests, of awareness, of unification at an advanced stage of production, which, in the interest of producers, eliminates in advance the obsolete, exhausted relations of production and repels them as unworkable in practice, even though they remain within the arsenal of historical possibilities.**[42] **Indeed, whether the more advanced stage of awareness can be retained or not depends upon the virulence of these preconditions. In this respect, the dialectical concept of progress rests not on an exclusion of what history has made outdated, but on its complete appropriation. This is the only way in which the concept of permanent revolution can be differentiated from the abstract logic of progress and substantively defined. It is not because of new types of contradictions and their extension into infinity, but on account of the historical presence of all old contradictions within the new ones that social upheaval becomes permanent. This is why a fully developed historical awareness is necessary for the constitution of a proletarian public sphere.** In this respect, the proletarian public sphere lies in

---

42. The analogy that is contained in the image of "withering away" or, more literally, "dying off" (*Absterben*) does not reflect the actual process through which the distribution of private property, the state, and outmoded relations of production *are sublated*. What is involved is not anything like the dying of individuals. Nonetheless, the image of "dying off" is repeatedly used in the writing of history with reference to societies, cultures, and epochs. But this is simply an image. Ancient Rome did not "die" because the Germans invaded, or because it was superseded by the Middle Ages. Rather, Rome lives on in the form of Roman law, administrative systems, ideas, national borders, populations that continue to survive within the newly developing societies. The life of a society does not simply end like that of individuals, except in the case of the immediate eradication of entire peoples. What is at the root of the Marxist concept of dying off is obviously the Hegelian idea of sublation, which simultaneously characterizes the negation of the given, its assimilation, and its continuation within a higher form of organization. Thus the state and private property form one level of social development, upon whose foundation the negating socialist forms of organization take shape. If private property, the state, and so on, were no longer present at all within this higher organizational context (because, for example, they had died), the entire socialist basis for socialism would subsequently fall away.

sharp contrast to every phase of the bourgeois, which has consistently excluded history. It is precisely when the bourgeois public sphere presents itself as laden with history—as, for instance, in the French Revolution's recourse to Antiquity, in Wilhelminism, in the "historical awareness" of the Third Reich—that its total indifference toward, and repression of, real history is evident. In contrast, the proletarian public sphere transforms the dialectic between living and dead labor—between living generations and all past generations in the history of the human race—into social forms of expression that can be understood by everyone. Karl Marx, *The Communist Manifesto*: "In bourgeois society, therefore, the past dominates the present; in communist society, the present dominates the past."

## The Medium of the Production of Social Wealth

According to Marx, commodity production also produces social wealth; it does so, however, on a "wretched basis." "Labor time as the measure of value posits wealth itself as founded on poverty. For real wealth is the developed productive power of all individuals."[43]

The wealth produced by capitalism can be appropriated only privately. It is not in reality available for a public appropriation by *all* human beings who are related to one another socially. The "immense collection of commodities," which the wealth of capitalist production represents, is itself a supercommodity of little use-value to its producers. Its overall use-value is just sufficient in ensuring the survival of the producers. The use-value produced by capitalism is, admittedly, not thereby exhausted, for it also has the tendency to threaten the individuals clinging to it with destruction—with mass murder and war. It is thus clear that use-value as produced by capitalism has a dual character: it is not only a property of individual things, but in it is reproduced the uselessness of the overall situation when it comes to creating human relations.[44] Thus, the concept of the production of social use-value is concerned primarily with the use-value of social relations. This category presupposes that, in its form, the totality of social production is governed by the production of use-value; it determines whether a social wealth is produced that *all* people can afford without being caught up in insoluble contradictions. Marx describes social wealth in this respect as the many-sided unfolding of the energies of the human species: **sociality—cooperation—freedom—awareness—universality—wealth of needs and of subjective human sensuality.** Each of these

---

43. Karl Marx, *Grundrisse der Kritik der politischen Ökonomie* (rough draft) (Berlin: 1953): 595ff.

44. On the concept of use-value in Marx and its meaning as a political and economic formal determinant, see Roman Rodolsky, *Zur Entstehungsgeschichte des Marx'schen Kapital, der Rohentwurf des "Kapital" 1857–1858*, vol. 1 (Frankfurt: 1968), esp. "Karl Marx und das Problem des Gebrauchswerts in der politischen Ökonomie," pp. 98ff.

human modes of expression requires a public sphere for its development; each represents an essential component of the proletarian public sphere. None of these concepts can be unambiguously defined under the existing conditions of production. Each of them denotes a specific and distinct direction of human development. Under the existing circumstances, they tend to fall apart and to mutually exclude one another.

Since the development of social wealth cannot be separated from individual enrichment of human beings, the diverse types of human energies cannot be realized if they remain merely specialized.[45] When they do develop as something specialized, this process is always linked with an impoverishment of the individual: in other words, social wealth in the sense of the development of proletarian relations of production and a proletarian public sphere can come into being only as a rich totality of many relations. Only in this way can the specific dialectic of the individual's potentials establish itself.

Given all this—since words do not, at the present moment, denote what would exist under changed conditions of production—universality embraces such varied things as the abolition of the division of labor, above all that between manual and mental labor, a concrete conception of the world, collectivity, unification of consciousness, and individuality. **Freedom** is understood as a material redemption of the emphatic concept of freedom, a concept that the bourgeoisie coined but never put into practice; it embraces autonomy, identity, and production governed by the producers themselves;[46] it is at the same time the medium of **sociality**, which entails a wholly different quality of modes of interaction and of the regulation of interests than those of existing society. Sociality would be expressed as the concrete mediation of a mutual dependency between an interest and the satisfaction of everyone else's interests, and hence represents the highest level of **cooperation**.[47] Something of what the anarchists understood as mutualism (reciprocal aid)

---

45. What Marx says about manufacturing also basically holds true for big industry: "In manufacture, in order to make the collective labourer, and through him capital, rich in social productive power, each labourer must be made poor in individual productive powers" (Marx, *Capital*, vol. 1, trans. Samuel Moore and Edward Aveling [New York: International Publishers, 1967]: 361).

46. It is precisely in the concept of freedom that it becomes clear that what is at stake is not simply the material fulfillment of the merely formal freedom of the bourgeoisie. The form and content of freedom cannot be kept separate from each other. The bourgeois concept of freedom is an exclusionary, negatory concept that presumes the fundamental existence of relationships of coercion and power. With the material realization of freedom, the form of this freedom is also altered. Voltaire characterizes the limited horizon of bourgeois freedoms when he says, "Ce mot de libertés, des privilèges, suppose l'assujettissement. Des libertés sont des exemptions de la servitude général." ("This talk of freedom, of privilege, presumes subjugation. Freedoms are the exception to a general servitude.")

47. The interests thus described should not be confused with the egocentric interests that the bourgeois public sphere attempts to regulate. What is at issue here is indeed the sublation of these purely egotistical interests that it has itself first produced as interests that are really worthy of humanity. See Karl Marx, *MEW*, vol. 4, p. 482: "In the place of the old bourgeois society with its classes and class

always crystallizes around this concept of the "social." None of these elements of social wealth can unambiguously be defined in an affirmative way. At the same time, these elements are **not utopian**, in the sense that they are not also products of existing society and they do not demand fulfillment.

The category of true needs must, under existing circumstances, have something enigmatic, intangible about it, because the truth content of these needs could be verified only once they were developed; nevertheless they exist as that which is developing. Because they do exist, the following sentence has a substantive meaning: the question of true needs entails the concrete imperative to guard against false needs.

## The Public Sphere of the Student Movement

Under the present conditions of the developing consciousness industry and the changing organization of commodities throughout the industrial process,[48] there are emerging impulses toward a public sphere that attempts to break through the context of exploitation. This is not a question of abstract alternatives: the capitalist process of production itself produces this countermovement. Within the context of a capitalist social order, the May 1968 movement in France and the youth and student protest movement in the Federal Republic can be cited as examples of such a form of public sphere.

The impulses underlying the student movement in the Federal Republic have in part been repressed and excluded from public consciousness; at best, people still recall the great mass demonstrations, the death of Benno Ohnesorg, the anti-Springer campaign, the confrontation with the police. This repression also determines the behavior of groups who were themselves actively involved in this movement.

One decisive motive of the student movement at the outset was the destruction of the clandestine practices of the traditional public sphere, in particular that of the university. The students strove for a fulfillment of the substantive content of a bourgeois-liberal idea of a public sphere by demonstratively forcing discussions. They wanted to bring experience, contexts of living, the historical present (Vietnam, the liberation movements in the Third World, their real experience as students) into a context of public discussion that was blocked by the formal public sphere. Communication and discussion were not the intention and function of the decaying public spheres of such institutions. Various interests were brought together in these spheres that used these institutions for defending themselves

---

contradictions, there will appear an association, wherein the free development of one is the occasion for the free development of all." Here the principles of social life and of the public sphere are really anchored in the value of the human being, as was *supposed* to have been the case in Kant.

48. See chapter 4.

against the attempts of society as a whole to regulate them—although, in fact, these attempts would have been made by outside groups acting under the guise of society as a whole.[49]

The interest of the students was almost totally opposed to that of the professors. The students were, in their entire context of living, incorporated into the university; by contrast, the professors were organized within the university only through that part of their work that related to teaching and self-government. An important sphere of their activity, the tasks connected with their research, remained more or less private. From their point of view, the university's limited form of a representative public sphere was quite satisfactory. As their whole life cycle is coming under the increasing threat of incorporation into the university—a situation that can scarcely be avoided given present-day educational requirements—the professors are becoming politicized and are organizing resistance against the democratic interests that students and assistants support.

The student movement was ignited both by concrete conflicts within the universities themselves and by events that affected the global public sphere. Its history, stretching from the campaigns against Germany's remilitarization and against the emergency laws, to the takeover of the VDS, to the dissolution of the SDS, will not be recapitulated here.[50] However, something of central importance for the proletarian public sphere is already displayed in the protest movement in

49. In the "Blue Report" (the report on university reform drawn up by the research committee on university reform, Hamburg, 1948), which was a cooperative effort on the part of, among others, Bruno Snell and C. F. von Weizsäcker, a committee was suggested for supervising the universities, in which public sphere, social forces, and the autonomy of the university were supposed to be linked together. What this did de facto was transfer a particular form of pluralism onto the university. This met with the resistance of those with the "Ordinarius" degree, who formulated their interests in the guidelines for the reform of university constitutions in the provinces in the American-occupied areas, the recommendations of a committee of experts, the *Schwalbacher Richtlinien*, ed. Karl Geiler, Walter Hallstein, Gustav Radbruch, Publications of the "Süddeutsche Juristenzeitung," vol. 6 (Heidelberg: 1947). The self-administration of the universities that was created by this and by Article 5 of the Basic Law attempted increasingly to force the state university administration away from university matters, and at the same time contained safeguards against the exertion of a direct influence by social groups. In practice, a powerful private economic interest found access into the special public sphere of the university through the emancipation from the state, an access that was expressed in the abundant parallel activities of the "Ordinarien." It is precisely this, among other things, that initiated the student critiques.

50. See, for example, issues of the journals *Neue Kritik* and *Neue Linke*; *Die Linke antwortet Jürgen Habermas* (Frankfurt am Main: 1968); Oskar Negt, *Politik als Protest* (Frankfurt am Main: 1971); Hans-Jürgen Krahl, *Konstitution und Klassenkampf. Zur historischen Dialektik von bürgerlicher Emanzipation und proletarischer Revolution* (Frankfurt am Main: 1971); Jürgen Habermas, "Demokratisierung und Hochschule—Politisierung der Wissenschaft," in *Merkur* 23 (June 1969): 197ff.; W. Schumm, *Kritik der Hochschulreform* (Munich: 1969); Peter Brückner, Alfred Krovoza, *Was heißt Politisierung der Wissenschaften und was kann sie für die Sozialwissenschaften heißen?* (Frankfurt am Main: 1972). It is characteristic of the process of repressing this important component of German political history that there have been no attempts made at a comprehensive bibliography or

its embryonic form: namely, a mediation between the **situation in the workplace** (including reflection on the meaning of subsequent employment) and the present **global context**. During the short life of these protest movements, this dialectic was not developed on either a practical or a theoretical level.

It is difficult to describe these mediations with any precision after the fact. It is certain that the immediate personal transfer of the experiences of the liberation struggles—from Vietnam, from Iran—occurred more rapidly via university students than in other spheres of society. This direct physical communication was accompanied by an abstract presence of liberation movements in the metropolises (as conveyed by the mass media). This presence encountered preformulated political and moral attitudes and judgments, which articulated the hopelessness of exerting any concrete political influence on the system. There emerged out of the contradiction between identifying with the liberation movements on the one hand, and the unlikelihood of being able to take part in the real struggle or offer help via the existing political channels on the other, a political ethic of refusal to compromise. This permeated all the campaigns of the first phase of the student movement—whether they were directed against Springer, against the tenure-based university system, or against the official visits of, for instance, Tshombe, the Shah. Such a mediation between the situation in the workplace and world events presupposes a **social sensibility** that is, in late-capitalist systems, cultivated only in universities. This sensibility does not stem merely from the fact that a person has more formal knowledge. It is just as possible for this type of knowledge to inhibit social sensibility. **However paradoxical it may sound, the cultivation of this form of sensibility is the product of a conservative mode of experiencing reality, which derives from the requirements of traditional learning, "education through academic discipline," autonomy, reflection on meaning, and so on. All human beings share a desire for consciousness and meaningful immediacy, but it can begin to be articulated only through the traditional, not the technocratically reformed, educational system. This desire comes into contact with a context of living that reveals itself to be, in virtually palpable terms, a nexus of crime and the achievement ethic. The worldwide strategy of preventive counterrevolution, as was adopted by the United States in Santo Domingo, Vietnam, Latin America, and Africa, visibly destroyed all those**

discussion. A bibliography would in any case, even if it included the numerous leaflets and working papers that were not published in the sense of publication technology, be completely inadequate, since it would not reproduce the actual contexts and discussions—that is, the element that is primarily practical and active. The accusation of pseudoactivism that was made by, for example, Habermas and Adorno (see Theodor W. Adorno, "Resignation," in *Kritik, Kleine Schriften zur Gesellschaft* [Frankfurt: 1971], for example, p. 148) did not in any way refer to the fact that the real character of this movement was not a consequence of their actions and praxis. [SDS (Sozialistischer Deutscher Studentenverbund) refers to the socialist student union; the VDS is the umbrella organization for all of the student unions in Germany.—*Trans.*]

**legitimating forms of the bourgeois public sphere—in other words, those very values that went hand in hand with a desire for higher education in the first place. A critique of real circumstances extends to each phase of the educational process as well and leads to a questioning of the perspectives that sustain this process. The need for a radical scrutiny of theory and practice allies itself with a critical theory that makes possible the reception of unorthodox socialist authors. This produces an interrelation, in terms of methodology as well, between social totality and individual interests.**

From the outset, the students were concerned that their political activities were being assimilated and integrated by the bourgeois public sphere. They did not wish to be reformists. This is, however, not just a matter of resolve. On the contrary, a political impulse becomes reformist under social conditions that do not allow for its autonomous unfolding. Under different conditions, this same impulse can take on a revolutionary flavor. Thus, even radical components of the protest movement allow themselves to be exploited by the publishing industry, regardless of whether the individuals in question refused to make business deals or participated in the process of exploitation. Bourgeois institutions and industries have adopted the experiences of the student movement—once again, regardless of whether they have to pay for them or not. Incorporation into a reformist context can be avoided only if one correctly estimates the outcome of the play of social forces. Individual political actions, gestures, and resolutions ultimately have no influence in determining which area of society, by virtue of the overall tendency, they will occupy. Furthermore, it was not the danger of reformism that led to a crisis in the student movement. **What happened, rather, was that—under the massive pressure of the surrounding bourgeois public sphere—aspects of the student movement that had initially acted as its constitutive features gradually became the factors that undermined the movement.** There were always two strands within each individual campaign of the student movement: mobilization via **the mechanism of political value abstractions; and the more difficult and slow constitution of emancipatory interests.**

Abstract mobilization, which relies above all on ethical and merely political impulses, necessarily creates a mechanism of exclusion that eliminates concrete interests because they cannot stand up to the legitimating political weight of world events. It is not possible to legitimate, in every instance, the abolition of examinations or the transformation of individual classroom syllabi in the same way one legitimates a concrete action that has a real or a supposed impact on liberation struggles. As regards the way these abstractions work, it is of little significance whether Vietnam, the struggle for the victory of liberation movements, or the domestic struggle on behalf of the working class is given precedence. What is essential to such abstractions is **that this accurate qualification and localization of the most important contradictions leads to a subordination of concrete interests in which the same contradictions are necessarily repeated as partic-**

**ular ones**. This is the reason why the concrete interests of students localized in the university were separated from large-scale political activities, such as the campaign against the emergency laws, that problematize domestic politics as a whole. A similar mechanism underlies the turning away of the majority of student groups from university issues in favor of infrastructural work in factories—a trend that is presently on the wane. Both tendencies are admittedly an expression of the same phenomenon: the inability of the intelligentsia to achieve a concrete relation to the context of living and public sphere of the proletariat.

It is difficult to put forward a single reason why the student movement, which formulated precisely the emphatic concept of **the production of a public sphere and of the incorporation of individual interests**, should have so neglected these two categories after the dissolution of the SDS. To understand this paradox and to grasp it as the key to the functioning of the proletarian public sphere, it is necessary to widen our perspective.

The valorization interest of capitalism cloaks the whole of reality with value abstractions, with a framework in which levels of attention and prohibitions on perception are bound. By means of these filters, the bourgeois public sphere excludes reality in diverse ways. The abstract negation of the valorization interest can result in a similar exclusion of reality, whose effect is comparable irrespective of the anticapitalist intention. **The result is a kind of political value abstraction on the part of the radical left. From the perspective of a Jacobin or socialist *ideal* or intent, the "real community," the whole "social essence" (Marx) itself becomes a context of valorization that eliminates all that which does not serve the aim of overthrowing society as a whole—an aim, sustained by pure will, that transforms anything suitable into mere raw material. Social practice interrupts the dialectic between individual interests and the totality of society, including the dialectic between concrete experience in the workplace and the experience of the contradictions that determine the world as a whole. The result is a duplication of reality. One aspect of this phenomenon is that the capacity for action by groups that consider themselves emancipatory is not increased, but rather diminished. Campaigns motivated by abstractly conceived politics do not have to clash concretely with the nerve centers of capital. Instead the outcome is, as a rule, a parallelism, which allows for the coexistence of goals formulated in revolutionary terms and of ongoing bourgeois conditions.** At both levels, the real interests of human beings become visible and form connections with the capitalist interest and the political legitimation interest alike. The explanation for this is neither treason nor opportunism. Rather, the correctly assessed weight of world events (Vietnam, the Black Panther movement, the suppression of the working class) leads to an inability to undertake small quantitative changes in immediate experience and in the workplace. These changes acquire meaning only in their relation to the total picture. Thus, if the interrelation between such concrete steps—which cannot be legitimated at every moment without destroying the situation—and the large-scale political fronts is interrupted, there is no longer any criterion whereby particular interests, in their subordination to abstract political goals, can be evaluated. **The reverse side of the value hierarchy is the instrumentalization of life interests, which are, however, the medium within which all transformation, including a global one, takes place.** Conversely, there is then also no criterion for measuring the limits of individual or group interests. Interests whose public status has been suppressed assert themselves all the more freely in the form of organic connections with legitimation values.

The consequences of such a derived constitution of interests are far more complex for anticapitalist movements than the consequences of the decay of the bourgeois public sphere are for capitalist society. **This is because groups that operate socially in terms of pure, abstract negation do not even participate in the abstract, effective universalizing and socializing tendencies of society. These are tendencies that create something like a public sphere, even when the bourgeois form of this sphere is decaying, or when it is not grasped as such.** What is at issue here is a general problem of every revolutionary movement that attempts to realize its aims within a surrounding bourgeois public sphere. Sartre has used the term "fraternité-terreur" to describe this experience: "A group forms itself in a heated situation, for instance in the face of a goal ("Storm the Bastille!"); immediately after the campaign, the individuals who make up the group uneasily confront one another anew and attempt in their freedom to establish a bond that could take the place of the direct bond produced during the campaign—in other words, a kind of agreement or oath, which in turn tends to constitute the nucleus of a series and to set up a relationship of reified contiguity between them. I have called this '**fraternité-terreur**.' "[51] Another aspect of the same situation is described by Adorno: "Repressive intolerance toward the idea that is not immediately accompanied by a recipe for action is rooted in fear. One must beware of an unmuzzled idea and of the attitude that is not prepared to sell it out, because one is profoundly aware of something that one cannot admit to oneself: that the idea is correct. An archetypal bourgeois mechanism well known to the *Aufklärer* of the eighteenth century is current once again, in an unchanged form: anguish about a negative state of affairs, in this case a blocked reality, is converted into rage against the person who points it out."[52] The situation described here—that on the one hand one must go on with one's existence, while

---

51. Jean-Paul Sartre, in a discussion with Il Manifesto in *Partei und Klasse*, p. 32. By "series" Sartre means forms of loss of individuality, isolation, and lack of consciousness such as result from processes of reification and alienation. "The same worker who finds himself part of an amalgamated group at work can be completely serialized if he is alone at home or in other life situations" (p. 31). Seriality is here the counterconcept to spontaneity, a sense of being part of a unified group.

52. Adorno, "Resignation," p. 147.

at the same time being in a position to grasp the meaninglessness of this individual existence—would be no different if we were dealing with industrial workers instead of students. **There are as yet no forms of life or experiences that allow one to sustain a state of consciousness even when the gap between this state and reality has become physically and psychically intolerable.** It cannot be denied that it is precisely the student movement in the Federal Republic that has gone the farthest in inventing modes of behavior to deal with visible gaps as visible gaps. Examples include Rudi Dutschke's notion of *informal cadres*, and the refusal of the most important leaders of the student movement to depict the social utopia in affirmative terms.

Within student groups, the abandonment of the emphatic concept of the public sphere and the mistrust of the sectarian nature of student interests (measured against the class interest of the proletariat) have been seen as signs not of disintegration, but of progress and insight. The calls to leave the universities and turn to infrastructural work in the community and the factory were in tune with this self-criticism. They were, however, also the expression of a rationalistic and moralistic context of legitimation that belongs to a bourgeois mode of production. The more highly the legitimation of one's own work could be rated, the more intense was the withdrawal from the postulate of a public sphere and the return to clandestine group work and isolation. The opposing answer in the historical situation after 1968 would have been formulated as follows: the radicalization of the limited interests of the students leads, on the one hand, to collective theoretical exertions in an anticapitalist spirit and, on the other hand, to a transformation of the intelligentsia in the universities that puts them, for the first time, in a position to ally themselves with the working class. **This process of transformation cannot succeed if even a few of the fundamental interests of the intelligentsia remain ill defined.**

A partial aspect of human labor, as it exists at all levels of development of society, is made autonomous by the professional intelligentsia. In the process, the intelligentsia has not voluntarily made itself the agent of capitalist interests throughout history. Rather, the division of manual and mental labor creates specific dangers for the mental worker, as well as an awareness on the part of the intellectual class that it is threatened.[53] These are the constantly recurring reasons

---

53. Bertolt Brecht repeatedly described the *entitlement to anxiety* of the members of the intelligentsia in the face of the threat of violence. The central European intelligentsia has existed since the founding of the first European universities within a massive context of terror (see, for example, the castration of the university teacher Abelard). Viewed from the standpoint of the ruling class, an aberrant intelligentsia has always been subjected to the most extreme physical punishment (torture wheels, being drawn and quartered, etc.). The retreat of the intelligentsia into professional groups and castes serves as a defense against this excessive pressure that is internalized by the intelligentsia. Here one could compare, for example, the actions taken against the intellectuals who were linked to the farmers in the German peasant wars. The "demagogues" and "student persecutions" of the nineteenth century,

for dependency. This historically determined dependency can only be broken by thoroughly politicizing the intelligentsia. **Without this, cooperation with the working class is inconceivable, because an appropriation and sublation of the social milieu of the intelligentsia, who come for the most part from the middle class, cannot be achieved by individuals but only collectively and politically.**[54] This situation is exacerbated by turning revolutionary activity into an illegal and professional activity. **There is no cure for the types of contradictions bred by an anticapitalist public sphere that is restricted to closed groups and under pressure from the surrounding bourgeois public sphere. Only the public sphere can simultaneously sublate both these contradictions and the pressure of formal bourgeois public sphere.** A group that pays for its opportunities with a lack of publicity will persistently distort and reduce the substance of its revolutionary activity. This is the most dangerous aspect of the resolutions passed by the ministers of the interior. These resolutions will do nothing to hamper the activities of the political organizations in question, but they will provide these groups with the absurd alternative of either abandoning the public sphere altogether or of renouncing their political goals.

## Workers' Protest Activities—Surrounded by a Disintegrating Bourgeois Public Sphere

One of the major contradictions of the proletarian public sphere, in its efforts to establish itself vis-à-vis the bourgeois, stems from the following fact: whereas it can be developed only by the producers of social wealth themselves, it is presently formulated in advanced industrial countries only by groups, such as the German and French students, who do not and cannot represent the productive class as a whole (in Italy the situation is somewhat different). In the course of their campaigns, the students have become aware of this—it was, however, not in their power to develop a social, collective praxis in light of this awareness. The experience of failure subsequently resulted in forms of self-criticism among the students that extinguished elements of the insights they had gained.

**For a proletarian public sphere—or a counterpublic sphere as the preliminary form—to come into being, three factors must work together: the interests of the productive class must be the driving force; it must be possible to create a medium of intercourse that relates the particular interests of the**

---

partial aspects of the persecution of the Jews, are nothing but the reactualizations of an agenda of terror that is already presupposed in the intellectual strata. The pressure leveled against aberrant behavior in the intelligentsia is an almost characteristic German phenomenon that can be linked today with certain constellations of interests in the second wave of persecution against the left at present.

54. See our analysis in chapter 1 in the section titled "The Fate of the Cognitive Drives: Experience through Production of Knowledge."

**productive sector and society as a whole to one another; finally, the inhibiting and destructive influences that emanate from a disintegrating bourgeois public sphere must not be overpowering during the development of a proletarian public sphere. In all these respects, the proletarian public sphere is none other than the form in which the interests of the working class develop themselves.** During the past hundred years, these three factors have never appeared simultaneously in any of the Western countries.

Unofficial strikes are considered an important indicator of the vitality of proletarian interests. What distinguishes them from the May movement in France or the student movement in the Federal Republic is not that they are **rooted in immediate interests**. Every major working-class movement takes these interests as its starting point, even during political strikes that are directed against a restriction of workers' interests or against the way their interests are being represented. The lesson of the political cretinism of social interests must be learned. The division into trade-union and political interests is a result of faulty development. What we are dealing with here are working-class interests that have already been diverted and administered in alien forms of organization.

What differentiates the May movement from the sporadic wildcat strikes that occur throughout the history of the labor movement is the way in which immediate interests socially unified themselves through the spread of mass campaigns, and thereby acquired a new status both in terms of the campaign itself and of the workers' self-image. With regard to the proletarian public sphere, as the specific interest-motivated campaigns spread—in other words, take on a grand social scale—the original interests must be identified in light of their specific role in a class society. This occurs less through slogans and programs specifically formulated for this purpose than by the translation of these circumstances themselves into practice.

Wherein lie the limitations of the wildcat strikes in the fall of 1969 in the Federal Republic and of the numerous wildcat strikes in England? In the fact that they fail to develop the potential for the political transformation of specific interests into those of society as a whole. Demands for wage raises, indeed even for an improvement of working conditions, are constantly reiterated and are taken up, criticized, or confirmed by the bourgeois public sphere in this abstract form. All attempts, for instance by political groups, to carry out this transformation from the outside on behalf of the workers merely cement this abstract quality. A concretization and fulfillment of these interests is, however, to be attained only by a consensus among those directly concerned.

The very fact that there is no such thing as a proletarian public sphere in the sense of a medium anchored in ongoing collective experience prevents individual campaigns and slogans from changing the consciousness of the workers. Within a developed proletarian public sphere, such slogans and programs could promote the crystallization of interests. At this point, it becomes clear that the proletarian public sphere is dependent on both the intelligentsia who, with their flexible centers of communication, are caught up in a process of transformation, and also on an autonomous counterforce, which secures proletarian communication against the bourgeois public sphere.

One of the reasons for the failure of strike movements restricted to wage demands no doubt lies in the principle that wage increases are certain to be balanced out by rises in prices. On the other hand, this same interest of the workers in a change in their own circumstances is more appropriately and fundamentally expressed in the demand for alterations in the speed of the conveyor belt, the abolition of shift work and piecework, changes in production methods. **Skepticism over the fairness of a wage cannot be politicized in the same way as can the workers' experience of the meaninglessness of an entire production process. In this concrete, meaningless situation, discontent at the overall situation of the worker in society can be articulated. Politicization presupposes that the opponent can be perceived in a concrete sense. Therefore, the unification of the consciousness of the masses presupposes the recognition of their own interests as objective, either by means of an organization that clearly delineates these interests or by means of an opponent who clearly refuses to satisfy them.**

The splinter groups of the left are presently emerging, above all, as the advocates and allies of the interests that are spontaneously expressed in wildcat strikes. Some sections of the left perform this work in the belief that they will become cadre parties in the future. While all of these groups constantly link their concrete political activity to their historical perspective, they also reify this link as the only adequate one in maintaining that all other groups will in time gravitate toward this focal point. Since they do not, however, discuss or communicate with other groups, who are to some extent setting out from similar premises, a kind of competitive relationship develops between numerous isolated, abstract initiatives. A proletarian public sphere between these groups cannot develop because they do not measure, correct, and interpret their own interests and needs against those of other groups.[55]

The wildcat strikes and the activities of the "class left" (the Manifesto group's term for all tendencies that see themselves as nonrevisionist) are the reproduction of individual struggles within a dominant bourgeois mode of production and publicity. These range from sporadic revolt to a sustained anticapitalist front. In this process, the spontaneous demonstrations, whose effectiveness is not a calculated factor, and those strategies developed by individual leftist factions that are formu-

---

55. What is described here does not refer to the entire concrete labor of these groups, but rather to the *form* of their public sphere. We are, however, of the opinion that the form of the public sphere will also have an effect on the perspective, the errors, and the possible failure of these types of labor contexts.

lated according to the most extreme criteria of instrumental rationality, tend to work in the same direction. Since they are fixated on individual focal points, the capacity for perceiving special, generally concealed contexts is enhanced; yet at the same time the social totality is blotted out in such a way that this concentration of energies must again lead to a weakening of political activity, because the total constellation is no longer a constitutive feature of each individual political step. This has dire consequences because, along with concentration on a focal point, the sense of the totality of social revolution is transformed into an anticapitalist alternative that is abstract and thereby merely fixated on its opponent. As a result of this, individual work is denied the necessary moment in which it can confront the power of the opponent in order to defeat him. New and essential experiences are gained, but in the process, other rich experiences are blocked that are necessary, for instance, for sustaining as a concrete possibility the notion of the production of social wealth by the producing class itself—the only genuine alternative to capitalism.[56]

No matter how the composition and function of the working class may have changed, it continues to be the material bearer of the production of wealth in society and therefore the subject of a new, humane social order. To assert this seems especially important in the present situation. It is necessary to distinguish between those social forces **that are in a position to accomplish a full-scale reorganization of society in the future and those that, under specific conditions, are primarily directed at overthrowing obsolete structures of authority.**[57] So it is plausible that the initial historical task of the intelligentsia is to destroy the eroded capitalist basis for legitimation and sketch the contours of a new society. However, their practical tasks would go beyond this necessary negative function only if, by a coalition with the working class, they were to produce a qualitatively new level of class struggle. The working class and the intelligentsia are caught up in a process that must change them both in such a way that they will be capable of forming an alliance. This process—for which the proletarian public sphere and its rudiments are a fundamental prerequisite and which itself produces the elements of this sphere—presupposes the cultivation of an intact and undistorted historical

---

56. The production of social wealth will not occur through an anticapitalist struggle. Rather, this struggle will contain an irreconcilable antagonistic element because of its fixation on an enemy who, because of his limited mode of production, cannot produce this wealth. "This is the motor works of the historical process, insofar as it can only be resolved outside of the concepts within which the contradiction presents itself" (Rossana Rossanda, *Der Marxismus von Mao Tse-tung*: 18).

57. See, for example, the function of trading capital and profiteering capital (e.g., B. Fugger, Welser) in the dissolution of the feudal system. The actual forces for the organization of bourgeois society lay, on the contrary, in the area of production. In his *Theory and Practice* (introduction to the new edition, [Frankfurt: 1971]: 9ff., esp. 14), Habermas poses the same question vis-à-vis present-day relations as follows: "Are the groups who bring into question—possibly in a passive way— compliance with important functions of the system identical with those groups who are able to act in a consciously political way in crisis situations?"

consciousness. In this respect, historical consciousness does not simply denote an actualization of a recollected past, for this would inevitably recall all the distorted lines of communication, too. It is, rather, the working through of the suppressed experience of the entire labor movement that has been mutilated by the bourgeois public sphere.[58]

58. This historical experience of the labor movement is also determined above all by defeats that exert pressure on the ability to remember. In this respect, the communicative distortions of the bourgeois public sphere only need to contribute odd jobs. The basic premise of the Manifesto platform deals precisely with the reactivation of the experience that is retained in the defeats. "Maximalism, reformism, and open class collaboration, or the reverse, spasmodic voluntarism and massive denial, are nothing but the various forms of this defeat" (Rossanda, *Der Marxismus von Mao Tse-tung*: 37).

# Chapter 3
# Public-Service Television
## The Bourgeois Public Sphere
## Translated into Modern Technology[1]

### Television as a Programming Industry

Public-service television is a programming industry. What sort of agenda does it have? The programmers maintain that it is above all else polymorphic.

"Open forms of programming are contrasted to closed forms." A concept of "pure" entertainment encounters pedagogical ideas; "apedagogic pedagogy" comes up against the desire for "greater politicizing"; the desire to use television to continue the traditions of the newspaper must confront the demand made on television that it perform a life-enhancing function.

Here are some examples of the multiplicity of opinions:

Dieter Stolte, director of the ZDF Department of Program Planning, "Auftrag und Management: Das Fernsehen als Produktionsproblem," in Fritz Hufen, *Massenmedien* (Mainz: 1970): "Today what are demanded are world-class interpreters built into a costly framework that corresponds to the affluent society. Costumes become the images for the generation that 'sets the tone.' Actions take place within large frameworks, that is, in giant spaces, and today no big entertainment show would make it without a twenty-member ballet. It goes without saying that special arrangements are also demanded and made for unusual performances, which not uncommonly assume the character of premieres" (p. 169).

Dr. Oeller, television director of the Bavarian Radio Network, in an interview

---

1. This chapter will address questions pertaining to public-service networks using the example of television. We have made this choice because a series of the problems involved would be duplicated for radio and television.

in the journal *kürbiskern* 3 (1971): "Communication is a public service for everyone. The following is to be kept in mind: the guarantee of entertainment, information, and educational programming. That is the primary provision of communication. Today it acts much like the provision of water, electricity, and gas. These are needs that are absolutely essential. And that is our social responsibility, which alone will determine our mandate" (p. 424).

Karl Holzamer, director of the ZDF, "Die Übung der Toleranz zwischen rationalem und 'emotionalem' Denken," in *Fernseh-Kritik, Unterhaltung und Unterhaltendes im Fernsehen, Mainzer Tage der Fernseh-Kritik*, vol. 3 (Mainz: 1971): "Lastly, in my opinion, is the demand that we orient our discussion toward reality, toward the matter at hand, and that, vis-à-vis our topic, we are also prepared to acknowledge that people have a natural need for diversion, for relaxation, for an unproblematic way of experiencing their human existence" (p. 12).

Gerhard Prager, director of the Central Department for Television Series and Film at ZDF, in the foreword to *Fernseh-Kritik*: "Ambivalent entertainment, that is, that which is aimed at relaxation as well as orientation, that does not pay less attention to surface attraction than to so-called deeper meaning, that serves a purpose but does not limit its means to a purpose—this will probably be found only wherever the much appealed to light hand responds to comic inspiration as well as the social reflex" (pp. 6ff.).

Walter Schmieding, director of the Berlin Festivals, discussion in *Fernseh-Kritik*: "But then why do we have these series all year long on German television in which families who discuss every topic imaginable are shown and yet in which none of the conflicts pertaining to foreign or domestic policy or sociopolitical issues ever come up? I remember with horror a series by Wolf Schmidt, in which the figure of Mr. Hesselbach had become a town councillor in some small town. The whole series took place in a German small town, but there was never any mention of the political situation there. No election battles were fought there, there weren't any political parties—there were only voluntary agreements made between citizens. These mendacious and reactionary images must have something to do with the fact that a fiction has sprung up in German television, the fiction that there is such a thing as entertainment, and pure entertainment at that" (p. 85).

Hans-Gerd Wiegend, superintendent of Youth Programming at WDR, creator of the series "Baff," "Unterhaltung—gesellschaftskritisch," in *Fernseh-Kritik*: "Pure entertainment is passé . . . In the news and current-events programs we are informed throughout the year about the Vietnam War, the peace negotiations in Paris, and we hardly notice that this terrible bloodbath has already become a commonplace for us. But if, on the other hand, we see battle scenes from Vietnam alternating with scenes of the negotiations in Paris—first the young soldiers and helpless children bleeding to death, then the ritual of diplomatic points of order—this close-up contradiction can again make us conscious of the existence of this war. This happened recently when coverage of the dead in Vietnam was followed by a beat dance from Soho. There was an outpouring of letters from outraged viewers. Their sense of piety had been offended, and the program editor knew that his news had 'hit home' " (pp. 117, 123ff.).

Erich Feldmann, dean of Media Studies, *Neue Studien zur Theorie der Massenmedien* (Munich/Basel: 1969): "*3. Gnosology of Television.* At the center of all problems that result from the founding of a science of television is the question of the validity of all the experiences and cognition that we gain from the communicative functions of the image media. We find ourselves in the area of philosophical inquiry that also belongs to film studies, facing the task of a critique of all image experience, which can proceed on the basis of the previous problematic of a theory of cognition, but must adapt its aporias and problems to the new specialization. A critique of this sort becomes a specific scholarly discipline within the framework of television scholarship. It can be characterized as a 'gnosology of television' if it is supposed to satisfy all the requirements of a critical examination of the sources, functions, object relations, and validity of visual experience. This gnosology may not be limited to the psychological analysis of cognition in Locke's sense or of transcendental elucidation in Kant's sense. Rather, it will initially strive for the interpretation of the development of the phenomenon of technically moved images, the scholarly processing of which can be treated as an examination of objects and characterized as an 'iconology' " (p. 57).[2]

Erwin K. Scheuch, "Unterhaltung als Pausenfüller. Von der Vielfalt der Unterhaltungsfunktion in der modernen Gesellschaft," in *Fernseh-Kritik*: "Entertainment as a claim made on the part of the public vis-à-vis the media is often evaluated as a specific factor by industry businesses. Justifiably so . . . In our research, countries such as Bulgaria, the southern areas of Serbia, and areas of the Soviet Union were included that were still primarily agricultural or preindustrial. Here there were times easily available for napping, an activity (if it can be called that) that occurs relatively infrequently for us. Television enters into these incidental activities, into this doing nothing, and to some extent functions as an alternative to napping. In view of this, even if cultural values are relinquished, television must be perceived as an immense activation of human beings precisely

---

2. See also Feldmann's theory of television programming (*ibid.*, p. 63): "The task of the television institutions consists in the setting up, processing, and transmission of programs for continuous offerings to the viewers. These programs form the production schedule with which the apparatus of the networks strives toward journalistic and cultural achievement and courts public favor. A scholarly evaluation of all conditions, objectives, creative forms, performance quality, and programming success is necessary to provide a systematic overview for the large as well as the small networks and to facilitate methodical planning as to which have cultural value and promise success within the public sphere. In the scholarly treatment of these questions, the special discipline of television *programming theory* emerges. It has above all else the task of taking up the continuance of contemporary culture in an analysis that registers and systematically orders traditional content within perspectives demanded by the times as well as the current cultural substance from the perspective of the zeitgeist." Feldmann had already published a theory of the mass media in 1962 (Munich/Basel: 1962).

when it is being enjoyed as simply the viewing of images, as compared to simple napping" (pp. 13, 45ff.).

Wolfgang Ernst, superintendent of the Infratest Institute in Munich, "Der Fernsehzuschauer und das Unterhaltungsangebot des Fernsehens," in *Fernseh-Kritik*: "Entertainment is that which entertains. And entertainment functions have varying contents that are group-specific, that is, what 'High Chaparral' is to one person, the readings in 'Der Spiegel' are for someone else. And the question of the effect of entertainment is expanded into the question of the effect of the mass media" (p. 54).

Friedrich Knilli, television critic, director of the Mass Media Department at the Institute for Language in an Age of Technology in Berlin, "Die öffentlich-rechte Lust am Show-Business," in *Fernseh-Kritik*: "Visual business and prostitution are among the oldest forms of business in the world. Often they cannot be separated. And if they are separated, the commercial satisfaction of visual pleasure is ersatz prostitution. The refinement and vulgarization of this ersatz erotica by the *mimus eroticus* is the history of visual advertising, not as a natural or cultural history, but as a history of the commercialization of visual erotics" (p. 56).

Hans Magnus Enzensberger, "Baukasten zu einer Theorie der Medien," in *Kursbuch* 20 (Frankfurt am Main: 1970): "If I say **mobilize**, I mean mobilize . . . in other words . . . make people more mobile than they are. Free like dancers, intellectually present like soccer players, astonishing like guerrilleros" (p. 160).

Götz Dahlmüller, "6 Themen zum Fernsehen," in *kürbiskern* 3 (1971): "The minimal agenda for an emancipatory television: the conscious tearing apart of the different areas of articulation (music, gesture, word, action, etc.), the pointing out of ruptures and contradictions between the images and what attaches itself to them and is superimposed upon them, which first makes possible the transparency and possibility for scrutinizing of the reality mediated by the media" (p. 457).

The multitude of views about the content of television presents itself as an immense collection of ideas that agree only on one essential point: that, far from being direct communication between human beings or groups, television is programmed. Only Enzensberger's interpretation deviates from this.

Radio and television do not possess a tradition going back to the bourgeois revolution. From the outset, they were not conceived as communication between free *citoyens*, individuals. Mass communication, in particular via television, is characterized by the way in which "a large heterogeneous audience more or less simultaneously exposes itself to utterances transmitted via media by an institution, whereby the audience is unknown to the station."[3] **In this respect, radio and television reflect a relationship between public sphere and individual that is**

---

3. Otto N. Larsen, "Social Effects of Mass Communication," in *Handbook of Modern Sociology*, ed. E. L. Foris (Chicago: 1966): 348. See also Ralf Zoll and Eike Hennig, *Massenmedien und*

**quite different from the one established by early bourgeois ideals.** A product of the structure of postbourgeois society, this relationship is governed by the fact that the wealth objectified in social production appears so omnipotent that relationships between individuals fade into insignificance. In terms of social importance, a conversation between two people cannot compete with a radio or television broadcast. In Germany, the political right was quick to recognize the potential of radio for mass communication and, as early as the 1920s and 1930s, gained control over this medium.[4]

In this respect, public-service radio and television networks in the Federal Republic have striven for a compromise. The delicate balance envisioned in the concept of the control of broadcasting by "relevant" social groups is, however, under constant threat—a fact that the Social Democrats are now beginning to take into account. Public-service television in particular embodies yet another compromise: the viewer is meant to be shielded from the full force of the programming industry, which constitutes just one special case of the overall primacy of production that is alienated from individual workers. For this reason, certain restrictions based on the charter of networks are imposed upon the programming industry. These restrictions have a variety of consequences. Television cannot exploit its potential for communication in the same way as the private consciousness industry. It is directed to take the public route; it must address its programs "to whom it may concern"—in other words, **it is confined to the transmission of generalized program material**. It is thereby following a norm that has always governed the bourgeois public sphere and that has prevented it from assimilating the immediate life interests of human beings. The reason why television has adopted this structure is not, however, to be found in the tradition of the bourgeois public sphere, but in a postbourgeois, sociopolitical decision. This combines the ruling public sphere's interest in control with a reformist regard for the autonomy of the viewers. The viewers are only formally subsumed by the public-service mass media. The public media are prevented from molding the viewers' needs in such a way that they become totally assimilated to the production logic of television; indeed,

4. See the critical interpretation by Jürgen Seifert, "Probleme der Parteien- und Verbandskontrolle von Rundfunk- und Fernsehanstalten," in *Kritik, Manipulation der Meinungsbildung*, ed. Ralf Zoll (Opladen: 1971): 124ff. It is important to also consider, vis-à-vis this opinion, the significance of radio and television in transformational socialist societies. This is particularly true as well for the Cultural Revolution in China. Here meticulous differentiations are made with regard to the social significance of political statements in accordance with whether these are made in the form of simple discussions, in the form of wall newspapers, in the official form of expression through editorials in party journals, or whether they are disseminated over the radio. It appears that dissemination over the radio is one of the most semiofficial forms of communication. Numerous examples of this can be found in the publications of the Publisher for Foreign-Language Literature, *The Great Proletarian Cultural Revolution in China* (Peking: 1966–1971): see, for example, vol. 10: 53, "Hongqi" commentator.

television relies on accepting these needs as it encounters them. The price of such considerations is that, in this generalized type of communication with viewers, television cannot develop their needs and interests in an emancipatory direction. This indicates that television is in a weakened position in comparison with the encroaching consciousness industry. Following Parsons, Dieter Prokop describes the exchange that occurs in the process of mass communication as an exchange of generalized receptivity against pluralism and as an "exchange of the willingness to ward off desires that threaten stability against the guarantee of formal diversity, while simultaneously maintaining psychic equilibrium and discipline."[5] Prokop defines this form of receptivity as an abstract-regressive organization of cognition. **The real interests and needs, which people would be prepared to fight for in a serious way, play no role in this organization.** This is why people would probably not defend the public-service networks, which are engaged merely in the production of program television, against a sustained attack by the consciousness industry.

What television can do as a medium of sense perception (equivalent to walking, making a phone call, talking, traveling, etc.) is revealed less by public-service broadcasting than by the communication of astronauts with ground control, by closed-circuit monitors in factories (visual control of a mechanized and automated production process), and, in the military domain, by audiovisual techniques of distance command, video links between airborne reconnaissance units, frontline troops and headquarters, and so on. What is striking about the majority of these telecommunications processes is that they are not tailored to programming. Rather, they function in a unidirectional fashion: they are **regulatory forms of communication that do not entail response.** When response is involved, it is restricted to an unusually narrow field (e.g., astronauts' communication).[6] Moreover, such unprogrammed communication is, without exception, nonpublic in character.

The limits that the bourgeois concept of the public sphere imposes upon emerging forms of human communication now become clear. From a technical point of view, the human senses are capable of being stimulated; from an ideolog-

---

5. Dieter Prokop, "Versuch über Massenkultur und Spontaneität," in *Materialien zur Theorie des Films* (Munich: 1971): 40.

6. In the case of extraordinary sports events such as the Olympic Games, it has recently become commonplace to set up enormous monitors in a stadium so that the audience can simultaneously follow the event taking place in that stadium and those that are taking place in others, including even sports events in entirely different cities. There thus develops a relationship between levels of reality that are taking place in proximity to one another (multidimensional reality). If in the process close-ups of the reactions of the audience are edited in, the illusion of interaction is produced. This is, however, really just a special case of programmatically controlled television, since the simultaneous transmission arrangement remains within the framework of an overall agenda that sets fixed limits on content for all sensual perceptions.

ical point of view, in the structures of control and in the restriction of the viewers' unfulfilled needs, it is nevertheless an accepted fact that communication occurs either privately (telephone) or nonpublicly (army videos). When it does involve the masses, communication is subject to programming restrictions. To grasp how unnatural this state of affairs is, just imagine that one could use the telephone only if one were prepared to employ prefabricated phrases. One would think it just as unusual if walking along the street were permitted only in marching formations. But this corresponds precisely to what is known within the context of television as "programming." The fact that this does not regularly occur to anyone with respect to television only confirms its extraordinary impact as a large-scale industry, which has entered into public consciousness at the expense of more universal possibilities.

A plausible discussion of the development of total telecommunication takes us into the realm of science fiction. **It would entail an expansion of the human senses, of our immediate experience, in corresponding to the actual level of social cooperation. Expanding the capacity for perception seems to be a prerequisite for all real social transformation. The problem, noted by Karl Korsch, with all forms of self-determination operating at the level of production (forms that Korsch calls "councils") is that they are aware of their own circumstances and interests, yet they know too little about the surrounding world. This problem can ultimately be solved only by expanding the realm of immediate experience.** Public-service institutions have paid little attention to these notions. This is in line with the climate of a transitional period, in which the masses are permanently mobilized yet prevented from self-determination (Habermas). In this respect, television programming is uniform rather than heterogeneous. It corresponds to a perpetuation of the bourgeois public sphere, which in this case seems to have been translated into concrete technology without possessing all the characteristics of the cumulative public sphere of production.[7]

Whether the networks can assert themselves against the expanding private consciousness industry, however, depends on their ability to connect with real desires for direct communication. Bright ideas or political resolutions cannot solve this problem. The first requirement is massive transformations in television's mode of production and relationship with the viewers. It is wrong to imply that such structural changes would be impossible under the public-service aegis of the networks. It is simply that, in the prevailing discussion, plans that call for

---

7. See chapter 1, "The Processing of Social Experience by the New Public Spheres of Production." From this perspective, one could see in the public-service television networks a variant of the early phase of the public sphere of production that is atypical for the overall development of the consciousness industry in the world and that takes into account general and legitimation interests to a great degree. It indicates that there are other realizable possible solutions than those that are purely capitalistic. However, these alternative solutions cannot develop definitively upon the foundation of the classical public sphere.

increasing the number of television channels and vigorously investing in the self-organization of the viewers are considered utopian.[8]

## The Television Screen's Appearance of Immediacy—The Reality of Television Production as an Industrial Enterprise

Television confronts the viewer in the form of a screen. The historical process of television production is not visible on this screen, however. The genesis of information and broadcasts, television's defining quality as a management-controlled production process, is foreshortened into an image of suggestive immediacy. No other medium transmits with comparable clarity the *appearance of both immediacy and completeness*, or is capable of putting merely the finished product onto the screen, instead of developing the viewer's awareness of the production process.

The real historical shape of television, the rhythm of its specific mode of production, must be examined in its archives rather than in any individual program on the screen. The social experience accumulated in television in the shape of limitless material, and information is accessible in a coherent form—a bird's-eye view as far as history and society as a whole are concerned—only to experts. The topical and sporadic nature of all broadcast material rules out any such overview, which would be the real and rich social product of the television networks.

A critique that concentrates on the screen alone cannot rise above the isolated quality of what appears on it. This is why a major part of television criticism remains either general (formalistic and cultural criticism) or on the level of content: that is, evaluation of an individual program with no critique of its conditions of production. Such critical strategies cannot, however, establish and elucidate the connection between television production and the laws that govern production as a whole. Written or oral critique must almost always remain ineffectual against the real products of a large apparatus. **Products can be attacked only with counterproducts. Television criticism must set out from the historical corpus of the medium, namely, television as an industrial enterprise. What is more, any self-determination of the viewers, as the foundation of a possible emancipatory development of television, must measure itself against this industrial dimension: that is, by what cannot automatically be detected within an individual broadcast. Television can be transformed not on the level of the individual program, but of its entire history, which determines that program.[9]**

8. Bertolt Brecht, "Radiotheorie," in *Gesammelte Werke*, vol., 18, 130: "Radio must make the exchange possible. . . . if you believe this is utopian, I ask you to think about why it is utopian."

9. Bertolt Brecht's statements are similar when he demands that radio be transformed from an apparatus of distribution into one of communication. See "Radiotheorie," p. 129: "Radio is to be transformed from an apparatus of distribution into one of communication. Radio would be the greatest conceivable communication apparatus of public life, an enormous system of channels, that is, it would be this if it were to understand how to not only transmit, but also receive, in other words, how to make the

There is no medium for such a critical perspective; neither television critics nor viewers possess or could acquire the necessary information. If anyone, it is the network employees who understand something about television as an enterprise and an apparatus. All criticism lacking such inside knowledge remains superficial and fails because, among other things, those responsible for television programs can reasonably point out that such criticism offers nothing constructive. The division of labor between the employees and the ostensible critics of television causes problems precisely in the case of public-service television, for it is mainly the critiques, not the market mechanisms, that prevent this industry from becoming autonomous and that confine it within the social framework of production.

## Short-Term and Long-Term Valorization Interest in the Mass Media

All television programs, no matter whether they are entertainment, news, or documentary, have a use-value and a commodity nature. Indeed, one can apply each of these categories to every television program in two respects, according to whether one is adopting a long- or short-term perspective.

Short-term capital interest is understood here and in what follows as that of individual capitalists; long-term interest, as the interest of the capitalist system as a whole, constitutes itself in complex ways and is not necessarily held by individuals. Short-term capital interest bases its valorization on use-values that can also have long-term significance (for instance, experiential content, the crystallization and expression of resistance, as in the protest song movement). Similarly, long-term capital interest, which expresses itself in varying degrees through notions such as the "common good" and the "public interest," has immediate, short-term, restrictive consequences, such as programming guidelines or censorship.

In television, there are as a rule no individual "capitalists": the social character of all commodity production is clearer here than in the private sector. In what follows, we will refer to a short-term interest in the case of television in an analagous manner to the interest of private industry, because one should distinguish between those commodities that can be sold quickly and those that do not possess a high degree of abstract exchange value. The topicality of news; the fullness of information; the tempo of events; the ability to generate high audience ratings; the rarity or inaccessibility of a news item; shock; violent contrasts—all these short-term commodity characteristics determine the quality of television. However, in every case they also engage experiences and therefore possess use-value. Without this use-value, programs would quickly become the source of ridicule or indifference.

listener not only hear but also speak, and how to bring him into the relationship instead of isolating him. Radio would accordingly proceed from the listener-recipients and organize the listener as a supplier. Therefore, all of the efforts made by radio to lend public concerns the real character of a public sphere are absolutely positive."

Gerhard Prager recognizes this fact when he states that it would be too much to demand of a network that it call its new division "the department of suspense" or "the department of interesting tidbits."

Many detective series or news items are deemed "good television" because a rule system, or a sequence whose normal outcome can be predicted by the viewer, is broken. Why do railway disasters, shipping disasters, deaths, political upheavals, and wars provoke unusual interest? It appears that the breaking of a reified layer of events evokes in the viewer a compensatory sense of his participation in what is going on in the world—a sense that does not really exist in the normal routine of production and everyday leisure time. Moments such as these create an illusion of history. For the viewer in front of the television set, the events of the day, his day's work, keep on running through his mind for an hour or two. His own immediate experiences, memories, the domestic situation around him constitute a diffuse whole. This is what the viewer really experiences as he is sitting in front of his set. This diffuse whole is not identical with the carefully planned and concentrated moment of the program on television, which is the outcome of days, weeks, months of work. No matter what is being shown, it is not identical with the experience brought to it by the viewer. Nevertheless, a process of exchange takes place. The viewer's diffuse experience, which he is incapable of organizing, is abandoned in favor of the program's prefabricated experiential model.[10] Underlying this is a mutual tacit recognition, preceding the actual process of exchange, of the independence of both levels: that of the viewer and that of the mass medium. By acknowledging the program as a kind of minimum offer, the viewer feels relieved of the need to do anything himself; in turn, the producer of the program acknowledges a minimum of the viewer's involvement and interest.

This results neither in a mere reproduction of the television experience, nor does the viewer's own experience find its identity in this way; instead, a third element is constituted out of the two processes. **In light of this, entertainment programs provide distraction only when they do not merely reproduce the daily round. At the same time, the possibility of projection is denied the viewer if**

---

10. For example: the viewer feels that he has been left in the lurch on this particular day. He had a particularly bitter sense of his isolation at work. Now he sees on television how the athlete Karl Schranz, who—as the viewer is already perfectly ready to believe—had been unfairly disqualified by the bosses of the Olympics organization, has received a massive outpouring of sympathy. All of Austria expresses its solidarity with Karl Schranz. To the extent that the viewer absorbs this experiential process and projects it onto his own, predominantly diffuse experience, he will also perceive a sense of genuine solidarity with Karl Schranz. "Just as we television viewers all support this man, so we would want to be supported by everyone else if we were being threatened." There is initially no contradiction in this projection. It is completely legitimate that people recognize their own needs for support from others by projecting them on to someone else. The contradiction lies in the fact that this process does not rest on any real behavior—the viewer will not be helped, now or in the future, in the way that Karl Schranz was helped. Therefore, nothing is altered in the viewer's own diffuse experiential world.

**such programs are too far removed from his experience.**[11] This marks the limits for broadcasting English and American shows, despite the fact that German audiences have become accustomed to them because of the current plethora of series. For instance, a "butler" is unable to provoke strong projections of humor in the Federal Republic, since for German viewers this profession is purely an idea they have laboriously had to learn.

When we speak, in the present context, of the "viewer's interest," the meaning of this concept is, in light of the television audience's position, an ambivalent one. **Entertainment programs would have a real function for the interest of the viewers, properly understood, only if the concept of entertainment were completely abandoned**; the viewers' interest would objectively be focused on the organization of their experience. However, the production process necessary for such an organization is not to be found in our society. It is thus correct to use the term "interest" to describe the viewer's interest in a real preliminary stage leading to a possible development of emancipatory television, even though neither the mere projection of wishes nor the possibilities of distraction or rejection can lead to the organization of one's experiential production (any more than simply switching off the television can). The utilization of the viewers by television and of television by the viewers for their respective unfulfilled needs is cooperation at a primitive level; but not even this level would be attained if one did not recognize the viewer's interest at this level merely because—seen ahistorically and in isolation from the actual viewer—it is ultimately not his real interest.[12]

---

11. The potential of the science-fiction film, which seems to distance itself considerably from real experience, is to be judged differently. In fact, it is precisely this genre that is able to react to the experiential mode of the fantasy that is forced back in the process of work and socialization. Only to the extent that this science-fiction film in turn severs itself from the experience of fantasy, dream, anxiety, and desire and begins to "flip out" or to render itself technologically independent does it come up against its limits.

12. See Dieter Prokop, "Versuch uber Massenkultur und Spontaneitat" 11ff. Prokop's comments also obtain for television shows, even though he takes his examples from the film industry. The same ambivalence exists for numerous other concepts; this is particularly apparent in the case of the concepts "ideology" and "production." Production as a concept of the critique of bourgeois economy must be formulated narrowly to be able to strike at the capitalist exploitation of labor power in the industrial process. Production as a concept within the context of the constitution of new productive forces and as the production of the species-generic wealth of human beings must, on the other hand, be defined widely and encompass the production of all areas of life, think *society as a whole as a factory*. Marx uses both concepts without ever drawing particular attention to this differentiated use.

A similar ambivalence characterizes the concept "ideology." In *Die Entwicklungsformen der Gesellschaft und die Wissenschaft* (Berlin: 1924), A. Bogdanow writes, "Ideology is the *expression* and the *conceptualization* of life. But in these societies [those that are more developed] life is fragmented; it is not the same in the various classes" (p. 13). From the standpoint of the bourgeois class position or that of other classes that do not represent the overall interests of society, ideology necessarily becomes a designation for distortions of the image of reality. It is not the concept or the designation that is altered here, but rather the standpoint of those upon whom it is brought to bear. Accordingly,

**The contradiction between long- and short-term interest is visible in every program, irrespective of whether it is news, documentary, or entertainment.** The contradiction is deepened by the ambivalence between the cultural-critical attitude of the majority of networks and their actual function as manufacturers of entertainment. Frequently, the network's profile comes into conflict with the type of viewer satisfaction it promises, whereby it modifies a program accordingly. In detective films, in many Westerns, for instance, entertainment comes in the form of sensationalism. At the same time, there is also reticence within the networks about intensifying sensationalism. Original types of television productions cannot develop, through such approaches, the radical aspect that characterizes filmic genres.

The appeal of sensationalism for the viewer lies in the fact that, with relatively weak libidinal investment, he can conceive of a situation in which he himself mobilizes all his sensual and intellectual powers at the same time. People whose work demands the highest degree of concentration coupled with only a partial use of individual sensual and intellectual capacities can suffer permanent difficulties in coordinating their individual faculties, which have varying degrees of usefulness for the production process. These people derive pleasure from the desperate situations that the hero tries to overcome by straining all his powers to the limit. Although television tends to provide the viewer with this form of satisfaction, it also keeps these feelings in check. It makes the viewer's feelings particularly malleable and prevents the mere projection of these sensations onto the televised events from forming into a reaction and thereby becoming part of individual experience. Evidently this is also related to the belief that too much excitement on television damages labor power, which must be ready for enlistment the following day. This is a fear in which the internalized self-control of the viewers and the programming considerations of the network coincide.

Another example is the entertainment programs where one has to guess a person's profession. As in blindman's bluff, the viewer is made to feel superior to the contestants because he knows the answer beforehand. Here the need to be more

---

categories such as "knowledge" or "interests" or "experience" must, on the one hand, also be able to be specified at the historical and concrete level upon which they move and relate to other social phenomena. On the other hand, they must be rendered transparent to the emancipatory potential that is contained in this concretization. The surest way to close off this potential for knowledge would be to use these concepts ahistorically or postulatively from the outset. The "real interest" of the television viewer exists for him (and thus for everyone who links into this interest) only if he can reach it from his present *position of interest,* however illusory it may be. That the dynamic relationship that is at issue here cannot be clearly grasped conceptually in so many words, since the concept or the designation also designates the movement itself, is a consequence of the tradition of thought and language that has developed thought and language as instruments of domination, and therefore possesses concepts for fixation, analysis, and "assessment" that can only indicate movement through the representation of movement within a context, that is, not at all with words of command.

intelligent than the machinery—a need that reveals itself to be an inversion of the extraneously controlled labor process—is initially taken seriously but then, thanks to the built-in silliness of the program itself, dismissed. The program incorporates its own distance from this procedure.

There is no less ambivalence in news broadcasts. A sensational news item (for instance about an air disaster) is broadcast; but it is not accompanied by programs that might meaningfully interpret this news in the light of social contradictions or develop it in relation to the viewer's own experience. It is only on such a broadened basis that grief, sympathy, incorporation into a historical context, or an autonomous reaction by the viewer become possible. The limits are established in this case not just by this contradiction, but also by the impotence of the viewer in front of his set. Commentary that retrospectively works a news item to death at the same level of abstraction at which it was originally reported does nothing to alter this situation. Insofar as experiences do manage to penetrate the items on the evening news, they are, in the commentaries, translated into an esoteric language that promotes the rapid consumption of events. The news commodities are not consumed because they are brought into any concrete relationship to the viewer but simply **because they were "there" in the first place**.[13] The commentaries simultaneously set the limits of a discussion of these news items by establishing the rules according to which they can be interpreted and also the structure whereby the news anarchy is ordered for the viewer. This is not, however, possible at the level of fragmented news, so that—with the exception of world events that relate to the viewers' experience—the result is news items that are low in use-value and virtually devoid of experiential content.

In other programs, the long-term valorization interest is capable of asserting itself more strongly, and temporarily suppresses the short-term. This seems to be the case with the principle of programming balance, with the tendency to avoid resolving conflicts that individual news items bring into focus, as well as with the fullest elaboration and reproduction of prevailing public criticism—insofar as it does not touch the foundations of society. Such principles are, however, unam-

---

13. A graphic example can be found in Michael Radtke, "Bundespolitik auf dem Bildschirm," in *Film und Fernsehen* 6 (1971): 4: "'A viewing of the new radio observatory tower of the Max Planck Institute in Effelsberg in the Eifel was on today's agenda for King Baudouin on the second day of his state visit to the Federal Republic. Ministry President Kuhn and the President of the Federal Republic accompanied the king on this excursion, which had been planned with a particular view toward Baudouin's special interest in technology.' This was the news in the main edition of the '*Tagesschau*' of April 28. During this comment, which lasted a few seconds, one could see *that* the giant parabolic mirror of the telescope was slowly tilted and *that* someone quickly explained to Baudouin the mechanism involved in this process (what was not shown was *how* this happened and *whether*, to remain with the example, the process was sufficiently explained to the king). All of this happened on a rainy morning, way down in one of these Eifel valleys. A few moments later I sat on the pillion seat of the superheavy Honda machine that transported this snippet of film with '160 Sachen' from Effelsberg to the Cologne offices of the '*Tagesschau*.'"

biguous only in relation to the dominant practice of the television networks. Measured against the events in society themselves, there is no such thing as programming balance.

When long-term commodity characteristics express themselves in the program as a whole, they have a particularly ambivalent effect. They "detoxify" and dilute the distortions that society manufactures out of its contradictions; they subdue the short-term commodity interest of television as a productive force, and create, in the process, mechanisms of censorship, dematerialization, and new, artificial relationships within ideology production. The content of experience does not remain the same, nor does it become wholly invalid by virtue of these interventions. One of the ways by which the long-term valorization interest expresses itself, as manifested in public-service television networks, is by generating a climate of possible and necessary solutions to individual conflicts. Television as an institution and a "medium of reform" is capable of maintaining all the subjects it treats in a middle-of-the-road perspective that cannot be radicalized. To sustain this view, Dieter Stolte, the director of the Department of Program Planning of ZDF, invokes Pascal: "To leave the center means leaving humanity behind."[14]

## The Juncture of Public-Service Television and Private Industry

Public-service networks are surrounded by private industry; they are thus in no sense autonomous in their production. There are numerous points of contention where the prevailing social system impinges on the output of public-service television production, which has a special legal status. This occurs through the transfer of such categories as **success with the public** and **profitability** onto the networks. These networks react like businesses monitoring consumer trends, by taking into account audience ratings and opinions. Although it is repeatedly emphasized within the networks that they do not wish to measure themselves by such purely quantitative criteria alone, the ratings function as a kind of TV currency that retrospectively determines the value of a program. Lately, a whole series of structural shifts within networks is becoming apparent.

The network charters also have a hand in forcing categories and practices to be transferred from the private sector onto public television. Here the **postulate of cost-effectiveness**, which entails a capacity for abstraction (for in order to come up with measurable units, one must first of all coordinate all factors) is at odds with the specificity of the majority of programs, for these programs cannot always be readily compared to others. The pressure of previous investments (for instance, studio capacity) acts—by virtue of the principle of maximum cost-effective-

---

14. Blaise Pascal, *Pensées*, trans. and ed. Ewald Wasmuth (Tübingen: 1948), fragment 378, p. 178. Cited in Dieter Stolte, "Auftrag und Management: Das Fernsehen als Produktionsproblem," in Fritz Hufen, *Massenmedien* (Mainz: 1970): 154.

ness—as a barrier to the development of more realistic filming techniques.[15] On the other hand, investment activity and the need—in competing with other networks—for operating with the most up-to-date equipment, lead to the belief in technology for its own sake, a trend that can be held in check only by a stringent application of the principle of cost-effectiveness.

Particular contradictions arise in formulating an overall policy within the network for dealing with **private suppliers**. These frequently monopolistic firms, which supply a major portion of import material—not just series but also lavish entertainment programs—seem to be able to deliver products at more competitive prices and more regularly than the anarchic free market is capable of doing. This fact binds the interests of the suppliers' monopoly with the notion of cost-effectiveness and with the desire of the network's management to run a uniform and orderly enterprise. This brings with it the considerable danger that the contracts that are drawn up on this basis turn out, in the long run, to be uneconomic for the network, and also infringe upon programming principles. In every case, such metabolic interchange between private interests and public-service television production cannot be rendered transparent according to the legitimation criteria recognized within television itself. The exchange is explained as follows: "These are legal obligations and therefore cannot be changed." This is the only explanation for many American series that are often expensive or would, according to their programming principles, never have been produced by the German networks themselves (for instance, the series of FBI propaganda films). In addition, a mutual interdependence between public-service networks and the monopolistic firms of the private sector develops. A consequence of this is that the television networks, unlike, for instance, newspapers, the theater, or radio, are big industries that tend to deal with other private firms at the level of their interests. The expansion of the consciousness industry and of the media cartel will most likely drive the public-service networks to marketing agreements and considerations that represent a further encroachment by the interests of private industry. The long-term result will no doubt be cooperation between the consciousness industry and the public-service networks of ARD and ZDF.[16]

---

15. Dieter Stolte, "Fernsehen von morgen-Analysen und Prognosen," in *Fernseh-Kritik, Mainzer Tage der Fernseh-Kritik*, vol. 4, ed. Bernward Frank (Mainz: 1972): 18: "The operational, efficiency-related necessity of rational use of the usual means of production (especially the stationary ones, like electronic studios and film studios) stands in opposition to the increasingly evident journalistic and artistic impetus toward authenticity, toward being right there, toward breaking out of the four walls of the studio into the streets and squares, the compulsion toward live reporting, toward individualistic expression using 'simple,' that is, chiefly mobile technical means, the stylistic element of the living camera, the trend from recordings toward film, from perfection toward improvisation. Or, to formulate it in catchphrases: industrial management contradicts the journalistic eros."

16. See Dieter Stolte, "Auftrag und Management," p. 157: "For if permanent cost increases, especially in the entertainment sector, should really lead [and why shouldn't they?!] to a situation in which the radio networks join into a cooperative relationship configured as usual with commercial interests,

Television as a productive force is constantly splintered due to the hierarchical administrative structure of the networks.[17] The cooperation between technology, administration, production, and editorial levels follows more or less monocratic paths but rarely coalesces in concentrated units of work. The separation of administration, legal departments, and technology from program production is thus favored. A further organizational factor is the mutual dependencies that arise out of interdependent ARD stations, as well as out of the compromises demanded by pluralistic control of broadcasting. Both develop selection mechanisms with respect to program content, since when unanimous agreement is necessary, it is the most entrenched and usually the more conservative standpoint that manages to assert itself every time. The problem of reaching agreements in general promotes purely quantitative decisions and makes qualitative changes in broadcasting and program forms difficult to implement. This is one of the reasons for the sluggishness of reforms in a medium that is faced with rapidly growing responsibilities and potentials. On the other hand, this selection mechanism is undoubtedly favorable to long-term capital interests and hostile to sudden incursions by short-term interests. All this is different from both state-controlled television in France as well as private television in the United States. The situation in the Federal Republic cannot be classified as either simply good or bad. Television as a productive force is constrained by the compulsion to make abstract decisions—and the lack of real decision-making that goes with this compulsion—which is a consequence of the pressure to reach agreements that characterizes any pluralist organization. At the same time, there develops a protective screen against annexation of this productive force by social groups. **Television pluralism does not suggest ownership or control over television by social groups, but the elimination of such ownership through the reciprocal control of each group by all remaining groups.** The orientation of television toward the happy medium, middle-of-the-road public opinion, nonradicalization, the limitation of expression, program balance, toward the so-called lukewarm character, results from this organizational

---

then 'live reporting, political, artistic, social, and sports events,' 'important opinion shows, hard documentaries, and the production of ambitious and engaged "television art" will have to be the decisive contribution of television to overall television programming.'" [ARD and ZDF are two major public-service networks in Germany. Since the publication of the German edition of this text, there has been a proliferation of private broadcast and cable networks alongside public-service television.—*Trans.*]

17. See Jürgen Seifert, "Probleme der Parteien- und Verbandskontrolle von Rundfunk- und Fernsehanstalten," pp. 124ff., esp. 132ff.

This structure of network management was developed under the statutes of occupation and historically juxtaposes two trains of thought: the traditional form of the state institution, in accordance with which the state radio had been organized in Germany since 1923, and the countermovement to this, which is what the occupational powers had in mind. Thus the radio networks have in their *internal management* the monocratic structure of state institutions, while in the *societal framework* they are, on the other hand, free corporate entities that move between the sphere of the state and that of social forces.

principle and could, under the social conditions in the Federal Republic, be changed only if other enormous disadvantages were accepted. A discussion about changes in the structure of television can therefore not be conducted in a generalized manner: "either pluralism or a wholly different form."[18] Rather, it must examine whether other structures of production and transmission—ones that would be closer to the productive base and better capable of realizing television's potential as an industry of production and transmission—could be organized that would widen access to the medium.[19]

## Levels of Societilization[20] of Television and Viewers

The inquiry concerning levels of societilization has two aspects with respect to television:

1. What role does societilization play in television networks as production industries?

2. How is the conflict between the societilization level presented on the screen and the viewer's needs for societilization (for that matter, the societilization structures) played out?

Within television networks, the individual groups of employees work at different levels. The largest consists of management and administration in the widest sense. In 1968, this group occupied a total of 836 of the permanent posts in ZDF (the Second Channel)—among them, some of the highest-paid jobs. The second largest group was engaged in the technical side and filled 614 posts. By comparison, the blue-collar work force (transport services, storage, etc.) came to 264; editorial, to 273; production, to 408. Salary structures within technical, administrative, editorial, and production departments are comparable.[21]

18. This version has been formulated by Oeller in *kürbiskern* 3 (1971): "Television is as little the school of the nation as the federal army can be the school of the nation. On the whole, television has no educational mission, for that would presuppose a general educational goal. And this is not possible because of the varying educational goals in society. Language is a social phenomenon. The same is true of communication. As such, it cannot become the private property of individuals. The difference in those who are communicating demands different educational goals" (p. 423).

19. This is the proper core of Enzensberger's theory of the media, according to which the mass media are supposed to be extended through *decentralization*.

20. [The word that appears in the German original, *"Vergesellschaftung,"* is generally translated "nationalization" (e.g., the nationalizing of an industry). The authors use the term, however, to refer to the process by which various areas relating to the present-day context of living, some of which have been deemed part of the "private" sphere, become absorbed by the dominant production interests of capital. The neologism "societilization" is used in order to distinguish between the more specific notion of "nationalization" and the broader meaning of "socialization."—*Trans.*]

21. See the bibliography and statistical data on this in Ralf Zoll and Eike Hennig, *Massenmedien und Meinungsbildung,* esp. pp. 37ff.

Television is no different from any modern bureaucracy with regard to management, adminstrative, and editorial staff. The tasks correspond to those in an apparatus of control and distribution that is predicated on individual creativity. Management, editorial, and programming have a dual nature, insofar as they also partly impinge on the domain of production. This domain, or television as a **management-led enterprise** that produces its own programs, corresponds to the level of individual artisanal production, as far as individual television plays and films are concerned; with regard to telelvisions series, it corresponds to relatively simple levels of manufacturing. Output ranges from shows with high budgets and elaborately staged and edited television plays down to series with sets that could be built in a day. The mode of production of these television plays and shows, especially insofar as they are produced in the studio, is not essentially different from methods of cinematic studio production or work in large theaters. The distinctions are merely based upon volume, routine, and experiences specific to television.

At the same time, the electronics industry, the spearhead of innovation, penetrates this sphere of production as the conveyor of technical expertise. The networks themselves possess a considerable capacity for technical development, above all in the central institute for broadcasting technology in Munich. The individual network orients itself according to the high scientific and technological level of the industry and competes with the other networks in what is increasingly becoming an international framework.

High technology impinges on the realm of the "creators," whose level of organization is still manufactural, and brings it into line with the late industrial stage of the medium. In this respect, cameramen and other studio technicians have a dual character: on the one hand, they belong to the artistic team; on the other, they represent technology. The writers, editors, and creative personnel are confronted by the technology of the television networks, not only in the shape of the technicians themselves but also by the dead labor objectified in professional expertise and in the achievements of the electronics industry—in other words, by a whole technical and scientific army. In the face of such economic power, the reliance of directors, writers, and actors on mere ideas can easily strike one as ludicrous. This is the underlying reason for the predominance of technology and of the industrial model itself, which determines television production, in particular the production of series, and which is expressed not only by its ready-made character[22] but also

22. The reduction through technology of possibilities for expression in television production is the reverse side of the fact that technology is actually considerably more advanced than is evident in the television programs. It possesses amazing capacities for innovation that open up the potential for television to develop forms of aesthetic expression unknown to any other medium. Recently, individual authors (*Autoren*) have begun to use these means (in the show "Baff" and in individual show episodes, for example, or in the case of Zadek), nonetheless failing to appreciate the full development potential of this technology with their exclusive privileging of formal tricks. The contradiction arises less

by its apparent opposite—the exaggerated insistence of well-known directors on special requests and *idées fixes*. A possible response to this situation would be for directors, writers, or editors to organize themselves. Forerunners of such an organization are the German Writers' Union (VS), the Authors' Publishing House, the filmmakers' syndicate and association of cinema and television directors, along with the producers' charters of the networks. One would need to develop these rudimentary forms of organization into a substantive, cooperative operation.

However, one should not regard the manufacturing mode of production used by individual television teams as merely backward. The industrial stage of this production will not consist simply of an intensification or rationalization of current procedures in the making of films and television plays. Rather, this presupposes a discipline, cooperation, and productivity in the creative and intellectual process that does not exist today. Nor can such forms of production be developed among the creators themselves; they demand motivation by the more evolved needs of the audience. In the context of the present situation, it is more correct to say that the artisanal production of individual items, which lags behind even the manufactural stage, is in a better position to respond to the consciousness and fantasy of concrete groups of viewers.

**The production of content and of aesthetic forms of programs depends more on the level of societilization of the viewers' consciousness and imagination than on the ideas and techniques of production teams. It is only when the "viewer factor" is industrialized that the potential of program making will be released. Until such time, all efforts in this direction will lead to abstraction, and thus to a further stablilization of the hierarchical relationship between television and viewers. A full realization of the potential of television would certainly no longer lead to the monologue form of program television.**

Television as a medium, as the coherent product presented on the screen, has a different level of societilization than do its individual components. Here the most advanced element, the technical medium (but not for technical reasons), absorbs the more backward modes of production. In its concentrated form, television has a "tempo" that corresponds to the time scale of a highly industrialized society.[23]

---

because of a lack of goodwill or simply because of the organizational separation of the technical and creative hierarchies, but rather, above all, because of the different levels of cooperation and societilization of the outdated creative and the highly advanced technical components of television production. Because of this, there develops a permanent cost and legitimation pressure vis-à-vis the production of television content that assumes the form of short tryout periods, the hasty economic use of studios, the adaptation of the authors' and directors' ideas about form and content to the technology, and so on.

23. We know that comments or questions from other family members irritate the member sitting in front of an engrossing television show. Concrete sexual or physical needs retreat for a time. The statistically calculated increase in the household use of water immediately after the end of an engrossing television show can be traced back, according to reports from the television networks, to the collective urinary behavior of the viewers. This is not because the concrete content of the broadcast actually possesses higher degrees of energy than the physically or libidinally structured body; rather, it corre-

The viewer does not relate to the individual programs; his experience does not automatically correspond with the individual experiences embodied in the programs. *He is dealing, rather, with the pluralistic package offered by a highly industrialized production process.* This does not prevent him from remembering and feeling things, from absorbing and comparing experiences, but such autonomous activity remains unorganized. Instead, the program output as a whole organizes the viewer's very existence, his time and his day.

## Wealth of Material, Lack of Time, Distortions of Communication

Among the most striking aspects of every television program are *wealth of material and the organized lack of time.* What retrospectively looks like manipulation by television almost always stems from the conscious or unconscious effect of these two factors. Like radio, television attempts representatively to reflect the entire world.[24] This takes place in individual time slots consisting of anywhere from a few minutes to an hour, with the exception of longer entertainment programs. Broadcasting hours can be increased to only a limited degree. There are, for instance, plans to move the ZDF news and thus the whole evening's viewing up by forty-five minutes; but even this proposal to increase broadcasting time has been highly controversial.

The phenomenon of the wealth of material in television is no more a matter of

---

sponds to the higher level of contemporaneity and production of television, which makes it possible to participate on credit in a transindividual, "important" moment that should under no circumstances be neglected. In this respect, but not as a television ontology, McLuhan is right: the medium is the message.

24. Precisely this view, that of comprehending the whole of the world, is, as we show in the other chapters, a characteristic of the bourgeois public sphere. Linked to this is the contradiction that such a state of perfection can only be reached once all of the information that disturbs the image of completeness (through, for example, particular precision) has been excluded. Also linked to this is the necessity that whatever is brought in the way of system-endangering information must, because of the ideal of the completeness of information, again be eliminated in whatever form. This results in a constant oscillation between too much and too little substance. Piechotta, in *Ästhetik und Kommunikation* 2 (1970): "At the base of the bourgeois mass media there lies a tendency to allocate reality into a totality of information and thus draw it into the parameter of its own sphere of production; there is an analogy here to the bourgeois ideology of reason, with which the whole world is supposed to be organized and put at the disposal of the bourgeois class. The reproduction of the world in the news forms the expression of the more intensive potential for production of the bourgeoisie vis-à-vis feudalism. Precisely the all-encompassing pretension of the bourgeoisie to align the whole world to the new mode of production concealed within it negative ramifications. The totality of information necessarily also encompassed that information which laid bare the characteristic violence of the bourgeois order and which had to turn as an inner compulsion against the universal news system that was itself coordinated with bourgeois interests. The circumstantial duress that is linked to the concept of total information is derived from the experience that the capitalist investment of private property generated a new type of power whose practical appearance supplies the dangerous 'substance' for news" (p. 32).

lack of coordination than it is in school. One reason for this is the major factor in the internal economy of the networks: the hierarchical career structure of the production staff and the television industry. This is the most important indicator of economic interests within broadcasting networks themselves. More posts can be created within the networks only if these networks increase their significance by increasing their program production. Since the posts are almost all defined by different areas of competence, this leads to a permanent increase of material. The principle of programmed television leads to a traffic jam: the impossible situation whereby the potentially infinite mass of material being broadcast must, in Germany, be forced through the needle's eye of two networks and the "mininetwork," Channel Three. The wealth of material is therefore also an indication of the apparently opposite principle, the **arbitrary process of permanently cutting out material**.

It is a fact that the standards used for selecting and organizing material (in other words, for limiting it) can only be established on the basis of the material itself. Since, from the very outset, the narrow base provided for broadcasting necessarily curtails the development of material, these materials cannot be ordered into comprehensive groupings that would allow them to be condensed. The control of the wealth of material is thus left to the very principle of lack of time: in other words, the material is mechanically and admininstratively divided up according to the limits of available broadcasting time. This is not a question of a clash between the total broadcasting time available and the totality of materials, but of a prestructured broadcasting time, in which the overall wealth of material and overall lack of time attempt to express themselves within particular slots and units. The result is that **the material's struggle for survival** is reiterated in each individual program.

This structuring is in fact anarchic in nature. It seems like order only in the context of the existing rules and conventions. The respective compartmentalizations can scarcely be explained on the basis of broader social structures, but, as a rule, on the basis of the history of television. It would be worth investigating how much of this rests on pure chance and how much was imported from other spheres, such as, for instance, radio or newspapers (where compartmentalization developed for quite different reasons). It is certainly correct to say that the prevailing circumstances determine forms of expression, ideas, and therefore also the way in which the mass media operate; but this merely describes a given state of affairs, without specifying the processes shaping it. **The dominant social interests do not assert themselves directly in the networks; one cannot claim, for instance, that the Federation of German Industry has a greater degree of influence in the networks than other interest groups do, or that it has a direct effect. Rather, such dominant interests, which control areas of production outside the public-service networks, assert themselves through the public-service structure of the networks, which is a contradictory form of organization based on the** model of the classical bourgeois public sphere. This structure produces a selection mechanism that makes it difficult for living impulses at the grass-roots level to establish themselves. Abstract organization, on the other hand, thrives more easily under these conditions.[25] The result of these selections makes television appear to be a reproduction of dominant conditions. A critique that restricts itself to this result alone fails to grasp the historical genesis of such modes of organization. Those directly involved in television work are most familiar with this historical process; a cultural critique that understands only the products, and not how they came about, is not convincing to these people.

Within the framework determined by the wealth of material and the compartmentalized time slots of the overall program, **television commodities** have some other general characteristics:

*a) Compression*

Measured according to the viewer's sense of time and the normal attention level, all programs seem to exist in a concentrated state. The time structure and experience organized in them are condensed in form. This form essentially excludes the structures in which events take place in reality. "What is, in the medium, considered 'entertainment' (detective film, game show, radio play, miniseries, sitcom) is involved precisely in *sensualizing* the subject matter, that is, in transforming it into a *condensed existence*, which no longer offers a link to social reality. (In this light, a close-up of the features of a murder victim in a crime film and the answer to the emcee's eight thousand Deutsche mark question are identical.)"[26] This phenomenon is due to the **difference in social tempo**

25. One example of such a selection mechanism is the fact that difficulties do not arise for any editor, department manager, or superintendent because he does *not* do something. A further example is the fact that television preorganizes its program criteria in the form of the abstractly formulated statutory goal of programming guidelines and program planning. It is not the particular individual products, the prototypes of new programs, but rather the programming will that precedes production, fashioned formulaically in the authorities of the network—that is, as a rule the level at which the legitimation of the program is tested. The abstractness and formality of this level prohibits the inclusion of all of those possibilities that one is only able to formulate once they have been tried out in production. Forms of expression that have already been tried out therefore have an advantage over those that have not yet been tried. This is not always the case. Often the programming planners ratify only that which has developed in the production, which never completely carries out what has preceded it as a program. In this case, however, productions that are very costly, productions with particularly immobile production apparatuses, especially studio productions, carry greater weight than productions that have come into being through improvisation with sparse means. The network can, in the latter case, cancel and replace the program without great losses to the network. However, the mobile productions made "on a shoestring" are precisely those in which innovations characteristically succeed.

26. Hans-Joachim Piechotta, "Antwort auf Enzensbergers Medientheorie," in *Ästhetik und Kommunikation* 2 (1970): 34.

**between lived existence, which is to a certain extent not yet industrialized, and the broadcasting output of a highly industrialized medium**. The medium's pressure to produce (as is apparent in the totality of television production, which is not directly visible on the screen) itself generates this concentration out of an overabundance of material, the pressure exerted by interests, throttled productivity, and so on, irrespective of what the television writers themselves have in mind.

The attention level demanded by these programs corresponds to that of busy professionals who are at the pinnacle of their social development. This does not mean that the programs are hard to understand, but that they rely on a speed of information, a level of tension, and a terseness that correspond to the attention level of managers and other important actors in social life.[27] Moreover, this does not only characterize the overall situation of television as an industry. Those individuals in television management who decide on whether or not to broadcast something are themselves so highly specialized and under such time pressure that they have a "feel" for this social tempo.

### b) Resensualization

Substantial parts of television's own output (television plays, shows, dramatized documentaries) do not mirror real structures but rely on the reconstruction of themes that have previously been investigated by academics or journalists. Scriptwriters, directors, and producers then turn these themes into something concrete again. Wide areas of television production in the studios and among suppliers, like the Bavaria Studio Company, act as such factories for "resensualization."[28] This method underlies family series, series about the resocietilization of criminal offenders, series about life in the German Democratic Republic, and so on. The problem is that the apparently concrete life depicted is, in reality, infinitely rich in determinations and structures; in the newly concretized model, nothing of this survives. To make up for this, new embellishments have been added to the basic plot.

The shifts in this process of reconcretization are bound up with the specific experiences of the writers, editors, and producers working in television. Actual

---

27. Here there develops a sort of Stuyvesant effect of the mass media. The intensity of the "big world" is reproduced in particular through the concentrated form of the program and experienced by the viewers as participation in the development of society. This is true of the all-day broadcasts that, for example, reproduced the no-confidence vote against the Brandt administration, as well as for the daily news or other brief broadcasts. In each of these cases, television offers a higher threshold of attention and contemporaneity than is normally present in the individual lives of the viewers. If, in the films from the 1930s, it is the stars, that is, individual idols of successful life, who assume the character of idols, here it is the whole of society, the worldwide framework of great events in politics and entertainment. The star quality of the world is thus its normal condition.

28. See Hans-Joachim Piechotta, "Antwort auf Enzensbergers Medientheorie," pp. 33–34.

structures are replaced by the structures determining the experience of television production. Because of the lack of other kinds of social practice, those working in this specialized domain cannot, as a rule, bring much of their own experience into play. With the help of their imagination, they create ever-higher levels of abstraction of their own private views of reality: in other words, they tend to replace real structures with a basic scheme, even though this scheme ("which looks like reality") and its genesis are not rendered transparent for the viewer.[29]

*c) The diverting of viewers' attention onto a sphere that is removed from society*
"The object is placed in a totality that is constituted in such a way that the object it contains is received in a manner similar to reality. The only fundamental difference is that the recipient is expected to concentrate upon a sphere that is removed from society. The division, for instance, between politics, culture, sport, and entertainment is indicative of this situation."[30] In the news, attention is also diverted through the very hodgepodge selection of news items. A train crash, a strike in Italy, the death of a philosopher, the abduction of a young girl, a controversy about the Deutsche mark (appearing in the form of a point-counterpoint between two politicians), a weather report, and so on—all of these items contain, in and of themselves, genuine information, but this information is cut off from its real social roots. This hodgepodge results in a fragmenting of attentiveness, together with a hybrid sequence of news items, which is distinct from each individual news item and wholly different from the events that are meant to be represented through the news broadcasts.

In taking on an increasingly abstract character, the news items turn into entertainment. Brief reports about fatal accidents do not cause a stir. If they are summed up on the evening news (for example, 87 dead in a plane crash, 500 Vietcong killed, the deaths of an elderly president and a famous scientist, two fatal car accidents), they assume the abstract nature of a body count, of a mere recording of casualties. It is impossible to get news items of this kind across unless one succeeds in stimulating in the viewer a sensual impression of the underlying human tragedies. For this purpose, real history would have to be told,

29. Karl Holzamer (in *Fernseh-Kritik, Unterhaltung und Unterhaltendes im Fernsehen, Mainzer Tage der Fernseh-Kritik,* vol. 3 [Mainz: 1971]: 115) cloaks the problem in a practical example when he refers to the fact that television staff members, who generally no longer travel by streetcar or public bus, apparently also emanate in the television broadcasts without being conscious of individual communication. What is at issue here is a general question: Can responsibility for editing, broadcasting, and artistic production be exercised at all in the top levels of the profession? Isn't a necessary relationship toward practice, which is at odds with the division of labor, part and parcel of this responsibility? This problem is repeated in the theater, in film, and so on. The specific professionalism required in these areas leads to an impoverishment of real experience. This is the decisive reason for the separation from the viewers, who of course are left in the real areas of life.

30. Piechotta, "Antwort auf Enzensbergers Medientheorie," p. 34.

for it alone constitutes news.[31] The succession of relentlessly critical documentaries, sports, and entertainment programs also creates such a hodgepodge, which structures itself according to the central notion of entertainment as the most general standard for communication in television.[32]

It is precisely the breaks between broadcast events that create the impression of arbitrariness. Neither television critics nor people working at the networks sufficiently take these junctures into consideration. The junctures constitute the moments of montage within the overall program and are more important in relation to the framework in which reality is perceived than in relation to the content of individual programs. They steer and direct attention, and thereby organize the possibilities for experience that must precede experience itself.[33]

The hidden perspective that this provides becomes more apparent if one looks at American television rather than German. For instance, there are between twenty and thirty television stations in densely populated areas of California. A small number of these are run by nonprofit organizations; the majority are financed by advertising. The individual viewer, who is shaped by his specific pattern of work and leisure, does not see any one program from beginning to end. In search of the best program—an imaginary amalgam of all programs, which he cannot, however, simultaneously monitor—he switches from channel to channel. His attention becomes fragmented through the mixture of extracts from heterogeneous programs. The viewer's desire for the best unified program leads him to an abstract level, namely, his complete indifference toward all programs. This corresponds to the viewer's growing indifference toward his own ability to be attentive. He abandons himself to what he is doing anyway: choosing between the individual chan-

---

31. It is evident that one could also condense *Oedipus*, the *Nibelungenlied*, the *Chanson de Roland*, any of Shakespeare's dramas, and so on, in such a way that they are reduced to a mere body count. This would be a parody.

If a sensually communicable news item does not emerge first off, the viewer will attempt to trace that which is offered back to the principle of television in which he most readily finds his way: he understands it as entertainment and distraction. The dynamization of abstract news value in the form of, for example, even more, or even more terrible, deaths, accidents, contemporary events will not help against this; the only thing that will help is the appearance of news that is really constituted within itself. News that corresponds to the inner movement of the viewer displaces the regression of the viewer to the entertainment mechanism.

32. See Heribert Schatz, "'Tagesschau' und 'Heute'—Politisierung des Unpolitischen?" in *Kritik, Manipulation der Meinungsbildung:* 109–23.

33. No doubt individual program directors and program planners exhibit a considerable, and even an artistic, understanding of this interface technology. The real possibilities for decision making from the standpoint of program planning are few, however, as a result of the scarcity of program-immanent alternatives. Precisely by switching between the individual program segments produced on a principle of divided labor (e.g., from variety shows to "serious" programming, from news reports to sports), the viewer's attention is not provoked, but rather exhausted. The occasional switches are for the most part unplanned, but result from the crowding of productions that are anarchic in their relationships toward each other.

nels. One obvious solution to this fragmentation is to choose from a television guide, but this already presupposes a structured interest, a level of attentiveness that has long since been deflected. One should not forget that television orients itself according to what is already an alienated life process of the masses. This life process is governed by the remaining spheres of socialization. One can provide evidence in claiming that—merely as an example—TV in California is the way it is because of how Californians are; conversely, one can deduce the way in which these people use television from the programs that are offered. What interests us is the form in which this interplay takes place, since all possibilities for a change in the current situation are dependent on this form.

## Limitations of Television That Derive from the Labor Process

"*Money*—a factor guiding both producers and the public, each without consulting the other—seems to be *entertainment*. Entertainment is the medium that embodies exchange abstraction in the mass markets of leisure. In the free market, in a competitive market, and also in oligopolistic competition, entertainment is certainly present as a by-product. But it is only in the wake of the restructuring of the market by the monopolies after 1930 that it becomes the institutionalized medium according to which producers and consumers alike orient themselves as if it were disposable income. The development of entertainment as a medium—which, as in the use of money, implies the existence of abstract, generalized structures of expectation in the minds of individuals—occurred on an empirical level after 1930, when the monopolies began to invest in public relations instead of in qualitative aesthetic innovations."[34]

This analysis, which has been developed in conjunction with Talcott Parsons, is relevant to the film industry and the expanding private consciousness industry, as well as to American private television. It does not, however, apply as much to television in the Federal Republic. Precisely because of its public-service structure, television maintains an unsteady relationship to the needs of its viewers. On the one hand, television does not cover over the expression of these needs with its own propaganda, even though it would have the economic means to do so. Rather, it makes repeated attempts to absorb part of these needs. On the other hand, television is in fact a medium of the consciousness industry, which is subject to the law of exchange described above: "The producers give the consumer 'pluralistic' cultural content, while the consumers give the producers a general 'receptivity.' "[35] This highlights the nature of television as the medium of a transitional epoch. **It is not impossible for television to take needs into account. One can determine what television can or cannot do only by examining its interaction**

---

34. Dieter Prokop, "Versuch über Massenkultur und Spontaneität": 34.
35. Ibid.

**with each individual need. However, a general boundary can be drawn that derives from the structure of leisure, which is determined by the labor process.** This has been explained by Habermas in his early essays on work, leisure, and consumption.

The labor process and family socialization produce needs, some of which can be directly satisfied in television by libidinal relaxation. Others, despite temporary satisfaction through the activity of fantasy, would give rise to severe disharmonies in daily life and the labor process. The latter group of needs must therefore be distorted and directed toward other illusory libidinal goals. In this case, laws governing television programming work together with desires for the repulsion of drives in the viewers themselves.

The first group of needs, those that can be satisfied by television, includes, among other things: rest; relief from work; "tuning out"; memories of primary nature; the equal use—which never occurs in the process of abstract labor—of all muscles, nerves, senses, and intellectual powers; recollections of childhood, and so on. Even imagining these situations proves to be a source of satisfaction. The example "recollections of childhood" implies the boundaries containing those needs that, when satisfied, lead to greater libidinal disharmonies than if left unsatisfied; on the other hand, the nonfulfillment of these needs is unbearable.

The second group includes the majority of sexual needs, the needs for omnipotence that are suppressed through our upbringing. Examples of this in the work domain include: the syndrome of violence toward machines and the values that hold the labor process together; the desire for an interruption of the time continuum; surprise. Evidently, the normal sequence of time, which is the form in which work and obligations are expressed—namely, the most important objectification of the reality principle—is identified as the main enemy.

These experiences cannot organize themselves individually or in the form of television programming. Under existing social conditions, they would all come up against barriers. They can thus be taken into account only indirectly; if they were taken directly into account, they would fail to be satisfying because their prestaged satisfaction would not be credible.

Of all needs, sexual ones are least structured in television, whether directly or indirectly;[36] at best, they are referred to through nineteenth-century forms of expression. The scale of existing needs in this field can be gauged from the "per-

36. The onetime broadcast of hard-core pornography during a documentary program on ZDF should be understood as having been motivated more by competition with ARD, that is, more by the need of the ZDF for original premiere programs than by latent viewer demands that play no part in such individual broadcasts; the viewers view the program as a sensation and at the same react with a necessary degree of defensiveness to the extent that they compare it with their own experience and/or are sensually gripped by the content of the broadcast.

sonals" in sex magazines. All these are needs that—were they not distorted by censorship in this society (including censorship by taste)—would be part of what could be described as the free unfolding of sexual needs. This would have repercussions for the cultivation of all human needs. For needs cannot be developed in isolation but only in their overall context: in other words, the development of all human needs is measured against the most repressed and least developed need.

Despite the softer approach taken by public-service television, networks try to at least partially satisfy the need to "escape" by providing "action" shows; through sensational news reports about disasters, torture, explosions; by exploiting the element of surprise, the need for an annihilation of the everyday environment, the time scale of production, and so on. This need to escape exists independently of television; that is, it entails experiences that television at most helps to structure. It makes no difference which explicit moral stance the relevant program adopts: whether the message of the program is "Anything is better than what we have now" or "No matter what it is, it's good, this world is good." Such explicit attitudes do not penetrate to the deep-rooted needs of the viewers; what does get through are the **form** in which customary experience is interrupted (contrasts, surprises) and the **means** for bringing about "hard action."[37]

Elements of the broadcast material that answers these needs for expression are dealt with in program discussions on television under the heading **brutality and violence**. What is especially problematic in this context is the ban on depicting

37. In the subdued incorporation of the human need to escape, there is a tendential separation of "content" and "form." This does not occur, however, within a certain practice; rather, the opportunity to assimilate the viewers' needs to express themselves varies in accordance with whether what is at issue is the "statement," the plot, or what Adorno describes as subcutaneous structure. For this reason, the subversive interaction between television shows and viewer needs remains without any public and conscious expression. In other words, that which is conscious of this shuts out this real interrelationship. Thus, the emancipatory potential that is contained in the need for escape from the oppression that is objectified in reality is not allowed to emerge. What develop are abstract forms of fantasy that tend toward regression and that do not tend to relate back again to real experiences—they can only be linked up again with clichés. If they were actually expressed, these needs for escape would surely provide the motor for incorporating the world into one's own experience, for adapting history to oneself. One could compare, for example, the gloomy perspective on the world that results from watching a TV crime show, or even after consuming one of the violent epics of despair that the film industry keeps on hand (such as *The Dirty Dozen*), with phrases from the Chinese Cultural Revolution such as, "Full of anger, the golden ape struck with his giant staff. Then the firmament of jade was once again free of dust." In the one case, eventually everything that can have any sort of human meaning—especially the lives of those carrying out the action—is laid to ruin by the satisfaction of needs for escape (for the most part by means of dynamite and secret agents) based on the division of labor. In the other, there is obviously a sense of trust that the breakdown of the normal life context will in no sense lead to destruction, but instead will finally liberate life. Beneath this complete openness to rebellion and escape, no emergence of the constructive qualities of the need to destroy reified reality is possible.

It is important to understand the immense tension between the cultural-revolutionary initiatives that exist in our world and the reform ideas of television that attempt to include "something more of viewer needs."

violence in television or film, as the government's draft **amendment to the criminal law** intends to secure. In light of the internal structure of the television networks, such a ban functions not just directly, in terms of the wording of the law, but also as a repression of the portrayal of brutality. This results in a selection mechanism that does not in fact prevent the portrayal of violence on television (e.g., the purchase of American crime series, whereby measured doses of violence are imported), but that leaves violence as social experience unexpressed. In this way, the potential for violence and aggression in society is by no means diminished; the social expression of this potential—in other words, its **public sphere**—is, however, denied. The rechanneled needs, which from the very beginning could only be indirectly satisfied, are thus even further repressed (not at a psychological, but at a social, level). To put it another way, there is a social necessity to continually express needs, in concert with the expression of all remaining needs. Such a production of experience in dealing with one's own needs is an indispensable prerequisite for any emancipatory transformation of society. Unstructured, unexpressed needs that are subject to rechanneling constitute the material for the law of the return of the repressed, which is valid not only in psychological but also in social terms: such needs are a quasi-ontological, conservative factor.

## Television and Criticism

The most effective form of critique in bourgeois society takes place via the market, whereby the needs of the members of society are formulated, regardless of how they are distorted by the market mechanism. Cultural criticism as well, which is practiced by the small, educated elite, only first became effective because of its impact upon the exchange value of cultural products.

Public-service television is a medium that is only indirectly controlled by the viewers via this market mechanism. The viewers are not capable of formulating qualitative needs and interests by relying upon the ratings companies or the social and parliamentary regulations of television pluralism. What other forms of critique are there to confront large apparatuses such as public-service television? **It is here that we discover why television is an institution that is characteristic of a transitional epoch, an era in which essential communication needs are no longer entrusted to the capitalist mechanism, but effective new forms of public regulation do not as yet exist.** Attempts, both on paper and in a practical sense, at regulating television councils, general directors, and department heads must face very specific types of obstacles. These critiques can rarely intervene usefully in the sophisticated apparatus of production; they merely interpret what the individual departments produce, as well as set the overall course by means of occasional interventions from above. They can supervise the output of television—within the limits of their purview and their special interests—but they cannot determine it.[38]

The producers' battles over network charters constitute a more substantial form of critique. In making claims for their right to codetermination, the producers are also attempting to develop a kind of **self-critique for television**. Under present circumstances, where there is no such thing as a self-organization of viewers, this represents an important attempt at an effective and informed critique of television's structures. However, the self-organization of television employees must contend with major contradictions. These contradictions do not stem from the fact that the charters cover the interests of only a section of those working in television. They arise rather because television comprises not only the networks but also the interrelationship between viewers and output. The issue of the producers' right to codetermination is only one isolated component among many, whereas a new form of public criticism of television can only be developed by taking all the components into acount as a totality. In the process, the dependence of television upon its own career hierarchy is intensified.[39]

Because television employees have economic interests in preserving and expanding their jobs, it is unlikely that their critiques and self-critiques will take into account the fact that television relies upon a fragmented division of labor and that it is shaped by programming, factors that play a key role in ensuring television's ineffectiveness. From the perspective of the individual salaried position, which can justify itself only by performing a function different from other positions, neither the totality of viewers' needs nor even so much as a single one of them can be grasped. Instead, the single need is divided into several components according to the needs of a differentiated classification of posts. What subsequently appears as a unified television program does not correspond with real needs but can, as a generalized product, only attempt to connect abstractly with the viewer's generalized form of receptivity. Exchange abstraction can hardly be elevated to the object of criticism in this type of self-critique performed by television employees. The limits of such a critique still exist, even though many network employees are in a position to evaluate the potential of an unfettered television, and the productive force revolts against its established boundaries.

Consequently, a comprehensive critique of public-service television can only

---

38. The attempt made by the new CSU [Christian Social Union] radio-network law in Bavaria strengthens these possibilities for intervention, but to the same degree destroys the productivity of the radio network.

39. Gerhard Prager, discussion contribution in *Fernseh-Kritik, Unterhaltung und Unterhaltendes im Fernsehen*: 82: "It has been substantiated in the public-service networks that, on the basis of long-term engagement with objects that remain the same, there is, in addition to the routine that can indeed in a certain positive sense be something like crystallized experience—that in addition to the routine, the career is exposed as a negative phenomenon."

be performed from an outside critical position. Yet it is precisely this approach that completely misses the mark.

When forms of **cultural criticism** take on television, an institution of the bourgeois public sphere in the traditional sense is confronting an apparatus of the modern consciousness industry. This apparatus does not respond to such a cultural critique but assimilates it by enlisting it as raw material for the redistribution of legitimations within the apparatus. Cultural criticism focuses to some extent upon individual programs. In doing so, it falls victim to the illusion emanating from the screen, which conceals the entire apparatus of production. On top of this, the majority of cultural critics operate in a selective manner and critique only those programs that interest them: that is, film critics critique films; drama critics, television plays; politicians, current-affairs programs and documentaries. In this way, criticism becomes a subsidiary of television and does not focus at all on the totality of the medium. The television section in newspapers is one product of this practice; here, a specific way of looking at television is developed, independently of the arts page or political commentary.

When cultural criticism does go beyond individual programs, it displays such extreme fluctuations in its judgments that an industrial apparatus like television can in no way measure itself against it. Opinions range from the notion that television, because it is modern technology personified, is progressive and has a generally emancipatory potential; to the conviction that, under existing social conditions, television does not allow for any fulfillment of viewers' needs (in other words, that television could have an emancipatory potential only in a socialist society); down to the manipulation theory, which maintains that one has to draw a distinction between emancipated television communication and attempts to assert the dominant interests via television.[40] These fluctuations come about because there is no interaction between the critique of individual programs, the analysis of viewers' needs, and an institutional critique of television. If there were, it would soon become evident that the "inescapable historical experience of conflicts and oppression, which works to constitute the object of perception, cannot itself be suppressed again."[41] It would also become equally apparent that the decentralization advocated by Enzensberger (if it is, as he suggests, universally demanded) would, under the prevailing social conditions, express itself as the further penetration of the consciousness industry. In other words, social forces would try to use this theory of delegation and decentralization in serving their own interests.

40. The latter position corresponds to the dominant opinion in most of the daily papers; the first version has been put forward by, for example, Enzensberger. The thesis that television could only be understood *in general* under present social conditions as an instrument of domination can be found among numerous leftist groups and in several reviews of Enzensberger's theory of the media.

41. Piechotta, "Antwort auf Enzensbergers Medientheorie," p. 33.

**The problem is that a critique of television cannot be formulated in literary or journalistic form, that is, in the medium of the bourgeois public sphere. A mode of production that is as self-sufficient as television can be critiqued only by an alternative type of production.**[42] This applies to the self-critique and codetermination of television employees, to the incorporation of the interests of the viewers, as well as to the effective expression of criticism from outside. All of these can play a significant part in changing the structures of television if they are concretized in an alternative body of broadcast material and new forms of organization. Public-service networks have a vested interest in such products, in which collective experiences are organized. Only if they develop products of this kind can they resist being overshadowed by the private program industry.

Whether intentionally or not, collective experience is organized in television. In the present situation, contact with this experience, via the screen and programming, is not available.[43] But even apart from the fact that there is as yet no medium for the playback of this experience, one essential organizational element is lacking: what can viewers do with the reproduction of their own experience when their immediate needs relate to the libidinal compensation of the alienated labor process and are not oriented by knowledge of the world?[44]

It is necessary, therefore, to discover how one can mediate in television production between the viewers' own experience and the satisfaction of needs —a mediation that is presently accomplished only by what are in part regressive fantasies devoid of experience. In this respect, every viewer need that can be determined empirically is ambiguous. There are no products corresponding to this stage of the organization of experience, either within television or outside of it (for example, in the activities of political groups). The oppositions culture/industry, politically committed commentary/entertainment, are not helpful in this case.[45]

---

42. It is therefore no coincidence that the particularly far-reaching and at the same time practical suggestions for changing television programming have up until now come from the networks themselves. See, for example, the recent article by Dieter Stolte, "Fernsehen von morgen—Analysen und Prognosen," in *Fernseh-Kritik, Mainzer Tage der Fernseh-Kritik,* ed. Bernward Frank, vol. 4 (Mainz: 1972): 15-32. In contrast, challenges from critical journalists, including those on the left, are often extensive but impractical.

43. This is just as true for the television employees, including the superintendents. The experience accumulated in television can only be read in the total television production, that is, in the programming that has been stockpiled over many years. This provides a record of information as well as an overall picture of the abbreviations, distortions, and abstractions of value from which the television team proceeds in any recording process. At base, the "commodity accumulation" of the television archive is something like a social whole exposed to specific distortions.

44. This problem arises in a similar way for television in the socialist societies in the process of transformation. This is the reason for the fact that numerous citizens of the GDR tune in to Western television.

45. On the concept of engagement and of the political option, see Theodor W. Adorno, *Aesthetic*

The expression of social experience in television production must confront the dominant interests in the mass media, too. It is not as if the contradictory features of concepts such as entertainment, documentary, social commentary, and so on, are not recognized in this context. It is just as impossible to produce experience or criticism in a "pure" form as it is to create a pure form of entertainment, which is the commodity value of television. What we are dealing with here is the problem of *television realism*. The mere reproduction of reality, for instance, the documentation of alienated labor, must take into account that people can derive pleasure from the appropriation of this experience only if they can actively transform the circumstances that oppress them. It is from such a possibility of action alone that interest in realism can be aroused. A similar problem affects criticism if it restricts itself to the mere reproduction of inhumane acts. While mobilizing the viewer, it simultaneously makes him experience the fact that, sitting in front of the television, he can do nothing to change the situation. For this reason, the critique of social conditions in television programs always conveys the limits of such a critique as well. Thus any emancipatory critical venture cannot, as a matter of principle, set out from the viewer who stays in front of his set. The interaction between viewer and program, which must play a role in the individual television product, has to orient itself according to a broader conception of the circumstances in which the viewer finds himself and not simply tie him to the screen. It may be assumed that any multimedia relationship—in other words, communication between network and viewer that makes it possible to have several television channels, correspondence by mail or phone, as well as viewers' organizations—would have fundamentally more potential for development.

At stake in all of these changes is the liberation of the imaginative faculty, of sociological fantasy. The viewers' imagination is the real medium of television. This involves activity within the imagination—just as, *before the bourgeois revolution*, the bourgeois mode of production was articulated as an overall social principle only in novels (Rabelais, Cervantes). In the process, the linkage between this ideological preparation of public opinion and the practice of bourgeois life and production remained superficial. It was others who paved the way for and introduced the bourgeois class's public sphere, and yet others who exploited this abstract freedom through production. **The situation is different when it comes to proletarian forms of experience. These are not based upon control over products but upon the experience of production itself: in other words, upon qualititative situations and notions of societal wealth, of which individuals must have a material sense if they are to produce it collectively. Consciousness, freedom, sensual substance must be**

*Theory.* See also the problematizing of the existing professional revolutionary who has been replaced by the industrial revolutionizing of relations in Gaston Salvatore's *Büchners Tod* (Frankfurt: 1972).

conveyed in those same individuals who occupy the social situation with their concrete lives. It takes a long time to develop products that correspond to this level of the social production of consciousness.[46] With the accumulation of this experience, one cannot wait for a societal leap to occur as if by magic.[47]

---

46. Dutschke meant this process when he spoke of "the long march through the institutions" that encompasses the readaptation of all areas of experience of social life, including the extent to which they are administered by institutions.

47. The following example will illustrate how communication revolving around this question occurs at present: a nonrevisionist appointee to a permanent position sits in an educational institution run by harsh conservatives and publishes, in a liberal weekly newspaper not generally read by Marxist-Leninists, an article in which the suggestion is made that the Marxist-Leninists should establish a mass-media department in their cadre party. This news will not reach the Marxist-Leninists.

# Chapter 4
# The Individual Commodity and Collections of Commodities in the Consciousness Industry

In analyzing the media cartel,[1] it is important to examine how the internal structure of a commodity is changed by the fact that it appears in a specific and coherent accumulation, which constitutes a new use-value and a new body of commodities. At the beginning of *Capital*, Marx speaks of the commodity as an elementary form: "The wealth of societies in which the capitalist mode of production prevails appears as 'an immense collection of commodities,' the individual commodity appears as its elementary form."[2] This definition of the relationship between the individual commodity and the total range of commodities presupposes the existence of an anarchic form of agglomeration. In some cases, such as the media cartel, it is scarcely possible today to speak of such elementary forms as one speaks in empirical epistemology of elementary sense perceptions. Although the total range of commodities does not have the form of a unified whole, in which the elementary forms are related to one another by structural laws, the individual purchaser of a commodity is nevertheless no longer confronted by this commodity in isolation or by an accumulation of individual commodities. Rather, he is party to a complex of services and commodities structured according to the interests of profit. The simplest of these forms, which can still be understood as "an immense collection of commodities" but in no sense follows an anarchic principle, is the department store (as a real body of commodities, which confronts a customer who believes that he is buying individual commodities). As a result, per-

---

1. For details see chapter 5.

2. Karl Marx, *Capital*, vol. 1, trans. Samuel Moore and Edward Aveling (New York: International Publishers, 1967): 35.

ceiving a commodity always gives rise to an association with the totality of commodities, so that the whole department store is potentially a commodity that
imposes itself upon the purchaser.

A process of transformation is evident here, which, acting behind the illusion
that an exchange society still exists, is effectively preparing the transition to a
**society based on compulsory exchange**. This type of society corresponds to the
stage of the commodity form described above.

The most extreme exertions of capital are necessary in mediating between the
advancing production interests and the needs of those working in the production
apparatus who have no possibilities for self-determination. People are unable to
develop a will of their own, but neither can the valorization interest assert itself
against their will. This stalemate is currently the basic form of conflict between
the masses and capital. For this reason, when subjects choose among individual
commodities, it is consistently interpreted as a sign of activity on their part.
Department stores that operate with a so-called **mixed calculation** provide proof
of this fact. These stores offer individual goods at extremely low prices; at the
same time, they price other items (often the majority) the same as or higher than
those offered by competitors or small retailers. In this way the maxim to "sell a lot
at high prices" can be realized without the purchaser being able to counter it with
his interest to "buy a lot at low prices." He can recognize, articulate, and satisfy
his real interests only by spending his time running back and forth between a
number of specialty shops and department stores.

The consciousness industry—when it appears in forms that can be anticipated—has an added element above and beyond the department store's accumulation
of commodities. **In the department store, the customer does not have to purchase a whole department for the individual commodity to attain its use-
value. It is different with the media cartel. Here the purchaser must literally
buy up a whole "department" to obtain the comparable use-value of the individual commodity. What is actually "for sale" are the life context and learning context that are preorganized in the media cartel. The media cartel is a
macrocommodity, which fuses the individual commodities of education,
entertainment, and information into one overall complex. Without this
macrocommodity, these individual commodities revert to an earlier phase of
valorization with respect to both their character as commodities and their
type of use-value.**

It is necessary to imagine the high degree of interdependence and concentration involved in the workings of the media cartel. As a rule, a corporation of this
kind owns the mass production of books, book clubs, shares in daily newspapers
and magazines, a central computer to which are connected facilities for the reproduction of novels, scientific publications, films, cassettes, television features, and
educational software. In addition to this, the central data bank (which also controls production facilities) serves a cable network, from which subscribers can

obtain all available scientific and encyclopedic knowledge in an audiovisual form by telephone or by watching television. At the same time, such an enterprise runs private technical colleges, private research facilities, vocational institutes, and local radio and television stations. All these programs are interconnected and interdependent; they communicate among themselves, advertise for each other, and are conceived of as a group. Within this system, there exists a fixed state of interdependence between the enterprise as a whole, the masses of readers and users organized by it, and the producers of software, regardless of whether the producers are employees or regard themselves as "free-lance." What is more, there is also an interdependence between the sectors of the enterprise responsible for publicity and the industrial sector that produces hardware—in other words, between the electronics industry and the sales vanguard that disseminates some of the hardware.

It is difficult for a customer to be selective when faced with this package. Thus, for instance, even if a student is at an advanced level, he will only be able to follow an advanced course if he has learned how it operates at the beginner's level. Individual courses have an educational value, in turn, when they fit in with other educational and entertainment facilities, and with the subsequent examination and course certificate.

The libidinal connections between learning process and entertainment, which make the products of the media cartel attractive to consumers, result from the organizational interweaving of fiction and documentary within a single product. On the other hand, without the media cartel's hardware and distribution network, a producer working for the media cartel can sell his products (e.g., a book, a scientific report, a training program, a film) only as a commodity that has no mass basis of equivalent value. The commodity is divorced from this distributor: it is an abstraction, a private object. It becomes apparent that the incorporation of commodities into the nonpublic public sphere of the media cartel is a constitutive factor of the individual product's use-value. This can determine, for instance, whether a commodity becomes an instrument of mass communication or a product that stays on the shelf, quite independent of the qualitative and quantitative aspects of the book, film, educational program, and so forth, in question.

Marx has interpreted this transformation of commodities in the case of one type of commodity, labor power. **The capitalist buys the labor power of the individual, but derives value through the cooperation of all workers. This cooperation is something qualitatively distinct, more advanced, and, by virtue of the moment of societilization, richer than individual labor power.** Marx describes this as follows:

Apart from the new power that arises from the fusion of many forces into a single force, mere social contact begets in most industries an emulation and a stimulation of the animal spirits that heighten the efficiency of each individual workman. Hence it is that a dozen persons working together will, in their collective working day of 144 hours, produce far more than twelve isolated men each working 12 hours, or than one man who works 12 days in succession. The reason for this is that man is, if not as Aristotle contends, a political, at all events a social animal.[3]

But this is by no means the only possibility for a transformation of the commodity form through the massing of complexes of commodities in service of a constructive and valorizing intent.

The transformation of labor power as a commodity is a transformation of the qualities of the workers. Similarly, the transformed commodity form, which the consciousness industry produces, is created from the contents and the needs of the consciousness of concrete individuals, who see themselves as customers. In reality, it is these people who produce the media cartel. Because these individuals, without knowing it, anticipate the media cartel through the nature of their needs, it should necessarily follow that they have a say about the activities of the consciousness industry. However, by virtue of the private appropriation and the outside regulation that are connected to the media cartel's development, capitalism generates a relation of production that robs those who participate passively with the media cartel of their status as producers.

Capitalism produces subjects who develop particularized modes of perception and specialized forms of labor that are in accord with the functioning of the production and valorization process. It is only on this basis that capitalism can sustain itself. At the same, because of their increasing societilization, these subjects also develop a fundamental need for a synthesis of these particularized modes of existence, a need that remains unsatisfied in the real production process. If these desires for synthesis were satisfied in accordance with their own social content so that they could lead to a general development of human powers, this could, in the long term, lead to the destruction of the basis that gave rise to these needs in the first place. **By consolidating the media cartel, capitalism is reacting to impulses toward an emancipatory development of human capacities. In view of capitalism's anarchic structure, the macrocapitalist (who does not exist as a subject) is unable to execute such a comprehensive and deliberate counterplan. He develops strategies, which are grouped together under the heading "consciousness industry," as a reflex action to mass needs, as well as to the movement of consciousness that is associated with these needs and that presents itself to him as a market gap.**

The agglomeration of commodities in the media cartel corresponds to the agglomeration of enterprises on the production side. This concentration, which constitutes both centralization and decentralization of production, is characteristic

---

3. Ibid., p. 362.

of the media cartel, but it also exists in all advanced sectors of industry. It by no means stands in opposition to the maintenance of exchange relationships between subjects or the preservation of those early capitalist modes of production that are typical of the intelligentsia's activities. Especially in those spheres that, if they become part of the valorization process, would be considered (from the perspective of valorization) excessively differentiated, a large industrial enterprise prefers symbiosis with numerous small firms, who are economically dependent on it but legally autonomous. These symbiotic forms of production, which are fundamental to capitalism, only seem to be early capitalist forms and to relate to subjects. It is in late-capitalist society's interest to produce such deviations. Accordingly, inventions by engineers working for the biggest American automobile manufacturers are not passed on to the research and development department, as it would be legally possible to do. Instead, the inventors are furnished with loans and subsidies and encouraged to set up small firms of their own. The invention is refined in these small firms until it is ready for production. If development is worthwhile, the large company takes over the small firm or acquires the patents for mass production. But if development is not worthwhile, it is not faced with the problem of having to close down some of its own departments. Instead, the company simply withholds any further subsidy. Thus, demoting the inventor is merely a part of the proper exploitation of his imagination and intelligence. The individual enterpreneur is not autonomous; rather, his situation indicates a decentralized form of one and the same late-capitalist, large-scale apparatus.

*Excursus 1 to Chapter 4*
# The Media Cartel and the Political Public Sphere—an Example of the Overdetermination of the Bourgeois Public Sphere by the Public Sphere of Production

Private economic media conglomerates would objectively be in a position to solve problems like that of educational capacities that are too narrow, the bottlenecking of professional and apprenticeship training, and insufficient capacities for scholarly training (the *Numerus clausus*) with the means available to them. Within the system of public poverty, the necessary investments can be siphoned off from state budgets only over long periods of time. The media conglomerates, on the other hand, are able to come up with the necessary capital on short notice. Here the interest of the media conglomerates in state-authorized commissions for the educational programs of the media cartel, as well as in competition-excluding controls and legislation, converge with the interest of the state in narrowing the number of unresolved communicative and educational problems. **The political public sphere and the media conglomerates are thus more likely to be partners than opponents**. The state, defined within the parameters of the bourgeois public sphere, is indeed not the site at which social resistance to the advance of the production interests of the media will form of their own accord. This is also the case wherever the media cartel places at the disposal of private interests, for example, infrastructures of the domain of education and scholarship that throughout their entire tradition have always been a publicly controlled domain.

The bourgeois public sphere that is characterized by its mechanism of exclusion would thus have only a slight chance of holding its own, even if it wanted to defend its weak substance from overdetermination by the public sphere of production of the consciousness industry. While the media concern influences the masses it organizes on a continuous basis throughout the year, the politician is limited to the election season. The political party must attempt to influence the formation of voter will by using conventional means—individual television speeches, public meetings, pamphlets—while the firms within the media cartel communicate with the potential voters on all channels and from all sides by way of entertainment, the news, and educational programming—always in the direct flow of communication. If indeed the tabloid newspaper (*Bild-Zeitung*) holds in check the expression of opinion of entire political parties in the question of press concentration, what will happen once private television, the press, educational programming with its own sales, entertainment cassettes, cable, and private data processing—manipulated under certain circumstances—are exerting a combined effect within one media conglomerate?

In contrast to the institutions of the bourgeois public sphere of one country, there are media conglomerates that form an international context within the EEC. Here *one* capitalism encounters *ten* national public spheres from which to pick and choose. The internationally entwined media conglomerate is able to quickly ascertain which of the individual EEC countries is making use of the least effective controls, or which will guarantee it the most opportune conditions for expansion. The media conglomerates will be able to synchronize the controls in all countries with the procedure in that country with the fewest controls by means of the EEC harmonization of the media area. The prerequisite for this is simply that the private media grow at a more rapid pace than the political EEC.

In the political discussions of merger supervision and media control, reference is made to the fact that it is quite possible that public controls are failing, but that state planning through specifically directed support measures can also effectively maintain viewpoints of general interest even as against the media conglomerates.[1] Public planning faces a specific difficulty, however. In the Federal Republic, for instance, there are five media oligopolies, including Ullstein Audiovisual (the Springer conglomerate) and Bertelsmann. Each of these oligopolies is in turn entwined with firms in the electronics industry, several of which have their home offices in the Federal Republic, others in the United States, Great Britain, the Netherlands, and Japan. The elimination contests for distribution among these combinations of oligopolies will be decided largely through technological developments that occur internationally in the electronics industry.

It is precisely in the initial phase of development, in which compromises appear to be possible between "common interests" and the specific capital interest of the media conglomerates, that the public planner is unable to determine which of the various coalitions he will promote in the final analysis. For instance, if he attempts to allow subsidies or tax breaks with public funds to the media cartel whose programming seems to him to coincide to the greatest degree with "common interests," or if he makes his authority available to it in the form of state-rec-

---

1. Cf. the minutes of the special party congress of the SPD of December 1971.

ognized educational commissions, he finds himself facing the risk that this firm—even if it conforms its program offerings entirely to the market—will fail because of developments in the technology industry; it need only belong to the wrong combination of international oligopolies. If, for example, the public planner supports the smallest oligopolies so as to encourage competitive economic structures, he must reckon with the fact that later on he will have delivered profits to the owner of the greatest market share, which the latter has accumulated through mergers.

# Excursus 2 to Chapter 4
# Individual Resistance
# to the Media Cartel?

The masses confront the media conglomerate not as an organized body, but as individual users. The business of the media conglomerate lies precisely in anticipating their organizational capacity within its logic. Human beings are able neither as individuals nor within the limited collective forms of the bourgeois public sphere to avail themselves of their central interest in codetermining what happens to their brains. They are reduced to the economically hopeless contradiction between the individual and the media conglomerate.

This contradiction is repeated in the relationship between the editors and programmers, the "media workers," and their conglomerate and the consciousness industry as a whole. In the classical media and traditional cultural production, these employees largely make use of their own means of production; in the case of disagreement they can change their situation, for example, transfer from television editing to the press, from the press to the radio station, from one publisher to the next, and in an emergency rely on the tentative alternative of self-publishing. This all changes in an economic context within which the network of an advanced mass communication, as it is dominated by the media cartel, demands the sort of capital investments that can only be realized in the form of a monopoly. Data banks, television satellites, combinations of several media presuppose concentrations of companies in which the means of production are separate from the living labor power. What changes here is **the working mode of the type of intelligence that produces within the media conglomerates**, precisely because of the specific allowance the media conglomerate must make for its chances for implementing a monopoly, for the actual disposition of the alienated consciousness of the masses, just as it is. **This intelligence must specialize. It is no longer subsumed merely formally by capitalism, but genuinely as well**. This means the division of labor, separation from the means of production, alienation from control of the whole product, being weaned off traditional forms of critique, no immediate contact with actual objects, and so on, as had previously characterized the working mode of intelligence. With this economic integration of specialized components of intelligence into the production process of the media conglomerates, these components also lose their ability to carry out their critique of media production in purely formal forms of codetermination and of company internal statutory struggles that imitate the bourgeois public sphere. Undoubtedly this process does not encompass the theoretical and social-critical forces that continue to function outside the media conglomerates. However, the most advanced communication networks are not available to these processes. Thus even those groups within the intelligentsia that organize their capacity to resist are at the very least separated from the most modern means of production.

Here the violence that emanates from the illusion of the consciousness industry as a whole can presumably not be as easily localized in the media conglomerates as in, for example, the tabloid newspapers. Within the Springer conglomerate, the personal and, to some extent, irrational ideas of the entrepreneur imprint the conglomerate. This corresponds to a phase of entrepreneurial concentration that Baran and Sweezy have described as that of the tycoons.[1] The media monopolies are increasingly less able to leave such a personal mark in the future. In their place will appear an insistent matter-of-factness (*Sachlichkeit*), an apparent social-political neutrality, as is the rule in modern management. The capital investments that the media cartel as it has emerged demands are incompatible with the risk posed by particular idiosyncrasies, a specific political leaning of a conglomerate. This does not mean that individual media firms do not now as before carry on biased propaganda, as does Springer, for example. But in the consciousness industry as a whole, these idiosyncrasies are transcended. The preparation of consciousness by the consciousness industry thus becomes indiscernible and covert.

It is largely impossible for human beings to behave autonomously toward the **varied programs of the media conglomerates**. These programs can, for example, link correct information with the wrong learning methods, valuable knowledge with a biased selection, educational opportunities with the disorientation

---

1. The term "tycoon" refers to the first capitalist magnates, the founders, highly individualistic cutthroats when it came to their methods for realizing their goals and eliminating the competition, tough men who were confused, however, when it came to their personal ideas. This gang extends from Peer Gynt (Henrik Ibsen) and August Weltumsegler (Knut Hamsun), who are only tycoons in their chimeric dreams, to Ford the First, the railroad empire magnates, Friedrich Flink, and Axel Springer. Cf. Paul A. Baran and Paul M. Sweezy, *Monopolkapital* (Frankfurt: 1970): 56ff.

of real experience, entertainment with a class perspective that is contrary to one's own interests. If, for example, difficult educational material is moderated by a beloved entertainment star, as is the case for an American media conglomerate, the media user will transfer his sympathy for the star onto the educational material; the subject-object relationship with which the learner is overtasking himself becomes opaque. Another media conglomerate transfers the propylaeum history of the world onto cassettes; the same selection of images and historical dates is thus programmed into educational cassettes, television programs, educational tools, discussion programs, courses of instruction, and parlor games. It is possible to imagine the uniformity of such a presentation of history by keeping in mind how even today press photos that are distributed by news services overdetermine the polymorphic image world of real political events. This tendency is increased for the media conglomerate because only it can intensify the commodity value of image sequences and the presentations of material through recognizability in such a way that it corresponds to its monopolistic interests in exploitation. Regardless of whether the conglomerate hereby produces a falsified image of history or whether it attempts to evade it through an insistent neutralization, in either case the polymorphism of real history is reduced to stereotypes, and tendentially to a trademark. A similar "processing" results in data banks that are affiliated with a media conglomerate. Investment in precisely this form of media conglomerate is lucrative only if it succeeds in overcoming the oligopolistic phase and establishes a monopoly. It is hardly imaginable that several alternatives will compete with each other here inasmuch as they are not compensatorily structured as public service. The media conglomerate will, however, attempt to fight such public-service competition. **A critique of such a data-bank medium as a whole could be carried out only through the production of alternatives**. This critique is especially difficult when what is at stake is not the correction of individual falsifications or errors, but rather a critique of structural errors in data processing or, for example, the noninclusion of facts or opinions that are represented by groups that are considered unaccountable or anticonstitutional at the moment by the codes of the data bank, or that are not considered for other reasons.

In such cases, where there is a mixture of truth and falsification, almost any reaction is equally unsatisfactory for the individual user. It would be equally pointless for him to cut himself off from a central social source of information and to abandon himself to his own uncontextualized personal impressions, or to declare himself in agreement with the fact that his consciousness is being filled up with information or with learning structures that will destroy it.[2]

One reason for the excessive amount of mixed programming in the media con-

---

2. Here we are not following the tendency to attribute to the media conglomerate the dissemination of only calamity. We are in particular not dealing with a *theory of manipulation*. A human being is cer-

glomerates, both with regard to the masses of users and to their own employees in these conglomerates, is the international entwinement of the consciousness industry. Exchange between the consciousness industries of various countries is played out almost exclusively in the form of **package deals**. In this way, market leaders secure their position at the forefront of the market, while on the other hand weaker oligopolies achieve a certain rudimentary reciprocity of exchange with these package deals. If, for example, a media conglomerate in the Federal Republic wants to include one thousand Hollywood films or one hundred Japanese films in its programming repertoire, it cannot select individual films, but has to accept, along with tried and true film classics (by John Ford, Howard Hawks, etc.), crime films that are nothing less than propaganda for the FBI. A portion of the mixed programming thus comes about mechanically, not as part of any editorial overview, simply because of the form of trade between big conglomerates. This tendency increases in proportion to the development of international concentrations of conglomerates.

The international structure of production and distribution of the media conglomerate simultaneously renders the employees of national media conglomerates particularly interchangeable. It makes available to the conglomerate a reserve army of international intelligence. An increasing abstraction in media production is also tied up with this development. The conglomerates are oriented toward international marketability. The ubiquity of the Walt Disney characters is but one example of the early phase of this development.

Even if individuals do not find themselves in an economic position that is comparable to that of the media conglomerate, from which they could resist (although they actually believe, on the contrary, that they do recognize their own needs and interests preorganized in this conglomerate), they are able to react as a mass. **This unorganized reaction makes itself felt as a specific inertia that acts as a barrier to the expansion of all mass media**. The media conglomerates exhaust themselves against this barrier. It has an objective nature inasmuch as human beings are held by their subsumption within the labor process and initially generate only insufficient attentive energies for the media conglomerate. The budgeting of leisure time sets fixed limits for the interests of the consciousness industry. In addition, there is the resignation and passiveness, the unconscious lack of expectation with which the masses react to leisure-time offerings as long as they are certain that the alienated context of work and daily life will not be altered by leisure-time activity. **The media conglomerates respond to this effective resis-**

---

tainly not one of Pavlov's dogs, who reacts only to stimulation from a consciousness industry; he is, rather, capable of resisting. But the media conglomerate also learns from this resistance. The problem lies in the fact that, in the mix of programming and the processing of his real needs, it is increasingly more difficult for a person to distinguish what his needs and interests are. He is thus not an "omnivore" when he loses the organizational capacities needed for his resisting the highly complex programming.

**tance in that they increasingly add the semblance of willful activity, of an alternative, and of a context of meaning to their product offerings**. At the same time, they attempt to sidestep friction in that they displace their product offerings to increasingly abstract levels of interest that, to the greatest degree possible, avoid contact with real contexts of constraint. They interpellate the need for compensation for the alienation of life and work relationships through the capacity for fantasy and dreams.[3] Precisely through resistance, the consciousness industry acquires a specific ingenuity, while this resistance itself is in turn incorporated into the forms of the media conglomerate, albeit out of context.

If the interests and needs of human beings for self-determining their conscious activity in the face of the media conglomerates can no longer be effectively expressed in the forms of the traditional public sphere, the next step is to assume that at least the **organizations of the masses** could do this. The wait-and-see attitude of the *unions*, for example, toward the development of the media is no different from the recalcitrance of the political parties or of the state. Here what exists is an entire range of what are to some extent contradictory reactions. In a central committee of the Federation of German Unions (Deutsches Gewerkschaftsbund), the members of which are primarily radio and television technicians, the union attitude toward the private-economy media conglomerates is determined by the fact that their primary concern is directed toward preserving the purity of the public-service structure of radio and television. Their recommendation: compromises in the question of new media in exchange for guarantees of the continued existence of the public-service networks. At the same time, a subsidiary of the Federation of German Unions that constructs public housing was already laying the cable that would make cable reception possible in one of their developments. This subsidiary inclines toward participation in the media conglomerate. In an individual union, on the other hand, it is believed that one is behaving correctly if one contains all initiatives regarding new media in order to not enable their further development through one's own activity. Here they trust that the media conglomerate will be derailed by the inertia and resistance of the masses. In the meantime, a large media firm prints up continuing education and work-training courses. These courses are sold to workers who want to move up professionally or to apply for work that requires specific training. The media conglomerate thus makes its profit. The entrepreneur of the company in question, and to which the educational cassettes pertain, displaces to leisure time educational processes that up to this point took place during work time. The cost of producing the cassettes is financed largely with public funds in accordance with the Labor Subsidies Law. Educational programs of this kind would, if they were publicly financed, have to take into account the long-term interests of workers in general education, work-related

---

3. Cf. chapter 1, "The Workings of Fantasy as a Form of Production of Authentic Experience. "

knowledge that will be effective long-term, as well as their interest in mobility (changing their place of employment, vocational rehabilitation). Instead, these cassettes contain narrowly delineated specialized knowledge tailored to the needs of individual companies. Although the union has a fundamental interest in codetermining production of the cassettes, and could support this particular codetermination because of the fact that highly trained workers themselves are in possession of a greater store of the working knowledge that is to be imparted, nothing happens.

It becomes clear where the specific weakness of the union mass organization lies whenever it follows the model of the bourgeois public sphere. It is then sharply separated from the very production from which it draws its strength. While the media enterprise creates products, the union is able to counter these products only with ideas and political demands. The one-sidedness of the products of the media can only be defeated by counterproducts.

*Excursus 3 to Chapter 4*
# The Public Sphere of Knowledge Production and the Media Conglomerate

The constitutional guarantee of the freedom of scholarly and scientific inquiry also contains a standard for the communication structures of the public sphere of knowledge production: it must be organized at base as a public service, that is, it must be accessible to everyone. The formal configuration of the universities corresponds to this standard in that they are public corporations with the right to self-management. Within this legal framework, private relations have repeatedly been crystallized—university teaching positions, the major clinics, the research projects that are supported by contributions from a third party also form quasi-private enclaves. In spite of this, a certain publicity [*Publizität*] has also traditionally been preserved in this part of scholarship. Under the priority of the public-service organization, it has nearly retained early capitalist communication structures—those of the community of researchers—well into late capitalism. This communication depends on contact between individual researchers, their organizations and organs of publication, which are as a rule run as small businesses. Correspondence courses, audiovisual university teaching aids, data banks, university information systems on the industrial scale would have a lasting effect on the **character of this public sphere of knowledge production**. The context within which their work is published cannot be a matter of indifference to the authors of scholarly or scientific works. Up until this point, the author could elude the danger that a work might form the ornamental apex of a private reactionary edifice of knowledge in that he has codetermined the framework for the publication of his work within the pluralism of publishers, journals, schools, institutes, and conferences. The fact that he has delegated the secondary rights to his books to the publisher, or that legal third parties can emerge in the case of scientific and scholarly works that are financed with the contributions of a third party, has no effect on this.[1]

In the phase of the media conglomerate, however, the probability now arises that these secondary rights will be accumulated and fed into data banks, educational programs, and information systems upon whose context the authors exert no influence. One media conglomerate is in a position to support several research institutes. Its commercial information systems sometimes provide information more quickly and comprehensively than those of the public sphere of knowledge production (libraries, specialized journals, conferences, documentation services). In the United States, such knowledge that is recorded in private-industry data banks is out of bounds for the social public sphere because of the fact that although the data banks remain formally accessible to everyone,[2] using them is dependent upon paying fees that only big conglomerates can afford. Here the principle of public access to scholarly and scientific material apparently reaches its limit.

The proper reaction to this danger cannot be the blocking by the media cartel of new research that has to do with scholarly and scientific pursuits. It is hardly plausible that a more effective system of distribution for research information, for which the media conglomerate has at its disposal the economically strongest capabilities, should be excluded simply because individual authors are protecting their copyrights. On the other hand, the organization of a complete body of research material within a system of information presupposes precedents that play a key role in the development of entire disciplines. Questions of the representation of scholarly minorities, contradictory views on teaching, and the problems of interfacing between the disciplines are examples of this. Does the media conglomerate make decisions in these matters according to criteria of production or distribution technology? Does it make any difference which individual researchers the media conglomerate recruits as advisors? All experience would indicate that structurations of this type in the public sphere of knowledge production are transformed immediately into relations of domination.

It is to be acknowledged that perpendicular to the antithesis of student protest versus technocratic university reform, an additional antithesis has formed: the production of knowledge at the industrial level opposes the production of knowledge at the traditional level of specialized craftsmanship. These two trajectories permeate all fronts and phenomena at today's universities. The one is supported

---

1. The university budgets include grants from private industry, nonprofit endowments, and so on—in other words, funds coming out of private budgets. These appear under the heading "Third Party Contributions."

2. The principle of public access enables the results of tax-funded research projects to be stored in the data banks.

by the need of researchers and scholars to apply their historically acquired experience, that is, the historical formation of their productivity, and to return in a moment of crisis to the tried and true forms of expression that they are sure they have mastered. The second trajectory, that of the industrial configuration of knowledge production, proceeds, on the other hand, from the challenge to knowledge production by real relations whose degree of complexity the individualistic mode of production of traditional scholarship based on competitive relationships does not comprehend. Both forms of knowledge production encounter certain limits to their productivity, albeit for opposing reasons. Therefore neither of them can be purely realized. In every university crisis, be it that the teaching facilities are inadequate, or that the legitimation of knowledge production itself is brought into question, regardless of whether it is a matter of qualitative questions or merely quantitative expansion—the responses are always attempted within a contradictory combination of intensified recourse to the configurations of traditional research productivity and the building up of an industrialized production of knowledge. In the course of these expansions and attempts at crisis management, the sluggish institutions of academic self-administration that also find themselves in a particular dilemma of legitimation must fail. What develop are forms of scholarly and scientific pluralism.

It is obvious to think of the pluralistic solution and thus the public-service form of organization for the alliance of the media cartel and knowledge production. The massive exploitation interests of the private media conglomerates that have an especially intense interest in scholarly and scientific material would oppose it. A guarantee of public-service structures of the scholarly public sphere even in the phase of the media cartel would have to prohibit a wildly expanding commercialization of knowledge production by the private media conglomerates. This guarantee would be deduced from the constitutional right established in Article 5 of the Basic Law, which instructs the legislator to economically safeguard that which he legally guarantees. Here the characteristic weakness of public-service guarantees and forms of organization would quickly become apparent—the weakness of any abstract, substance-excluding bourgeois public sphere vis-à-vis the material interests of the public sphere of production. **Public-service organization tends to bring forth from out of itself private relations of power and to privatize itself, just as the private interest of the public spheres of production, that is, that of the media conglomerates, tends to transform itself into public authority.**

It is easy to recognize the weakness of a pluralistic organization of the university if, under present circumstances, one were to examine the overdetermination of the universities by the private enterprise of projects, consultants, and freelancers. Academic authors to some extent work more for third parties—for example, their publishers—than they do for public research and teaching at the university itself. This situation is radicalized to the extent that a developed consciousness industry is evaluating knowledge production comprehensively for the first time. This is reinforced by tendencies such as the exodus of research from the context of research and teaching.

## Public Service or Private Structure of the Consciousness Industry?

Is it possible to maintain the public-service structure of knowledge production, education, and television if, at the same time, most of the other domains of the public sphere are being overdetermined by the private consciousness industry? Would it be possible to at least compensate for the overwhelming influence of the private mass media with public competitive enterprise? In political discussions of the mass media, these suggestions constantly are heard. For each of the individual public spheres whose public-service structure should be maintained, this means energetic reforms, expansions, adaptations. For television, this is a matter of a stronger emphasis on educational programming, greater flexibility in the programs; in the case of universities, it is one of developing a public media cartel indigenous to higher education; in the case of the unions, an intensification of the unions' own professional training and adult education programs. In each of these public spheres—television, scholarly and scientific inquiry, the unions—what is at stake is a bourgeois public sphere that has been carried over into concrete relations. Their specific structural flaws likewise extend into the necessary procedures of adaptation. The weaknesses grow along with the strengths. Thus the recommendation that the media conglomerates be confronted with mere prohibitions or with competition that is merely compensatory do not get to the heart of the problem.

Thus, following the ideas of the culture ministry conference and the universities, a public higher-education media cartel is being planned. With this decision in favor of centralization, difficulties pertaining to agreement between the individual universities are evidently bypassed; a procedure that is part magisterial, part pluralistic, facilitates what seem to be practical solutions. However, with this centralization, the plan excludes the considerable concrete interests of researchers in a public sphere of knowledge production that is organized in such a way that each individual researcher has immediate access to it and that no separation of scholarly and scientific production and publication opportunities occurs. A central public higher-education media cartel separates out the specific public-sphere interests of researchers, which nonetheless should be brought into play against the private structure of the media conglomerates.

The public-service form of organization is an important but relatively superficial means for constructing (from out of the thought of the traditional public sphere) a dam against an excessive concentration of private-economy media. It should not be overlooked that a portion of our society's potential for resistance that cannot be expressed politically is articulated in the public-service or nonprofit structure; above all else, the long-term capital interest can be better expressed in the public-service form than in an open opposition to antagonistic social forces, in the course of which there is no eventual agreement so that the long-term capital interest disintegrates. But the antagonisms themselves are not changed by the organizational shortcut. Now as before they permeate the public-service organization that appears to be uniform, but that is not, in terms of its substance. At the same time, the price that must be paid for the formal unification of all interests in these organizations is that they are expressed in a reciprocally devalorized, pluralistic form. This situation is responsible for the characteristic inflexibility of the big public-service networks, among which the radio stations are not alone. It prevents them from linking the interests that are organized within them (e.g., those of the viewers, the author colleagues, or the scholars in the case of the universities, the workers in the case of the unions) in such a way that their energy really supports the organization. The extent of illusion in these agreements between the organization and those who are being organized is evident in the weakness of these organizations as soon as they come up against real capital interests.

# Chapter 5
# The Context of Living as the Media Cartel's Object of Production

The term consciousness industry[1] includes a number of different groups of organizations:

1. The traditional media, which, mediated by a political sphere, are a product of a lengthy dispute between social interests and the interests of the media in their own growth (for instance, press, publishing, cinema, adult education, radio, television, etc.);[2]

2. Advanced, for the most part privately organized media, such as the cassette industry, videodiscs, cable broadcasting, satellite data banks, and the media cartel. These media have to do with very different types of innovations with extreme-

---

1. The designations programming industry, illusion industry (W. F. Haug), and culture industry (Horkheimer/Adorno) have also been used instead of "consciousness industry." Each of the various designations corresponds to a specific stress of inquiry, and yet they cannot be definitively distinguished from one another. In what follows we will use the term "consciousness industry" as a generic term that refers to the whole of public-sphere work and mass media, regardless of which individual agendas they follow and which programming hardware they use; the individual programming industries such as, for example, public-service television, the private media cartel, and so on, should be differentiated from these. In contrast to these, the concepts "culture industry" and "illusion industry" encompass complex syndromes and qualities of the consciousness industry that we want to analyze precisely in their elementary relationships. It should be possible to break down "illusion" and "culture" into their proletarian and bourgeois components. We will not in the process fail to appreciate that for Haug as well this desire for a more precise designation was decisive in his choice of "illusion industry." But to us it seems more useful to proceed using the term that foregrounds *the specific raw material and mode of appropriation of this industry*, that is, human consciousness.

2. See chapter 3, "Television as a Programming Industry." It should be noted that the public-service-bound television agenda does not extend to a consciousness industry that directly preorganizes

ly diverse effects. The range of products offered by these media rests, on the one hand, on a **transformation of the form of enterprise** (media cartel); on the other hand, we are here faced with **new technical and organizational developments**, which relate to the production of hardware and to its mode of distribution (cassettes, videodisc, cable broadcasting, local FM radio, satellite). It looks like, in the future, videodiscs will be sold as merchandise while cassettes will be distributed through a lending system. Cable broadcasting is based on the principle that subscribers pay a fee to link in to audiovisual information networks. Associated with this are plans for private local radio and television stations. The use of FM for local transmission is extremely expensive, though it does free one from the problems of the international distribution of transmitting frequencies. By contrast, satellite signals can be received everywhere and can be transmitted on an intercontinental basis. Media corporations that are able to implement several of these technologies—or, for that matter, **all of them**, including those of the traditional media—are engaged in establishing **cartels**.[3]

Private media that are organized in a complex way, above all the media cartel, are not as yet factors determining the market in the Federal Republic.[4] As we will

the consciousness of the viewer; it remains in place precisely because of its public-service connection to the threshold of the program offerings, however intensively these offerings may affect the actual conscious activity of the viewer. The socialization effect of all these media in turn builds on the socialization and educational consequences of the parental home, school, professional training, and workplace, which also possess media characteristics.

3. See chapter 4, "The Individual Commodity and Collections of Commodities in the Consciousness Industry." Since what is at stake in the context of this book is the fundamental relationship between this private consciousness industry and the concept of the public sphere, the exposition of the individual plans, models, and statements of fact regarding the media cartels, cassette television, and so on, has been eliminated. For an overview of the rapidly changing situation, see Dieter Prokop, *Massenkommunikationsforschung I: Produktion* (Frankfurt: 1972): esp. 136ff.

4. A statement by the audiovisual subsidiary of the Springer conglomerate, Ullstein A. V., reads as follows: "Since closer consideration has revealed that the electronic audiovisual do not even exist at present, our firm—as is widely known—boldly bypassed this technical impediment and announced that, together with the mail-in photoprocessing firm *Quelle*, it would sell standard narrow-gauge films as 'the ideal launching of the audiovisual future' beginning in the following summer. Since, however, it has in the meantime been determined that these films are still too expensive to initiate the new age, we decided to consider the matter further" (quoted from *Die Zeit*, 2 April 1971). It thus appears as if only the producers of "soft ware," such as Videothek Wiesbaden or Ullstein A. V., are marking time for the present. In part they push forward with production stockpiling, in part they develop preproduction independently. For example, Ullstein A. V. of the Springer conglomerate is developing photo albums in which both text and image "are expanded to the latest state of the art; through simultaneously listening to the appropriate records, the multimedia effect can be increased even further. The photos that are pasted into the album can be supplied upon request in white or chamois, with either a flat or a deckle edge" (*Die Zeit*, 2 April 1971). This situation characterizes the dependence of the producers of the "content" on the current initial stage of the *hardware* industry. However, this hardware can only be introduced onto the market if the simplest, most promising technological processes have been put in place in the research and development departments competition that is currently to be found, since

demonstrate below,[5] one should not conclude from this that these advanced forms of the consciousness industry are not growing. Characteristic of the media cartel's development is that it initially expands only tentatively, but then, after the electronics industry has started manufacturing hardware and distribution networks have been built up, growth occurs at a frenzied rate for a time. In the United States, the media cartel is one of the most rapidly growing branches of industry. The reason that these media initially develop in this way lies in the fact that, although the publishing companies appear to be the protagonists of this industry, the most important investment interests are those of the electronics industry, which produces the hardware.[6]

## The Sensuality of the Classical Media

The traditional mass media have developed, according to a division of labor, relatively independently of one another.[7] Viewed in isolation, they are either not particularly capital-intensive or, insofar as they have great resources at their disposal,

---

mass production begins as soon as the hardware is introduced, and up until that point a development phase in this industry is possible only "in the prototype." The oligopolistic structure of the market contributes to this with extremely harsh competitive conditions between the great oligopolies. This also makes overdetermining planning of this consciousness industry impossible. Since an extremely powerful interest depends in turn on such planning, concealed cartel- and syndicatelike market agreements will sooner or later result here, into which the interests of political, religious, and other groups with claims for a controlling voice could enter. Among these other groups will also be individual institutes for whom the question of the media cartel is of central concern. These institutes are being erected to some extent at the moment (for example, the Institut für Kommunikationsforschung e. V. in Bonn). The outlook toward eventual participation in such a pool, along with the simultaneous fear of no longer being able to win a connection with development, lead to a complication of the discussion and to the willingness to compromise that weakens the position of all groups, in whose interest it would be to unequivocally cling to public-service or nonprofit structures for the consciousness industry as a whole.

5. See the final paragraph of this chapter.

6. One substantial factor is that the organization of the "demand," that is, the context of needs that accommodates this consciousness industry, seems particularly suited to the "export of capital toward within" in the sense of an expanded exploitation of the domestic markets. See the category of "inward imperialism" in chapter 6, "The Latest Stage of Imperialism: Inward Imperialism." There is therefore much to support the contention that the interests of the hardware producers in a high production-expansion of information hardware would also not be sufficient to explain the extremely rapid growth of the consciousness industry in the United States, and that what was at issue here was a general form of expansion within capitalism that *discovers for itself the raw material and the basis for exploitation that is consciousness.*

7. In the case of radio and television, the connection between personnel and institution was particularly strong during the founding phase of television, since at this stage the supervisory bodies had jurisdiction simultaneously over radio and television, and some personnel were transferred over from the radio stations into the television departments. Nonetheless, a medium developed that was independent of radio. What has in the meantime been considered "legal" for radio and for television has referred to precise distinctions and to the division of labor.

are structured like public institutions.[8] They are dependent on the specific traditions, which developed **separately**, of such diverse areas as the educational system, the churches, culture, electronic information storage, freedom of the press, and entertainment. Science only plays a marginal role in these types of media. If one wishes to conceptualize these institutions in a systematic way, one must begin by noting that the majority of them are subsumed under capital; that is, that these media also realize the interests of capital in a mediated way or that, should a conflict arise, they would work to limit the productive force of, for instance, the networks.[9]

**The development of these media corresponds to a reception situation in which people's entire perceptual system is itself, through a division of labor, fragmented. The senses are enlisted in a specialized manner: radio monopolizes hearing;[10] books, newspapers, and television develop reading and seeing, film is concerned with movement (above all in film's authentic phase of development as silent film); and, lastly, education incorporates learning processes, noting, memorizing, and recalling.** Entertainment, education, and information exist side by side as similarly specialized areas, as if there existed specialized systems of perception that corresponded to them. In the process, states of attentiveness, as well as of distraction, are treated like new, specialized senses

---

8. One exception to this is apparent in the case of film, which is organized as a private industry and simultaneously functions with an extreme degree of calculation (exceptions to this are the *Autorenfilm*, the "alternative cinema," and the political film). Nonetheless, the production of the individual films is a craftsman's mode of production in the form of the workshop: planning and financing apply to individual works (with the exception of distribution-dependent productions). For the most part, production management is reduced again after the closing of film production to the diameter of a small office. In spite of the high degree of calculation, what is at issue here, from the long-term perspective, is a seasonal operation that is not capital-intensive. This fact is obscured by the "publicized production costs," which, in the case of film, become a quality of the product and, in the U.S. film industry, for example, make up a substantial portion of the trade value.

9. This is expressed, for example, in the principle of subsidizing that is more or less silently respected by all public-service or nonprofit institutions—that is, they are active only where they do not supersede private business interests. This limits the activities of adult education in particular.

10. Radio appears in retrospect as the medium within which National Socialist propaganda was expressed most effectively. The reason for this phenomenon can lie in the fact that the senses as they emerged historically are mutually correcting. The more comprehensively a mass medium addresses humanity, the less it is able to lie. The concentration of all news and impressions onto one single sensory organ, the ear, renders suggestion independent, in contrast to the way the sensual supervision of everyday human experience normally functions. The effect of radio in the 1930s is codetermined by a series of additional factors. Hearing is the mode of apprehension that can be most intensively developed as a long-distance sense. In addition, the acoustic intelligence, presumably cultivated through interaction with the original objects, possesses a particular capacity for abstraction, imagination, and transferability from one sensual situation into the other. While the eye has the tendency to register everything that it can see as an immediate impression, the ear has historically been trained to differentiate impressions—that is, to understand them as not being immediately bound to a fixed location. It "goes along with them."

and combined into an entertainment sense, a current-events and news sense, and so on.[11] In addition to the five senses, as many new senses develop as there are program products that have gained acceptance among the viewers.

Such a division of labor between the various receptive capacities of a human being was, along with a specialization of the senses, necessary for a particular stage of capitalist production—that stage of the production process referred to as "Taylorism." In this stage, the individual particles of historically evolved labor power are divided up and rearranged for valorization by means of time-and-motion studies and planned work organization. Sequences of movements are separated from the sensory apparatus as a totality so that human beings become available for a new synthesis in the interests of technologized production.[12] The organization of the traditional media corresponds to this organization of the sensory apparatus, an organization that was not originally created by the media. The issue here is that people are incorporated by the traditional media as autonomous beings, although in social terms this autonomy is yet to be achieved. An individual is no longer, as in the case of primary experiences, addressed in all his historical sensory characteristics, of which Marx says: "The cultivation of the five

---

11. Television functions as a gauge for these senses: how much has a certain program cost, which topoi and important personalities (stars, politicians) appear today on the viewing screen, which programs do I recognize as having "an effect on the public," which do I reject as "not affecting the public"—this *sense of programming* largely overdetermines the real sensual activity of the five senses. It attempts to mediate the abstract relationship between the programs and does not proceed from the relationship of the viewer himself to the program. The television journals are engaged above all with these combined viewer senses and attempt in turn to preorganize them for the programming.

12. In the process, the senses that are impoverished in individuals by specialization and division take on a certain regularity that is released from the sensual apparatus, necessary in order for a rich and concrete totality of the sensual apparatus to develop in overall human development. Marx also expresses this ambivalence in relation to, for example, the division of physical and intellectual labor. The human being develops in the course of his or her production within the division of labor (together with the impoverishment of his individual, complex powers) the wealth of generic powers. On the other hand, there simultaneously develops a mutilated movement that does not contain, but rather only impoverishes, this twofold relationship of individual impoverishment and social enrichment: "If it [the class of so-called unskilled workers] develops a one-sided specialty into a perfection, at the expense of the whole of a man's working capacity, it also begins to make a specialty of the absence of all development" (Marx, *Capital*, vol. 1, trans. Samuel Moore and Edward Aveling [New York: International Publishers, 1967]: 350).

In numerous slapstick films from the silent era, public enjoyment (at this point in the history of film, the public was primarily made up of workers, and in North America an immigrant public from the urban lower classes) was due to the fact that in film, a labor experience that is founded on the specialization and impoverishment of the sensual apparatuses (that is, on the rendering independent of sequences of physiological movements without any meaning for the individual) is assembled into a new pattern that does not appear as such in the world of work: the libidinal components of repressed omnipotence, the rapidity of movements, the admitted lack of meaning, the confusion and disorder that are experienced on a daily basis, and all of this within a *context of cooperation*, which even the most rudimentary film plot—as opposed to the management experience of Taylorism—reproduces.

senses is the work of all previous history." This historical second nature is—as in the labor process of Taylorism—dismembered by the media, but it is not put back together at a higher historical level of individuality, that of a socialized human being. He remains, as it were, at a halfway stage, a half-finished social product. He cannot react to the media in a "natural" (that is, historical) way, nor is he a "synthetic human being" who, himself a totality, deals with the totality of all media. In this sense one can say: traditional mass media do not render human beings sensual.

If the organization of the human sensory apparatus is altered because of ongoing developments in production, the media continue, for a time, to give the old answers that have been programmed into them. They share that moment of inertia in the human sensory apparatus that resists change. In the end, however, the media cannot continue to produce the old reception needs of their own accord when people have these needs less and less; it is in the media's own production interest to start searching for new avenues.[13]

## The Sensory Reception Basis of the New Mass Media

Taken individually, the new mass media are merely quantitatively different from the traditional ones; taken as a whole, they are qualitatively different. Initially, innovations such as the cassette industry, the data banks, or the mass communications companies that make up the media cartel indicate the intensification of existing communications processes. They subsume domains that were formerly part of the public sector under short-term private capital interest. This is particularly serious since it is related to the privatization of the infrastructures of the educational realm.

The new mass media are in a position to dispense with pluralism and to deliver

13. These efforts to respond to new forms of perception crystallized, for example, in the WDR's [West German Radio] much-discussed program "Baff," in which the integrated elements of entertainment, journalism, information, reportage, shock, and lampooning (which interpellate the whole perceptual system) are bound up into a total show (*Gesamtshow*). It is assumed that this program exerts a strong effect precisely on young people, but there has been no qualitative investigation of whether this is indeed the case. As a rule of thumb one can say that the more important the networks consider a theme to be, the more intensively they will rely on a traditional mode of reception of specialized sensory information, doing so on the assumption that in this way the viewer will be able to "test" the individual units of sensory information. On the other hand, they permit new forms of expression that are "emotional" but not capable of being precisely rationalized in their form of reception in entertainment or youth programs, which they deem to be of lesser consequence. It is highly doubtful whether solutions that are based merely on an increase in the already overpowering (measured against the nonorganized viewer) means of television will be able to produce a connection between the new forms of viewer perception and the media's forms of expression. Rather, an adaptation of the media would only be possible here in cooperation with self-determining viewers, for whose self-determination the organizational forms and economic framework have thus far been lacking.

their output directly to individuals and households. **Their programs do not merely comprise an abstract all-purpose package ("to whom it may concern") but are able to make individualized needs, the needs of target groups, and thereby whole contexts of living, the object of a focused opportunity for exploitation.**[14] This is why, viewed in isolation, the cassette industry, satellite broadcasting, and electronic data storage merely deliver more perfect forms of existing types of communication; individually, they must contend with the considerable inertia of the masses, whose energy and receptivity are, as before, absorbed by the labor process. They suffer from this friction and are just as incapable of fully realizing the productive force accumulated within them as is public-service television. Things look different when one examines the overall effect that the interaction between these various new media has, especially in terms of the media cartel. **Within this totality of the consciousness industry, the media respond to a changed structure of perception on the part of the viewers, a structure that is not produced by them but by the new production process.** Thus one must distinguish between the initial stage of development of the new media, at which point it is difficult or impossible for these media to develop individually, and their more advanced stage, during which corresponding and qualitatively new potential needs grow among the mass viewership.

Because of technological changes, people today are faced with demands for cooperation of a new kind. The reified traditional division of labor between the individual sensory functions can no longer serve to meet these demands. One must have specialized sensory functions to respond to multiple technical stimuli, and these functions cannot be fully engaged without the remaining sensory activities simultaneously becoming active. Thus, for instance, supervisory and regulatory tasks require having a general overview of all the possibilities for change within the overall apparatus. This type of task does not only demand a specialized sense perception. The response to control lights, to the interruption of individual procedures, the reading of instruments, and so on, constitute a sensory combination that runs counter to the specialization necessary for individual work sequences. This attentiveness is both specialized and holistic at the same time. It presupposes that individual activities are executed with precision, that individual information is exactly perceived, and that this work process involves both a high level of abstraction and a superficial monitoring of the overall situation. In a more general way, even driving a car in heavy traffic entails this specialized, holistic attentiveness. This type of attentiveness does not imply a Gestalt perspective, which would not be concrete enough, or a mechanistic isolation of the individual senses, which would not take the totality of the process into account. The historically developed interconnection between the perception of the meaning context,

---

14. The contradiction becomes clear if one contrasts this with how television emits its transmissions *publicly*—that is to say, aims them toward an undetermined number of receivers.

the specific work situation, physical and mental activity, and the nerve and sensory apparatus is thereby broken and reassembled in the interest of valorization in a manner quite different from the rationalized labor process of the 1920s and 1930s. This rational process still exists today as a nonsynchronous thought, but not as a dominant tendency. The degree of integration of the senses that is actually necessary becomes clear if one examines how susceptible this new stage of production is to interferences and breakdowns.[15]

This changed form of organization, which is marked by the activation and the overstimulation of the **perceptual faculties**, is accompanied by a specific transformation of the receptive forms and the processing of perception. This is due to **shifts in the libidinal realm**, in socialization, and in work motivation. These shifts are caused by changes in the legitimation context and by a tendency, stemming from these changes, toward a reprogramming of the historically learned life cycle. This crisis affects first and foremost the performance principle itself. The postponement of drives in the interest of long-term success is no longer unproblematically accepted. What Lothar Hack has described as the "new immediacy" has emerged: needs must be satisfied immediately, because one perceives that the material possibility for satisfying them is present. The lack of legitimation that many structures of society suffer from; the senselessness; the panic that is expressed periodically, especially by the entrepreneur, that the door is about to close ("the economy is collapsing"); the general mood provoked by the worldwide trend toward inflation—all these factors contribute to the opinion that "one can afford to live because the necessary means exist, and no one doubts that they may not be available much longer if it comes to a crisis situation."[16] The ruling apparatus is unable to counteract this mood— which, after all, is based on real experience—through meaningful, long-term planning, because it is not itself convinced that this system is capable of long-term development. It could derive long-term identification only from the collective history of society, yet this is precisely what must be suppressed by the

---

15. Thus, for example, the difference between "slow go" and normal work in the strike behavior of radar specialists and airplane pilots seems to lie in the difference between the specialized individual use of the senses and their integrated, informal collaborative use. The increase in delays is achieved through isolating the parameters (for example, telephoning instead of addressing someone directly, formal verbal exchanges instead of eye contact, agreement within a parameter that can be recorded on tape, in a renunciation of the constant changing of the parameters that makes it possible to transmit information more quickly, etc.).

16. A similar structural change in the motivational apparatus seems to arise during senseless wars. It corresponds to the mood after 1943, expressed in the commonplace, "Enjoy the war, because peace will be terrible." The ideologies of the dominant class do not reproduce what are merely falsifications, but rather contain even in their instrumental form real experiences inasmuch as they have never been optimistic up to this point. They promise the Twilight of the Gods, the end of the world, and terrible ruin, without this information being perceived in its conjunction with identifications and short-term gratification as part of its own content.

dominant powers. A mass state of expectation, which rests on collective social experience, cannot be satisfied by rhetoric, tricks, or medium-term plans. All this complements the changes in the libidinal and informally organized structure of mass loyalty, which express themselves in undirected movements and dispositions that can, in turn, develop in ambivalent, reactionary, or emancipatory ways. In each of these processes energies are released, while others are harnessed in new ways.

The sensuality of the program and social senses, which have flourished under the production process—like the "sense of possession" described by Marx—continually absorbs earlier forms of sensuality into itself and reproduces them at its level. **Once basic material needs (hunger, thirst, shelter) are satisfied, the empirical needs also have the tendency to produce that unity which is charactistic of them in objective forms of satisfaction. They look for a context of meaning and thus respond primarily to products that provide not individual satisfactions, or individual use-values, but that offer whole cycles of them in the form of a context of living. Under these conditions, the media cartel now makes its appearance from the object side. It amasses all these tendencies and organizes them from the outside.**[17] In a proletarian public sphere, the connection between needs and senses would necessarily be secured by forms of human activity. By contrast, the media cartel organizes the unity of the two by

---

17. If these needs for meaningful immediacy are absorbed from the prevailing relations of domination, what results is a sort of synchronous perpetual present of life without history. I am in a position to fashion my life in such and such a way: if in my real life I come up against difficulties, I will trade in the medium. In this way I appear to be the master of my fate. Instead of "grasping fate by the throat," as even Beethoven still recommended, I will, if anything goes for my throat, seek out another. In this sense I am also the master of time. As the hero in the Western or the gangster film, I have at my disposal prebourgeois predatory instincts; as the chief of the criminal police, in the role of the television politician, commentator, expert, I take part in the industrial disciplining of present time (*Jetztzeit*); as an alien from space, I duck into the future; I have—in a different sense than that of man's year-round state of sexual arousability—sexual encounters at any time, and so on. What is at issue here is not only the fluctuation between real life and the media; rather, within real life itself I am in a position to fluctuate in such a way that I enter into a relationship with a woman in the spring, experience the high point of this relationship with another woman in the summer, separate from a third woman in the fall (in case the relationship becomes too complicated), and reconcile with a fourth woman in winter (still within the cycle of my feelings). I myself have "experienced" the four stages of *one* relationship—only the objects have changed. This new Don Juanism does not have at its roots the libidinal economy that Wilhelm Reich describes; rather, its social foundation is the choice of channels that is one characteristic of the programming senses that have emerged. This is a case of the further development of the human qualities that Robert Musil describes in their zero phase in *The Man without Qualities*. From the perspective of the traditional life cycle of the nineteenth century, this new human quality seems "formless," negative. In reality, it is **positivity with an alternating content**. It is apparent that this syndrome of qualities corresponds much more readily to the abstract system of relations[hips] of capitalism than the "sensuality of possession" that drives classical bourgeois humanity toward the process of exploitation.

relying upon an alienated reality, upon what human beings are not, what stands in their way, acts as the source of their purely abstract unity as individuals,[18] and tears their needs apart. People are united as individuals, but they experience this union through capital. They can recognize each other only via this apparatus. Collectivities are formed, but without self-regulated interpersonal relationships; forms of satisfaction develop, albeit passive ones. That which exists is organized, but there is no autonomous activity. To be more precise: the semblance of this autonomous activity is attached retroactively.

The potential productivity of consciousness, which up until now had been employed only selectively in the labor process, is given a place within the framework of the production process as a whole. Not only work behavior is to be organized according to capitalist criteria of efficiency, but human beings are meant to follow the same principles in their overall behavior outside of the labor process, too. That phylogenetic potential that humans have, one that is determined by the labor process, is to become, at another stage, the object of capitalist valorization.[19] This is why the media cartel is an extreme threat to any self-organization of human experience in the forms of autonomous, proletarian public spheres. **The raw material, out of which the public sphere can form itself, becomes the very object that is processed by the media cartel.**

In discussions of these problems taking place within the mass media themselves, the response is that such an account is exaggerated. The claim is that the media cartel and the impact of the consciousness industry are being overestimated; further, that the growth of the consciousness industry is being held in check by the blockages of the masses in the labor process and in their inherited, reified habits. There is, it is said, not enough leisure time, not enough perceptual and life energy to respond to the media cartel. This way of looking at things provides a particular opportunity for deception and self-deception. It fails to grasp the characteristics of the consciousness industry already mentioned above: its nonlinear, erratic growth. The uniqueness of the industry stems from the fact, among many other things, that when this industry offers up its product to the public, the actual societitilization of the human sensory and consciousness apparatus becomes readily apparent. The opportunities for the development of consciousness and of human capacities become so clear—if the development of the consciousness industry extends over a longer period—**that a private appropriation at the**

---

18. Someone putters around, sits in the corner bar, sits with his wife, engages in recreational sex, plays with his children, goes on vacation, makes use of local public transportation—all of these activities are linked together only by the fact that one and the same person carries them out. These individual, fully heterogeneous partial needs are found in individuals, but they do not form a concrete context of expression.

19. The structures that Adorno and Horkheimer describe or presuppose (especially radio and Hollywood) in the chapter on the culture industry in *Dialectic of Enlightenment* still characterize in this respect a preindustrial phase of the consciousness industry.

**moment of a tangible societalization could be met with insurmountable resistance**. For this reason the media enterprises have already evolved a dual strategy on the eve of this development. On the one hand, it is repeatedly stressed in the press that the media cartel and the cassettes are probably not going to achieve the expected level of success, that they are being overestimated, and, moreover, that means for regulating them will be found in good time. On the other hand, the production needs of the electronics and computer industry, which manufactures communications systems, lead to an aggressive takeover of the market once output gets under way. This does not allow for any gradual integration of diverse social interests, as was, for instance, possible during the infancy of radio and television. The software producers[20] themselves would have an interest in long-term distribution, for only in this way could they direct attention toward new communications systems. The interest of software producers, which is declining in comparison to that of hardware, will not assert itself against the output needs of the industry that distributes communications systems and is, in addition, weakened by the certain knowledge that only accomplished facts can serve to secure the principle of private appropriation. The early capitalist who built the railways had the highest interest in going public, so that he could—thanks to an overestimation of the social consequences of his railway line—obtain credit wherever he wanted. In contrast, the late-capitalist enterprise that runs the consciousness industry must conceal the social effects it has, and must strictly underestimate its influence so as not to erode the base of its private initiative. Almost all publications and broadcasts of the media cartel and the cassette industry are governed by this single-minded underestimation.

---

20. The publicist firms that produce the programming are characterized as "software" producers. In contrast to this, the electronics industry, that is, the "hardware" producer, produces the technological hardware.

# Chapter 6
# Changes in the Structure of the Public Sphere
## Capitalist "Cultural Revolution"—
## Proletarian Cultural Revolution[1]

The manifestations of cultural revolution that are tied to recent developments in China should not be considered exotic and restricted to Chinese society. The cultural revolution in China and protest movements that are emerging in late-capitalist countries have some common elements. Analyses of the connection between the Chinese Cultural Revolution and the counterrevolutionary aspect of recent movements generally tend, however, to overlook the fact that the relations the protest movements are challenging are also undergoing a cultural revolution, albeit with opposite aims and content.[2]

The objectification of structures within human subjects, the historically devel-

---

1. Cultural revolution is the radical revolutionizing of forms of production and thought, customs and emotions, within which life interests are expressed. Capitalism revolutionizes this culture just as radically as this proletarian cultural revolution does—in the opposite direction. In leftist groups, the term "cultural revolution" takes on an unequivocally emancipatory perspective. However, the exclusive use of the concept in the emancipatory sense obstructs a perspective on certain actual developmental capabilities of capitalism. Deciding between capitalism and the proletarian cultural revolution does not take place at the level of words and designations. It is therefore also correct to speak of a capitalist cultural revolution, just as Marx always characterized the revolutionizing of modes of production by the bourgeoisie as a *revolutionary* change.

Capitalist cultural revolution is clearly totally incompatible with that of the proletariat in its substance and in its phenomena. Thus, for example, one cannot say "capitalist *or* proletarian cultural revolution." The grammatical "or" presupposes a possibility of subsumption, an overarching concept, that only history, and not grammar itself, could produce.

2. The Chinese Marxists emphasize this. There is no relationship to the status quo in this fundamental question. Either the proletarian cultural revolution organizes the masses, or the masses "take the path of capitalism."

160

oped cultural organization of the senses and faculties, are themselves a material ground that must be transformed if people are to become capable of making a collective effort to overturn the relations of production. The sensibility of the masses, which has been sharpened because of the cultural revolution, is focused on the two essential crisis points of social life—namely, that one is "prepared for natural disasters and prepared for an outbreak of war." The cultural-revolutionary public sphere, the organized experience of the masses, is meaningful as a type of self-defense against the internal and external nature of human beings and against what is, in the form of the social, capitalist global context, second nature. The enemy confronts the people not just as an external opponent, for instance, as an imperialist, but is also embodied in dead labor, in the people's own prehistory, as well as in human beings and their relationships to one another. The tools of the class struggle itself—consciousness, strategy, the level of societitization, which has been brought about in an alienated manner, the organization of human senses and faculties, indeed, in certain circumstances, party organization—are enemies and at the same time instruments of struggle with which the people free themselves from their opponents. The splitting up of these universal, contradictory faculties by the production of proletarian culture and society demands resistance on two fronts. Such resistance is only possible in a cultural-revolutionary public sphere that recognizes and advances this struggle on two fronts within each individual element of social life.

The splitting of the human being into private and public is bound up with the blind manner in which previous history has determined societitization. Societitization is to be accomplished now in a deliberate and planned way. A public person comes into existence who is no longer a slave to nature, who no longer regresses into the private. In order for this to happen, the modes of behavior that determine the content of human cognition and consciousness must first be transformed, for traditional forms of cognition and consciousness are grounded upon a merely technical relationship to nature.[3] If planning, consciousness, and work are rooted in an egocentric social attitude based on mastery over nature, then the subject-object relationships (nature and all those

---

3. One of the few Western European theoreticians of Marxism to have recognized this entwinement of mechanisms of social domination and exploitative behavior toward nature and developed the full complexity of its theoretical and practical consequences is Ernst Bloch. According to Bloch, society will be able to organize itself by reasonable principles only once the productive powers of history are brought in through nature that has been liberated for coproductivity. Here Bloch picks up on an agenda in Marx, in which the relationship between man and nature is characterized by the dialectic that is inherent to both. The humanizing of nature cannot be separated from the naturalizing of humankind: "Only here has his *natural* existence become his *human* existence, and nature become human. *Society* is thus the perfected essential unity of man with nature, the true resurrection of nature, the realized naturalism of man and the realized humanism of nature" (*Die Frühschriften*, p. 237).

objective complexes that confront the subject as a second nature) that are determined by such an attitude,[4] fuse into one hermetic block. As is the case with external nature, one cannot comprehend the nature within us, the nature of history, of the class enemy, and of one's own people, in terms of its inherent dialectic between subjects and objective complexes through such an approach. Not even the most radical application of the dialectical method can, under the conditions determined by self-imposed reification, develop a double political front. Dialectics in this case become a slogan attached to a practice that excludes dialectics.

In this sense, the cultural revolution, which translated literally means "changing the mission" (*Ko-ming*), is an overturning of the relation of the masses to themselves, to work, and to nature. Nature and social (second) nature of a mankind that is organized in a nonproletarian way must, in this perspective, remain unpredictable until one succeeds, through a cultural revolution, in arranging the senses and faculties of human beings so that they come to represent social tools with which the masses learn to rework nature and second nature, including their own prehistory. Therefore the **object of production** of a society that has been transformed by cultural revolution is not primarily material goods but human relationships, society, the public sphere, and new habits.[5] This is the motive for the repeatedly emphasized motto "politics comes before economics" with which, borrowing from Lenin, Chinese Marxists preface all their individual arguments.

Capitalist development also revolutionizes habits, cultural patterns, the struc-

---

4. In an analogy to social development, one can say that the fundamental structure of the construction of subject-object relationships between people is determined by a relationship between mother and child in which qualitative moments play a decisive role. In the successful bond between mother and child, the mother enters into the nature of the child, and the child into that of the mother. Protection, safety, security, learning the first satisfactions, reciprocal mimetic relationships—all of this is located within a context of satisfying the needs of the child. The first object relations are therefore relations between human beings, and in the case of successful childraising they are not based on domination and control. This interrelationship is not sustained for the remainder of the life process, however. The overdetermining factor, and that which determines the subject-object relationship of adults, is labor within the alienated process of production. Within the subject-object relationship, behavior is opposed to nature as a dominant behavior in that objects are merely the object of processing and control. The human relationship toward the primal object that is acquired early in primary education becomes a means out of whose forces self-domination and the ego are constituted, which are precisely the supports for the technological mode of operation that dominates nature. Within the bifurcated construction of the "cultured human being," the original knowledge of qualitative, libidinous human relationships that include nature lives on as discontent with culture, not as social practice.

5. For Marx, it is not only the mode of production, but above all the *object of production* as well, that is different in socialism from what it is under capitalism. Socialism concerns itself primarily with the production of life relationships, relationships between human beings and with nature, with the production of society; capitalism primarily with the production of material and immaterial goods.

ture of the personality, senses and faculties, and consciousness. The entire production of the last two to three hundred years has socialized people to an increasing degree. Societilization itself becomes a fundamental human need, virtually an anthropological category, because people become ill if they have to live in isolation. On the other hand, this societilization under alienated conditions rooted in nature is always tied to a simultaneous need to be free of these conditions and to regress to private forms of existence. These private forms offer relief from the pressure of alienated societilization. The most virulent expression of this tendency to seek relief is found in National Socialism. In order to prevent the anarchic privatization that corresponds to alienated societilization, a supplementary societilization is imposed in the form of community, *Volk*, and so on, which simulates primary relationships between human beings. In this process, social modes of behavior that have already become outmoded, such as the norms of a society based on plunder, are reactivated. All attempts by bourgeois class society to reappropriate the archaic levels of human and individual development merely result, under the existing conditions of alienated societilization, in repression.

A cultural-revolutionary movement under capitalism does not dissolve the old relations and build new ones. Capitalism has the same relationship of exploitation toward those human faculties that are handed down by tradition as it has toward nature. It moves in two opposing directions: on the one hand, it revives historically obsolete, but apparently securely mastered, earlier stages of behavior and culture, only to dispose of them in the course of capitalism's crisis politics; on the other hand, it abstracts from all historical tradition and from the context of living, and establishes a new beginning in the form of computers and of the closed worldview of the mass media.[6] With each of these changes of direction, with each new impulse, tradition, the security that rests on culturally evolved behavior, and social experience are all lost. This movement of capitalism is mechanical and unintentional. It rests not on analysis and synthesis but on decay and overlaying; it destroys the interests that capital has in an evolved cultural context, just as it destroys proletarian and emancipatory interests. Capital is not capable of reaping the full benefits of its earlier activity if, in its hectic surge forward, it leaves behind its own beginnings. Moreover, it does not leave any structures intact long enough to enable proletarian experience to crystallize and proletarian history to sublate itself. In its mode of operation, in its tendency to destroy the living raw

---

6. Here there emerge as many origins as there are shifts within the process of exploiting capital or in interests of domination. This tendency in the bourgeoisie had already begun in the French Revolution with the new calculation of the year that was maintained for a full five years. *Capitalism can be understood as the period of permanent cultural origination.* In art, this corresponds to the compulsion toward avant-gardism, to the politics of the successive establishments of the Reich and the republic, to an economy based on cycles of crisis, the catapulting of labor power from the work process as well as the pulling of ever-newer reserves of labor power into the labor process, the exploitation of which *is always only begun.*

material of which the cultural context *and* its transformation consist, capitalist "cultural revolution" cannot be reconciled with proletarian cultural revolution. It is directly related to the direction in which capital is expanding at any given moment. The cultural-revolutionary effect of capitalism is different in classical than in present-day imperialism.

## Violence, the Nonpublic Sphere, Objective Illusion, Accumulation

In those regions of the world where it is a question of capitalism's transparent economic interests, for instance in Latin America, the illusion with which interventions are meant to be legitimated plays almost no role. Special CIA units and propped-up military regimes are publicly provided with contracts that protect immediate capital interests.

Things are different with the illusion associated with the American intervention in Vietnam. The statement of loyalty to an ally, of aid to the weaker party and to those under attack, the proclamation of defeats as victories, the systematic destruction of a country, to say nothing of the claim that human rights were being protected—this conglomerate of blatant lies, distortions, falsifications, sentimentalizations, and so on, can sustain itself only within a framework of a public sphere characterized, in essence, by the manufacture of illusion. The effectiveness of this illusion is particularly astonishing because the concealment of material interests is not the primary concern here. When Marx says that the idea has always been ridiculed if it was not associated with interests, it no longer applies to this new form of illusion as it did to that of the classical bourgeoisie: the illusion itself and the violence associated with it take on a material form.[7]

The strictly nonpublic nature of the sites of production, the public-relations activities of corporations, and the consciousness industry provide a third type of example. A power relation develops in these cases that only needs to produce an illusion of violence in order to be effective. People can switch off the televison, they can refuse to believe the public-relations activities of the corporations, and they can freely choose their workplace—all these freedoms are, however, pure illusion. Depending upon how much people make use of these freedoms, they are punished accordingly.

---

7. The ambiguity of the Vietnam War tears apart the lives of concrete human beings. On the one hand, this war has an immediate effect on all of those who are ensnared within it, the American soldiers as well as the Vietnamese, in terms of their existence and their fates. They are killed, wounded, involved in war crimes, crippled. What makes this war into a bloody play, on the other hand, can be seen in the fact that arrangements can be made at the political level simultaneous to the end of the war that either declare the previous action to be meaningless or create a situation that already existed before the war (as in Korea).

Whereas the functions of violence and illusion are thereby in part reversed, all earlier systems throughout capitalist history remain viable as well.[8] The development does not culminate in outmoded phases of capitalism dying away and new ones asserting themselves, but in **accumulation**: there is no linear direction to the development of capitalism, insofar as it is endeavoring to resolve its internal contradictions by means of this expansion. In its place, **there emerges a simultaneity of overlapping attempts at resolution, which can coexist only because they are linked with one another by a level of objective illusion that is inherent to the structure of the bourgeois public sphere.**[9]

## Classical Imperialism and its Public Sphere

In *Imperialism, the Highest Stage of Capitalism,* in which imperialism is described as the "eve of the socialist revolution," Lenin noted five features that have been significant for all subsequent Marxist discussions of imperialism: "(1) concentration of production and of capital, which has reached such a high stage of development that it creates monopolies, which play the decisive role in economic life; (2) fusion of bank capital with industrial capital and the emergence of a financial oligarchy on the basis of this 'finance capital'; (3) the export of capital, as against the export of goods, gains particular signficance; (4) international monopolistic associations of capitalists are formed, who divide the world up among themselves; and (5) the dividing up of the globe among the capitalist superpowers is completed."[10]

When these contradictions take on an explosive form, a world war breaks out. This world war or a social revolution are the forms of public sphere appropriate to this phase of imperialism. They render public the crisis situations that multiplied

---

8. Cf. chapter 2, "The Reversal of the Functions of Power and Illusion."

9. It would therefore be incorrect to understand the function of illusion in highly industrialized societies as a homogeneous quality. The common illusion is rather the result of the disintegration of the bourgeois public sphere, on the one hand, while on the other that of the nonpublic sphere of technological-factual power relations, and, third, the product of a public-sphere labor that is delivered separately, in addition to the nonpublic production and reproduction context of society. Ultimately, it comes down to the fact that the capitalist context of exploitation appropriates the social substance concentrated in the bourgeois public sphere, in forms of education and in the areas of socialization. The contradictions that thereby arise produce their own additional illusions. The reasons for the emergence of objective illusion are therefore extremely varied. The objectivity of this illusion is indicated in, among other things, the fact that, through it, capitalism and all of its public-sphere characteristics are structurally transformed. According to the most extreme impression, the *image of the jungle* is most appropriate to this total context. However, it is actually a matter of extremely rational relationships within an irrational total context.

10. V. I. Lenin, *Der Imperialismus als höchstes Stadium des Kapitalismus*, Verlag für fremdsprachige Literatur (Moscow: 1946): 108.

during the preparatory stages of the war in a nonpublic manner through cabinet politics and secret deals.

At stake during the phase of colonial expansion and the period of classical imperialism that followed it was a dividing up of the territories worth investing in by capital, as well as an attempt to eliminate competition on a world scale. The extreme example of such competition is war between the great imperialist powers. In the majority of cases the classes waging this war cannot achieve their economic and political aims. The imperialist systems are driven economically toward the establishment of a world market, but they are not in a position **to establish this world market politically. This is the reason why a global public sphere does not develop on the basis of the real relations between countries.** Instead, there emerges a global public sphere of idealist postulates, such as Wilson's Fourteen Points, the League of Nations, international treaties as public sphere, which, however, always concern only matters of detail, such as sovereignty over airwaves, territorial waters, copyright, maritime law.

Today this constellation has fundamentally changed. The existence of socialist societies restricts the political and economic foreign-relations activities of the individual capitalist countries to a considerable extent. This also has consequences for the form that the capitalist global public sphere takes: it has become a kind of programming public sphere, whose homogeneity is essentially determined by opposition to the public spheres of socialist societies. This greater homogeneity does not indicate that the problem the capitalist class has in expressing itself politically (which has been discussed in previous chapters) has been overcome. This public sphere is a derived, secondary one, which has all the effective mechanisms of the traditional public sphere and the public spheres of production.

## The Phase of Imperialist Mass Mobilization (Fascism, National Socialism)

National Socialism is inconceivable without the experience of the First World War and social revolution. In terms of arms buildup, war, and competition, National Socialism follows classical imperialism. One can interpret it, based on many of its features, as an attempt to revise the results of the First World War under improved circumstances. However, the social organization of National Socialism is marked by characteristics that go beyond classical imperialism. A whole series of these characteristics relates to the severing of historical ties and the violent destruction of the framework of the "blockaded nation." A manifestation of this is the destruction of the organizations of the labor movement, as well as the rejection of the standards determined by the bourgeois superstructure, such as the constitutional state, ethics, intellectualism. At the same time, that which in classical bourgeois society falls outside the framework of the public sphere—the horizon of experience and the consciousness of the masses, which originated under repressive conditions—is drawn into a process of mobilization. In other words, the political plays a primary role in fascism. Competition arises between the **traditional agencies of socialization**, such as family and school on the one hand, and **socially organized education** on the other, such as Jungvolk, Hitler Youth, Labor Service, Wehrmacht, and Nazi party organizations. National Socialism maintains the parallel existence of both, because it is just as dependent on the traditional products of family ideology, education, and class differentiation as it is opposed to such traditions. In the process, educational institutions and families do not remain intact (as is exemplified by the system of informants, sending children to the country, etc.). On the other hand, the primacy of politics is only an illusion. It does not permeate the economic and social processes in reality because the unifying tendency it contains, an ideology of the *Volk,* only unites the existing contradictory elements on a formal level. These contradictory elements are in constant motion. The system is not based on specific connections between the contradictory elements, but rather on all of them at once. This produces a perennial state of flux which also gives the impression of political mobility, that is, something constant, and at the same time it gives the impression of **dynamism in a system that is inherently static.**

As a result, politics appears to the masses as a spectacle full of twists and turns, as history, even if none of the contradictions are resolved in reality. This interplay with the aggregate of social contradictions enables people to **switch back and forth between their historically inherited identities: they can be robber, policeman, farmer, worker, comrade, soldier, and bourgeois homeowner. In spirit, they return to the simple life while being members of a highly industrialized, armed nation at the same time.** In this respect, National Socialism siezes upon the history that has been objectified within people. It opposes all "decadence," which registers on a sensory level the processes of differentiation within capitalism; it appeals to the "intact sensuality of earlier epochs"—less with regard to the five senses, which are the concrete expression of world history, than to the sense of possession, which constitutes the five senses in a unified form.[11]

---

11. Cf. the interrelationship between the theorem of human shapelessness developed by Robert Musil, which refers to this historical phase, and to the possibility of recourse to an "intact sensuality" as a specific component of a period of decline. In "The German as Symptom," Musil writes: "This need for the unequivocal, repeatable, and fixed is satisfied in the realm of the soul by violence. And a special form of this violence, shockingly flexible, highly developed, and creative in many respects, is capitalism. To describe this I have already advanced the broader concept of an order that takes account of selfishness. The principle of order is as old as human association itself. Whoever wants to build in stone where people are concerned must use violence or desire. This reckoning with people's bad capacities is a bearish speculation. A bearish order is trained vulgarity. It is the order of the modern world." In Robert Musil, *Precision and Soul: Essays and Addresses*, ed. and trans. Burton Pike and David S. Luft (Chicago and London: University of Chicago Press, 1990).

The impulse against intellectualism is related to this. National Socialism does not turn against intellectual labor simply because, as a system based on mass deception, it has to protect itself against possible revelations by the intelligentsia. Under National Socialism, this group would have no opportunity to enlighten the people; it possessed, in any case, no authority among the masses. What happens, rather, is that the close links between the intelligentsia and the bourgeoisie, which had been the dominant class until 1933, are dissolved. This separation is achieved, on the one hand, by the fact that National Socialism integrates a specific, strongly anticapitalist intelligentsia into the ranks of its own propaganda (e.g., the Black Corps), on the other hand, that campaigns of terror were instituted against specific professional groups among the intelligentsia (e.g., the trials of doctors and monks). Moreover, this phase shows that capitalism in the guise of National Socialism is attempting to free itself from the bourgeois class, which no longer appears capable of legitimation. The "Night of the Long Knives" is directed against that which can clearly be recognized as bourgeoisie. In the "extermination of the Jews," a specific bourgeois mode of accumulation is fetishized and, *pars pro toto,* persecuted. This process is favored by the fact that, under the pressure of the crisis, the bourgeoisie itself is in danger of dissolution, of dividing into the most diverse splinter groups—a mechanism that underlies the competitive principle of the bourgeois mode of production. Confirmed once again in their state of isolation, the bourgeois are reintegrated as national comrades. Thus the existence of the bourgeois class is not changed, but rather the class, in having a consciousness of its own, is eliminated as a coherent way of life.

This separation of National Socialist society from its own momentous bourgeois past is also accompanied by a rejection of the notion of a society based on contractual freedom and exchange. **Compulsory exchange is instituted in its place.** This is the most important feature of this period: the property-based society separates itself from the subjective will of the property owners. The direction of the whole is determined not by the needs of the market or of real human beings but by what is produced, by where the needs of historically developed industry are taking it. In the process, the compulsory exchange of society is introduced in a mechanical form: by legal coercion, direct threats of violence, state control and direction of companies, a police state. Violence and propaganda coexist. From the outset it is impossible to say whether the policies of the National Socialists are implemented by violent means or by mobilizing the masses.

During the entire time of National Socialism, the masses could not be convinced that relying upon the notion of a chimerical future in order to sustain presently existing contradictions must lead to a dead end, to war and inevitable defeat. It is defeat alone that retrospectively negates the National Socialist system in the consciousness of the masses. However, this negation involves a process of repression that again destroys the experience connected with recognizing how National Socialism attempted to solve the contradictions of capitalism. Public consciousness associates National Socialism with Stalingrad and the events of 1945. All developments of capitalism that do not bear these marks of defeat are not automatically grasped as an extension of the fascist phase of mobilization. And even with respect to these moments of extreme catastrophe, it is doubtful whether the masses have really become aware of what was being done to them even at the high point of National Socialism.

What is the reason for this incapacity to convert immediate experience into social experience? National Socialism promoted a particular human faculty: a sense for the outstanding achievements of industrial firms, of military apparatuses, and also of individual fighters, for the reorganization of material and human beings. It managed to give workers self-confidence in their own powers—by recourse to forgotten types of past activities: plunder, violence against other peoples, standing the test, using everything one has, playing the hero, but also displaying initiative, being practical, finding solutions, ruthlessly drawing connections between disparate areas, and so on. **National Socialism mobilizes, in a technically effective manner, labor power as a whole, whereas capitalism is capable of exploiting it only piecemeal.** The self-confidence of the masses, which rests on this, is, however, set in motion without regard for their autonomous goals and interests. This very division between power and goals continued to determine the behavior of the working class in the period of reconstruction after 1945.

If an industrial firm is destroyed—as in the years between 1942 and 1945, or in the period immediately after the war when everything was dismantled—it becomes apparent that the workers are soon prepared to rebuild. At this exceptional historical moment, when the goal is to abolish hunger and to boost output, property relations are irrelevant to workers. Yet, in the process, they overlook the essential point: by rebuilding the industrial plants, they are simultaneously reproducing the relations of production.[12] In concentrating on **one single** domain of experience and regarding this alone as decisive, the workers lose sight of the frame of reference from which a proletarian public sphere could be constituted, one that would render the existing system of domination transparent. This individual moment of experience is, without a doubt, of central importance to them. However, in isolation, that which is in and of itself **revolutionary**, in this self-activated type of reconstruction, takes on a conservative function. Only the workers were in a position to rebuild the factories—that was their unique strength.

---

12. Cf. the examples provided by Eberhard Schmidt in *Die verhinderte Neuordnung 1945-1952. Zur Auseinandersetzung um die Demokratisierung der Wirtschaft in den westlichen Besatzungszonen und in der Bundesrepublik Deutschland* (Frankfurt: 1970).

## The Latest Stage of Imperialism: Inward Imperialism

The present scope of capitalist countries' foreign spheres of influence appears, compared with classical imperialism and the imperialism of the 1930s, to be fundamentally restricted. It is true that the so-called underdeveloped territories become, as before, objects of exploitation (capital export, export of commodities, taking over of sources of raw materials, development aid, control of currencies by means of the world monetary system, etc.). But the capitalist countries are no longer faced with the alternatives, in the traditional sense, either to start wars against one another or to collapse.[13] New alternatives are provided through a higher level of organization of capital in supranational economic blocs such as the EEC, capital absorption, inflationary tendencies, and redistribution between the economic, political, national, and supranational sphere of complexes of contradictions that contain the potential for crisis. **Imperialism is directing its energies inward.** In the urban areas above all, it turns even human beings and their contexts of living into an intensified object of imperialist expansion and of the higher concentration of valorization. It does so by means of organization, force, and imposed illusions, characteristics similar to those Lenin described in outward-directed imperialism.

These contradictions are publicly expressed, in a most extreme way, through the colonization of consciousness or through civil war. What precedes and follows this clash is the compartmentalization of the individual and of social groups into faculties that are organized against one another. This is apparent, *in a more basic form,* in the following situations: television suggests an autonomous human being who develops his critical faculties, but yet the public sphere of production provides no room for critique. The consciousness industry and the educational system develop human faculties that find no adequate expression in the labor process. In advanced capitalist industries, the labor power found **within an individual** is simultaneously mobilized and disqualified:[14] the individual fluctuates between states of extreme concentration and ones in which the majority of human senses and faculties are dormant. The tendency toward a complete silencing of the intellect, to the extent that it represents a danger to the system, is paralleled by its

13. This is not absolutely valid, however. Since the energies that both world wars brought forth have not been absorbed, but rather intensified, it is also possible that capitalistic countries will wage war against one another or that there will be a global war against the socialist countries. Cf. also C. F. v. Weizsäcker, *Kriegsfolgen und Kriegsverhütung* (Munich: 1971), esp. the introduction on pp. 3ff. This investigation proceeds on the assumption that the intimidation mechanism upon which the equilibrium of the blocs is presently based can lose its effectiveness in the 1980s. In spite of the newfangled ways out of this situation that are described in what follows, it is therefore an illusion, which has a devastating effect on consciousness, that wars are no longer possible, or are only improbable, on an international scale.

14. Cf. chapter 5, "The Sensory Reception Basis of the New Mass Media."

complete activation for individual functions. Herbert Marcuse's notion of "one-dimensional man" is not sufficient for describing this state of affairs.[15]

The contradictory nature of the public horizon of experience structured by capitalism also strikes individuals who are oppressed by the system and who engage in protest movements against it. It is conceivable—the events of May 1968 in France confirm this fact—that challenges to the capitalist system in the form of strikes, sporadic uprisings, and revolutionary movements are capable of actualizing themselves **at any given moment precisely because** the abstractly aggregated faculties of individuals are inwardly organized against one another. For this reason, a range of human faculties can momentarily coalesce in such movements and turn into a sudden potential for resistance whose power can in no way be explained as deriving from the complex of functionally organized faculties. However, not all remaining faculties are thereby incorporated into the movement. The tendency toward revolutionary unification and transformation of people remains fractured. The revolt movement displays the same fluidity as the system of domination. In this respect, none of the forces associated with the capitalist context of contradictions and its public sphere—neither capitalist nor anticapitalist ones—has the capacity to form a political system. Each of these opposing tendencies—either to revolt against the system or to adapt to it—encounters resistance among the masses. Both of these tendencies lose considerable force because of the friction arising from this resistance. None of the tendencies that will be described below develops without deviating from the pursuit of its original goal: each of these is characterized by its variability and its search for new ways to resolve contradictions, without having either the possibility or the will to transform its foundations. Consequently, both the way in which capitalism manifests itself and the form of the protest movement change. The new tendencies of capitalism thereby become apparent only after the fact, because within the localized settings of individual countries they are overshadowed by earlier levels of capitalist development. It is, however, wrong to interpret this structural transformation of the capitalist context of contradictions from the perspective of its unsuccessful localized variants. Instead, one should trust that the process as a whole will, in the long term, be capable of yielding the most intelligent and, under capitalist conditions, the most progressive solution.[16]

---

15. Within class society, man seems one-dimensional from the perspective of a mature existence that would be worthy of man. As a whole man, he can react here only in a one-dimensional way. The reason for this one-dimensionality lies in the fact that the multifaceted faculties that developed historically in individuals in a variety of ways cannot be organized and expressed in their complexity within the capitalist system. Their real, multidimensionally torn faculties are expressed abstractly and therefore *seem* one-dimensional.

16. Thus, in the Weimar Republic, for example, the attempts made to solve problems made by a Hugenberg, a Brüning, or a von Papen appear to be especially narrow-minded and premature. This in no way alters the fact that they are the expression of a system that then founds National Socialism

## The Transformation of Commodities into Fantasy Values

In his *Critique of Commodity Aesthetics*, Wolfgang Fritz Haug writes: "Henceforth, something doubled will be produced in all commodity production: first, the use-value, second and in addition to this, the appearance of use-value."[17] Based on the relatively high level of social productive forces, this second aspect of commodity production, that of the fantasy value, is becoming more and more important. It presupposes that tangible social wealth manifests itself in a type of **leisure that is not a mere reflex of work behavior**. This is because a fantasy production mediated by commodities has specific types of limits imposed upon it in light of work discipline and the draining of work time of its human content. Society must not just be turned into an **immense collection of commodities** in objective economic terms, but also in a way that can be **concretely perceived by the individual**. The individual must be linked to these commodities not only through physical contact and the consumption of goods, but also through imaginary consumption. It is only then that commodities themselves take on the character of a public sphere. The commodity becomes, as a sensual-suprasensual thing, a means of transforming articles of use into fantasy products, which do not merely function as the object of consumption but indicate a worldview as well. The object of the realization of this commodity on a mass scale is consciousness. The consciousness industry makes use of the economic opportunity, which the overall development of commodity production provides, for its own specialized output. The libidinal fantasies of human beings, their hopes, wishes, needs, are no longer set free, are no longer capable of developing themselves in accordance with random interests, but are concretely occupied with use-values, with commodities. In this process, advertising does not manipulate, it merely seizes an opportunity. The function played by ideologies in the early phases of fascism, since there were scarcely any use-values available for distribution (the estates for the

---

under conditions that have been altered very little objectively. "Progressive" capitalist solutions here have nothing whatsoever to do with the emphatic concept of progress, and under certain circumstances can consist predominantly of relations that are historically outmoded.

17. Wolfgang Fritz Haug, *Kritik der Warenästhetik* (Frankfurt am Main: 1971): 16. See also p. 57: "Capitalism is based on a systematic quid pro quo: all human goals—even mere life itself—validate the system only as pretexts and means (they do not validate it theoretically as such, but rather function de facto in this way economically). The perspective of capital exploitation as the end in itself for which all of life's efforts, longings, drives, and hopes are only means to be exploited, motivations that can be used to ensnare people, and which an entire branch of the social sciences labors to inquire into and utilize—this perspective of exploitation that is absolutely dominant in capitalist society is diametrically opposed to what human beings in and of themselves are and want. To put it quite abstractly, that which mediates human beings with capital can only be illusory." In the following, Haug's categories ("the technocracy of sensuality," the category of illusion, collective practice, and the illusion industry, etc.) are presupposed.

Knights of the Iron Cross were yet to be conquered), today takes on a material, immediately visible form. This form entails the combining of concrete libidinal fantasies, needs, and the psychodynamic economy of the individual, and the integrating, more or less nonforcibly, of this economy into the context of valorization. At this level, it is no longer a question of the mere restriction of the private sphere but of the differentiated forms in which this sphere is valorized as a whole.

The bearer of labor power as a commodity reacts to a compactly packaged product whose individual use-value qualities are concealed. A feature develops in this case that was always a characteristic of commodity production and that expressed itself in the form of packaging and advertising. Both the exotic and the life-style associated with the commodity have always played a defining role in shops specializing in colonial goods, in imported tobacco, and so forth. But it is only at the level of the consciousness industry and of the media cartel[18] that these impressions combine into an overall context of the individual commodities themselves. The shop selling colonial goods merely provides the frame for varied types of commodities; in the department store, in television programming, in the media cartel, and in the total manifestation of a commodity-producing society, the commodities are mediated by the fantasy production linked with them. How powerfully a worldview, an imaginary nexus of meaning, is thereby suggested can be gauged when one imagines how somebody from a noncapitalist society or an underdeveloped country reacts to the range of fantasy products of a highly industrialized commodity world: consider the impact of German television or advertising on GDR viewers or newly arrived immigrant workers.[19] Human beings are subject in this case not merely to a "seduction" that is external to them, for the libidinal forces that impel them toward the commodity nexus are their own. Their imaginative faculty is distracted and simultaneously enriched. The promise of the commodity world, which under the existing conditions of appropriation cannot be

---

18. Cf. chapters 4 and 5 on the consciousness industry and the media cartel.

19. Two different tendencies can be differentiated in this context: (1) the tendential disappearance of the use-value in fantasy value, and (2) the linking of broad, imaginary life desires to relatively limited use-value characteristics. Example for (1): The promise made by Henri IV that every peasant would have a chicken in his pot on Sunday referred to chicken pots with specks of fat. The business of fried chicken franchises, whose hormone-injected chickens are produced at a rate of 33 million annually, indicates that the nutritional value of these chickens has nearly disappeared, and according to the dietetic calorie table amounts to nothing. It is the idea of the chicken that is being eaten here. Example for (2): Almost all cigarette advertising is founded on the inclusion of emotions, universal contexts, undisturbed nature, that is, on desires that exceed the limited horizon to which the use of cigarettes is linked. Both examples concern commodities that are not integrated with other commodities. Only at the level of the totality of commodities, shopping centers, and the media cartel do the individual fantasy values come together. They link up not merely with individual feelings and moods, but with history, the life cycle, and social meaning.

fulfilled, leads people's consciousness to extend beyond the borders of this commodity world.

The individual has two ways of making use of this surplus consciousness for his private existence. He can attempt, either privately[20] or through collective activity (for example, by joining political groups), to break out of society. His other alternative is to satisfy his wishes on his own through education, self-actualization, or the motivation to better himself. Both strategies cannot, as a rule, be pursued. This provides the opportunity for the consciousness industry to assert itself by offering the synthetic third way: it removes libidinal wishes that cannot be satisfied within the system from reality, where they could have a destructive impact on the capital interest. It stops people from searching for individual use-values and confronts them with a balanced totality of commodities that maintain the socially produced libidinal energy in an economic equilibrium.

A mere negation of this nexus, as advocated by progressive forms of cultural criticism, achieves little. Since fantasy production represents a specific mode of action of the majority of workers as well, criticism must work through this fantasy production. Where it remains external to it, the economic exploitation of commodities that are transformed into fantasy values continues without interruption. It is possible to dissolve this nexus only by taking up, within a proletarian public sphere, these promises of meaning and totality—promises that reproduce, in a highly sensitive manner, actual wishes, some of which remain uncensored by the ruling interest—and by incorporating them into the autonomous forms of action of the workers. This necessarily results in breaks and in a consciousness of the difference between a practical possibility for action and one that is merely fantasized in the commodity nexus. This applies not only to the workers but also to the population as a whole.[21]

20. Drugs, which today are linked to a retreat into a subculture; a retreat into criminality, which also leads to its own subculture. The civil, libidinally subdued form of expression: a retreat into the entertainment media. What occurs here is a back-and-forth oscillation: a return to the adaptive behavior of predatory society, demoralization, plans for a new world; the same force can be expressed in shoplifting at a department store, a wildcat strike, or resignation.

21. Cf. Haug, (ibid., p. 158), who identifies the energy that is satisfied in the efficacy of the illusions of the commodity context as potentially socialistic and suggests interpretations to transcend the mass-effectiveness of advertising and the context of fantasy, thereby directing a critique against illusion and its surrogate character. Haug refers here to the "commodity poem of advertising" in contrast to the "impotent antiadvertising of the poets." Actually, the masses are better able to orient their experience around the fantasy content of commodity contexts than around an art that comes into being without their participation. This characterizes an aporia of authentic art as well, but cannot be used against the radicality of advanced works of art so long as an organization of proletarian experience does not take place within the proletarian public sphere. They remain "viceroys" of an autonomous production of fantasy that will comprise social experiential content for as long as the production of fantasy of the masses takes place only within a context of blockage, that is, as long as it is unorganized or organized by capital interests.

## The Conservatism of Feelings and Its Exploitation in the Consciousness Industry

The feelings, perceptions, illusions of the masses, as these have developed within the alienated context of living, are processed in the sensationalist press, pulp novels, television, as well as in the combined product packages we can expect from the media corporations. In this process, the consciousness industry encounters a state of affairs that it has not given rise to: the unequal development of the productive forces of feelings, perceptions, illusions, and of the productive force of the intelligentsia. These factors have different historical tempi and also develop in different directions. Marx speaks of the "unequal relationship of development of material production, for example, artistic production. Generally, the concept of progress cannnot be grasped through the usual distraction."[22]

Authentic artistic and intellectual forms of expression—which are only partially determined by commodity production—have, at various stages of the development of bourgeois society, repeatedly tried to objectify social experience. Organizationally, they are one step ahead of the developing experience of the masses, just as in their creations they also transcend the level of the social productive forces and relations of production. This authentic art remains, however, largely without an audience; in part it speaks to small, educated strata and progressive criticism. While it is producing, the actual producers of social experience, the masses, are incapable of an autonomous reply. A level of differentiation and of organizational capabilities vis-à-vis experience develops, upon which overall social cooperation cannot be founded. So it is not surprising that, under these circumstances, the most progressive forms of articulation of social experience, regardless of whether they are artistic or intellectual, are themselves vulnerable to mutation, and are thus incapable of providing more than outlines and plans.

The consciousness industry is unable to enlist this form of intellectual activity in a direct way. It is precisely the advanced degree of objectification that separates the works of the intelligentsia from the experiential capacity of the masses, which remains unorganized. This is why the consciousness industry attempts to incorporate sections of the intelligentsia in serving its own demands; it trains specialists for dealing with the fantasy production and experience of the masses at the appropriate level of organization.

The articulation of the needs, perceptions, and feelings of the masses occasionally falls behind the level of productive capabilities of society as a whole, of the consciousness industry, and of authentic intellectual production.[23] This does not

---

22. Karl Marx, introduction to *Grundrisse der Kritik der politischen Ökonomie* (Berlin: 1953): 29.

23. These three formal phenomena of the social productive force characterize in turn completely different trajectories and levels of development. *Technical-industrial progress* cultivates abstract governability, "technical rationality"; the *consciousness industry* attempts, through a reconcretization,

apply to experiences and fantasy production per se, which are far and away richer than the consciousness industry and the intellectual avant-garde, but to the possibilities for organizing this experience and fantasy. This possibility to organize depends, for one thing, on the way in which the connection between libido and reality is constructed through authority relations within the family, in primary socialization. In the later course of life at school, and especially at work, it becomes evident that the family situation and the relationship with primary objects are not the principle governing social reality as well. The seemingly intact family context is ruptured either from the outset or, at the latest, when one enters the real work process. By contrast, this family context is still determinate in terms of those needs of fantasy that remain unarticulated and their special mode of organization. The more abruptly family socialization as a relationship between real human beings is destroyed and the person is incorporated into the work process, the less time these fantasies—which are bound to earlier stages of development— have to organize new, more "realistic" subject-object relationships and modes of experience. Because they have never been fully satisfied, they do not have the power to dismantle the old types of authorities (e.g., the image of the father, the longing for an ideal, secure world, etc.) from which they originally developed their capacity for organization; only in this perspective is "love a conservative drive," the activity of fantasy a mechanism that conserves. This is why the political right can rely on the fact that commodity interests, which exploit this state of affairs, work to cement the existing forms of rule, and why attempts by the masses to assert their fantasy can be redirected into conservative channels. The consciousness industry, which takes feelings, perceptions, and illusions as they are, thus almost always acts as a stabilizing factor; as a rule, it strengthens superego structures or identification with roles from the past. **Conversely, the political left must first of all reorganize fantasies in order to make them capable of self-organization.** In the process, it encounters the authority structures mediated in the family, which convey self-forgetfulness and obedience, at any rate an ambivalent relationship toward self-determination. So it appears as though the left has a monopoly on rational language, the capacity for conceptualization, analysis, and abstraction. The political right and the organs of publication associated with it seem, by contrast, to have a monopoly on myths, dreams, and images; in other

---

through its specific "world of entertainment," to attend to the regressive emotional needs of human beings and to exploit them; the authentic *production of the intelligentsia*, particularly that of art, literature, and music, attempts to actualize mimetic experience that has been blocked; it struggles against taking repose in regression as well as the guardianship of technical rationality. It attempts with meager economic allocations to emancipate "the material," the artistic objects with which it deals; its economic means and forms of communication are in any case not sufficient to noticeably alter the relationships between people and this artistic material or the relationships between people themselves in the same way.

words, they control the most important means of organization by which intuition, experience, and wishes can interact with one another in a satisfactory manner.

This situation cannot be reversed by the type of professional intelligentsia employed by the consciousness industry, the advertising agencies, or propaganda departments. This body of specialists is defined by the fact that it deals with the undeveloped fantasies and experiences of the masses and merely administers them. At stake in a proletarian public sphere is, however, a transformation of those forces among the intelligentsia with expertise in the production of authentic artistic and intellectual works. This places them in a position to establish a cooperative relationship between the intelligentsia and the material needs of the masses. Without the process of transformation, which can succeed only on a collective basis, the experiential raw material and the expertise in its organization remain separated. Admittedly, this is only the first phase, for subsequently the self-organization of proletarian experience must take the place of mental labor based on the division of labor between intellectuals and masses.[24]

## The Dialectic of Real and Formal Subsumption of the Public Sphere under Capital

The production process is, as Marx says, the determining factor, and specifically in its polarized guise of labor and valorization. If one takes, for instance, the cassette industry and the media cartel as the most developed manifestations of present-day capitalist production, the following question arises: Which historically new contradictions of capitalist production and reproduction make it necessary for the existing system to integrate the residues of the liberal public sphere, including individual domains of autonomy, into the valorization process?

First of all, it can be maintained that the new stage of societilization of capital, which also leads to an increasing societilization of the directing functions of the production process,[25] results in a one-dimensionality that is fractured because it rests on magnified internal contradictions. As the ruling system is actually stabilized, it becomes increasingly less legitimate. The fundamental contradictions between expanding societal production and continuing private appropriation can apparently be resolved, even just temporarily, only if the valorization interest penetrates into all pores of society.

This new level of societilization can be more precisely defined by two characteristics: first, by the **transition from formal to real subsumption**; second, by a compulsion, corresponding to the stage of development of the productive forces,

---

24. Cf. the assessment of the proletarian cultural movement in the Soviet Union after 1917, in commentary 14.

25. Cf. Helmut Steiner, *Soziale Strukturveränderungen im modernen Kapitalismus* (Berlin: 1967).

toward **increased training of mass labor power, including that of the intelligentsia**.

Marx does not apply the categories of formal and real subsumption of the labor process under capital to institutions. Under conditions of formal subsumption, the capitalist appears as the chief overseer of society as a whole. The realms of the public sphere are under the command of capital and function primarily in its interest. Capital influences legislation via parliament; it influences the content of daily newspapers through advertisements and investments; and it influences the publisher as to the content of his newspaper. Where there is real subsumption, politics and the public sphere adopt the **form** of the capital interest as well (public structural planning to further industrial concentration; the incorporation of periodicals, broadcasting networks, educational programs, and private schools, together with their users, into the media cartel's nexus of products and advertising).[26]

The formal subsumption of the public sphere under capital suggests that the specific mode of production of, for instance, the mass media is related only loosely and often in a merely technically mediated fashion with the capitalist process of production. Under such conditions, it cannot as yet be maintained that substantive activity in these domains of the public sphere is unequivocally integrated into the interest context of capital. Real subsumption suggests, by contrast, that hitherto relatively autonomous domains are integrated into the valorization context and that the use-values, information, and ideologies produced in this context are directly employed to stabilize the system of rule. This does not, of course, mean that such a real subsumption could, in a social system that contains hybrid forms of control over the production of use-values,[27] come into being without a polarizing impact

26. On the concept of formal and real subsumption, see Karl Marx, *Resultate des unmittelbaren Produktionsprozesses* (Frankfurt am Main: 1969): 45ff., esp. 47: "It is in contrast to the latter that we designate the previously noted subsumption of the labor process (that of a mode of production that had already developed before the introduction of capital relations) under capital as the formal subsumption of labor under capital. Capital relations as compulsive relationships, in order to force overtime work by increasing the length of the work period—a compulsive relationship that is not based on any personal relationships of domination and dependency, but rather develops simply out of various economic functions—are common to both modes, but the specifically capitalist mode of production knows other ways for increasing the surplus value. On the other hand, surplus value can only be generated on the basis of an available mode of production, that is, a given development of the productive force of labor and the mode of labor that corresponds to this productive force through increasing the work period, that is, in the mode of absolute surplus value. The formal subsumption of labor under capital is thus appropriate to this as the only form of production of surplus value." And, p. 60: "That which is generally characteristic of formal subsumption remains—the direct subordination of the labor process, in whatever mode it is carried out technically, to capital. But upon this basis, a mode of production arises that is technically and otherwise specific, that transforms the real nature of the labor process and its real conditions—the capitalist mode of production. Once this mode is introduced, the real subsumption of labor under capital occurs."

27. Mixed forms would include, for example, commonly accessible apartment construction, public television, commonly accessible forms of private schooling, the establishment of resocialization and of commonly accessible social work, child-care centers.

on the relevant domains of the public sphere. Indeed it may even be assumed that capital is of itself **not interested in directly subjugating all these domains under the norms of the valorization process**. This applies, for instance, to basic research in universities and institutes, to schools offering general education, and to sectors of art and entertainment. Wherever the individual capitalist incurs costs that, because of more general types of needs can also be met by the state, there is an interest in financing expensive and long-term investments through taxes.

Capital can subsume labor power in a real fashion without transforming itself. If, however, it absorbs institutions, the public sphere, and contexts of living for its enrichment, it then transforms itself as well. Once enriched by this subsumed societal raw material, it is no longer capable of resolving its contradictions according to purely capitalist criteria. As a result of this, there develops a specific dialectic of real and formal subsumption. Examples of real subsumption are planning, the production of use-values of public benefit, the subsumption of intellectual activities in the consciousness industry, the real subsumption of the labor power of the intelligentsia, and so on. A particular area of real subsumption is in the structuring of state policy by means of supranational economic communities such as the EEC, which need to be only formally subsumed in order to bring about the real subsumption of entire branches of industry, sectors of the population, regions, and domains of the public sphere. An important element of this context is, however, the **transformation of realms that are already subsumed in real terms into ones that are merely formally subsumed**. This phenomenon can be found at two diametrically opposed poles of the context of capital. A reorientation of the capital interest is taking place with respect to the family; socialization in early childhood is no longer wholly entrusted to this realm. There is an attempt to determine socially the very earliest conditions amid which human labor power is growing up. In light of this, the regulating of industrial discipline through a total, repressive control over sexuality and eroticism, that is, real subsumption through the inhibition of drives, and so forth, is less significant. The release of sexuality under a purely formal type of supervision is in accord with this tendency toward intervention in early socialization. This is expressed in the manifestations of repressive desublimation, the pornography wave, debates on censorship, etc.[28] At the opposite pole, that of the most abstract form of the capital interest, the EEC, a related tendency can be found. To the extent that major international economic transactions are rigidly controlled, those firms supplying large corporations and individual businesses (down to a gas station), can take on a purely formal relation to capital.[29] In this respect, formal and real subsumption are not mediations of the

---

28. Cf., for example, the farce represented by the "Voluntary Film Self-Monitoring Board," after the monitoring forces that were interested in censorship (church and state) have been eliminated from it, so that now it is the film industry itself that provides official certification that a film is not offensive.

29. See chapter 4.

context of capital that follow one another in a linear fashion, but rather, they complement one another, one merging into the other. The interaction between the centralization and decentralization of the power monopoly, as of that of illusion and power described in chapter 2, have their structural origins in the dialectical relationship between formal and real subsumption.

## Primary and Secondary Exploitation

The theory of disparity is based on the probability that those conflicts that can be actualized are those that are furthest removed from the central power relations, from capital. On the other hand, this theory holds that private property as an institution mobilizes the most effective forces against any attempt at change. Conflicts are tolerated at those points where they are of least danger for the maintenance of capitalist class relations. Such conflicts are located primarily in those spheres that concern not only a single class but all members of a society. This raises the question of context, which has already been posed by Marx in *The Communist Manifesto* and, subsequently, in the third volume of *Capital*: namely the problem of the relationships between primary and secondary exploitation.

When Marx speaks of secondary exploitation, he has in mind, given the economic conditions of the nineteenth century, groups that are hardly the main perpetrators today. In *The Communist Manifesto,* he says: "No sooner is the exploitation of the laborer by the manufacturer, so far, at an end, that he receives his wages in cash, than he is set upon by the other portions of the bourgeoisie, the landlord, the shopkeeper, the pawnbroker, etc."[30] In *Capital,* he relates this in general terms to individual consumption: "That the working class is also swindled in this form, and to an enormous extent, is self-evident; but this is also done by the retail dealer, who sells means of subsistence to the worker. This is secondary exploitation, which runs parallel to the primary exploitation, taking place in the production process itself."[31]

When Claus Offe confronts the disparity between life spheres in comparison to the old class hierarchy as the new form of social inequality, he is identifying an essential element of late capitalism. In the meantime, however, secondary exploitation is no longer restricted to the traditional sector of consumption, nor to the spheres of public poverty (such as transport, hospitals, old people's homes, schools, kindergartens). What is, rather, specific to the tendencies described in this book is the fact that, along with the whole field of leisure, human conscious-

30. Karl Marx and Friedrich Engels, *The Communist Manifesto*, trans. Samuel Moore, ed. and intro. A. J. P. Taylor (London: Penguin, 1967): 88. Cf. also the classic literary representation of this function in Gustave Flaubert's *Madame Bovary* and in the novels of Balzac.

31. Karl Marx, *Capital*, vol. 1, trans. Samuel Moore and Edward Aveling (New York: International Publishers, 1967).

ness itself becomes a target for exploitation. It is precisely because secondary exploitation also takes hold of people's wishes, hopes, and ideas that a close connection is established between primary and secondary exploitation. The latter can also be detected in the classical phase of capitalism, where it has a specific function; however, in late capitalism it acquires a new quality, for it is based on the fact that, in the context of primary exploitation, an accumulation of societal wealth is produced that threatens to become independent of the immediate capital interest. **This new level of development marks the attempt to draw the centrifugal tendency of this societal wealth back into the context of primary exploitation and to make just as much or even more profit here than is possible under the conditions of primary production.** In the process, there is no deliberate linking of the two spheres of exploitation. Rather, they enter into an anarchic, competitive, and contradictory relationship with one another. What is common to them is the interest in maximizing profits. This interest turns them into antagonists. A linear accumulation, a parallel intensification of profit, is impossible. If secondary exploitation is intensified, it draws attention and labor power away from the primary production process. Conversely, the blocking of labor power and of the context of living by the labor process is the only real limit to the expansion of secondary exploitation.[32]

### Tendencies toward an Enrichment of the Context of Capital: Planning, the Institutionalized Production of Use-values, the Context of Living as an Object of Production

If the transformation of commodities into fantasy values involves the mobilization of material illusion, then what is at stake in the following case is the incorporation of realms that have hitherto not been directly appropriated by the valorization interest—realms that accrued to the capitalist production process as if they were natural products. The tendency to institutionalize the production of those use-values that are of benefit to the public within the overall capitalist context—either by making it communal, making it part of the public sector, or by creating public-service organizations—**constitutes what can be experienced even by individuals as a practical critique of the "natural" and universal validity of the principle of private property.** Public-service television,

---

32. In this context the question arises as to whether a bipartite intensification of exploitation will not come up against the spontaneous defensive powers of those who are affected. For until now, it has been precisely leisure time that has served as compensation for the alienated labor process. If this compensation loses the semblance of freedom in that it is again subordinated into the context of economic exploitation—and this will happen even if the mass media cooperate in separately producing the semblance of freedom—capitalism will lose an important component of its ideological legitimation. The result of this could be that the claim to freedom will be carried forward in the process of production.

the housing policy of local authorities, public institutions (hospitals, old people's homes, kindergartens, etc.), are not spheres of production yet, in an environment that is structured by capital, these spheres are perfectly capable of being enlisted in the interests of the system. Capital interests impinge, at an individual level, as suppliers, as producers, and as utilizers of newly created infrastructures, into these domains of public interest. A vivid example is urban renewal. It is public knowledge that private property no longer has the sole initiative in this area. It has become clear that in a series of fundamental spheres of human life, projects planned and organized on the basis of cooperation between private and public funds are not merely feasible, but are the only viable ones that exist. This allows for a concentration of economic forces that could not be accomplished by capital alone. At the same time, superstructures develop against which the individual is impotent. The horizon of expectation of what society is capable of is extended, but it is not organized in the form of autonomous activity by the masses.

These tendencies crystallize around the question of the genesis of labor power as a commodity: in other words, the societilization of education, child-rearing, and family socialization. This applies to preschool education, the expansion of the state school system to include extended social projects. As far as the educational system is concerned, there is no linear development here. The stage reached by the productive forces no doubt demands increasing societilization of those institutions that shape labor power as a commodity. This requires adapting the educational administration, which derives its essential norms from the eighteenth century and its most important contents from the nineteenth century, to the actual state of social development. The societilization of education and training (which is clear from the fact that the system has to finance these institutions through taxes) entails, under existing conditions, the danger that the intended synchronization of school and university with big industry will be subverted through the efforts of these institutions to attain autonomy. What this means politically, especially in light of the experiences of the student movement, is that the students and pupils who are unified through this context can develop communication structures that, in the long term, jeopardize a technocratically based reform of these institutions. Against the backdrop of the advanced consciousness industry and of the media cartel, the reprivatization of education and training counteracts this trend. The purpose of this reprivatization is to overcome the difficulty of achieving a real subsumption of educational institutions under capital by means of technocratic reforms. This is achieved by harnessing learning processes to prefabricated programs on a private level. This would have a dual advantage for the valorization interest. First of all, it would not lead to communicative and collective learning processes; the isolated individual would be confronted with content whose ideological function could scarcely be discussed or critiqued. Moreover, sophisticated, individualizing didactic methods could organize learning processes more rapidly and effectively than any public institution within the educational system could, given the lack of teachers and facilities.

## Intellectual Activity as the Most Important Raw Material and Possibility for the Realization of the New Range of Products

Whereas in classical imperialism the almost limitless exploitation of the earth's raw materials is the object of the "appetite of capital" (Marx), there appear to be limits to the influence on the amount of libido available for inward exploitation. If eighteenth- and nineteenth-century capitalism is concerned with the simple valorization of labor power, which excludes all the remaining faculties and activities of human beings, the consciousness industry concentrates on valorizing the private sphere, a human being's libidinal interests, his fantasy and his consciousness. The theory of the preservation of psychic energy is applicable in this case. It cannot be expanded any more than can a plot of land. **It is unlikely that it will make do, in the long run, with surrogate forms of satisfactions or that it will allow itself to be diverted, by a reality principle in whatever form, from its own type of realism in finding satisfying situations.**

In its early stage until the middle of the nineteenth century, capitalism fed off extensive exploitation. This was followed by the phase of the capitalist mode of production proper, the production of relative surplus value, that is, of the heightened productivity of labor, allied with a reduction of work time. Under the pressures of the present situation, exploitation, upon which the valorization interest is dependent, is being intensified. On the one hand, consciousness, the perception of symbols and aggregates of commodities, and the socially shaped libidinal economy are subjected to a rationalization. Individual needs, however sketchily developed, are directed toward more rapid production and more rapid exchange, toward the reproduction of labor power that brings with it faster satisfaction. On the other hand, the consciousness industry simultaneously—although motivated by an independent profit interest—makes the human brain into the object of its valorization. Third, the productive intelligentsia is alienated from its existing mode of production—which is on an artisanal or, at any rate, manufactural level and which is libidinally charged and focused on the product as a whole—and subsumed under abstract, industrialized work processes. At this moment of development, the intelligentsia experiences what primary accumulation signifies for the working class: the separation of intellectual activity from its means of production. Since the intelligentsia is capable of anticipating this process, it is unlikely that more than isolated groups of intellectuals will allow themselves to be subsumed by this form; others will vigorously resist just such a development. This danger is the material cause for a transformation of the intelligentsia, one that puts it in a position to enter into a cooperative alliance with the mass of the population.

In all of these cases, the human brain is occupied as the core of human labor,[33] the determinant of all modes of production. This gives rise to an explosive contradiction: namely, that, on the one hand, something is to be done, purchased, made known; on the other hand, this same capital interest uses up the basis of these efforts of labor, consumption, and knowledge as its raw material. Through the capitalist valorization of the worker's consciousness, his means for expressing the consciousness of his class position are taken from him. It is true that, in the present situation, these means of expression are partially distorted, blocked, and bound in linguistic forms that do not lead the worker to full class consciousness. Further, every historically explosive situation confirms that the worker can overcome a tendency toward apathy, a divided consciousness, and resignation. This brings us to the stage at which his means of expression, which by and large rest on collective experiences, are taken from him (by attaching them to alien interests). **Objective alienation is joined by an alienation from the awareness of this alienation.** By means of the industrialization of his consciousness, what he thinks, what he imagines, and so forth, are radically separated from what he actually does in alienated labor. Unless alternative forms of proletarian public spheres are formulated and collectively realized under these conditions, the danger exists of a further dissociation of the working class. To be sure, certain factors, some of which have already been mentioned, work to counteract this trend.

Traditionally organized capitalist production was based on the valorization of labor power. Since this was only partially geared to the capital interest, labor power as a commodity related to capital as to something alien or opposed to it. There existed, so to speak, an external relationship that offered the worker a large number of possibilities for evading the interests of capital. Under the new circumstances, a contradiction develops: on the one hand, the context of capital with all

---

33. Cf. Karl Marx, *Capital*, vol. 1, trans. Samuel Moore and Edward Aveling: 178: "But what distinguishes the worst architect from the best of bees is this, that the architect raises his structure in imagination before he erects it in reality. At the end of every labor process, we get a result that already exists in the imagination of the laborer at its commencement. He not only effects a change of form in the material on which he works, but he also realizes a purpose of his own that gives the law to his modus operandi, and to which he must subordinate his will. And this subordination is no mere momentary act. Besides the exertion of the bodily organs, the process demands that, during the whole operation, the workman's will be steadily in consonance with his purpose" (translation modified). And in *Resultate des unmittelbaren Produktionsprozesses*, p. 48: "The general authorities of the labor process, as they are represented in chapter 2, such as, for example, the administration of the objective conditions of labor in material and means as opposed to the living activity of the laborers themselves, are independent of any historical and specifically social character of the process of production, and for all of the possible developmental forms of the attributes that remain equally true, indeed, unalterable natural attributes of human labor. This is irrefutably shown in the fact that they are valid for those who work independently, not in the context of exchange with society, but rather only in that of an exchange with human beings producing nature, such as Robinson, and so on. There are in fact, therefore, absolute attributes of human labor generally, as soon as it has worked its way out of a purely animal character."

its demands and norms is transposed directly and from outside into the worker's intellectual organization and aims at grasping it as a whole; at the same time, pressure within the work process and the earlier forms of the context of capital persist.

To be sure, the linking of the human brain to a particular interest, namely, the production and realization of surplus value, is something specific that cannot be organically connected with his overall physical and mental organization, regardless of how individual faculties and forms of expression may be divided and organized against one another. The overall organization of the human being resists being reduced to *one* interest that presents itself as the whole. In this respect there is a difference between labor power that is controlled by the will, the technical enlistment of the human brain, and its real mode of functioning, which has its foundation in the libidinal economy. The site of living labor, in even its most attenuated form, would still be the human brain. Beneath this threshold, a human being would function like a dead thing. The notion that human evolution could forcibly be made to regress to the amphibian stage is nothing more than an ideology. Total regression—for instance, to an automaton—is, notwithstanding literary invocations (Huxley, Orwell), out of the question. Not even late capitalism would have any use for individuals whose behavior is reduced to mere reactions. From such a reduction of thought and behavior there would develop a situation so diffuse that it could take on an explosive character at any time. In his novel, *The Rebellion of the Hanged*, Traven described this experience as the point of no return: "But as brutally and heartlessly as people might be oppressed, as much as they might be mesmerized by the rumble of drums and trumpets, there is, at any given time and place, a limit, where neither force nor brutality nor divine sublimity nor promises nor demagoguery continue to be effective. Life has lost its value; for man, no matter how lowly, still demands more of life than simply to eat and procreate and toil for the gods, while raising their ire in the process. When the oppressed and tortured man begins to feel that his life has become close to that of an animal's, that it could not get much closer, then that limit has been exceeded, and man loses any reason whatsoever and acts like an animal in order to win back his human worth."[34]

## Proletarian Publicity as a Form of Resistance against Real Subsumption under Capital

"Consistent materialists have nothing to fear" (Mao Tse-tung). It remains to be seen who in capitalist society can afford to be a consistent materialist. In its "materialist instinct" capital follows a path of increasing abstraction. It has the tendency to separate itself from all purely human qualities that hinder the more sophisticated organization of the process of valorization—it separates itself from

---

34. B. Traven, *Die Rebellion der Gehenkten* (Frankfurt: 1950): 196f.

use-values, human needs, the interests of the workers, and, finally, from its own bourgeois class, which brought capitalism into being, and so on.[35] If capital were capable of consistently following this path toward what is as a whole a dead system, toward an ever-purer representation of the context of property and capital, the possibility would exist of eternalizing existing power relations. However, in order to advance along this path, it must increasingly absorb contexts of living, living labor, human raw material. Capitalism cannot avoid dirtying its hands with human beings. Herein lies its extreme instability.

Precisely when capitalism makes human consciousness and contexts of living into its most important raw material, into the site of its realization, it is creating conditions that tend at almost every moment toward a revolutionary explosion. Revolutionary movements also play a role in the specific instability of the societal nexus, although in a different way. During the first phase of every anticapitalist movement, the movement, in stabilizing itself, must fall back on regulative relationships, organizational norms, and the forms of public sphere of a dead apparatus. Life that reacts with violence is not able to organize itself as life; it strives to absorb so many dead, albeit universalizing, tendencies that it becomes unstable. This is why there is, in this phase of development, no balance, no stasis of forces, no status quo.[36]

In contrast to conditions under National Socialism, the organizations of the working class are preserved during the stage of imperialism. Their capacity for articulation, however, is diverted from its main object, namely, proletarian experience as a totality. Without the development of a proletarian public sphere, even the outgrowths of resistance, its rigid characters, serve to strengthen the system. Therefore, the question of organization, correctly formulated, concerns, in Western European countries as well, the core of proletarian cultural revolution: the organization of collective proletarian experience. If this is not organized in the forms of proletarian public spheres, it provides raw material for new processes of appropriation by capital.

---

35. Cf. the preliminary stage of this in National Socialism. In National Socialism, society separates itself from individual attributes of the bourgeois context of living.

36. Marx discussed this problem in reference to the behavior of the revolutionary proletariat vis-à-vis the existing state apparatus: in his analysis of the Paris Commune, he says that the bourgeois state could not simply be taken over, but would instead have to be smashed by the revolutionary class. This is correct, but only with the qualification that a proletarian public sphere is established within the revolutionary class in anticipation of later social functions, in which experience is organized as a vital component without seeking help in the abstract systems of mediation of the class state. If there is no such form of public sphere, the danger exists that in the apparent destruction of the old state apparatus, the old functions are reinstated. The people's commissars become ministers, the soviet officials become low-level bureaucrats.

# Commentaries on the Concept of Proletarian Public Sphere
## 1. The Proletarian Public Sphere as an Organizational Model for the Whole Nation (the Development of the English Labor Movement)

In the first half of the nineteenth century, the English working class attempted to take power in an industrially advanced country. This attempt ended in defeat.

Marx derived almost all the categories of his critique of political economy (primary accumulation, the working day, machinery and heavy industry, joint stock companies) from the English situation. Nonetheless it is striking that there is no political theory of the class struggles in England in the elaborated form of the *Class Struggles in France* and the *Eighteenth Brumaire*. The *Communist Manifesto* too has as its concrete object not so much the German Revolution of 1848 as the English situation. What needs to be done is to update the experiences of this strand of the history of the labor movement, which both made possible Marx's theoretical elaboration and—after its defeat—brought English reformism into being.

In his book *Die Entstehung des Proletariats als Lernprozeß* (The emergence of the proletariat as a learning process), Michael Vester reconstructs the history of the origins of the working class in England during the period from 1792 to 1848.[1] He has shown how cycles of learning and current struggle follow one another in such a way that the English working class is initially fighting above all to consolidate autonomous structures of communication. This has to do with the rights of association and assembly of those incorporated into the particularized context of anarchic commodity production. Between 1800 and 1840 there develops some-

---

1. [Michael Vester, *Die Entstehung des Proletariats als Lernprozeß* (Frankfurt am Main: 1970). See especially pp. 21–23, 174ff., 300ff., 346–49, 357ff., and 394ff.—*Trans.*]

thing equivalent to a proletarian form of communication independent of commodity production, which in part integrates, refashions, and redirects elements of popular culture with a view to the constitution of the proletariat as a class. For its formation as a class for itself, this autonomous communication network, which is independent of bourgeois forms of the public sphere and of state regimentation, is of central significance.

Michael Vester, *Die Entstehung des Proletariats als Lernprozeß* (Frankfurt am Main, 1971), pp. 21f:

"Due to the heterogeneity of the situations, the unity of the working class could only be reached indirectly, as coalition. The development of a communicative countersystem stood in close interaction with the development of substantial objectives. For only intensive, continuous, and broad communication realized in their own press, educational, protective, and action organizations sufficiently made possible the articulation, exchange, examination, and further development of views. The right to communication was a central object of conflict between the establishment and the workers' movement. The flip side of laissez-faire was a strict regulating of the freedoms of correspondence, speech, press, assembly, and association, which was initially practiced violently, later increasingly manipulatively. In fact, specifically oppression, above all under the emergency laws of 1792 to 1818, taught the movement the necessity of better solidarity. As a consequence of this oppression and of the discontinuous progress of the industrial revolution, the workers' movement could not continually expand and develop, but only in cycles that, in each case, ended with a defeat; after their evaluation, a renewed and, in the main, also qualitatively more progressive attempt followed. The evaluation of failures was essentially the task of the leading theoreticians, journalists, and organizers of the movement. And their strategies had to undergo a test relative to their receivability and practical feasibility in the following wave of struggle. The most significant contributions to the theory of the early workers' movement were achieved by the 'workers' intelligentsia,' a group of urban and, in part, rural tradesmen and industrial specialists, either from their own resources or as interpreters of theoreticians who originated from other classes."

pp. 23f.:

"In the first two cycles of struggle (1792–1819), the workers' movement primarily turned against the old oligarchy; through labor-protection legislation or voting concessions, this was to reverse by political means the structural crisis of small producers, which at that time ruled the thinking of the social movement, and restore the old values of individual autonomy and communal solidarity. The oligarchy attributed the opposition movement to ringleaders and not to structural problems. They could therefore suppress the movement only on the surface through their prohibitory measures. In the next two cycles of struggle (1820–32), the workers' movement turned itself toward a new opponent, toward self-consolidating capitalism, and correspondingly reinterpreted its mutualistic, autonomistic conceptual objectives. Now affirming the industrial mode of production, it strove to overcome the capitalist relations of production through cooperative decision-making structures. Parts of the movement, however, still promulgated a restorative anticapitalism, and the majority participated in the election battles of the middle class—thereby aiding those to victory and themselves to disillusionment. Through these experiences, the class consciousness of the workers was consummated, that is, their insight that only through mutual solidarity and independent action in relation to the upper classes would they be able to permanently improve their situation. In its new understanding of the economy, the workers' movement had in fact accepted the effectivity postulate of the bourgeois economy, but not the capitalist form of ownership. The 'moral economy' was replaced by the vision of a cooperative surplus economy. The last two cycles of struggle (1832–48) would bring confirmation of that previously gained class consciousness. From 1832 to 1834, a syndicalist-leaning trade union movement attempted to improve its situation by direct economic action and, in part, to achieve cooperative control over the means of production. Frustrated by lockouts, the movement then attempted to realize its social goals indirectly through Chartist voting rights agitation. Also now, the political and economic means available for struggle were not sufficient for it to constitute itself as a class to the nation. From the 1840s on, capitalism stabilized itself for several decades by virtue of a long, new growth cycle and corresponding political regulation measures such that it could also resist larger disruptions and continually reestablish its objective and equilibrium through automatic control. In contrast, the workers' movement lost its revolutionary will and adopted as its purpose the consolidation of its economic wage agitation organizations.''

pp. 174ff.:
"One month later, on August 16, 1819, the movement reached its high point and turning point. A chain of mass rallies carried out in a disciplined manner raised the morale of the movement and, at the same time, disturbed the establishment. 'The peaceful behavior of so many thousands of unemployed is not natural,' commented General Byng, incensed by the phenomenon of the working classes having begun to solve their organizational problems. The 'transformation of the rabble into a disciplined class' was due not least of all to the experience of failure with underground and revolt actions. The mass demonstrations, with their hundreds of group leaders, bands, banners, and so on, revealed an organized exploitation of the traditions that stood available to the movement, in the form of army veterans, trade unions, auxiliary classes, and Jacobin rituals. On August 16, following a weeklong drilling of peaceful demonstration forms, a mass demonstration was staged on the St. Peters Field in Manchester consisting of 60,000 to

100,000 workers, who were bloodily scattered by the cavalry units known as 'heroes of Waterloo.' The slaughter, since designated as 'Peterloo,' resulted in 11 dead and over 400 injured.

"Both in its actual course and in its psychological aftermath, Peterloo became one of the formative experiences of English history. The shock rested upon the fact that the event fully fulfilled the description of a massacre: the masses were drilled for nonprovocation—on account of which women and children were present—and reacted to the intervention of the hussars with nothing but panicked flight. A fifth of those injured by saber cuts and trampling were women. The very fact that the Yeomanry—the mounted constabulary of Manchester's propertied middle class—were involved gave the action the character of blind class hatred. Peterloo, sanctioned by the government, proved itself ultimately to be a moral victory for the martyrs: the whole of England found that with the attack on the defenseless, the liberal conceptions of 'fair play' were sorely violated; no one could remain neutral; the protest gatherings increased and took place at more locations than ever before; in September, the speaker from Peterloo, Henry Hunt, was received in London by 300,000 people. The emergency laws, which were strengthened at the end of 1819, could not prevent employers and local authorities from becoming more tolerant and finally, in 1824, the impotence of the gag measures was legally recognized with the lifting of prohibitions of association.

"In December 1819, parliament enacted the infamous 'Six Laws,' which aimed at crushing the radical communications system. The laws forbade military drills, again restricted the right of assembly, facilitated house searches, broadened judicial powers, increased the punishment of blasphemous and inciteful criticism, and subjected the radical popular press to a newspaper tax, which raised the price of a single copy to at least 6 pence. The subsequent judicial action, the largest in English history, brought the leaders and journalists of the movement into prison. Political radicalism was incapable of resistance. In the industrial regions, workers equipped themselves with pikes, staffs, and pistols, without considering this to be much more than maneuvers."

pp. 300ff.:

"An important agent was the radical popular press. From 1816 on, there emerged subscription clubs, reading rooms, reading clubs, and informal reading groups, for example, around workers reading aloud at work. The coffeehouses of London developed into distribution points. Into the 1830s, editions, as a rule, ran up to 30,000 copies despite expense-increasing surtaxes. The audience was mustered either commercially (i.e., drawn by sensational reporting) or from specific organizations such as churches and 'Mechanics' Institutes' or from passively or actively engaged individuals. The battle for press freedom was very closely connected with the movement of the working class, the more so as a parting from the radicals of the middle classes became unavoidable with the rise of critical political economy. The pewtersmith Carlile would not be dissuaded from continuing with his periodical *Gamlet* by repressive measures. His approximately 150 helpers, who spontaneously drew to him (and thereby proved the virulence of a commensurate culture), accrued to themselves 200 years of prison sentences in toto. The 'unstamped' press then initiated by Hetherington—that is, the press that refused the statutory newspaper tax—brought the number of persecuted journalists and distributors to approximately 500. The newspaper distributors, among them also women, developed their own 'folklore,' characterized by missionary traits, an unshakable performance in court, and tricks that circumvented the law—for example, the sale of straw, which 'by chance' was packed in newspapers.

"The ideology of the working class, maturing in the 1830s as a consequence of the struggle for communication rights, valued especially highly the freedoms of press, speech, assembly, and the individual. Its enlightened belief in the multiplying effect of the word found its historical confirmation in the rapid expansion of the radical organization, which locally usually rested on a core of tradesmen or specialists, serious and respected representatives of self-taught culture. The general school system was too underdeveloped or decayed to offer points of contact, although the 1820s had brought certain improvements, in the Sunday schools as well.

"The critical media of the muses were foreign to the culture of the tradesmen. Popular theater continued the lively and trivial tradition of the annual fair and could become a site of unrest when, for example, the audience refused to sing the national anthem. Humor and satire and, above all, caricature—which in the meantime had become a highly developed art of allusion—found great resonance and were legally scarcely prosecutable.

"The rather morally reserved basic attitude of the tradesmen corresponded to certain traditions of Methodism and of the Utilitarianism related to it. They concerned themselves chiefly with the natural sciences, moral principles, and political economy and were concerned not to be unreliable sexually, financially, or in family life."

pp. 346ff.:

"'The General Convention of the Industrious Classes of Great Britain' met from February 4 to September 14, 1839, in London and Birmingham and concerned itself above all with violent tactics. The term 'Convention' recalled the French Revolution as well as the English tradition of constitution-amending assemblies. Elected the previous year in popular assembly, the government understood the gathering of the fifty-three delegates as a counterparliament and held the military in readiness. The assembly agreed at the outset not to take part in the free-trade agitation of the middle class; this question distracted from suffrage, and cheapened grain would only result in a lowering of wages, that is, one-sidedly benefiting the employers. Three fractions emerged over the question of which measures should be seized upon rejection of the petition. The legalistic right, around the delegates of Birmingham, soon lost sway. The left, under Julian Harney, began its own agitation for the election of a parliament of the nonvoters, which was to be protected by the armed poeple on its way to the lower house. They were scolded for this by the convention majority. The majority group was led by O'Connor, O'Brien, and Lovett and affirmed constitutional forms of struggle and resistance. In this, O'Connor presumably thought more of street battles, Lovett of demonstrations and legal confrontations. In April, the convention no longer expected a rapprochement by the ruling classes and declared the arming of the people to be justified. During the week of Pentecost, a popular assembly concerning 'ulterior measures' was to occur.

"The growing agitation of the masses in central and northern England provoked countermeasures by the government. By May, it had here come to uncoordinated armed actions and military exercises and to an attempted revolt in Wales. The government mobilized its agents and garrisons. In the country and in several cities, such as Birmingham, it introduced the rural police, previously unknown there. With that, it provoked the increase of armed tendencies among the Chartists. In May, the petition already bore 1.2 million signatures.

"To avoid a violent resolution, the Convention met beginning on May 13 in Birmingham. It answered the government in a manifesto composed by Lovett with the slogan: 'violent, when it so must be.' The manifesto formulated the questions that the popular assemblies were to answer by July 1. This concerned passive resistance such as refusing to make savings deposits, withholding rents and taxes, opposing newspapers, and the general strike; demonstrative measures such as the spontaneous election of Chartist candidates; and finally, sanctions such as 'constitutional' arming and readiness for defense, but only in the case that the government were to begin with violent repression. The delegates swarmed out and received the unanimous agreement of numerous popular assemblies.

"Their great enthusiasm for these measures rested on a mistaken estimation of the attitude of the military. The latter was under the command of General Charles J. Napier, who sympathized with the Chartist opposition against the economic and political establishment. He affirmed the goals, but not the violent means, of the the Chartists, granted the assemblies full freedom and his soldiers the right of participation, which he himself also used. When in July the Convention discussed and decided on the general strike, he paraded before several Chartist leaders the superiority of his own weapons and battalions in order to make clear to them the societal power relationships under which he himself suffered and noted:

'The workers have no means to go into idleness. They will plunder, and then they will be hanged by the hundreds. . . . They talk of physical force. Fools! We have the physical force, not they. They talk of their 100,000 men . . . What could 100,000 men accomplish with their pikes and flintlocks against my cannon shot . . . ? Poor people! How little they understand of physical power! . . . What should I do? Would that I had gone to Australia!'[2]

"In his opinion, the workers needed above all education, bread, and milder Poor Laws. While his officers restrained themselves, he could not always prevent measures of repression by local officials. The magistrate of Birmingham deployed a club-wielding security force of one hundred from London on July 4 against an illegal workers' assembly; the workers hammered these into retreat. Various Chartists, among them Taylor, Lovett, and Collins, were arrested; military and police controlled the city, scattered assemblies, and thereby provoked confrontations and acts of violence against the property of enemies of the Chartists. It did not come to plundering.

"The Convention returned to London, where on June 14 the first reading of the petition had taken place. It was rejected 235 to 46 against Attwood's motion. Disappointed by the result and by the radicalization of Chartism, Attwood withdrew from politics. The Convention was placed before the necessity to act. A protest strike of 25,000 miners from Newcastle against the Birmingham arrests enlivened the general strike debate. Most delegates saw this strike as the first step toward a civil war, which, according to Benbow's fashion, would solve the social problems. On July 16, the general strike was set to commence on August 12. A little later, O'Brien returned from the provinces and reported that the people in fact were not prepared for the general strike. So that those willing to fight would not set off needless blood baths, the Convention announced the transformation [of the strike] into a several-day demonstration, which in fact took place at many locations. Particularly the trade unions, which did not believe themselves to be organi-

---

2. [Vester cites W. Napier, *The Life and Opinions of General Sir Charles James Napier* (London: John Murray, 1857, vol. 2, p. 69) as cited in Max Beer, *Geschichte des Sozialismus in England* (Stuttgart, 1913, p. 341). There is here a degree of source dissonance: in the English edition of Beer, *A History of British Socialism* (London: G. Bella, 1921, vol. 2, p. 74), Beer cites Napier as follows: "'The Chartists say they will keep the sacred month. Egregious Folly! They will do no such thing; the poor cannot do it; they must plunder, and then they will be hanged by the hundreds; they will split upon it, but if they are made to attempt it they are lost. . . . Physical force! Fools! *We* have the physical force, not they. They talk of their hundred thousands of men. Who is to move them when I am dancing round them with cavalry and pelting them with cannon-shot? What would their 100,000 men do with my rockets wriggling their fiery tails among them, roaring, scorching, tearing, smashing all they come near? And when in desperation and despair they broke to fly, how would they bear five regiments of cavalry careering through them? Poor men! How little they know of physical force!' " A fusing of two passages in Napier, the first is a journal entry (p. 63): "Journal, July 25th. The Chartists say they will keep the *sacred month*. Egregious folly! They will do no such thing; the poor cannot do it, they must plunder and then they will be hanged by the hundreds: they will split upon it, but if mad enough to attempt it they are lost." The second is from the referenced page 69, though truncated (beginning in Napier, "[t]hey have set all England against them and their physical force: fools! We have the physical force, not they. . . ."). For the remainder of the quote as it appears in Vester (re: pikes and flintlocks or Australia), I find no reference within ten pages save the allusion on p. 74, the August 23 journal entry beginning,"I was mad not to go out as governor of Australia. . . ."—*Trans.*]

zationally or financially prepared, were called on to participate in order to guarantee a bloodless course of events. It came only to minor incidents, but already in August to the arrest of 130 Chartist leaders.

"As the interest turned again to the local organization, the Convention soon became functionless. It closed with the passing of a 'Declaration of Rights,' which was composed by the emigrant German jurist Schröder. Its 39 articles revealed an extraordinary knowledge of the constitutional literature and legal history of England since the Middle Ages, which were appealed to as witness for Chartism, and were in fact studied and cited by many accused Chartists and simple workers.

pp. 349f.:

"While O'Connor could delay the development in Yorkshire, several thousand Welsh workers attempted a revolt on November 4, 1839. Their attempt to seize Newport, based more on moral than material necessity, became known in time to officials. The workers were quickly beaten into retreat by rifle fire, which claimed ten dead and about fifty wounded. The leaders were accused of high treason, sentenced to death, and reprieved to lifelong deportation. This was the signal for a wave of arrests, which removed nearly all leaders from the Chartists. From April 1839 until June 1840, a total of 380 English and 62 Welsh Chartists were arrested. The action left behind a broken and disorganized movement."

pp. 356f.:

"The only result was that the establishment quickly convinced themselves that, with lower wages, the masses must have cheaper foodstuffs: in 1846, the corn tariffs were rescinded. Cole provides the laconic commentary: 'Strikes during a sinking economy can, however, scarcely have success except when they become revolutions.'

"Chartist agitation separated from the strike movement again ended in persecutions. The government mobilized troops and arrested approximately 1,500 Chartists, of whom about 600 were sentenced in October to imprisonment or exile. In the trial against O'Connor and 58 comrades in March 1843, the conspirators were judged less harshly, taking into account the self-control of the workers given their plight. Thereafter, the membership of the NCA sank below 4,000, and apathy among the now disorganized workers of the north increased to such an extent that the *Northern Star* had to be moved to London."

pp. 357ff.:

"While the 'National Charter Association' was mainly occupied with its land plan, the elections of 1847 and the agitation of the continental refugees in London introduced a new awakening of Chartism. Several Chartists had success in the nominations, and O'Connor was surprisingly elected an MP in Nottingham. In

1844, the emigrants had joined together into their own organization, under whose influence Chartism developed into a section of the international revolutionary movement. Particularly appreciated by the Chartist intelligentsia was Frederick Engels, who had collaborated since 1843 with editors of the *Northern Star* and was accepted as a Chartist. His friend, Georg Weerth, who, like himself, was commercially active in the radical north, had represented the Chartists at the Brussels Free Trade Congress. In November 1847, the London Congress of Communists, at which the Chartists were numerously represented, commissioned Engels and Marx with the drafting of *The Communist Manifesto*.

"Carried along by enthusiasm for the emerging revolutionary Internationale, the *Northern Star* forgot earlier experiences with undifferentiated slogans and declared on January 1, 1848: 'The tactic of moral means is moral humbug when it cannot rely on physical means of force.' The Chartists again began to secretly hoard weapons and conduct military training.

"The French February Revolution triggered excited mass meetings in the entire country, and the NCA assumed the agitation for a new petition and a national convention. Also according to the old pattern, the government mobilized its informants, provocateurs, troops, and police. O'Connor proclaimed the people's charter and land reform as goals and drew up the constitution of a smallholders' democratic republic. He boasted that the charter became meaningful first through his 'firm social program' and already saw himself as president of the new republic. The Convention passed the petition in April and once again held that the people were ready for battle: '—forcibly if we must!' Phrases of violence and uncoordinated preparations for battle caused the government to bring together in London approximately 500,000 soldiers, police, and special constables from the whole of southern England. When the petition was transported to parliament on April 10, O'Connor himself obliged, following its proclamation to call on the 50,000 demonstrators to be peaceful and to return home. Although O'Connor claimed 5.8 million signatures, an investigative commission counted only 1.98 million, among which were many forgeries. On July 3, 1849, the petition was rejected 222 to 17."

pp. 394ff.:

"The changes became traumatic, experienced as catastrophes. The socioeconomic structural changes, the political oppression, and the severe experiences of their own praxis of resistance cut deeply and lastingly into the consciousness of several generations, who were themselves, or through their families, originally rural dwellers. From Paine to O'Connor, yearning for land repeatedly broke through, and the anticapitalism movement bore, in its form of the rebellion, characteristics of a peasants' movement. The land question played a significant role even in Owenism, which, as a decisively pro-industrial tendency, cherished the utopia of the rural environment, leisure, changing venue in labor, and of freedom of movement itself. With urbanization and habituation to the industrial system, the old value patterns were increasingly displaced, and in the crisis of Chartism, the workers turned to a new trade union and cooperative movement. This was more stably organized and more disposed toward peace with capital. The employers for their part could give up their politics of starvation wages as their economic position was better secured and they no longer needed to fear attack on their entire system. The wage percentage of the national income in no wise rose, but the standard of living of the workers began modestly, but noticeably, to climb. In place of desperate mass movements of revolt, formally organized associations stepped in, which negotiated over labor as a commodity and entered into contracts without calling the commodity society itself into question. This change documents, as Hobsbawm substantiates, 'a partial learning of the rules of the game.' Workers learned to view labor as a commodity that, under historically specific circumstances, was to be sold to a free capitalist economy; but where they additionally still had a possibility, they fixed their wage-scale demands, and the amount and quality of labor, according to noneconomic criteria. Industrialists became familiar with the value of intensive versus extensive labor exploitation and also, to a lesser extent, with work incentives, yet still measured the degree of labor exploitation according to standards of habit or experience (by custom, or empirically)—when they did this at all. Hobsbawm dates 'the complete adaptation to the rules of a scientific management' to the conclusion of the great depression of the departing nineteenth century.

"Marxian theory can be understood as one of the results of the long learning process of the emerging workers' movement and also, as Korsch indicates, bears birthmarks of this genesis, for example, in Jacobin accentuations."

The Chartist movement set itself the goal of constituting the nation as a whole in social-revolutionary terms as a proletarian public sphere. This impulse within the English labor movement is quite distinct from the revolutionary activity of the French workers in the nineteenth century, just as, conversely, English capitalism and the industrialization impelled by it asserted themselves more consistently than on the Continent.[3]

---

3. "In England—and the biggest French factory owners are petty-bourgeois in comparison to their English rivals—we really do find the factory owners, men like a Cobden or a Bright, at the forefront of the crusade against the banks and against the stock-market aristocracy. Why isn't this the case in France? In England, industry predominates; in France it is agriculture. In England industry demands "free trade"; in France, it demands the protective duty tax, the national monopoly alongside the other monopolies. French industry does not control French production, and thus the French industrialists do not control the French bourgeoisie. . . . In France, the petty bourgeois does what the industrial bourgeois would ordinarily have to do; the worker solves the problem that would ordinarily be that of the petty bourgeois. And who solves the problem of the worker? No one. This task is not solved in France; rather, it is proclaimed." Karl Marx, *Die Klassenkämpfe in Frankreich 1848–850, Marx-Engels Werke*, vol. 7, p. 79.

Accordingly, what was at issue was not merely the attempt at a political revolution but beginnings of a social revolution. The forms of the public sphere associated with this did not exclude as backward any spheres of society. The movement spread from the industrial centers across the whole country: the bourgeoisie could not simply mobilize the provinces against the vanguard revolutionary movement of the Chartists. The self-confidence and militancy were rooted in the experience that the workers were more capable of organizing production than was capital. This impulse was expressed in particular in **Owenism**, in the willingness of the workers to cooperate in the face of the industrial nexus.

After the defeat of the Chartist movement, the notion of public action by the workers is almost completely reversed. Throughout the subsequent phase, the forms of struggle are trade unionism, Fabianism, and the shop steward movement. There is no longer an attempt to create a public sphere embracing the whole nation; indeed, political struggles on a national scale are avoided. There is an internal link between these defensive organizations. The shop steward movement[4] creates autonomous cells of resistance against capital and the trade union bureaucracy. The most important characteristic of trade unionism is the wholesale particularization of individual unions;[5] it is a form of resistance against the attempt by capital to separate central union organizations, which can come forward as national negotiating parties, from the rank and file and their concrete interests and to drive them on to more and more abstract levels of negotiation. **Decentralization, the way in which struggles are reduced to sporadic issues, the constant search for practical terrains of conflict, correspond to real experience of struggle.** The workers would rather abandon the image of state policy, of the pseudopublic sphere representing society as a whole, than the basis of their own experience. Accusations of political cretinism, the divorcing of the representation of economic interests from politics, revisionism, fail to grasp this process. On the contrary, the development of the universal and thoroughly political ambitions of the English labor movement in the early nineteenth century and the apparent reversal of this ambition in the laborism of the late nineteenth century and of the twentieth century **together**

---

4. Cf. J. Rosser, C. Barker, M. MacEwen, H. Scanlon, K. Coates, *Arbeiterkontrolle und Shop Stewards*, a response by the English working class to the bureaucratization of unions, trans. and ed. by the "Basisgruppe," Wedding, (Berlin: 1969), and Rudolf Kuda, *Arbeiterkontrolle in Großbritannien* (Frankfurt am Main: 1970).

5. This is not contradicted by the fact that all of the unions are consolidated in the TUC (Trade Union Congress). This integration of all workers' organizations, which are also completely heterogeneous, is precisely the social expression of the maintained autonomy of individual unions. Likewise, the corporative affiliation of the unions with their masses of members to the Labour party does not indicate a tendency toward centralization, but is rather an expression of the protective and defensive function of the individual unions vis-à-vis the overdetermining domain of state policy.

constitute the experiential nexus of the English labor movement.[6] This is governed by the fact that the working class in England is faced with a capitalism that is, in economic terms, comprehensively developed. There is no corresponding development in political institutions. On the contrary, these institutions, including the imperial nexus of Empire and Commonwealth, appear especially improvised and geared to nonpublic rule.[7]

This example makes clear how the category of the proletarian public sphere differs from the bourgeois public sphere. In the light of the reflection of the overall English development in its parliamentary and societal public sphere, the period from the Ten Hours Bill to the present emerges as a **slow, linear process of small advances and setbacks**. Development occurs via compromises. Aggregates of proletarian interests are absorbed in the bourgeois public sphere and transform the English public sphere so that, as in the case of strikes, it differs clearly from Continental bourgeois public spheres. The population at large expresses tolerance toward the interests and struggles of the workers and reacts in a disciplined way to disturbances of its own context of living linked with these struggles. On the other hand, the labor movement as well adopts the checks and balances of the bourgeois public sphere. It is this pragmatism, which is regarded as characteristic of the English situation, that underlies the image of progress by small steps. Via this progress, material interests assert themselves against one another, as it were hydraulically, by following the line of least resistance. The picture is not dialectical; it displays hardly any breaks; innovations are not brought about through

---

6. It is therefore incorrect to view the practical revisionism and syncretism of the English workers and their organizations, which have been maintained over many decades, as a consistent character trait. The experience that is bound up in this behavior can have a completely different effect in new situations, and again take up seemingly forgotten components of the English labor movement. This will be obvious if one observes, for example, the practices of the coal miners in their strike in the winter of 1971–72, which deviated completely from Continental labor struggles. An additional perspective that must be included here is the fact that within the framework of an integrated European economic community, the practice of the English labor movement can have a completely different effect than in the English national context.

7. This fact is for the most part overlooked because it is concealed by the everyday, practical functioning of nonpublic mechanisms of domination in the colonies as well as in the home country. However, the most important conquests of the empire were made by societies and individual persons in private capacities. Even the government management of World War II took place in the form of an almost private top management; only partial areas of this policy are subject to parliamentary control and are actually understood under the key word "policy." Apparently the futility of the fascist movement in England was grounded in this limited configuration, even mimicry, which perpetrates the impression of political control in the English tradition. This tendency has determined English politics since the seventeenth century and was the foundation for the emancipation of the bourgeoisie. Cf. Jürgen Habermas, *Theorie und Praxis* (Neuwied & Berlin: 1967): 52ff: "While for Thomas Paine human rights are organized around property, Rousseau's theory is able to express in the form of human rights the metabolic relationship with nature, the inclusion of the human being in the production process, the denaturalizing of the human being, and thus the transcendence of domination."

extremes, but improvements and setbacks appear from the outset to take the middle course.

**This mirroring is, however, a product of the vantage point of the bourgeois public sphere; it does not correspond with the movement of the real experience of the masses.** The latter becomes visible only once one applies the ground rule of the proletarian public sphere: namely, that the public sphere as an organizational form of the societal, collective horizon of experience is not merely a category of the present but absorbs the totality of historical experience. This reveals that experience follows a course of breaks and extreme changes of direction, in other words a dialectical course, even if within the bourgeois public sphere it appears to be linear on account of this public sphere's mechanisms of exclusion. What needs to be investigated is why the historical nexus of experience before the defeat of the labor movement is predicated on a proletarian public sphere that embraces the nation as a whole, and why after the defeat—because of additional experiences—this same "self-confidence" is articulated in the form of particularism. Neither does the offensive stance of the Chartist movement rule out defensive struggles, nor can one correctly understand subsequent revisionism if one regards it merely as a symptom of the decay of the original self-confidence. The unwillingness of the masses to abandon their own experience—their anti-utopianism—points to the fact that a common historical experience, a continuity, underlies these two opposing forms of behavior by the English labor movement.[8]

One result of the historical defeat of this labor movement was the fracturing of a public network of communication under proletarian control. This gives rise to a specific obstacle to the development of workers' interests. Faculties, interests, and sporadic defensive actions fall apart into unrelated fragments. Insofar as the workers and their organizations make use of the universalizing norms and institutions offered by society (such as newspapers, parliament, political parties, television) in order to stabilize and articulate their interests, they are cut off from their experiential base. At the same time, these forms of the bourgeois public sphere, of state regulation, are characterized by a specific lack of substance and by a characteristic **public poverty** (and not just in a financial sense). This makes it especially difficult to ally qualitative proletarian experiences with the universalizations offered in society. If, on the other hand, the workers hold on to the principle of self-experience, then they can only bring together the dispersed fragments of their interests and experiences to a partial extent. New factors must be introduced, for

---

8. Cf. the expectation on the part of Lenin and Trotsky that there would be revolutionary movements in England in the 1920s. This expectation was based on an analysis of the whole historical context of experience, the *potential* that was manifested in the English labor movement. As long as a labor movement does not separate itself from the principle of self-experience, the actual course of history does not say anything final about its underlying potential.

example, impressions about the success of the international labor movement, in order to produce anew the blocked context of the proletarian public sphere.

The bourgeoisie must not support itself by its former experiences. As long as it controls the means of production and the alliance with state power still operates, the ruling knowledge of the moment suffices. Just as its defeats prevent its further development, its victories necessarily act as precedents for future victories. The opportunistic orientation of capitalist production and the abstract context of its public sphere enable a rapid readoption of old experiences after every crisis, just as they ease a sudden change to new practices. Without this state of affairs the violent upheavals within capitalism, to which generations adapt themselves only with difficulty, could not be understood.

The working class's mode of experience operates in the opposite manner. Concrete experiences of struggle, of successful or failed revolutions, can communicate themselves only in the medium of a historical continuum, an inherited framework of ideas and actions. To the extent that internationalism is losing significance, autochthonous developments in individual countries are on the rise. The internationalist horizon of the labor movement is further curtailed by the fact that **international capital tends, economically, toward the formation of a world market, but is prevented by its own barriers from constituting this world market politically.** The internationalist plane is not automatically recognizable as political by the working class, the political class par excellence, because the class enemy does not occupy this plane in reality.[9]

---

9. See Mario Tronti, "Alter und neuer Internationalismus," in his *Extremismus und Reformismus* (Berlin: 1971, pp. 55f.): "We have observed that today the political initiative of capital finds itself in a state of crisis: a specific type of political crisis, whose fundamental causes lie in the failure of an explicit international strategy. The United States is seeking a way, but it doesn't seem to be in a position to find it. The Soviet Union does not seem to be seeking one. Since Kennedy, capital has no longer found an adequate consciousness vis-à-vis the global problematic." "The lack of a cycle of class struggle at the international level is relative above all to the second factor—the low level of political intensity of international capital. The capitalist response is bifurcated. One cannot attribute all of the difficulties that the workers' struggle sees itself confronted with to the lack of a subjective organization. Precisely this lack of organization on the part of the workers is a phenomenon that results from the political backwardness of capital and that to an extent reflects it" (pp. 56f.).

# 2. Lenin's Concept of the Self-Experience of the Masses

The proletariat makes experiences on its own; their evaluation is carried out by leaders, theoreticians, writers, who in their mode of production are located in a substantive and, by intent, emancipatory context but who, in formal terms, constitute a bourgeois public sphere.

It is interesting that in his assessment of the English labor movement after 1917 Lenin sets out from a precise grasp of English experiences.[1] He does not transpose the Russian model onto the English situation, but develops the organizational questions of party building from the need to take into account the specific constellation in England and, in particular, to resolve organizational questions through the **self-experience** of the English proletariat. This need for self-experience on the part of the working class results from the inadequacy of all attempts to demonstrate to the workers from the outside that they have been led astray by traitors and that their interests are not being properly represented. Against this, Lenin stresses the principle—and this in the core of his critique of left-wing communism—that only those experiences are politically significant for the liberation struggle of the working class that the workers themselves make with their so-

---

1. This primacy of self-experience provides an important perspective for the interpretation of Marx's work. The entire experience of the labor movement before 1850 seems to be filtered through its elaboration in Marx's work. Here the separation between proletarian experience and the processing of this experience, a processing that nonetheless is fundamentally based on this experience, is repeated. It is not enough to go back to the classical bourgeois economists, the early socialists and philosophers, in order to understand Marx's interpretations in their context. Rather, Marx presumes precisely the practical experience of the English labor movement—that of the Chartists, for example—which is an experience that cannot be portrayed literarily.

called traitors. They must themselves recognize that their revisionist leaders are through their actions betraying their class interests. The correct theoretical insight that an institution or organization (such as parliament, trade unions, political parties) is **historically** obsolete says little about whether it is also obsolete for the **practical experience** of the masses. So long as reformist solutions of their problems appear possible to the masses, they will prefer these to revolutionary solutions that are laden with risks. They must themselves recognize that the greater risk is associated with reformism (e.g., Kerensky's war policy)—only then will they decide on the revolutionary alternative. A proletarian party is not one that calls itself thus but one that recognizes this state of affairs and acts accordingly.

V. I. Lenin, *On Britain* (Moscow: Foreign Languages Publishing House, n.d.), pp. 466f.:

"On the contrary, from the fact that the majority of the workers in Britain still follow the lead of the British Kerenskys or Scheidemanns and have not yet had the experience of a government composed of these people, which experience was required in Russia and Germany to secure the mass-scale passage of the workers to communism, it undoubtedly follows that the British Communists *must* participate in parliamentary action, that they must, *from within* Parliament, help the masses of the workers to see the results of a Henderson and Snowden government in practice, that they must help the Hendersons and Snowdens to defeat the united forces of Lloyd George and Churchill. To act otherwise would mean placing difficulties in the way of the revolution; for revolution is impossible without a change in the views of the majority of the working class, and this change is brought about by the political experience of the masses, and never by propaganda alone.

'To go forward without compromises, without turning'—if this is said by an obviously impotent minority of the workers which knows (or at all events should know) that if Henderson and Snowden gain the victory over Lloyd George and Churchill, the majority will in a brief space of time become disappointed in their leaders and proceed to support communism (or at all events will adopt an attitude of neutrality, and for the most part of benevolent neutrality, towards the Communists), then this slogan is obviously mistaken. It is just as if 10,000 soldiers were to fling themselves into battle against 50,000 enemy soldiers, when the thing to do is to 'stop,' to 'turn,' or even to effect a 'compromise' so as to gain time until the arrival of the 100,000 reinforcements which are on their way and cannot go into action immediately. That is the childishness of the intellectual and not the serious tactics of a revolutionary class.

"The fundamental law of revolution, which has been confirmed by all revolutions, and particularly by all three Russian revolutions in the twentieth century, is as follows: for revolution it is not enough that the exploited and oppressed masses should realize the impossibility of living in the old way and demand changes; for revolution it is essential that the exploiters should not be able to live and rule in the old way. Only when the '*lower classes*' *do not want* the old way, and when the 'upper classes' *cannot carry on in the old way*—only then can revolution triumph. This truth may be expressed in other words: revolution is impossible without a nation-wide crisis (affecting both the exploited and the exploiters). It follows that for revolution it is essential to secure, first, that a majority of the workers (or at least a majority of the class-conscious, thinking, politically active workers) fully understand that revolution is necessary and are ready to sacrifice their lives for it; secondly, that the ruling classes should be passing through a government crisis, which draws even the most backward masses into politics (a symptom of every real revolution is the rapid, tenfold and even hundredfold increase in the number of members of the toiling and oppressed masses—hitherto apathetic—who are capable of waging the political struggle), saps the strength of the government and makes it possible for the revolutionaries to overthrow it rapidly."

pp. 526f.:

"What is an organized minority? If this minority is truly class-conscious, if it is able to lead the masses, if it is capable of answering every question that comes up on the order of the day, then essentially it is a party. And if comrades like Tanner, whom we particularly reckon with as being representatives of a mass move-ment—a thing which cannot, without stretching a point, be said of the British Socialist Party representatives—if these comrades are in favour of a minority existing that will fight resolutely for the dictatorship of the proletariat and that will train the masses of the workers in this direction, then essentially, such a minority is nothing but a party. Comrade Tanner says that this minority should organize and lead the whole mass of the workers. If Comrade Tanner and the other comrades of the Shop Stewards' group and of the Industrial Workers of the World (I.W.W.) admit this—and in the conversations we have with them every day we see that they do—if they approve the proposition that the class-conscious communist minority of the working class must lead the proletariat, then they also have to agree that this is the sense of all our resolutions. And then the only differ-ence that exists between us is their avoidance of the word 'party' because of a sort of prejudice held by British comrades towards political parties. They cannot con-ceive of a political party being anything else than a replica of the parties of Gompers and Henderson, of parliamentary bosses and traitors to the working class. And if they imagine parliamentarism to be what it actually is in Britain and America today, then we too are opposed to such parliamentarism and such politi-cal parties. What we need is new parties, different parties. We need parties that will be in constant and real contact with the masses and that will be able to lead these masses."

pp. 462f.:

"But the writer of the letter does not even ask, does not deem it necessary to ask, whether it is possible to bring about the victory of the Soviets over Parliament without getting politicians who stand for Soviets *into* Parliament, without disintegrating parliamentarism *from within*, without working within Parliament for the success of the Soviets in their forthcoming task of dispersing Parliament. And yet the writer of the letter expresses the absolutely correct idea that the Communist Party in Britain must work along *scientific* lines. Science demands, firstly, that account be taken of the experience of other countries, especially if these other, also capitalist, countries are undergoing, or have recently undergone, a very similar experience; secondly, it demands that account be taken of *all* the forces, groups, parties, classes and masses operating in the given country, and not that policy be determined by just the desires and views, by the degree of class consciousness and readiness for battle of just one group or party.

pp. 528f.:

"But in this case, in regard to the British Labour Party, it is only a matter of the advanced minority of the British workers collaborating with the overwhelming majority. The members of the Labour Party are all members of trade unions. The structure of this party is very peculiar, unlike that in any other country. This organization embraces 4 million of the 6 to 7 million workers belonging to the trade unions. They are not asked what their political convictions are. Let Comrade Serrati prove to me that somebody will prevent us from exercising the right of criticism. Only when you prove that will you prove Comrade McLaine to be wrong. The British Socialist Party can freely say that Henderson is a traitor and yet remain within the ranks of the Labour Party. What we get here is collaboration between the vanguard of the working class and the backward workers—the rearguard. This collaboration is so important for the whole movement that we categorically insist that the British Communists should serve as a connecting link between the Party, i.e., the minority of the working class, and all the rest of the workers. If the minority is unable to lead the masses, to link up closely with them, then it is not a party and is of no value whatever, no matter whether it calls itself a party or the Shop Stewards' National Council—so far as I know the Shop Stewards' Committees in Britain have their National Council, their central leadership, and that is already a step in the direction of a party. Hence if it is not disproved that the British Labour Party consists of proletarians, then we get collaboration between the vanguard of the working class and the backward workers; and if this collaboration is not undertaken systematically, the Communist Party will be worthless and then there can be no question of the dictatorship of the proletariat. And if our Italian comrades cannot advance more convincing arguments, then we shall have later on to finally settle the question here on the basis of what we know, and we shall come to the conclusion that affiliation is the correct tactics.

# 3. The Ideology of the Camp: The Public Sphere of the Working Class as a Society within Society

One of the defining characteristics of the empirical public sphere of the working class, both of its maximalist positions as of the communist and social-democratic parties of Western Europe, consists in the fact that it views society as divided into two great camps. Such a division does indeed exist. It is in part called for by the ruling classes. What concerns us is not how this division can be overcome but to demonstrate that the division fostered by the system cannot be made into an affirmative strategic-political element of the interests of the working class without abandoning the universal goal, indispensable for the class struggle, of a new organization of society as a whole.

The concept of camp can already be found in Marx, albeit with a specific meaning. He says in *The Communist Manifesto:* "Our epoch, the epoch of the bourgeoisie, possesses, however, this distinctive feature: it has simplified the class antagonisms. Society as a whole is more and more splitting up into two great hostile camps, into two great classes directly facing each other: bourgeoisie and proletariat."[1]

Marx is here speaking of camps as two great classes "directly facing each other," in other words, that are linked with one another by class struggle. This is no doubt not so much an analytical statement about the overall class structure of bourgeois society as a reference to a practical constellation of antagonistic social forces. What is elaborated here is a political-revolutionary contradiction, not the

---

1. Karl Marx and Frederick Engels, *The Communist Manifesto*, trans. Samuel Moore, ed. and intro. A. J. P. Taylor (London: Penguin, 1967): p. 80.

element that actually constitutes society. If the classes themselves were, each for itself, the constitutive element of society, this would already be the moment of decision. However, one class with a developed mode of production, the bourgeoisie, is confronting the other camp, which has no mode of production of its own. The proletariat cannot be understood as a camp because it lacks an essential factor, namely control over material production. This is why the "camp" cannot be seen as something positive within which one can establish oneself—even if only with a view to anticipated struggles.

The concept of camp is today mainly used in an international context. One important element of the self-image of the whole Eastern bloc consists in the repeated affirmation of the common interests of the socialist camp. But there is being repeated here at a global level what, in its structure, already occurred in the individual Communist parties in the late 1920s. The autonomy of production in an individual socialist country is abstract. Even if a total closing off in the economic field were to succeed, if trade with capitalist economies were not necessary, the political-military pressure of the capitalist powers would suffice to distort the production of the socialist camp. A socialism of heavy industry is not merely a planning decision but was, at a specific historical moment, the necessary response to enormous capitalist pressure.

As a result of this pressure, there develops a spiraling demand for security and delimitation. This demand creates a permanent compulsion toward the mediation of all forces that stand outside the camp but in some respect feel themselves to be allied with its interests, and it makes clear options necessary for each individual and party. Within this camp mentality, differences of political position, the smallest deviations from the general line, and indeed criticism become insupportable, because the autonomy is unstable and in fact under constant threat. What the Stalinist party organization does with individual communists who transgress or call into question these clear, that is, generally formal demarcations (this as a rule entails avowals of loyalty to decrees and programs), corresponds to the attempt of the ruling power within the socialist camp to pledge the various parties working under specific conditions in other countries to its line of foreign and defense policy. How stable this mechanism of camp mentality is can best be seen in the way in which it continues to be effective in wholly altered circumstances—today the Soviet Union would, on account of its economic and military power, have no further need to enlist the aid of the Communist parties.

This camp mentality, as a subjective position adopted by individuals, is the form of expression but not the basis. The mechanism, which determines all the institutions of the labor movement, has the same root as its opposite, the syndicalist component that is present beneath the surface of the labor movement: both derive from the workers' need for solidarity.

The social democracy of the Second International took up this collective need on the part of the workers and transformed it into principles of organization.

However, what at the grass-roots level is a need for mutual protection, cohesion, and solidarity, at the abstract organizational plane of public sphere, party, and nation ossifies into a schema that, reacting back onto the base, destroys solidarity, demarcates individuals and groups from one another, and reunites them in a merely mechanical manner. This results in a split between union members and non-members, between party and proletarians, between economic and political perspectives; it is on the basis of this split alone that the opposition between the vanguard and the mass of workers has fateful consequences.

Following this mechanism, the democratic element in democratic centralism is, in rapid sequence, inevitably attenuated. Whereas essential interests do not enter into the bourgeois public sphere and are thereby shielded from incursions by this sphere, the public sphere of the camp made up by workers and their parties from the outset absorbs the most important proletarian interests, in particular that of solidarity. This lends substance to this public sphere and strengthens its impact on proletarian interests. On the other hand, in its abstract form this public sphere cannot realize the interests it has absorbed; it is therefore no less of an anticipation, an illusory synthesis of the whole of society, than is the bourgeois public sphere.[2] Like the latter, this camp must therefore attempt to block a living public sphere, since this would negate the illusory synthesis. Today the Communist parties are no longer required as auxiliaries against counterrevolution but to maintain legitimation, to neutralize the critical public sphere of their own camp. As we have said, this is not simply a matter of blindness but also of the incontrovertible need of those who are organized to live in a context of meaning that can be publicly represented. If it is impossible *not* to yield to this need on the part of the masses, and if it is equally impossible to satisfy it in reality, the result is a specific contradiction. This does not permit the formulation of a "flexible politics of a society in a state of transformation that is surrounded by a capitalist environment," and escapes instead into "permanent revolution" *or* "socialism in one country." The latter ideal types are harmonizations that operated at an infrastructural level as permanent exclusions of real relations and real human beings.

The masses' underlying structure of needs, which even a bureaucracy has to take as given (it cannot generate it from within itself), is extremely complex and rests on components that have developed historically. The original needs and the conditions under which they arose no longer exist; the needs are caught up within the power strategies of classes and groups. If a bureaucracy comes into being on this basis, there develops an exchange relation of a particular kind: the promise to secure boundaries within which only the masses believe they can meaningfully

---

2. Cf. also chapter 2. What concerns us here is an analogy. We in no way fail to appreciate the fact that an illusory social synthesis with the content of a worker's state cannot be equated with the illusory synthesis of a bourgeois public sphere.

live, including a minimum of material provision, is exchanged for generalized agreement on the part of those organized.[3]

The sealing off of a socialist camp from the surrounding capitalist society interrupts, if it is successful, the movement of social contradictions in yet another respect. These can resolve themselves only from within the overall mechanisms of society; this is, however, not to suggest that this same resolution is still possible in the individual spheres of a society divided into camps. If anything, in these partial spheres they can solidify as permanent unripe contradictions, even where in the overall framework of society they tend toward resolution. Every illusory synthesis that splits up a unified context of production thus preserves contradictions, develops into a mechanism that again and again manufactures unripe conflicts that tend never to resolve themselves.

Therefore, there are—in advance of any specific content—categories of public sphere that rule out a revolutionary resolution of contradictions. In line with this the category of proletarian public sphere can be defined as follows: **it does not denote specific forms and contents but applies the Marxist method such that no raw material of social revolution, no concrete interest remains excluded and unresolved. It thereby ensures that the medium of this resolution and transformation of interests is the real context of production and societilization as a whole.** This also entails that the categories through which needs and interests can be grasped as particular ones do not transpose themselves onto the categories that denote the totality of society, which is not identical with these interests but the medium in which they can move. **The proletarian public sphere is the correct application of the various categories by means of which living interests generalize themselves without destroying, as dead interests and norms, the whole living substance that they wish to organize.** A prerequisite here is not merely reflection on the question of organization in general, but rather, this question of organization itself embodies constant reflection on the dialectical relationship between organizers and organized as the applications of the materialist method to the organizations of the working class.

## The Interest in Control

A governing interest of bureaucracies is control. They operate according to the maxim, "trust is good, but control is better." Control can be exercized only when the ways in which individuals behave can be brought under a common denomina-

---

3. Cf. the entirely similar organization of the public-service television stations. These organizational forms from a period of transformation denote an unstable equilibrium. They cannot remain hybrids over the long term. Either they broaden the principle of social responsibility that is a component of its public-service form of organization, or they revert to the situation of the capitalist society that has created them or tolerates them. In the latter case, they establish a context of domination that is particularly congruent and complex.

tor: that is, when the manifold possibilities of individual expression are reduced to attitudes that are capable of being predicted (and by means of the mechanisms that the bureaucracy has at its disposal). This basically corresponds to the bourgeois legal framework, to the generality of laws. In this respect, this need for control is not specific to bureaucratic organizations but is a characteristic of every abstract structuring of society. Marx's principle in the *Critique of the Gotha Program*— where he states the conditions for the sublation of the bourgeois legal framework: from each according to his capabilities, to each according to his needs—is allied with the material liberation of individuality and is at the same time irreconcilable with bourgeois commodity production or bureaucratic rule. What we have in mind here are by no means merely the terroristic deformations of bureaucracy but precisely its typical, that is, functioning, guise.

The bureaucracies of the working class would not be capable of asserting this interest in control among the masses were there not within individuals a corresponding need for security. We are not here dealing simply with the internalization of bureaucracy or rule. Rather, the more that individuals become impoverished in social expression, the more they must also mistrust their autonomy and fall back on regimented and ready-made supports. Insofar as they develop their expressive richness, by contrast, they gain in self-confidence that would enable them to deal with social issues in an autonomous manner. **This would not entail individualistic fragmentation but precisely what Marx describes as "free association of producers."** On the other hand, there develops within individuals—who, owing to the suppression of their interests and their possibilities of expression, cannot answer for what they do—a fear that is grounded in social experience (behind which, in addition, individual neurotic fears assemble). Between this fear and the control needs of the bureaucracy, which through its normative ventures takes away further expressive opportunities from individuals, there is a widening gulf. Once the suppression of expression has gone beyond a certain point, the pressure of the producers' material needs—along with those that are, in light of the stage of the productive forces, ripe—grows so powerfully that, in the face of delegation and seesawing, centralized controls have to be lifted. **What is understood in existing socialist societies as liberalization is the ongoing attempt to reduce excessive tension in this way.** In the process, sectional interests are permitted public expression, while other interests continue to be excluded. This mechanism works in a different way from bourgeois competition, but it has similar effects. It does not lead to a return to capitalism, but like the latter it stands in the way of the development of socialist relations of production. Both the loose and the strict common denominator are an expression of the commodity situation in existing socialist societies.

The public sphere of the working class in capitalist countries as a **society within society** manifests its specific conflicts at three levels. **At the level of perception and consciousness it restricts the social horizon of experience for all**

**classes. At the level of political organization and of class struggle it entails the totality of social contradictions in a public sphere conceived as a camp not being visible in its full concreteness.** The class enemy's potential contradictions can be grasped only in a schematic way.[4] Third, **the working class's dealings with the bourgeois public sphere**, at the center of which stands the nonpublicly determined interaction between production interests and the power accumulated within this public sphere, cannot be learned. The workers are subject to the influence of this public sphere, which becomes particularly prominent at times of crisis. Elements of this public sphere penetrate into the organizations of the working class, where their bourgeois origins are not recognizable.

As we have described in the main body of this book, if the public sphere is interpreted in bourgeois terms, this confuses the energies of the working class. The more that the bourgeois public sphere itself has congenital defects, the more the working class is impelled to define itself through institutions in which no link can be achieved between proletarian interests and those of other social strata, in which the working class can neither assert nor express itself. At the same time, tied to this public sphere is the control of actual instruments of power, which embrace, for instance, the waging of war, state economic intervention, control of information, police, and the judiciary. If the working class is unable to bring this public power under its control, the latter's potential falls into the lap of fascist forces, whose diffuse organizations, linked in a purely abstract manner, thereby acquire a real foundation resting on experience of rule. Power itself holds the divergent energies of the fascist camp together.[5] It is thanks to this that they are in a position to translate their nonpublic, terroristic actions before seizure of power into a societal language that can count on a response that corresponds to the emotional reaction to traditional state authority, but here accrues to the fascist regime.

---

4. Marx states very clearly what is meant by the totality of contradictions: "The result which we have arrived is not that production, distribution, exchange, and consumption are identical, but rather that they all contribute to the articulation of a totality, differences within one unity. Production overdetermines itself in the antagonistic determination of production as well as overdetermining all the other factors. The process always begins again anew from it. . . . A determined production thus determines determined consumption, distribution, exchange, the *determined relationships of these different factors vis-à-vis one another*. Of course, *in its one-sided form*, production is also determined by the other factors. For example, whenever the market, that is, the sphere of exchange, is expanded, production increases in accordance with these parameters and is more deeply graduated. Production changes with changes in distribution, such as the concentration of capital, varying distribution of the population in cities and in the country, and so on. Finally, consumption needs also determine production. There is a reciprocal affective relationship between the various factors. This is the case in any organized whole" (Karl Marx, "Einleitung zur Kritik der politischen Ökonomie," *Marx-Engels Werke*, [vol. 13, 1857]: 630f.).

5. Cf. Franz Neumann, *Behemoth. The Structure and Practice of National Socialism 1933-1944* (New York: 1966); Angelo Tasca, *Glauben, Gehorchen, Kämpfen. Aufstieg des Faschismus* (Vienna: 1969); O. Bauer, H. Marcuse, A. Rosenberg, *Faschismus und Kapitalismus* (4th ed. Frankfurt: 1970).

No fascist system has ever been overthrown without an external war, and not even the timely reaction of the Spanish working class was able to defend the Republic against the potential of the right once the latter had taken hold of sections of the Spanish public sphere and power structure, in particular the army.

Workers' parties and Marxist theory have always had difficulties in correctly appreciating this dialectical relationship of the working class to the public sphere and the power potential of the bourgeois state. One reason for this may be the experiential structure of the working class itself. In sociology, the self-image of a great part of the working class in capitalist industrial societies is characterized as dichotomous consciousness: in other words, these sectors of the working class assume that society is split into above and below and that this is the case in all societies and could not be otherwise. According to this hypothesis, hatred of the work forced on them and their inability to recognize the objects they produce as the products of their own labor render them **indifferent to the question of how society functions outside of their immediate sphere of production**. They may be interested in overthrowing these social circumstances, but not in a deep grasp of the laws according to which the latter operate.[6]

This disposition makes difficult a mode of behavior that, in apparently contradictory fashion, demands two things:

1. taking control of the public sphere, not in order to possess it but to prevent its occupation by the class enemy;
2. constructing a counterpublic sphere of the working class.

Both strategies require nearly diametrically opposed forms of conduct: discipline and spontaneity. The control of the bourgeois public sphere demands what is—measured by the production and life experience of the individual worker—a virtually artificial mode of conduct, which may be imparted to the intelligentsia or students through their learning processes but that, for those who do not participate in the system of rule, represents no direct experiential possibility. It is thus essentially a task of the organizations of the working class to direct attention to this point of **preventive control of the bourgeois public sphere** and the instruments of power associated with it, to convey the appropriate motivation and expertise, and at the same time to regulate the interest emerging here so that it does not result in an orientation toward a public sphere that is of no use to the working class.

A motivation for this difficult process of experience formation on a highly abstract terrain can probably be developed only by examining the historical defeats of the labor movement because of their lack of experience in dealing with

---

6. Here we are concerned with a behavior exhibited by workers in situations that our society offers them. We are not describing a characteristic inherent to the working class, such as would take effect in situations that link experience and practical action.

the bourgeois public sphere. **The enlistment of experiences from contemporary struggles always comes too late to close this gap.**

In what follows, we will analyze three historical crises of the labor movement in which **a sealing off against the bourgeois public sphere** and, following from this, a failure consistently to estimate the instruments of power and the real or apparent characteristics of this public sphere, served as a major factor in the defeat.[7]

1. In the revolutionary movement in Italy in 1919–20, the parties, in which the majority of the working class was organized, did not place themselves behind the concrete actions of the workers at the infrastructural level (factory occupations, taking over production under workers' control, strikes, taking up arms). The parties postponed the overthrow of the capitalist system to a later, "more ripe" point in time. At the same time, they gauged the mood within the working class and the forces in the parties such that an involvement in power appeared out of the question. But only such an involvement would have placed the Italian public sphere in a position where it could have brought the counterrevolutionary terrorist actions of the fascists under control. As neither a counterpublic sphere, nor a political translation of the power of the socialists and the working class within the framework of the central public sphere of the bourgeois state, was established, a situation arose in which this position, which was termed **maximalism**, fell victim to preventive counterrevolution and fascism was able to seize a public sphere that the working class had only indistinctly perceived.

2. After the First World War, Austrian social democracy perpetuated a specific tradition of the Second International: to concentrate socialist forces within the capitalist system and to organize their context of living in the form of **a powerful oppositional society within society** (socialist municipal policy, housing developments, cooperatives, socialist newspapers, paramilitary units, etc.). This secessionary tendency of **Austro-Marxism**, in which the workers continued to be subject to capitalist production, renounced the hegemony of the working class within Austrian society as a whole in favor of what appeared to be possible in practice: coexistence in the sphere of leisure time. It concentrated social-democratic energies at a few universally recognizable sites and made possible from February 1934 onward the destruction of socialist resistance at the hands of the militia, the army, and the clerical-authoritarian government, who found themselves in possession of the bourgeois public sphere.

3. With its own press, military bureau, armed units, women's, youth, and sporting organizations, its own trade union initiatives, and so on, the **KPD in the Weimar Republic** also appears to be a society within society. The party's share of the vote in Reichstag elections grew. While the workers and voters it organized continued to be employed in capitalist factories, its electoral policy enacted an

---

7. See commentaries 4–10.

intensive demarcation from the social democrats ("social fascists"), the bourgeois public sphere, the National Socialists, and to some extent from the trade unions as well. This attitude on the part of the KPD, which was dominant especially from 1925 onward, contrasted with the original ideas of the Spartacus group, which were oriented toward the whole of the working class and of the interests incorporated in German society.

**Power could not be won** by means of the KPD's Robinson Crusoe attitude, which the party stuck to as its numbers grew under its left and ultraleft course. At the same time, **none of the movements of the class enemy could be foiled**: neither the cabinet policies of Brüning, Papen, and Schleicher, nor the taking over of the bourgeois public sphere by National Socialism.

The immobilism of the Italian party leadership in 1919; the rigid and resolute sealing off of the KPD after 1925; the attempt by the Austrian social democrats to organize relations of solidarity outward from the context of living within the bourgeois framework, that is, to practice socialist politics from within the private sphere—these correspond to quite distinct points of departure and social situations. We are not attempting to draw parallels, nor is it possible to derive a single concrete lesson from them. What we are trying to do is to define **a gap in the experience of the labor movement**, in which, in all three instances, the crisis of the latter is specifically expressed. The materialist concept of the public sphere, within which revolutionary politics ineluctably takes place, cannot exclude sectors of the class enemy's reality or of the surrounding system as bourgeois forms that have been overcome so long as these forms—as is the case with the bourgeois public sphere and its public instruments of power—retain a material character. Even the illusion of a bourgeois public sphere still possesses this material character and represents, overriding all demarcations, a medium for the consciousness of the masses until another continuum of the public sphere is developed. **The proletarian public sphere can leave out nothing whatever for it derives its energy from its grasp of this total context.**[8]

---

8. It is clear that the march of the Chinese communists to Yenan and the building of an independent army, production, and Soviet public sphere there represent a completely different reaction. When the People's Republic of Yenan was founded, it differentiated itself from imperialism and from the regime of Chiang Kai-shek, but it always analyzed its own position within the context of these public spheres that surrounded it. At the same time, it was also completely autonomous, which is to say that it determined its production and the political expression of the contexts of life and interests contained within it itself. On the other hand, the Italian, German, or Austrian workers in the historical situations alluded to of 1919, 1925, or 1934 were still immediately entwined in the capitalist process of production, and they were not in possession of a form of political expression that could be communicated to the whole of society. The contradiction lies in the fact that the renunciation of reality that is bound up with the delimitation of boundaries cannot lead to real autonomy. Here the manifestation of the renunciation of reality is, as a rule, the symptom that follows from the renunciation of a revolutionary concept. At the same time, this symptom intensifies the incapacity to reclaim revolutionary positions.

# 4. 1919: Maximalism in Italy; 1934: Austro-Marxism—Two Sides of the Same Phenomenon

Angelo Tasca, *The Rise of Italian Fascism, 1918–1922,* trans. Peter and Dorothy Wait[1] (New York: Howard Fertig, 1966): p. 52:

"At the general election of November 1919, the Italian masses showed their disapproval of the war and their need for social justice by voting for the socialists and the *Popolari.* These two parties alone had between them a majority in the new Chamber: 256 out of 508 seats. . . . Of the 156 socialists, 131 had been elected in the north, in the Po valley and in Tuscany; only ten came from the inland districts of the south, five of whom were from Apulia. The Islands [of Sicily and Sardinia] returned no socialist deputies. The socialists, however, were nearer to power than the figures showed by the extent to which they could interpret the will of the whole Italian people and voice their profound discontent. Three courses seemed open to them: to leave parliament and have recourse to direct action in the country; to remain there while creating a second power in the country to replace it; to win over in parliament and in the country the allies which were indispensable to the accomplishment of the democratic revolution."

---

1. Angelo Tasca, founding member of the Italian Communist party, wrote *Nascita e avvento de fascismo, L'Italia da 1918 al 1922,* the French version of which appeared as *La Naissance du fascisme.* [The English translation cited here has been somewhat modified.—*Trans.*] The book is one of the only consistent analyses of the defeat of the workers' movement by Italian fascism, binding fac and theory, from a Marxist perspective.

Benito Mussolini in *Popolo d'Italia,* issue of 26 February 1920, cited in Tasca, *Rise of Italian Fascism,* p. 53:

"The marvelous victory at the polls has simply shown up the inefficiency and weakness of the socialists. They are impotent alike as reformers and revolutionaries. They take no action either in parliament or on the streets. The sight of a party wearing itself out on the morrow of a great victory in a vain search for something to apply its strength to, and willing to attempt neither reform nor revolution, amuses us. This is our vengeance, and it has come sooner than we hoped."

Tasca, pp. 54f.:

"The manifesto issued in August [1919] by the maximalist section, which dominated the party,[2] plumped for revolution without any transition period. . . . 'The proletariat must be incited to the violent seizure of political and economic power, and this must then be handed over entirely and exclusively to the workers' and peasants' councils, which will have both legislative and executive functions.' The maximalist resolution that was approved by the majority in Bologna explains it: the party must strive 'in the constituencies and the institutions of the *bourgeois* state for the intensive propagation of the principles of communism, and for the rapid overthrow of these instruments of *bourgeois* domination.' Thus the 156 deputies and, a few months later, the 2,800 socialist communes were apparently to confine their energies exclusively to revolutionary propaganda and sabotage of the state. In actual fact the socialist deputies and mayors devoted their best efforts, as in pre-war days, to the advocation of public works, the creation of syndicates and co-operative enterprises, and to everyday, sometimes excellent, administration. Everything went on as if there were no distinction, or connection either, between this practical and almost shamefaced reform and the maximalist proclamations. Everyone worked on his own by way of a strange, formless division of labor."

pp. 73–74:[3]

"The maximalist party leaders, unmoved, continued to sleep on their paper schemes for soviets. The National Council at Florence had directed the party executive in January 1920 to draw up within two months definite plans for Workers' Councils. At the National Council in Milan in April—long after the time limit had expired—the 'need for soviets' was once more affirmed, and the party leaders once more called upon to 'create these proletarian organizations.' To lighten their task, they were supplied with a set of regulations for drawing up soviets, wherein, in a few dozen clauses, every provision for their efficient functioning was laid down. Only the soviets themselves were missing. . . . Was it in

---

2. This was the Italian Socialist party, which also joined the Third International.

3. The complete text of the resolution can be found in *Almanacco Socialista*, 1910, pp. 458–70.

order to seize power and destroy the counter-revolution at birth that the party leaders had to impose these soviets from above, in bureaucratic style? On the contrary, it was chiefly to 'obstruct and paralyse the experiment of social democracy,' to prevent 'the establishment of the bourgeois parliament,' and to destroy those illusions of democracy—'the most dangerous kind.' With these objects in view they must 'intensify and complete their preparations for the forcible overthrow of the bourgeois state and the inauguration of the dictatorship of the proletariat.' 'Complete their preparations': this was not easy, for how could they complete what had never been begun?"

pp. 75–76:

"On August 30 the management of Alfa-Romeo cleared out its workshops in Milan and shut its doors in order to suppress a wildcat strike. The Federation[4] ordered its members to occupy the factories, thus snatching their most formidable weapon from the employers' hands by forestalling and preventing a lock-out. The occupation of factories, often represented as some critical stage of revolutionary fever, was in its inception simply a substitute for a strike which had become too difficult, and a more economical method of enforcing labor's new collective contracts. The Federation leaders had chosen the line of least resistance, and they thought that the occupation would provoke government intervention, while some of them, though they did not admit it, cherished the hope that its political outcome might lead to the socialists taking a share in the administration.

On August 31 the workers occupied 280 machine shops in Milan, and in the next two days the movement spread all over Italy, at times even forestalling the orders of the leaders. It began with the metallurgical trades, but the factories wanted raw materials and accessories supplied by other industries, so, to ensure the continuance of their work, these had to be won over. The control of the factories passed into the hands of workers' committees, who did all they could to maintain output. In this they had only themselves to rely upon, for all the engineers and nearly all the technicians and clerical staff had left on the order of the directors. Work in progress went on well enough, nonetheless."

pp. 77–78:

"The workers now faced a difficult decision. Should negotiations with the employers, now prepared to yield on every point, be resumed? A negative answer would give the signal for a general insurrection, since it was no longer possible to keep the workers in the factories without giving them something further to aim at. The only way out was by escaping in a forward direction. Armed insurrection was out of the question, for nothing was ready. The workers felt safe behind the factory walls, not on account of their arms, often ancient and inadequate, but because

---

4. The metalworkers' union.

they look on the factories as hostages which the government would hesitate to shell to bits in order to dislodge the occupants."

p. 82:

*"The 'posthumous and preventive' counter-revolution.*[5] The end of the factory occupations left both the workers and the employers with the feeling that they had been beaten. In addition to the collective agreement the workers had gained 'syndical control of industry.' But what was this vague committee set up by the September 15 decree in comparison with the mirage they had seen during the weeks spent in the occupied factories?

"The employers had been forced to give in without a soldier or a gendarme stirring to dislodge the workers from the factories; they had been made to sign blindly an agreement which they had recently refused to discuss, and submit by Giolitti's orders to the control of industry. Both sides were equally disgruntled and saw no hope in the future, but the industrialists and landowners were livid with rage and ready for anything, willing to sell their souls for revenge. It wasn't long before the offices of hundreds of working-class and socialist organizations were destroyed all across the country; the homes of 'red' and even 'white' workers went up in flames; the bloody persecution of 'reds' of any kind had begun."

p. 217:

"A similar thing occurred with the strike in late July of 1922. Not only was the July strike ten days too late, but it followed on a campaign in which maximalists, communists and anarchists had described it as the 'necessary and sufficient' means for turning the tables and beginning to liquidate fascism without any help from the state or having to make 'compromises' with 'non-proletarian' forces. The authors of the appeal for the general strike had taken careful precautions in drawing it up to show the connection between the movement they were starting and state action, upon which they called to defend their outraged liberties as a way of building a bridge. But if the working classes and the state were to work for a common end there had to be a connection between them, some sort of 'collaboration.' By calling the general strike on July 31, however, the working classes materially severed their connection with the state. Even supposing (let us make this hypothesis in spite of the fact that it would have been quite unjustifiable at the time) that the state had decided to cope with the fascist gangs, it would have been entirely paralyzed by the strike in the public services and the railways, while the fascists, with several months' advantage in distributing their forces, could cover a wide area in their columns of trucks. 'A solemn warning to the government of the country,' said the secret committee's manifesto. But neither to those who took

5. The formulation is taken from Filippo Turati. Cf. as well L. Fabbri, *Contro-Rivoluzione Preventiva* (Bologna: 1922).

part in it nor to those who suffered it did the strike appear merely as a 'warning.' There was practically no government in existence as a result of the cabinet crisis which had now lasted a fortnight; besides, the 'warning' could not be conveyed to the 'government,' for the strike had destroyed all points of contact between the workers and the state."

It is evident that Marxist analysis in modern Italy (e.g., the Manifesto group, Potero operaio, Scienza operaia) is today seeking to reappraise the historical experiences of the years 1918–22. Italian capitalism has often been described as a delayed capitalism: even today it still possesses backward elements, side by side with forced developments that have grown especially rapidly. At the time of the revolutionary movement of 1919 Italian society was not an economic unity. The south had practically no industry, the north was industrialized in places; small-scale industry had developed in central Italy. This regionally divided economy, which was to some extent not even in a clear context of socialization or cooperation but simply coexisted under a common national umbrella, was not autonomous as a national structure of production. This means that none of these three Italian economies, neither the agricultural, the industrial, nor that based on small industry and manufacture, could exist without export or import with other countries (supplies of coal and iron, exports of fruit from the south, export of workers to the USA, etc.): a precarious balance ripe with crisis potential. A national conception of socialist reconstruction was, under such conditions, out of the question. Labriola's critical Marxism thus consistently set out from an internationalist and revolutionary position.

After 1918 too the situation in Italy seemed unsuited to a socialism in one country. Let us compare the Italian situation with that of Russia in 1917. Here the proletariat was concentrated in a few centers, above all Leningrad and Moscow. In essential elements the structure of industrial and agricultural production was, partly because of the relative isolation of Russia, autonomous. Unlike the Socialist party of Italy, the Russian party had been able to sustain without interruption its internationalist position even after 1914 and possessed a theory that responded to the situation of world war.

On account of the seemingly indissoluble economic interests of the Italian regions, two wings developed in line with international socialist debate (which was not geared to Italian problems). One wing sought practical, reformist solutions, which were intended gradually to transform the Italian situation so that a conception of revolutionary politics would be possible. This faction was rapidly subsumed under the category of right-wing social democracy and compelled to act accordingly. By contrast the majority in the party committees did not see themselves as being in a position to indicate practical measures so as to bring together in a socialist sense the interests of the rural workers of the south, the small entrepreneurs and their employees of central Italy, and those of the industrial centers of the north. What were not taken into account in this process were the unifying tendencies of the war and the subsequent social upheavals. Even in this situation the Italian Marxists strove on the one hand to keep to the "pure and orthodox" Marxist doctrine and on the other to import the Soviet model into Italy. This policy of the majority of the party leadership soon cut itself off from the concrete situation in Italy.

In the politically and economically fragmented situation in Italy in the years 1919–22, revolutionary conditions were subjectively and objectively present. A change came about rather unexpectedly. In international debate, above all within the Comintern, these questions were not treated as specific to the Italian situation:[6] Zinoviev's postmortem of the events of 1920 reproduces the essential points of the Comintern's analysis; Lenin too regards the left-wing infantile disorder of the Maximalists in Italy primarily from the point of view of their relationship to parliamentarianism. Within the committees of the Italian Socialist party the parallelism between practical reformists and theoretical Maximalists stood in the way of a definitive analysis or a decision in any one direction.

We cannot in retrospect judge whether in light of the factory occupations of 1920 or 1922 an offensive or defensive strategy by the working class would have fitted the situation. If the defensive option was correct, it would have presupposed two things: on the one hand, a determined struggle against fascism, on the other, an attempt **to prevent the state and the public sphere from allying themselves with the latter**. This strategy applies not only to the Italian situation or to the fascism of the 1930s and 1940s, National Socialism included; **it also holds good for every form of transfer of the economic contradictions of capital onto the political level, where a kind of real subsumption of public sphere and state under the interests of capital begins to manifest itself.**

**An essential element of a successful socialist strategy always consists in separating the capital interest from the state. Situations can arise where it is necessary simultaneously to wage an offensive strategy against certain aggressive sectors of capital and a defensive struggle to maintain certain social and political possibilities for action and constitutional rights.** For instance, one cannot uphold the idea that where press and freedom of opinion, the very existence of reformist parties, the autonomy of scientific knowledge, and so on, are under direct threat, this will result in the masses discovering, through their disillusionment, the true nature of the system. The conviction that the more repressive the terms in which society presents itself, the more favorable are the conditions for socialism is one of the most fateful mistakes of the labor move-

---

6. Cf. for example, the minutes of the second and third congresses of the Communist International, especially the presentation of Zinoviev that is included in *Protokoll des III. Kongresses der Kommunistischen Internationale*, Moscow, 22 June–12 July 1921, Bibliothek der Kommunistischen Internationale, vol. 23, Hamburg, 1921, 2 vols., reprint 1970; here, vol. 1, pp. 166ff.

ment. As a rule, it is no more than a preconception on the part of ultraleftist groups within the intelligentsia.

In this regard, here are some more passages from a more general analysis by Tasca:

Angelo Tasca, "Allgemeine Bedingungen der Entstehung und des Aufstiegs des Faschismus," in Otto Bauer, Herbert Marcuse, Arthur Rosenberg, *Faschismus und Kapitalismus, Theorien über die sozialen Ursprünge und die Funktion des Faschismus,* 4th ed. (Frankfurt: 1970), p. 170:

"Fascism is a postwar phenomenon, and any attempt to define it through parallels with historical events that 'came before,' such as Bonapartism, will remain futile and run the risk of leading to confusion. . . . In countries that, unlike the United States, the British Commonwealth, or the USSR, do not have at their disposal a large domestic market, crises prove in varying degrees to be 'hopeless' crises. Under these conditions, economic discontent is easily linked to nationalistic needs and the myth of a 'place in the sun.' On the one hand, one insists on concentration on the national economy and thus the aggravation of its artificial and parasitic tendencies; on the other, the illusion arises of breaking through the 'encirclement' and seeking a solution through violence beyond its borders. The capitalist economy, which has for the most part lost its specific incentives, now no longer 'oscillates' between crisis and prosperity, but rather between self-sufficiency and war."

p. 172:

"Three factors come together here to prepare the way for fascism: the intensification of the class struggle, its increasingly political character, and the relative equilibrium of the forces that oppose it. If the first two factors are given, the last one will play a decisive role. The equilibrium of the forces that oppose each other paralyzes governments, regardless of whether their components are formulated as a national union, 'leftist cartel,' or social-democratic majority. If this equilibrium lasts too long, if it does not lead to a higher form, erratic, blind changes are released in which a certain propensity for tenacity, the defense of threatened privileges, and the hopes of the classes that are set in motion and stimulated by the crisis are all found simultaneously. Since the working class waives its right to go beyond itself legally, it tends to form a 'second power' within the state and in opposition to it, while the bourgeoisie grasps at either a 'reactionary transformation of the state' or fascistic violence."

p. 176:

"Fascism is pure reaction, but a reaction that manipulates mass methods that are effective only in the postwar situation. It attempts to displace the struggle onto its opponents' territory, to undermine their influence on the masses. Hence the use of demagogic slogans and socialist terminology: Mussolini's newspaper was for a long time called the "socialist daily," and his party referred to itself as national-socialist. This creates new situations in which the old political crises frequently do not see their way clear."

p. 178:

"The working class, the masses of the people, must endeavor to isolate fascism from the state, to neutralize and combat the influences and accomplices that intend to put the state at the service of fascism. Fascism is able to do nothing without the state, and less than nothing against it. On the other hand, antifascism will succeed only with difficulty if it is forced to struggle simultaneously against the whole of the state and the whole of fascism. The Italian communists who announced in 1921 that 'the struggle is playing itself out between proletarian and fascist dictatorships'; the German communists who in 1932 pretended to be the solution to the battle 'on two fronts,' against both Weimar and Potsdam, ended up by fighting neither against fascism nor against the state. The antifascist struggle is a three-way struggle: the antifascist front, which must be extended as broadly as possible; the fascist bloc, which must be undermined if possible; and the state, whose means must be mobilized in defense of democracy. Victory over fascism is only possible by means of a political strategy that takes these three elements into account and succeeds in arranging and constituting them in such a way that 'power' finds itself on the side of democracy."

p. 179:

"There is no longer any place in such a system for the disastrous illusion, long nurtured by the communists, that fascism will provoke progress in that it eliminates the 'democratic illusion.' The Italian communists actually announced in May 1922: 'It is true that the white reaction is scoring short-lived victories over an enemy who thus pays the penalty for his wicked machinations, but it eliminates the illusion of a liberal democracy and destroys the influence of social democracy on the masses.' And in the decree issued by the presidium of the Communist International of January 1934 on the German situation, one reads: 'In that the establishment of the openly fascist dictatorship dissolves the democratic illusions of the masses and liberates them from the influence of social democracy, it accelerates Germany's progress toward a proletarian revolution.' This is not the place to provide a thorough critique of this concept, which the Communist International never revoked in spite of many 'about-faces,' and it may suffice to observe that fascism not only disposes of the 'illusion of democracy' but also the subject that cultivates it, the socialist workers' movement. The same can be said of fascism as is said of a 'perfectly successful operation': the patient did not survive, and thus has been liberated from all his 'illusions,' and ultimately from any illusion whatsoever."

# 5. Austro-Marxism (1918–34)

The representatives of Austro-Marxism are clearly the opposite of Maximalists. The Austrian social democrats have tried to incorporate the bourgeois public sphere, the traditions of philosophy, the law, ethics, and so on, into their reflections. Their program, which in the specific Austrian situation soon failed, is the first example of a long-term social-democratic reformist and infrastructural policy. The thinking that underlies the theories of the Austrian social democrats can still be found today in the social democracies and individual socialist countries; this applies in particular to the focus on the balance of blocs, the stressing of ethical and general humane norms. It can be said that, with the exception of China, every socialist country today contains its share of this realpolitik and idealism, which the Austro-Marxists were the first to combine into a program.

Otto Bauer, "Das Gleichgewicht der Klassenkämpfe" (The equilibrium of class conflicts), in *Austromarxismus. Texte zu "Ideologie und Klassenkämpf,"* Otto Bauer, Max Adler, Karl Renner, Sigmund Kunfi, Béla Fogarasi, and Julius Lengyel, ed. and intro. Hans-Jörg Sandkühler and Rafael de la Vega, Europäische Verlagsanstalt (Frankfurt am Main: 1970), p. 85:

"The Ascendency of the Working Class, Equilibrium of Class Forces, Restoration of the Bourgeoisie—these are the chapter titles in my history of the Austrian revolution. One sees the analogy between my depiction of the Austrian Revolution of 1918–22 and Marx's depiction of the French Revolution of 1848. But one also certainly sees the differences that emerge from these, namely, that in terms of number, class consciousness, organization, and experience, the Austrian proletariat of 1918 stood far above the French proletariat of 1848. In Paris, the ascendency of the working class of 1848 lasted only a few days; in German-speaking Austria of 1918–19, it lasted a whole year. In 1848 Paris, the period of equilibrium between class forces lasted only a few weeks; in German-speaking Austria from 1919 to 1922, it lasted three years. In Paris, it was a time of chaotic confusion without lasting result; in German-speaking Austria, it was a period in which the proletariat strove for accomplishments that have outlasted it. In Paris, it was a time of illusions in 'Fraternité,' of the brotherhood of opposing classes; in Austria, the proletariat entered this time without any illusions, in full knowledge that the temporary cooperation of the classes is not a means to a lasting eclipse of their contradictions, but rather merely the result of a temporary equilibrium between their forces; not a means for overcoming their class conflict, but rather only a means for the provisional stabilization of their results."

pp. 91ff:

"The general crisis of traditional parliamentarianism is a form of expressing the equilibrium of class forces. . . . "

"The statement of *The Communist Manifesto* that state authority is merely the executive of the bourgeois class—in 1847 the description of a tendency of future development—is today for some countries still only the description of a past or preceding historical period. But the class state of the bourgeoisie was not followed by the dictatorship of the proletariat, but rather, by a state of equilibrium of class forces that expressed itself politically in very diverse state forms. This experience makes it probable that there will be a transitional period in which the forces of classes maintain equilibrium with one another between this and the period in which the state will be a class organization of the proletariat."

p. 95:

"Kelsen's whole critique denies the characteristic difference between the pre- and postrevolutionary state. It does not want to recognize for the past any such characteristic difference because it intends to shake faith in characteristic changes of the state in the future. It does not admit that the state, until 1918, was an organization of control for the bourgeoisie, because it does not want to recognize that in the future the state must become an organization of control for the proletariat."[1]

---

1. Bauer refers to a discussion of his book *Die österreichische Revolution* (Vienna: 1923) by constitutional lawyer Hans Kelsen, "Dr. Otto Bauers politische Theorie," in *Der Kampf. Sozialdemokratische Monatsschrift* (February 1924). (See also Kelsen, *Sozialismus und Staat. Eine Untersuchung der politischen Theorie des Marxismus,* 3d ed. [Vienna: 1965].) Constitutional lawyer Kelsen developed the position of "pure legal doctrine" in legal and state theory. This doctrine proceeds

*Philosophisches Wörterbuch* (Philosophical dictionary), ed. G. Klaus/M. Buhr (Leipzig: 1965), p. 66:

from a strictly formal and logical interpretation of law. It refers to the attempt, starting from neo-Kantian ideas, to establish constitutional and legal orders transcendentally in that all social, ethical, or political standards or all other forms of expression of interests are excluded. This represented the most far-reaching attempt in the area of constitutional law to "purely" represent the exclusionary principle of the bourgeois public sphere. Kelsen was the author of the Austrian federal constitution of 1920. Kelsen's attempt to develop the state and law as one formal instrument, neutral vis-à-vis the class struggle, does not ignore the Marxist analysis of the state or the advocacy of constitutional law and interests. Rather, "pure legal doctrine" is meant to make of the state and law just one means that would correspond to the particular requirements of class equilibrium. Thus, the *paths* upon which Bauer and Kelsen want to direct the state for this equilibrium are different, but their *goal* is the same. Dominant opinion in legal and state theory has never followed Kelsen, but rather has represented in effect the more intermediate standpoint represented by Bauer (Radbruch, Anschütz). A significant counterview-point to Kelsen's theory can be found in Carl Schmitt, *Verfassungslehre*, 4th ed., 1965 (1st ed., 1928), pp. 8f., 55, 252, 386: "The state doctrine of H. Kelsen presents the state as one system and one unity of legal standards, clearly without the least attempt to explain the factual and logical principle of this 'unity' and this 'system,' and without confronting how it is, and in accordance with which necessity it so happens, that the many positive legal requirements of a state and the various constitutional-legal standards form such a 'system' or a 'unity.' The political *being* [*Sein*] or *becoming* [*Werden*] of state unity and order is transformed into a *functioning*, the contrast between what *is* politically and *what should be* is consistently increased by the contrast between what *is* in substance and what *functions* according to law. But the theory does become understandable if it is viewed as the last offshoot of the aforementioned genuine theory of the bourgeois constitutional state, which sought to make of the state a constitutional order and therein glimpsed the shape of the constitutional state. During its greatest epoch, the seventeenth and eighteenth centuries, the bourgeoisie gained the authority to create a real system, that of the law of individualistic reason and natural law, and formed standards that were valid in and of themselves from concepts like private property and personal freedom, which are valid above and beyond any political existence, because they were *right* and *rational*, and thus contain a genuine element of what *should be,* irrespective of the existing, that is, positive, constitutional reality. That was responsible normativity; here one could speak of system, order, and unity. For Kelsen, on the other hand, only *positive* standards are valid, that is, those that are *really* valid; they are not valid because they *should* properly be valid, but rather only because they are *positive*, irrespective of qualities like reasonableness, justice, and so on. Here what *should be* suddenly ceases to exist and normativity is broken off; instead, there appears the tautology of a crude factuality. Something is valid if it is valid and because it is valid. This is 'positivism.' Anyone who seriously contends that 'the' constitution should be considered valid as the 'basic standard' and that all other standards should derive from it may not take arbitrary, concrete conditions as the foundation of a pure system of pure standards because they are established by a particular position, recognized and thus characterized as 'positive,' and thus only de facto effective. A normative unity or order can be derived only from theses that are systematic, normatively responsible without regard for 'positive' validity, that is, theses that are *correct* in and of themselves because of their reasonableness or justice." It is important to recognize that Carl Schmitt's analysis takes place from the conservative perspective oriented toward the actual existence of the state, that is, toward the actual disintegration of the bourgeois public sphere. From the social standpoint of the ruling class, Schmitt is able to effortlessly separate himself from the idea of the state and of law. Kelsen, on the other hand, makes his "last attempt to save the logic of state and law" from a "leftist" standpoint. Kelsen's main writings include: *Der soziologische und der juristische Staatsbegriff* (1922); *Hauptprobleme der Staatsrechtslehre, entwickelt aus der Lehre vom Rechtssatz,* 2d ed. (1923); *Allgemeine Staatslehre* (1925).

"Austro-Marxism—manifestation form of revisionism, of the revisionist deformation and adulteration of Marxism through centrist and opportunistic leaders of the Austrian social democracy. A peculiarity of Austrian Marxism was that its representatives (F. Adler, M. Adler, V. Adler, O. Bauer, K. Renner) sought in a demagogic manner to conceal behind 'radical' phrases and with the help of a 'Marxist' terminology their antisocialist goals and their enmity toward Marxist theory and the revolutionary workers' movement under the pretext of the 'completion' and 'further development' of Marxism."

Hans-Jörg Sandkühler, Rafael de la Vega, in *Austromarxism*, p. 8:
"Austrian social democracy turned away from Marxist principles at the second party congress in Vienna (1901) and embarked on a clearly opportunistic and revisionistic line that reassumed the essential elements of the Gotha Program of the SAPD (1875). The ideas of Lassalle and Blanc were advanced in particular by Viktor Adler, who also launched the slogan 'community of interest' [*Interessengemeinschaft*] between social democracy and the Hapsburg crown.

"Eduard Bernstein's 'Bible of Revisionism' (*Die Voraussetzungen des Sozialismus und die Aufgaben der Sozialdemokratie* [The prerequisites of socialism and the tasks of social democracy]), published in 1899, in which he advances a thorough revision of the central teachings of Marxism (criticism of the theory of pauperization, reconciliation of the classes, a peaceful growing over into socialism, the task of the Marxist dialectic in favor of a criticistic ethic of Kantian provenance, etc.), was translated into practical politics by Austrian social democracy, although several of its representatives took the field against Bernstein—if only with words."

Max Adler, *Das Soziale in Kants Erkenntniskritik* [The social in Kant's critique of knowledge] (Vienna: 1920), VI:
"[Not to play Kant off against Marx], but much more, rather, to think through the theoretical work of Marx *just as it is,* but with a logical consciousness sharpened via Kant's critique of knowledge in order to first call attention to all the elements of thought that lie in it that make it possible as a *theory of social experience.*"

Max Adler, *Gesellschaftsordnung und Zwangsordnung* [Social order and order of coercion], in: *Austromarxismus*, p. 202:
"In the imperative [*Im Sollen*], we have before us the *socializing form* of will [*des Wollens*]."

The Austrian Republic, which was established as a rump after the separation of the nationalities, consisted of regions with wholly heterogeneous economies. The various territories and provinces blocked one another within this state framework.

It seemed out of the question that a *volonté générale* could come into being out of the conflicting interests of the agricultural regions, the isolated capital Vienna, and the industrial areas. The individual parts of the country were not even in a network of cooperation and exchange. This was why the government, set up in 1919 with the participation of the social democrats, attempted to attach Austria to Germany, to assert an internal conception of socialism resting on that of the Second International. When this policy failed, there seemed to be only one opening for socialist policy, the one for whose realization no societal consensus was required: namely, the organization of the everyday life and leisure of the social democrats and thereby of society into two great blocs—that of the bourgeois and Catholic forces, who were in possession of the state and the public sphere, and that of a new society within the old. This was to be achieved by **self-help by the social democrats at the infrastructural level, whereby the process of production was once again excluded from this infrastructure**. This is a politics of practical compromises in a situation that is politically hopeless. The problem lies in the fact that none of the compromises brought about an uncontradictory development of workers' interests or a control of the bourgeois public sphere, above all because the core, the production process, could not be organized in an autonomous manner. Austrian social democracy experienced several defeats and was practically eliminated by the clerical-authoritarian victors in 1934.

The attempt at a **politics of class equilibrium** is something other than the principle of **twin rule**, which allows for a more long-term learning process on the part of the masses. Twin rule must rest on the production sphere itself. The Austrian theory and practice of class equilibrium was a precursor of the modern proportional system. According to this pluralistic political principle, on whose basis countless reformist institutions are today organized (municipalities, television networks, universities), in case of a real equilibrium between both sides the interests of neither can be realized. A **compulsion to compromise** dominates, such that, instead of one or the other interest being realized, a third term comes into being. But normally it does not even come to this, for the equilibrium does not exist in reality, and the proportion and theory of equilibrium merely conceal the real dominance of one of the two sides. This is a general experience of the labor movement. The experience of Austrian social democracy in 1934 is thus no different from that of the SPD in the Federal Republic today in their dealings with the ZDF television network, even if the political constellation is entirely different and hence scale and manifestation appear to be incomparable.

In brief, the struggle of the Austrian social democrats after 1918 was as follows: In 1918 they formed a coalition with the bourgeois parties; this gave them control of the defense ministry and the militia of the new republic. Simultaneously a series of reforms, the so-called Hanusch Laws, were passed. They missed the opportunity to nationalize the East Alpine Coal and Steel Company, as was scheduled in the social-democratic program and appeared possible in the situation. It was in this armaments depot that the radical right Heimwehr was equipped, a private army that was the instrument of the destruction of the Socialist party. The grand coalition came to an end in 1920.

July 1927 saw a violent confrontation of military units from both camps, the workers' militia and the Heimwehr. It was now not the Heimwehr that was fighting against the workers in the outlying suburbs of Vienna but the police and the army, who employed heavy weaponry. The final defeat came about in February 1934. It is significant in our context of camp mentality and the relation of counterpublic sphere to bourgeois public sphere that the camp of the Austro-Marxists could not be defended and that it was, precisely, a confused relationship to its members that determined the form of the defeat.

Joseph Buttinger,[2] *In the Twilight of Socialism: A History of the Revolutionary Socialists of Austria* (New York: Draeger, 1953), pp. 3f.:

"On October 17 the Heimwehr leader most strongly bent on violence, Emil Fey, major and knight of the Order of Maria Theresia, was named secretary of state for security. . . . In mid-March, he abolished representative government entirely, under the flimsiest of all pretexts known to the history of coups d'etat: since the last session of parliament could not be formally adjourned because of the resignation of all presiding officers, calling a new session was said to be 'illegal.'

"When his parliamentary opponents, on March 15, made one attempt to have the people's representatives meet anyway, Dollfuss called out the police. He also had the Heimwehr march on that day and actually mobilized the federal army, to intimidate the Social Democratic Party leaders who in turn had mobilized their own para-military formation, the Republican Defense League. Yet the most effective means of breaking their wavering will to resist was not the threat of force but Dollfuss's confidential pledge of early negotiations which would 'disentangle the situation.'

"On the very next day the government dissolved the Social Democratic Defense League in Tyrol. Two weeks later, on March 31, the League was banned throughout Austria. By then, pre-publication censorship had been imposed on the Vienna *Arbeiter-Zeitung,* the central organ of the Social Democratic Party. In April the constitutional court, the tribunal with jurisdiction in questions of constitutionality, was paralyzed, in May the holding of elections forbidden throughout the country. On May 20 Dollfuss founded the Fatherland Front, his

---

2. Joseph Buttinger was one of the leaders of the illegal Austrian social democracy from 1934 until the annexation into the German Reich. His presentation can serve as the most thorough and detailed account of the events. He also provides clarification of individual names and organizations on pp. 624ff.

organization of political unity under authoritarian leadership, which was to replace all parties.

"The summer saw parts of the Fascist para-military formations incorporated in the state enforcement machinery as a so-called Volunteer Defense Corps."

p. 5:

"On Friday the 9th a public 'peace' debate had taken place in the Vienna City Council, between Social Democrats and moderate leaders of the Christian-Social Party. Dollfuss replied on the 10th, in an interview with the government-supporting Catholic newspaper, *Reichspost*. Once more, he spurned every effort to reach a compromise with the Social Democrats, approved the provincial putsch movements, and disavowed as not expressing his views the conciliatory speeches of certain politicians otherwise close to him."

p. 10:

"Bauer immediately summoned the party executive. At nine o'clock it met for its last session, not quite at full strength, in an apartment on Gumpendorferstrasse. Politically it was already dead. It seemed as though blind fate had placed what was left of the party's once so formidable power in the hands of the small combat command. It did not matter that Bauer's motion for a general strike call and Defense League mobilization was almost voted down; events took their course regardless of the decisions of the executive. Bauer ordered the combat command to its assigned post. He sent the general strike directive to the union leaders. He told Felix Kanitz, the propaganda director, to have a long-drafted combat manifesto printed at the designated plant. After ten o'clock he also came for a moment into the *Arbeiter-Zeitung* offices; but for the editors he had no orders about armed resistance.

"While Leichter fumed at being suddenly sentenced to inaction, Bauer ran into the first of the unforeseen technical obstacles on which his combat command would so soon founder. The premises set aside for it by City School Board Chairman Otto Glöckel—some of the board's office rooms on Vienna Hill—were not free."

pp. 11f.:

"On the ground that 'Social Democratic union members at the power plant' had walked out, the government proclaimed martial law: 'The federal government, ready to draw on its entire resources, has taken all measures to nip these systematic plots of bolshevist elements in the bud. . . . At the Sandleiten settlement in Ottakring shooting started at one o'clock; at one-thirty the police stormed the municipal gas works in Leopoldau; two o'clock brought the first clash at the Reumannhof on Margaretengürtel. During these hours, the party charged with 'systematic plots' saw the accustomed lines of communication between its upper and lower echelons severed, one after the other. When direction and a clear view were most urgently needed, the separation of leaders and followers was complete. In the most trying hours of their political life, the sudden turn of events robbed the rank and file of active Social Democrats of the voice of their leaders, the protection of their community, and the consoling authority of institutions they habitually obeyed in all matters of social action. Splintered into a thousand little groups bound more by friendship than by the common party life of the past, the suddenly leaderless following now sought delivery from its unaccustomed isolation in confused talk and aimless action. . . . Tens of thousands of Defense Leaguers, Athletic Leaguers, factory workers, streetcar employees, railroad workers, Young Fronters, Young Socialists, members and officials were running from place to place on the afternoon of the 12th and in the night that followed, asking what they could do, where their rendezvous was, or where else they could join an armed unit if the designated spot was already held by police."

pp. 13f.:

"After a long search Leichter[3] and Pollak finally found the technical aides of the combat command in a hall of the Vienna Hill settlement. The command itself had found makeshift quarters in an Akazienhof superintendent's apartment, but Leichter and Pollak did not get that far. Nor had the aides any use for editors. The excited Leichter no sooner produced his manifesto than he was told with the supercilious air that fighters have for writers—not only in critical combat situations—that Deutsch, through his connection with the Inva Printing Company, had provided for all propaganda needs of the combat command.

"Indeed, as early as nine o'clock Felix Kanitz, the party propaganda director, had sent a Defense Leaguer named Charlie Peutl to a printing plant in Margareten with orders to have everything set to put out the combat manifesto. An hour later, at ten, Kanitz and Peutl came up on Vienna Hill across the fields between Meidling and Favoriten. They too had to search for a long time before they found the makeshift quarters of the combat command staff. It was past eleven when Kanitz sent his messenger back to the printer with the text of the manifesto. En route to Triesterstrasse, Peutl was rather surprised to see Julius Deutsch, the 'military chief' of the resistance, sitting at the broad window of a tavern at the settlement corner, staring out into the gloomy morn. The streetcars came to a halt just as Peutl reached the Gürtel, and at the printer's it turned out that the 'unforeseen' power failure had stopped all presses and thus foiled the printing of the combat manifesto too. . . . Construction Workers secretary Holowatij, the most reckless of all later underground members, offered to turn out the unprinted manifesto on a mimeograph apparatus removed from his office, demonstrating that he would not

---

3. The editor of the *Arbeiter-Zeitung*, later a founder of the first central committee of the illegal party. [Note by Negt and Kluge—*Ed.*]

let a chance to act be spoiled by reflections on whether the action made sense. When the full text proved too long for two pages, Holowatij and his helpers, after brief debate, decided what to cut.

"It was not quite five when Peutl and another comrade stood on Vienna Hill at the door of the combat command post, with a few thousand copies of this document. Leighter and Pollak had just arrived, Holowatij was there too. His tale of relieving the 'cowering Kanitz' of the combat manifesto's manufacture could make the two leading party journalists only more embittered at the failure of press preparations for the struggle. Twenty-four hours earlier the party had had eight printing plants, seven dailies, and eighteen weeklies; to run the thousands of multigraph machines in party, union, and cultural organization offices there were innumerable people who had vainly hunted all day for a chance to do something."

pp. 21f.:

"Far beyond the realm of politics it shaped the lives and thoughts of its active members. The police announced on March 28 that fifteen hundred associations had been dissolved as falling under the ban on the Social Democratic Party. Hundreds of thousands of men, women, young people, and children had spent the best part of their chiefly proletarian lives in these organizations. They were filled with dreams and activities all of which orginated in this party's 'idea.' Its broad organizational structure had room for all trades and professions. It enabled all ages to organize their entertainment requirements, their educational plans, their purposes in life, their cultural desires, their hobbies, even their follies, and to fuse them 'ideologically' with the aims of the party, in serious or ridiculous fashion. . . . If the convictions, energies, prejudices, vanities, and sacrifices of these people had sufficed for the continued existence of the party, it would have been assured even in these hardest times.

"To the disciples filled with the party's spirit, the fact that it was imperishable followed from their fundamental 'Marxist' view. In this view the realization of the party's aims was a historic necessity."

# 6. Camp Mentality of the KPD before 1933

From its foundation, a central problem of the KPD in the Weimar Republic was to develop a political identity that reflected both the revolutionary strategy it was to follow and the potential origins of its members. Up until the phase of its so-called Bolshevization there was, if one takes its controlling organs as the yardstick, no truly unified political line. It was difficult to determine in detail which coalitions between sections and individuals were responsible for a recent decision or for a specific course. Up until 1925–26 there was basically a struggle between individual sections over the organizational and political identity of the party.[1]

One of the fundamental reasons for this search for political identity was that there was not only a high degree of fluctuation in membership (by contrast with the constantly growing number of voters, at least until 1926), but the members were in part, or in many places primarily, made up of unemployed persons, who no longer had any links to factory production. In 1932 only 11 percent of KPD members were factory workers. This was, it is true, stabilized in the wake of the Comintern slogan, Bolshevization of the Communist parties. But what emerges

---

1. Thus the offensive actions of 1921 and 1923 were clearly intended to convince the masses of the revolutionary character of the Communist party. An extensive listing of sources and bibliographical material, including newspapers and journals for the entire time period, can be found in Hermann Weber, *Die Wandlung des deutschen Kommunismus*, 2 vols., (Frankfurt am Main: 1969); here we refer to volume 2, pp. 364ff.; Karl Dietrich Bracher, *Die Auflösung der Weimarer Republik. Eine Studie zum Problem des Machtverfalls in der Demokratie*, 3d ed., (Villingen: 1960), and the bibliography cited therein; *Illustrierte Geschichte der deutschen Revolution* (pirated copy: 1969).

more and more strongly during this period is the sealing off of the Communist party as an independent camp within society as a whole. No doubt a certain degree of political identity was thereby attained, but this was from the outset fractured, and in two respects. As a section of the Communist International, the KPD separated itself from the real experiential context in which it stood as an organization, as well as from the individual experiential basis of its members. When the party was waging a defensive struggle against social-democratic revisionism on one side and the right on the other, it drew its strategy from an over-identification with the Stalinist policy of "socialism in one country." Thus a declaration of December 1924 proclaims: "The Communists have only one fatherland and home, and that is Soviet Russia!" The price of this coalition within a homogeneous camp is a separation from living social reality, which would have made wholly different policies necessary in Germany than, for instance, in France or the Scandinavian countries.

This policy within a camp was wanting in two respects. Describing the social democrats, whose organizations united masses of workers, as social fascists—as the left wing of the National Socialists—blocked any possibility of a united front against fascism, and not only at the level of the leadership. In fact, it became apparent that even where the factory cells were declared the organs of a united front at a grass-roots level, this united front was never intended seriously, for it was always defined in such a way that it could have meaning only where the Communists were in command. Thus Walter Ulbricht wrote at the time (in his article "The next organizational tasks of the Communist parties"): "In Germany we can see during the tariff campaign a fundamental strengthening of factory agitation. This was an attempt, through the creation of organs of a united front within factories, to mobilize broader masses of workers under Communist leadership. If the successes are only small, this goes back above all to the fact that in the past not enough attention was given to political work in factories." The moderate effectiveness of this and similar initiatives toward a united front at the grass-roots level derived not so much from the fact that they were unpolitical in nature but rather that external agitation without roots in the experiences of the workers themselves does not suffice to separate the masses from their reformist organizations.

On the other hand, because the workers were diverted from the experience of their own social reality and were obliged to identify with the Soviet Union, the traditions, psychic states, and so on, of socialist thought were scorned. These could then be adopted and exploited by National Socialism. Ernst Bloch and Wilhelm Reich recognized early on the danger in an underdeveloped socialist fantasy. They made it clear, for instance, that the ideologies of home, fatherland, community, and so on, which were gaining influence in the working class, could not be divorced in a rational manner from the workers. These ideologies are forms of expression that must either be restructured to take on a socialist meaning, be sublated, or be relinquished to the enemy. Under no circumstances can they remain in a politically neutral space.[2]

2. A conclusive analysis of the danger of National Socialism was submitted very early on (in 1922) by the Communist theoretician A. Jacobsen in "Der Faszismus," in *Die Internationale, Zeitschrift für Praxis und Theorie des Marxismus* (1922; reprint Verlag Neue Kritik, November edition, no. 10, pp. 301ff.): "Things have to be stated as they are. Today fascism is by no means a movement that is supported only by bourgeois elements and the lumpenproletariat, but has its foundation in the broad masses of farmers and the petty bourgeoisie, and even the workers, whose ideology is petty-bourgeois and syndicalist. . . . Now, the warnings for Germany. In spite of the fact that fascism exhibits many specifically Italian characteristics, its essence is international. Picking up the threads of bourgeois nationalism, of the social decline of petty-bourgeois strata and the masses of workers, it finds its firm ground above all wherever the masses, disappointed in their socialist leaders and not recognizing the contexts, attempt to change their position in the national framework and believe that they have found a way to do this in a renewal of moral discipline. . . . Let us not mistake the danger. It is a warning signal that the National Socialist Hitler has gathered thousands of workers behind his flag in Upper Bavaria and Munich, and is able to force the resignation of Lerchenfeld through the pressure exerted by the masses that stand behind him. Also symptomatic is the platform speech of the German Nationalist Hergt at the party convention in Görlitz, in which he recommended the shifting of party activity away from the Reichstag back toward the people. The German Communist party should heed these indications of an ideological changeover within layers of the petty bourgeoisie and the workers, for if it does not it will suddenly find itself facing a movement, the danger of which cannot yet be estimated."

# 7. "Social Fascism"

One of the most consequential means of expression of the camp mentality is the reduction of all social groups that are outside the German Communist party into one unified complex of fascist forces. What Lenin constantly emphasized—that it was necessary in the class struggle to exploit even the minor contradictions within the enemy camp—is practically prevented by such a polarization of forces. One could almost say that the label of social fascism has as its goal the obviation in advance of every level of compromise with social-democratic groupings. In this the fundamental difference between the organizational forms of political rights and the reformist workers' organizations was overlooked, but not only this: the difference between Brünings's parliamentary bourgeois regime and fascism was also ignored.

Trotsky rightly pointed out that social democracy, no matter how it may objectively have encouraged fascism, is by its structure the expression of workers' interests. He made clear that fascism cannot by any means restrict itself to destroying only the workers' leaders and organizational nuclei but, for self-preservation, must work toward eliminating all autonomous forms of organization of the working class so that any chance of an independent crystallization of the proletariat is prevented. **In this devastation of the organizations of the working class, this reduction of the proletariat to the amorphous state of individuals no longer autonomously linked to one another,** Trotsky saw the essence of the fascist system. That fascism and social democracy cannot be equated at this level is evident. In consequence, there is—if one takes society as a whole as the object of analysis—not a single argument to support the idea that social democracy, in particular its leadership, is the chief enemy of the revolutionary labor movement.

How little this camp mentality and the social fascism thesis are an expression of the real experience of the labor movement can be shown with particular clarity in the phase of class struggles preceding the October Revolution in Russia. In the face of the counterrevolutionary military actions of Kornilov, the Bolshevik party did not for a moment hesitate to help the Mensheviks, and set up revolutionary defense committees, which the Bolsheviks joined as a minority. Their minority position within these committees in no way prevented them from playing the leading role in revolutionary mass actions, from determining the direction of the struggle, and, in so doing, to help those workers influenced by the Mensheviks and the Social Revolutionary soldiers.[1]

---

1. This compromise is by no means a matter of the so-called lesser of two evils. What is at stake, rather, is the *concentration of the struggle against one opponent, with whom compromises and coalitions are excluded.* A dialectical method consists precisely in consciously exploiting the contradictions that exist within the enemy camp in order to effectively allow the movement of the matter in one's own interests. Lenin emphasized this element of cunning in dialectical thinking as a decisive element in the class struggle. This capacity for cunning no doubt also includes the capacity for pulling back, for breaking up one's own camp, for the surprise compromise, for *disorganizing the enemy's forces through a strategy of intensifying their inner contradictions.* Trotsky provides an example of this: "In the days of the Kornilov march, Kerensky turned to the sailors of the cruise ship *Aurora* with the request that they take on the task of protecting the Winter Palace. The sailors were all Bolsheviks; they hated Kerensky. This did not prevent them from diligently guarding the Winter Palace. Their representatives visited Trotsky, who was a member of the 'Kresty' and asked, 'Shouldn't Kerensky be taken prisoner?' Yet the question had a half-facetious character: the sailors understood that Kornilov would first have to be eliminated in order to be able to settle accounts with Kerensky. Thanks to correct political leadership, the sailors of the *Aurora* understood more than Thälmann's central committee." (Leon Trotsky, *Schriften über Deutschland*: 227).

# 8. Fetish "Politics" and Working-Class Politics

The fundamental question concerning a proletarian public sphere that is encapsulated in a camp is which characteristics of workers are organized to prevent connections and fusions with bourgeois modes of life. It emerges that at this level of the abstract organization of characteristics, the relations between proletariat and bourgeoisie are relatively clear and transparent for the individual. Individuals are able unequivocally to identify with the working class and its party by dissociating themselves from the bourgeois class. But the difficulty with this clear demarcation is that a multitude of characteristics of living individuals are left in an unorganized state in which, wholly outside of the control of the party of the proletariat, they can enter into specific connection with bourgeois ideas, attitudes, and character structures. At this level of material infrastructure, of the psychic organization of individuals, there develops a nexus of interests and needs that determined enemies need only recognize to be able to use to their own ends. This momentarily reveals that the organization of isolated characteristics of workers at the level of clear demarcations is illusory. It is therefore not surprising that fascist movements have, from one day to the next, masses at their disposal who join a current that drags them away from their camp.

Under the conditions of the camp, a whole series of attenuations, which were originally forced on the organization and the struggle by the enemy, cannot be overcome. This applies to the category "proletarian," which is deduced from the reified proletarian character, in other words from the human labor power ravaged as the object of capital. It applies, furthermore, to the primacy of state politics. Originally, the adoption of the concept of politics is a response to the excessive pressure exerted on the workers' organization by the bourgeois contradictions that cannot be resolved economically and are therefore transposed into political relations of authority. In this form of organization, such contradictions take on a logic of their own. The mechanism of classification, which decides on what can be a focal point of struggle and organizational activity and what cannot, is based on the meager possibilities of connection between the merely objectively defined concept "proletarian" and the state-defined "political": the one curtails the other. Thus the interests of proletarians that do not seem relevant in terms of state politics disappear as no less marginal than domains capable of politicization that do not at first glance look proletarian (e.g., childrearing, sexuality). These become the object of mass organizations that are only affiliated to the party, in which such diverse facets as women, sport, culture, antifascism, childrearing, and perhaps national consciousness find themselves juxtaposed. These reifications limit the amount of social substance and experience that is capable of expressing itself in the organization at all. The strategy and tactics produced by the latter are an expression of the limits of this substance. Their economism, their state-orientation, their conformism cannot be overcome by mere resolve, for instance, by adding on the correct theory and a consideration of the subjective factor among the masses. There is, rather, within the proletarian public sphere organized as a camp, no motivation or material base of experience for a comprehensive extension of the political and theoretical horizon.

A clearly defined demarcation between politically conscious and unconscious masses underlies this thinking in terms of a camp. This demarcation is, however, itself a fundamental characteristic of idealist thought. A proletarian who is, today, class-conscious can by tomorrow—if he obtains no specific responses in his everyday situation in political form (in other words, an orientation toward the future within the context of his life history)—be a supporter of a fascist movement. Conversely, the daily experience of having no future can rapidly transform unemployed persons who are given a perspective of real and lasting change into class-conscious proletarians. The decisive problem here is concealed by the fact that it appears as though long-term behavior on the part of workers could come about through appeals and plausible arguments for socialism, for instance, through the theory of crisis: in other words, through an ethical or scientific awareness. *But in such a case this behavior is based on internal mechanisms of character and libidinal economy on which bourgeois society too is based and which it has produced. This explains why, at decisive moments, workers act contrary to the expectations of the party leadership.* In this respect, fascist leaders reveal themselves to be the more consistent materialists. For them this eclectic materialism comes easily because they make no effort to unite workers' interests around emancipatory goals. **They can allow themselves an opportunistic materialism precisely because they practice a politics of adventurism.** Among Marxist theoreticians, it is above all Wilhelm Reich who insisted on this point.

Wilhelm Reich (Ernst Parell), *Was ist Klassenbewußtsein? Ein Beitrag zur Diskussion über die Neuformierung der Arbeiterbewegung*, Verlag für Sexualpolitik (Copenhagen/Paris/Zurich: 1934; reprint, no publisher, n. d., 1968), pp. 36ff.:

"Fetish 'Politics'—

"The political layman understands the term 'politics' as referring to diplomatic discussion between the representatives of major and minor powers among whom decisions are made as to the fate of mankind; he can say with justification that he doesn't understand it at all. Or he understands politics as parliamentary deal making between friends and enemies, but also as mutual swindling, spying, cheating, and decisions made in accordance with the formula 'business as usual'; he also has no understanding of this, it disgusts him quite often, and he thus develops the liberating opinion that he 'doesn't want to have anything to do with politics.' In so doing, he doesn't see the contradiction in the fact that this activity of which he is justifiably contemptuous will continue to make decisions that affect him, and that in spite of this he will continue to complacently allow these momentous decisions to be made by people he considers swindlers. . . .

"To anyone schooled in Marxism, it will be immediately clear that bourgeois politics must always be demagogic, since it can only make promises to the masses, but never fulfill them. Revolutionary politics contradicts this in that it can also fulfill, in principle undemagogically, everything it promises to the masses. Wherever it is demagogic or has a demagogic effect, one can assume with certainty that this has been at the cost of fundamental revolutionary principles."


p. 11:

"Someone who had conducted himself very quietly asked a leading functionary, who proclaimed himself to be an especially ardent advocate of the class consciousness of the German proletariat, to name five concrete elements of class consciousness and perhaps also five elements that were hindering its development. 'If one wants to develop class consciousness, and why it doesn't develop of its own accord under the pressure of every sort of need, so what is stopping it?' The question seemed logical. The functionary was initially a little astonished by the question, hesitated for a moment, and then responded decisively, 'Well, obviously, it's hunger!' 'Is the hungry SA-man class-conscious?' was the immediate counterquestion. Is the thief who steals a sausage out of hunger class-conscious, or an unemployed man who joins a reactionary march for two marks, or a kid who throws a stone at the police during a demonstration? If, in other words, the hunger upon which the German Communist party has built up its entire mass psychology is not in and of itself an element of class consciousness, what else could be? What is freedom? What does it look like concretely? How is the socialist freedom different from the nationalist freedom that Hitler promises?"

pp. 38ff.:

"Why didn't Litvinov [1] address the masses?

"Revolutionary politics is, in its content and language, either the expression of the primitive, unacculturated existence of the broad masses that is bound up with life, or only calls itself revolutionary and will be futile and reactionary in its effect. Even when it makes proposals that are fundamentally correct, it will remain uncomprehended by the masses and thus have an objectively antirevolutionary effect."

p. 40f.:

"In his writings and speeches, Lenin always turned to the broad masses. This gives us the answer to our question: Can revolutionary politics ever succeed in defeating bourgeois politics if it utilizes the latter's way of speaking, its tactics, its strategies—in other words, if it utilizes bourgeois methods? It will never succeed using these methods. It will only stray into the labyrinth of politics and lag along after events, and be *even worse* at it than the bourgeois politicians. There is only one choice: *cut through* the tangled knots that bourgeois politics has set up as a labyrinth, so that, rather than simply aping bourgeois politics, revolutionary politics confronts it with its fundamental principle. Turn incessantly, with untiring simplicity and clarity, to the masses; speak the thoughts of the masses, those that have been thought and those that haven't been thought out, give them expression; destroy the respect of the masses for 'high-level' politics; don't take the swindle seriously, but rather mercilessly and untiringly expose it; speak in the language of the masses; don't adapt the masses to 'high-level' politics, but politics to the masses, democratize it, simplify it, make it accessible to everyone. Lenin's statement that every cook must be capable of administering the state contains the fundamental principles of social democracy. 'High-level politics' can only exist because revolutionary politics has adapted itself to these politics in its form, language, and logic, even though the content of these is revolutionary, because it has not turned toward the masses, but instead treated them like a child that has to be convinced, that finally has to realize and also 'realizes more and more,' that someone is playing it for a fool."

---

1. The Foreign Minister of the Soviet Union.

# 9. The Proletarian Public Sphere and the Election of Hindenburg

The problem of the false relationship of the party to the bourgeois public sphere and its instruments of power was clearly shown in 1925 in the presidential election for Ebert's successor. Whereas the bourgeois public sphere from the outset—if one disregards the Center as a melting-pot of various bourgeois forces who were looking for a middle way—appeared as a united front and amassed a total of 13 million votes for Hindenburg, the left and the left center fragmented into 7.5 million for the social democrats, 1.8 million for the Communists, and 8.9 million votes for the Center. For the second ballot the leadership of the Communist party, with backing from the Comintern, stuck, no doubt predictably, to its own candidate, Thälmann, who obtained 1.9 million votes. In this way Hindenburg, with 14.6 million votes, was elected Reich's President ahead of the Center candidate, Marx, who gained 13.7 million. Thus the electoral behavior of the KPD was decisive for the election of Hindenburg.

The election signaled the unification of the traditions of the Wilhelmine Reich with those of the Weimar Republic, of the high command of the Reichswehr with the authority of the Reich's President, a president who himself came from this military tradition. The Reichswehr, the state, and the political right, along with the republican center (comprising the democratic Hindenburg voters) now stood together against the working class until 1933; the content of politics was derived from compromises between heavy industry and large landowners. What the Communist leadership had failed to grasp was the fact that even a civilian like the Center candidate Marx would have contributed to bringing together the dissociated forces of the bourgeois public sphere in a manner distinct from that made possible by a right-center bloc with simultaneous full synchronization of state, Reichswehr, police, and capital. Even without the decisive addition of the National Socialists, such a bloc, with the Brüning, von Papen, and von Schleicher administrations, had to be directed against all working-class politics. Because the united right once again held public and state instruments in its hands, it became difficult in an economic crisis to transform proletarian interests into political interests. In this respect the right-wing bloc in no way echoed the real mood of the country. It consolidated itself, however, thanks to the purchase of the Ufa film fortune and the Scherl press concern by the leader of the German nationalists, Hugenberg. The KPD reacted to all these developments with self-deception about the consequences of this concentration of power.

Two elements of this development are important for us: first, the underestimation of the instruments of power of the bourgeois public sphere assimilated to the state; second, a blind clinging to one's own candidates, who stand no chance of election but who define the identity of one's camp.[1] The nonpublic sphere within the latter then serves as a barrier—after defeat—to this election being grasped as a test of one's own powerlessness. There is, however, a distinction here between the experience of reality of the proletarians who remain in the party camp and make use of its systems of information, and of those who, as before, fall prey to the bourgeois public sphere and have to regard the election battles of the KPD as defeats, whereas within the KPD camp they count as important stages. An additional notion here is evidently that a strengthening of the reactionary camp does not have to be avoided because precisely through such strengthening the masses will learn to grasp the pointlessness of any compromise. This takes on an extreme form in the interpretation of the victory of National Socialism, which came to be regarded as the last rearguard action of the bourgeois public sphere before the proletarian revolution. What is correct about this notion is no doubt the fact that the masses learn from the spectacle of bourgeois politics. In his analysis of the ultraleft in the English labor movement, Lenin stressed, as we have seen, that it was senseless to try to leapfrog over the autonomous learning processes of the proletariat by means of arguments and slogans.[2] However, he was setting out from a practical situation in which the workers could trace the futility of reformist solutions to the fundamental contra-

---

1. The futility of the Thälmann election is immediately apparent if one imagines a Thälmann victory, which was objectively impossible. It would have been the equivalent of a civil war, in which professionalized power, that is, the Reichswehr, would presumably have decided the issue. The candidacy carried on with the firm expectation that it would not come to this. But it must have a devastating effect on the imaginative capacities of the masses if the goal of an election battle—Thälmann moving into the palace of the Reich's President, Thälmann as the commander in chief of the Reichswehr—is already objectively impossible to imagine.

2. Cf. commentary 2.

dictions of capitalist society through the reformist initiatives of a social-demo-cratic party. **So long as the masses continue to consider that social-democratic solutions are possible, they will not abandon the reformist parties. That such solutions are impossible is not a matter of persuasion but of real experience. This experience cannot be gathered through fighting social-democratic practice at any price—even at the price of the right taking power. From the actions of fascists or the extreme right the masses learn nothing whatsoever about the hopelessness of reformism**; with a public sphere that corresponds to their structure of perception, to some extent they do not even notice this phenomenon. That this has never been comprehensively discussed is an expression of that narrowing of perception that grasps only the immediate neighborhood of one's own camp and cloaks the whole of the rest of society in abstract analyses through which no further experience or immediate perception penetrates.

This is, to be sure, not only a problem that the Weimar KPD had to solve but a contemporary syndrome of any leftist party that is subject to a camp mentality. The basic structure of this contradiction within Marxist parties can be found today in a multitude of groups that espouse radical, nonrevisionist programs, as in Communist mass parties, where it is not a decisive factor whether these display liberal traits, like the Italian Communist party, or have stricter programs, like the French Communist party. What we are dealing with here are not characteristics of institutions per se or the structures of perception and consciousness of the working class. What is interesting about the practice of the PCI and the PCF is that the more concrete is the experiential sphere in which, for instance, the candidates of different parties have to work together (at the regional or municipal level), shifting coalitions in actual fact come about whereby the various groupings of the left cooperate in removing right-wing candidates. At the level of society as a whole, however, the abstract demarcation into camps remains.

# 10. Learning from Defeats?

In the history of the labor movement, there are defeats that represent a store of experiences for all subsequent periods—as, for example, the defeat of the Paris Commune. Other defeats remain wholly without experience; they have destroyed experience and left traumatic fixations. Examples of this are the defeat of the German labor movement in January 1919, the failure of the offensive actions of the KPD in 1921 and 1923. Yet other experiences, such as the destruction of all organizations of the labor movement in Germany after 1933, signal both: experiences in the interests of immunization (admittedly, in the main only after the defeat of National Socialism) and loss of proletarian historical consciousness.

Within Marxist writing, the relationship between defeats and experience is most often interpreted in the exaggerated form that Marx, in his *Critique of Hegel's Philosophy of Right*, terms "esoteric." The data that can be assembled into a meaningful context—which, in other words, give the defeat a meaning in retrospect—are extracted. The result is a compulsion toward an optimistic perspective that brackets out the destruction of experience. To admit the latter would mean that one was not following a reliable and consistent policy. This esoteric interpretation stands alongside what is the kernel of the Marxist approach, which is to investigate each situation with a view to its real materialist experiential content, **and in which the esoteric method has no place**. These two lines of Marxist analysis are completely irreconcilable; either one is correct **or** the other.

In the article "Democratic Pan-Slavism," Marx writes: "One single courageous attempt at a democratic revolution, even if it is stifled, will expunge whole centuries of infamy and cowardice from the memory of other peoples and will instantly rehabilitate a nation, however deeply it may have been despised."[1] In *The Class Struggles in France,* he states: "The workers were only able to gain this victory at the price of the terrible defeat of June."[2]

At the same time, the hopelessness of the individual attempts at revolt, the massacres that the army inflicted on the demonstrating workers, have left a deep impression. The heroic conception of the revolution, including its defeats, should, in Marxist discussion, not conceal the question of which defeats of the working class strengthen the fighting spirit and which inhibit the development of political awareness and class consciousness for a whole epoch. What is the working class supposed to rely on if not its own experiences? The only plausible reaction to the experience of defeat is for it to avoid the situation with which the defeat was associated. The masses never entered into struggles in order to free themselves from infamy and cowardice. These are motives that moved, for instance, the Polish aristocracy in the nineteenth century, who wanted to save Poland. Such motives are idealistic. A similar stance on the part of a workers' organization would fundamentally contradict the "materialist instinct."

Nevertheless, the compulsion develops, again and again—precisely for consistent workers' leaders—to follow, in situations that seem hopeless, a reaction in which the masses already find themselves. It was thus that Liebknecht justified keeping to the January struggles in 1919. After the failure of the March initiative of 1921, Clara Zetkin ended her speech at the congress of the Third International, in which she set out her opposition to the offensive strategy, with the words: "And if I demand of the congress that it undertake a thorough and conscientious examination of both theory and tactics during the March action, I am demanding this out of a conviction that our analysis must be: an arming for new and severe struggles, irrespective of either defeat or victory, for defeats too can be fruitful if they are defeats of the proletarian masses in the face of a superior enemy, if they are defeats of which the proletariat can say with pride: We have lost everything, except the honor of having fought, of having stormed forward in a revolutionary manner!" (*vigorous applause*).[3] This turn of phrase is repeated by individual groups within the student movement when they regard the latter's defeat after 1968 as a success in terms of learning, according to which falling back onto splinter groups represented an experiential gain.

---

1. Karl Marx, *Der demokratische Panslawismus,* in *Marx-Engels Werke,* vol. 6: 281.

2. Karl Marx, *Die Klassenkämpfe in Frankreich,* in *Marx-Engels Werke,* vol. 7: 21. Cf. also the final passage in Engels's introduction to *Die Klassenkämpfe in Frankreich* (p. 526). Engels refers here to the defeats of the Christians that finally led to the victory of Christianity under Emperor Constantine. The ambivalence of this consoling reference is especially clear, since the state Christianity of Constantine (this so-called victory) destroyed everything that the Christian revolutionary party had fought for in the years of their constant persecution and defeat.

3. Clara Zetkin, in *Protokolle des III. Kongresses der Kommunistischen Internationale,* reprint vol. 1, p. 300.

But in all these cases no real historical experience is released. It is covered over by the ethical abstraction. The only truly major defeat that brought about an adequate response—in other words, a materialist analysis—is the Paris Commune, which is today kept alive by the Chinese Marxists as a symbol of the possibility of bitter defeats. This is why a verse of Mao's can read: "The Internationale, tragic song."[4] The red flag too retains its meaning for a developed proletarian public sphere only to the extent that the history of this symbol, with its diverse experiential contents, remains living. It is not a mere symbol of activation.[5]

Whether a defeat absorbs emancipatory experience depends not on its retrospective interpretation but whether the struggle was objectively necessary and hopeful. Historically hopeless struggles, such as the Peasants' Wars, the struggles of January 1919 in Berlin, and the March action of 1921, or struggles with incorrectly conceived goals, will never enhance social experience and the capacity of the masses to organize, to improve. In this respect, the Peasants' Wars strengthened the backwardness of the German peasantry, as did the Jacquerie (the numerous hopeless revolts by French peasants up to the eighteenth century).[6] Emancipatory lessons are an indication that historical struggles possess an invaluable material subsoil; this is not absorbed by the fact of defeat and continues in subsequent experience. Struggles that rest on abstract strategic thinking, such as those of March 1921, neglect precisely this material underground.[7]

Horkheimer and Adorno define social stupidity as the scar tissue of historical defeats: "The coercion suffered turns good will into bad."[8] Sensibility is destroyed if it constantly comes up against insurmountable resistance. Such deformations "can build hard and able characters; they can breed stupidity—as a symptom of pathological deficiency, of blindness and impotency, if they are qui-

---

4. Cited in Joachim Schickel, *Die Mobilisierung der Massen. Chinas ununterbrochene Revolution* (Munich: 1971), p. 75. The entire verse reads: "Millions of workers, peasants: all marching double-time, / Kiangsi unrolls before us like mats, Yenan and Hupei are ahead. / The Internationale, tragic song; / a whirlwind, fallen upon us from heaven."

5. Apparently, the red flag was first raised as a signal by Lafayette's national guard on the battlefield of Paris. This signal meant: Fire at will upon the masses of people who have gathered to demonstrate. This meaning was reversed later when the flag was appropriated by the people.

6. Cf. the emergence of the Danish peasants, who responded to the political defeat of Denmark after the war of 1864 with the introduction of rural adult education.

7. The reasons for hopeless struggles that never would have been undertaken had it been really possible to examine the overall material context can be based in a spontaneous reaction on the part of the masses, who assess the situation incorrectly, such as the revolutionary movement of July 1917 in Russia. The struggles can also be actuated under orders from higher leadership—under certain circumstances linked with errors in transmission; an example of this is the Hamburg insurrection of 1923. But the masses can also be reacting to the open provocation against their rights, which sets in motion a mass potential at the wrong point in time so that it can then be defeated.

8. Max Horkheimer and Theodor W. Adorno, "The Genesis of Stupidity," in *Dialectic of Enlightenment*, trans. John Cumming (New York: Continuum, 1972): 258.

escent; in the form of malice, spite, and fanaticism, if they produce a cancer within."[9] **But societal sensibility needs some resistance to work against if it is to constitute itself as an experience for itself.** Learning processes resulting from defeats must therefore be examined with a view to two different types of experience: destructive and emancipatory. If only one or the other of these aspects is manifest, there is generally an error in the analysis.

9. Ibid., pp. 257–58. In certain respects, the ideal type of the "hard-as-steel Bolshevik" as it appeared with the German Communist party in the 1920s, especially during the Ruth Fischer-course, is reminiscent of this character formation. What is at issue is a propaganda image, something calculated. This Bolshevik—who completely deviates from the image of the intellectuals who worked together with Lenin in the Bolshevik faction—is characterized by an abstract hardness, insensitive because he is "implacable." While he accommodates all of the party's twists and turns, he himself remains completely unchanged. He allows himself to be sent into any country in the world, into any concrete situation in which he has not grown up and in whose experiential context he does not live; there he engineers uprisings that end like the defeat of Canton. His behavior is just as abstract as that of the character mask of the bourgeois on the opposing side. André Gorz (in *Weder Bolschewik noch Gewerkschaftler*) describes the configuration of this character and that of the syndicalist labor leader. In Arthur Koestler's *Der Yogi und der Kommissar*, the comparison is made possible by the stereotyping of this image of the professional revolutionary that cannot exist in reality, because only the abstraction of a revolutionary can be compared with the abstraction of a yogi. Thus the subsequent byproducts of historical defeats continue to distort the real content of experience. In this form, "historical experiences" of the labor movement enter effortlessly into the bourgeois public sphere.

# 11. The Temporal Structure of the Experience of Historical Struggles

The blocking of linguistic expression, of symbols, of gestures, of relationships between human beings too, is rooted in particular situations and contexts of action. Even apparently invariable linguistic patterns or forms of expression among workers acquire, in specific conditions free from the restrictions of the normal work and life situation, a wholly new direction. The temporal structure of experiences that are made in real situations of struggle can neither be grasped quantitatively nor in the qualitative scheme that, for instance, applies to primary socialization. What we have, rather, is a form of compression of time, which entails that the experience of contexts becomes, as it were, sensually manifest. One day, one hour, can determine victory or defeat. Temporal continuity is exploded, and indeed in such a fashion that reifications, blockages of the consciousness and behavior of the masses—which under normal conditions could not be overcome by years of educational work—suddenly fall away like shells. Solidarity—which one could not have expected toward a strike or an uprising on the part of any individual peasant, white-collar worker, artisan, and so on—comes about as if taken for granted. The most important reason for such a collective liberation of uninhibited communication and of linguistic energies is that the reality principle that is experienced as a permanent censorship of their individual behavior and thinking is, for the moment, put out of action in its entirety so that they can behave as if an alien reality confronting them did not exist. At any rate, this compact reality, which in normal life fences them in and keeps them under control, is so far removed from their field of vision that they are able to bring contents of their own experience into the form of communication and relationships between human beings. All these changes generally take place not through following directives and slogans that come from outside, but rather they are part of a context that is rapidly organizing itself, **in which each individual behaves in the way that he has always behaved in his fantasy, in his wishes, in his libidinal goals.** The complex organization of this experience is described by Merleau-Ponty in his *Phenomenology of Perception:*

> The day-laborer who has not often seen workers in regular employment, who is not like them and has little love for them, sees the price of manufactured goods and the cost of living going up, and becomes aware that he can no longer earn a livelihood. He may at this point blame town workers, in which case class-consciousness will not make its appearance. If it does, it is not because the day-laborer has decided to become a revolutionary and consequently offers a value upon his actual condition; it is because he has perceived, in a concrete way, that his life is synchronized with the life of the town laborers and that all share a common lot. The small farmer who does not associate himself with the day-laborers, still less with the town laborers, being separated from them by a whole world of customs and value judgements, nevertheless feels that he is on the same side as the journeyman when he pays them an inadequate wage, and he even feels that he has something in common with the town workers when he learns that the farm owner is chairman of the board of directors of several industrial concerns. Social space begins to acquire a magnetic field, and a region of the exploited is seen to appear. At every pressure felt from any quarter of the social horizon, the process of regrouping becomes clearly discernible beyond ideologies and various occupations. Class is coming into being, and we say that a situation is revolutionary when the connection objectively existing between the sections of the proletariat (the connection, that is, which an absolute observer would recognize as so existing) is finally experienced in perception as a common obstacle to the existence of each and every one. It is not at all necessary that at any single moment a representation of revolution should arise. For example, it is doubtful whether the Russian peasants of 1917 expressly envisaged revolution and the transfer of property. Revolution arises day by day from the concatenation of less remote and more remote ends. It is not necessary that each member of the proletariat should think of himself as such, in the sense that a Marxist theoretician gives to the word. It is sufficient that the journeyman or the farmer should feel that he is on the march towards a certain crossroads, to which the road trodden by the town laborers also leads. Both find their journey's end in revolution, which would perhaps have terrified them had it been described and represented to them in advance. One might say that revolution is at the end of the road they have taken and in their projects in the

form of 'things must change,' which each one experiences concretely in his distinctive difficulties and in the depths of his particular prejudices. Neither the appointed order, nor the free act which destroys it, is represented; they are lived through in ambiguity. This does not mean that workers and peasants bring about revolution without being aware of it, and that we have here blind, 'elementary forces' cleverly exploited by a few shrewd agitators. It is possibly in this light that the prefect of police will view history. But such ways of seeing things do not help him when faced with a genuine revolutionary situation, in which the slogans of the alleged agitators are immediately understood, as if by some pre-established harmony, and meet with concurrence on all sides, because they crystallize what is latent in the life of all productive workers.[1]

1. Maurice Merleau-Ponty, *Phenomenology of Perception*, trans. Colin Smith (London: Routge & Kegan Paul, 1962): 444–45.

# 12. Class Consciousness as a Program Concept That Requires Development by a Proletarian Public Sphere

For Marx, class is an analytical category and at the same time a category of reality. It is a tool, and simultaneously the application of this tool. It is not a mere scheme of classification that sorts individuals according to origin, social milieu, place in the production process. Class denotes, rather, a concrete historical process of the growth, change, and sublation of the conditions of life to which the masses are subjected. In this light, it is relatively unimportant whether they have consciousness of this or not. This process, whereby the class represents itself, runs through individuals, so that one cannot speak of this or that person representing the essence of the class along the lines of "Thälmann and Remmele are the gold of the working class" (Zinoviev). Empirically acting class individuals are subject to the conditions of existence of the **class**, without thereby being able to remove themselves from the influences of society as a whole and other classes. The real struggle of real individuals is in only exceptional cases identical with the class struggle between bourgeoisie and proletariat, which continues as a social process through individuals even where the social forces are confronting one another in political struggle or in civil war.

The concept of **consciousness** has a different background. Consciousness is, for Marx, tied to individuals. There is no supraindividual subject to which it could be ascribed. Marx also employs the concept in the sense of conscious being, which runs through the heads of finite human beings.[1] The production of this con-

---

1. Karl Marx, *The German Ideology* in *The Marx-Engels Reader*, ed. Robert C. Tucker, trans. T. B. Bottomore (New York: W. W. Norton, 1972): 118: "Consciousness can never be anything else than

sciousness occurs socially: via the forms of concrete reality, history, socialization, libidinal economy, the psychic structure of the individual, education, direct experiences in the work process, and the repercussions and interactions of all these levels. If one wishes to use the concept of consciousness at all in the present context, it must be grasped as the result of these components, which contain both conscious and preconscious elements. Against this program of individual behavior oriented by the unity of the proletarian way of life, what in everyday parlance is understood as consciousness can be entirely marginal in actual class struggle. There are situations in which consciousness can be attributed to proletarians who nevertheless march in a direction opposed to their class.

**Class and consciousness** are real categories, which derive from two entirely different, mutually opposed historical contexts of thought. **The Marxist tradition draws them together into a single term so as to outline a program.** This program is concerned with the mediation between the coming into being of the proletarian context of living, along with its subjective, "conscious" side on the one hand, and the practical sublation of this proletarian context of living on the other. The dialectic contained in this concept consists in the fact that it is geared to totality, but must at the same time grasp the entire empirical experiential context of the working class if it is not to become a mere classificatory category. Our critique of this concept takes into account the demand for it to be given material substance.

In Marxist orthodoxy, class consciousness is fixed as an end result. In this form, the concept prevents the resolution of concrete mediation between social totality, class situation, transformatory praxis, and the historically evolved way of

---

conscious existence, and the existence of men is their actual life-process." The concept of consciousness in Marx emerges from his critique of Hegel, for whom consciousness is not at all mere conscious existence and also does not limit itself to the intellectual capabilities of individuals. Marx uses consciousness without precisely delimiting it from the actual actions of individuals. The consciousness of the proletariat is simultaneously action. Both forms of activity are not treated as if they were identical, but neither is there a specific level of mediation between them. This corresponds to the expectation that, because of the objective position of proletarians, their becoming conscious of their alienation will be enough to move them to action. The possible, originally direct, relationship between consciousness and action has become more complicated with the advancement of social development. Social action is in possession of a multilevel base in the socialization, libidinal economy, in the psychic makeup of the person, in alienated labor similar to that of consciousness. The historical development of this base did not occur synchronically. The different positions that consciousness and action take in the process of production under the division of labor result in accelerations and retardations. These concepts, which are used in the scholarly study of education, refer to the following actual state of affairs: maturity in terms of the formal capacity to think can coincide in the case of secondary-school pupils with a particular delay in the degree of maturity of the structures of libido and character. All of the nonsimultaneities in the development of the faculties of children that can result in education only when taken together are designated with the terms retardation and acceleration. The analogy in our context must certainly take into consideration that what is at issue here is not a perspective on individual psychology, but rather on society and history.

life of the proletarian. The part played in psychoanalytic theory by rigid ego-psychology (Hartmann, Erikson)—which basically attempts to define satisfactory achievements of conformity, the fixing of a single psychic agency as the major control agency vis-à-vis libidinal drives—is, in Marxist orthodoxy, regularly played by a rigid consciousness theory that is in essence only the other face of a rigid economic objectivism. Class consciousness as the control instrument of the reality principle and realpolitik has its support in the organization of the centralized party.

It makes no difference within this class consciousness whether **consciousness** is governed by **class interest** or vice versa—in either case one *or* the other is absent as a dialectical regulator. If consciousness takes on the function of a controlling agency that governs class interest, the capacity for the practical articulation of the latter is crippled and activity is geared to present reality. This is typical of communist parties that are struggling for their identity and survival in capitalist societies; they encounter the problem that, in its embryonic form, class interest generally contains unrealistic traits, if one takes capitalism as an expression of the reality principle. An element of this is the self-confidence—corresponding to the child's sense of its omnipotence, which is, however, destroyed by "realistic" bourgeois education—to envisage and practically to strive for taking over the means of production by the producers **before this has become social reality.**[2] The class interest becomes realistic only when it has gripped the masses and has, in retrospect, proved itself to be the stronger force. By then, however, another reality principle is already dominant.

The reverse mechanism can be seen in the so-called "rebellion of the will against intellect and consciousness."[3] One of the prejudices based on this mechanism maintains—as it were in a kind of distribution of energy—that one cannot allow oneself to be concerned with theory in critical situations; the latter is, where the goal is the need to do away with immediate material pressures, a luxury: "At a time of emergency measures, diversity must yield to unity!" The development of the concrete mode of production, in which the elements fragmented according to the division of labor come together again, is postponed until a time after the revolution.[4]

These attenuations describe a type of organization that permanently restricts

---

2. Marx says that "theory becomes a material power as soon as it stirs the masses." It is necessary, however, that the masses be able to produce the libidinal prerequisites that will put them in a position to avail themselves of the theory.

3. Cf. Alfred Meusel, *Untersuchungen über das Erkenntnisobjekt bei Marx* (Jena: 1925; reprinted by Rotdruck: 1970): 11f.

4. It is possible to repeat this reference to the future after the revolution, however. Thus, for example, in the Soviet Union between 1917 and 1920, it appears to have come down to deciding politically between the emergence of the cult of the proletariat and of cultural revolution *or* the elimination of illiteracy. In accordance with the maxims of concentrated thinking, it is argued that the development of

the capacity for experience. Whereas the old Bolshevik party of Lenin grasps the party as an effective instrument **within** the revolutionary process of emancipation of the proletariat, after Lenin's death the **theory of revolution** is reduced to a mere **theory of the party**. There thus ensues a narrowing of the spectrum of experience whereby the element of the democratic—in other words, the needs, ideas, actions of the working class, which always amount to a diversity that is not completely controlled—retreats into the background in favor of the centralist aspect. In the process, however, centralism too is damaged. This type of party is faced with the following dilemma: either it burdens itself, as the imagined producer of all social circumstances, with the substance of the actual community, in which case it will fall victim to immobilism; or the party sets itself against society, forms the nucleus of an avant-garde that is dragging society along behind itself, in which case it excludes—similar to a bourgeois public sphere—the very conditions of life it wishes to change. There develops here a parallelism, characteristic of many socialist societies in transformation, between "political" agencies, economic practice, and the private way of life of the masses, which is fully grasped by neither. In both cases, there comes into being below the level of the idea of party unity an actual degree of decentralization that makes a transformation of society by the party impossible. One can liken this to the parallelism of a currency system divided into an official and a black-market currency.

Lenin had understood the party as an organization that seismographically registers the real life interests of the oppressed classes. If there is an agency that penetrates the jungle of ideological infiltrations, diverted interests, and absorbs the real-life conditions, this should, according to Lenin, be the proletarian party and the mass organizations directed by it. However, the party in its distorted form achieves the opposite. It is becoming more and more evident in the industrially advanced socialist societies in transformation, in which the apparatus of industrial production, dead labor, is assimilated to the party apparatus, that the **real life interests of the workers express themselves in a coherent manner**—in other words, as political interests—only spasmodically, and can enter into the party **after the fact** only through confrontations with the state and party apparatus. It is not that the Polish workers' party has not changed since Gdansk; it changed, however, in retrospect. Just as under bourgeois conditions the relations of production accommodate themselves to the state of the productive forces, so political circumstances follow the course of social development.

By comparison, the Leninist party appears to be the socialization agency of a

<hr>

a proletarian culture could not be achieved so long as the seemingly essential interest in the transcendence of illiteracy has not been realized; in reality, however, it is quite possible to imagine that the mobilization of cultural proletarian energies can also have a decisive impact on furthering the campaigns against illiteracy; the illiteracy campaign, on the other hand, links the proletarian cultural revolution to concrete objects. On the cult of the proletariat, see commentary 14.

still-embryonic shaping of proletarian will; it sets **the direction in which development will proceed**. This is not important as a principle of success, but it corresponds to the need to set in motion the dialectic between particular social movement and the totality. The merely retrospective ratification of **individual** impulses of a proletarian uprising (for instance by changes in personnel, individual party reforms) does not bring about a unified transformation of the proletarian context of living but allows the sporadic articulation of the interests of the working class and the administration of the legacy of the labor movement by the party to coexist. The party begins to work when the real social movement is already at an end. **The reason for this is that the party develops a form of action that is separated from the production context of the living labor of the working class.** It allies itself with the way in which objectified dead labor functions instead of being the organizer of the working class as the greatest productive force (Marx), whose object is the production of conditions of life and forms of social intercourse themselves. It is not by chance that Marx speaks of communism as the production of the latter.

# 13. Class Consciousness as a Mechanism of Pigeonholing—Georg Lukács

Lukács's starting point is the tendency of capitalism to establish itself as a commodity-producing society that potentially subsumes all objects, modes of behavior, and forms of consciousness, and transforms them into exchange relationships. The limit to this universalized exchange production—a limit inherent in the system—consists in the fact that it produces a specific form of commodity by which the commodity context is simultaneously completed and potentially broken up: in other words, labor power. There arises at this point the objective possibility that this "talking commodity" turns its consciousness against the context of exchange. Whereas in bourgeois class consciousness subject and object fall apart, since consciousness is always consciousness of alien objects, according to Lukács they come together in one person in the proletarian. Because he recognizes the commodity character of his labor power, the proletarian is simultaneously subject and object. When the worker knows himself as a commodity, his knowledge is practical. That is to say, this knowledge brings about an objective structural change in the object of knowledge. In this consciousness, and through it the special objective character of labor as a commodity, its "use-value" (i.e., its ability to yield surplus produce), which like every use-value is submerged without a trace in the quantitative exchange categories of capitalism, now awakens and becomes *social reality*. The special nature of labor as a commodity, which in the absence of this consciousness acts as an unacknowledged cog in the economic process, now objectifies itself by means of this consciousness. The specific nature of this kind of commodity has consisted in the fact that beneath the cloak of things lay a relation between human beings, that beneath the quantifying crust there was a qualitative, living core. Now that this core is revealed it becomes possible to recognize the fetishistic character *of every commodity* based on the commodity character of labor power: in every case, we find its core, the relation between human beings, as a factor in the evolution of society.[1]

The use-value quality of labor power as a commodity that gains consciousness of itself is in a position to recognize other use-values and to define relations between human beings that rest on the universal production of use-values. That the worker is simultaneously subject and object is a correct insight at the **empirical** level of proletarian self-experience. But Lukács hypostatizes this experience into the **springboard of the class consciousness of the proletariat as a whole**. Thus the proletariat's recognition of labor power as a commodity allegedly embodies at the same time the objective recognition of its historic mission. The hypostatization is most clearly revealed in that, at the individual level of the subject-object relation, the proletarian is, in the production process, in fact linked with the social totality and the concrete experience of his position. The machine that the individual worker handles, operates, is occupied with every day, confronts him as something alien, which exerts pressure and compulsion on his life. If the experience of the machinery were merely the experience of alien objects, then the worker would see in them only the element of this alienation. In order to be able to recognize the machinery he encounters as what it is in reality, namely, objectified dead labor, he must be able to perceive the contradiction between labor power as a commodity and his living labor.

At the level of the proletariat as a whole and thereby of class consciousness, an experience and insight that correspond to that of the individual proletarian cannot be achieved by mere addition, but only by an organization that mediates a world-historical consciousness with individual experience. But such an organization, as described by Lukács in the model of the party, stands outside the production context in which this experience alone can be constituted; the party has, rather, the

---

1. Georg Lukács, *History and Class Consciousness: Studies in Marxist Dialectics*, trans. Rodney Livingstone (Cambridge, Mass.: MIT Press, 1971): 169. A process of self-reflection such as the one Lukács describes here will certainly not take place in this way for one single member of the proletariat—and certainly not within the conceptual language he uses. Lukács deduces the concept of the proletariat and the worker from the proletariat that has been made the subject of historical changes. In Lukács there is an inclination to use a typifying method that is similar to Max Weber's "ideal type." Lukács himself refers to this problem: "In this context it is unfortunately not possible to discuss . . . the relation of historical materialism to comparable trends in bourgeois thought (such as Max Weber's ideal types)" (p. 81 n. 11). Precisely when he speaks of typical interest positions to which class consciousness is imputed, there is evidence of this undialectical methodology. This typifying methodology is particularly incorrect if the attempt is made to analyze the concrete life context within which the individual member of the proletariat is positioned as a bearer of the commodity that is labor power. The proletarian life context is not only an object of empiricism that occupies itself with the individual worker, but also the object of any study that examines the historical production of labor power as a commodity as a collective social process (see also Lukács's definition of class consciousness).

function of sorting already constituted proletarian experiences into historically relevant and random ones. As it does not develop any real sensorium for the latter, it is a sure means of ascertaining differences in theory and drawing the organizational conclusions.

Lukács's correct, materialist standpoint consists in the fact that in the category of labor power as a commodity the individual proletarian can arrive at a consciousness and a critique of commodity production. This perspective is, however, concretized and developed by Lukács in the wrong direction. Instead of developing the experiential levels of the individual proletarian **downward**—toward the predispositions of his consciousness, socialization, education, libidinal economy, mode of life, and so on—he overrides the latter's element of consciousness (which constitutes only a potential) by a historical construct that follows a pattern of linear progress.[2]

---

2. Cf. Lukács, *History and Class Consciousness*: "The relation with concrete totality and the dialectical determinants arising from it transcend pure description and yield the category of objective possibility. By relating consciousness to the whole of society it becomes possible to infer the thoughts and feelings which men would have in a particular situation if they were *able* to assess both it and the interests arising from it in their impact on immediate action and on the whole structure of society. . . . Now class consciousness consists in the fact of the appropriate and rational reactions *imputed* (*zugerechnet*) to a particular typical position in the process of production. This consciousness is, therefore, neither the sum nor the average of what is thought or felt by the single individuals who make up the class. And yet the historically significant actions of a class as a whole are determined in the last resort by this consciousness and not by the thought of the individual—and these actions can be understood only by reference to this consciousness" (p. 51).

# 14. The Bourgeois Ideal Association and the Party Question

An important difference between the socialist and capitalist mode of production is the fact that the object of production is altered.[1] The most important object of production is not the production of material goods as, for instance, in heavy-industry socialism, but the production of human relations, of society, of the public sphere. The necessary cultural revolution in thought, experience, life, and work practice is precisely among groups that could attempt such a reorganization in an emancipatory sense, overlaid by another question: the party question.

In bourgeois society, the interests of the bourgeois block the development of those of the *citoyen*, the *volonté générale*, even if only in an abstruse form. The interest of the bourgeois in privatization—"the longing for the island that belongs to me alone," for a house, a factory of one's own, for private education, uniqueness, individual immortalization—allows the interests of the *citoyen* to be realized only in atrophied form. These express themselves in the nineteenth century above all as specific enthusiasms (fleet building, Richard Wagner societies, keeping animals, sports, singing, weltanschauung, unification of the whole of Germany). **The organizational form of this residual *citoyen* is the bourgeois ideal association.** A "multiple individualism" comes into being that—for a time—attempts to free itself from regimentation of society as a whole by the pressures of commerce.

---

1. Karl Marx, *Nationalökonomie und Philosophie*, in *Die Frühschriften* (Stuttgart: 1968): 254: "We have seen how significant the wealth of human needs, and thus also a new mode of production as well as a new object of production, are in socialist theories."

This ideal association is a consistent image of the bourgeois public sphere. The members do not act for themselves but by means of the **committee**. Within their real, total context of living, in particular their production interest, they remain outside the association, but organize within the latter a **partial interest** (from rabbit breeding, to sports, to politics). The association constitutes a **formal public sphere** governed not by the will of the members, which comes into being in an ad hoc fashion, but by the generalized shaping of will that is formally laid down in the **statutes**. It is only indirectly, through the association's **register**, that the will of the members becomes binding for all. The life interests of the members, such as the coming into being of "relationships," friendship, are mere adjuncts, not the purpose of the association. This association structure is the only organizational form of bourgeois society—apart from state and family—that is fully established, noncommercial.[2]

In the structure of their organizations and their tradition of assembly, the workers' parties, in particular social democracy, have followed this associational model. This model suffered from the outset from the difference between ordinary members and the committee, from the impossibility—inherent in the structure—of establishing the general will of the members other than by statutes or formal decrees; the association structure does allow for collegiality within the committee, but is otherwise noncooperative and noncollective. It allows only for the makeshift combination of an interest that is in itself diffuse and underdeveloped. **It is the opposite of the model of a factory**, where the employees work and the board does not: in the association, the committee works but the members do not. Compare the rigid and formalistic structures of the association with the extremely flexible freedom of contract that applies in the economic world. Compare, further, in legal terms, the virtually **amorphous situation of struggle in the factory** with the **peaceful world of the objectified implementation of statutes within associations.** The parent organization of large firms hardly ever has the character of an

---

2. The noncommerical or "ideal organization" is covered in paragraph 21 of the *Bürgerliches Gesetzbuch* [Civil Code—referred to as "BGB" below—*Trans.*]. This organization is different from the commercial ones of paragraph 22, which, as a rule, can exercise their legal powers only under state sanction. A definition of the term "organization" is not provided explicitly in the BGB. In a commentary by Palandt (BGB, 31 edition, Section 1, Associations, 1. General Regulations, Introductory Remarks, number 1, page 21), the term organization is defined as follows: "an association of persons that is of an intended duration and has a corporate constitution, and that is regarded as a unified whole and therefore carries a single title and *exists independently of changing individual memberships.*" Legal ties exist primarily between members and the organization or the party organ of the organization; in contrast to this, the legal ties *between individual members* are completely insignificant. The bylaws are binding regardless of whether the member is familiar with them or not, and so on. The notion of "ideal organization" does not suggest that the ideals of the members are realized through the organization, but rather it signifies an area removed from the realm of the commercial organization or the capitalist association.

association; it follows, as did the earliest trade unions, the model of the BGB company.[3]

No element of even the communist parties of the West or of Lenin's party has in any way altered the basic model of the Social Democratic party, that is, of the political workers' association, even though the object is the revolutionary reshaping of society. The only change is that the revolutionary practice of Lenin and the Leninists at the outset entirely overlays the merely organizational limitations of the association structure. With the crisis of the revolutionary movement, however, the latter's inherent tendencies once more come into play. The rule of the apparatus, the mutual exclusion by one another of members of the central committee, the feigning of a general will of the party, which is, however, determined by the central committee alone—all these are characteristic features of the bourgeois association structure. The structure of the party does not correspond to the collective work program of socialism; it is not an expression in organizational terms of the production process itself and of its revolutionary transformation. It possesses, on the contrary, bourgeois mechanisms of exclusion as regards the production process and the context of living. It is an extension on a gigantic scale of a scheme that, in its historical origins, permits only "multiple individualism on the model of Robinson Crusoe."

This organizational schematism has hitherto collectively been transcended only by the Chinese Marxists during the Cultural Revolution. Admittedly, the Proletkult movement already called this organizational model into question between the years 1917 and 1920. The conflict between the Proletkult and the central committee of the Soviet party centered on the question of the autonomy of the cultural-revolutionary movement.[4] So long as Soviet society manifests itself in the shape of a workers' state, thus of the **State**, and so long as the civil war makes the military and state-political mobilization of all forces against the class enemy necessary, the cultural-revolutionary movement must—so the leaders of the Proletkult, such as Pletnev and Bogdanov, insisted—be organized in an **autonomous** manner. The Proletkult organizations, which for a time numbered more members than the Communist party of the Soviet Union, were thus, for a

3. The BGB takes the associations of the so-called BGB companies as the standard for all corporate organizations. This more loosely defined organization stands in contrast to the stock corporation, the limited partnership, the general partnership, the cooperative, and the organization as specific, specialized types of associatons. The BGB Company is defined simply by the fact that a number of persons come together for the sake of realizing common goals.

4. Cf. Eberhard Knödler-Bunte, "Chronik zur politischen Entwicklung des Proletkult 1917 bis 1923," in *Ästhetik und Kommunikation 1972* 5/6, pp. 153–90, and V. Pletnev, "An der ideologischen Front, mit Randbemerkungen Lenins," in *Ästhetik und Kommunikation 1972*, pp. 113–26. For other texts on the Proletkult, see the second, revised edition of *Bibliographie deutschsprachicher Literatur zum Proletkult*, ed. E. Knödler-Bunte, manuscript of the Institut fur experimentelle Kunst und Ästhetik (Frankfurt am Main: 1972).

period, also organized independently of state and party. **The Proletkult section in the Soviet ministry of culture was elected and controlled by these organizations.**

Revolutionary struggle on cultural terrain is, so the majority of Proletkult organizations maintained, produced in a different way from military struggle against the class enemy or political struggle. Its organization differs from all forms of organization within the economic sphere. If the day-to-day slogans of the civil war or of the transformation of the Soviet economic base were transferred to the cultural-revolutionary struggle, this struggle would cut the masses off from future cultural emancipation. The problems of the present overwhelm the future, which comprises the opposite — the sublation of existing proletarian culture.

The party contested this demand for autonomy and administratively eliminated it in 1921. In the process it opened up a whole chain of contradictions. Superficially, the Proletkult movement displayed several false lines of development, which rested on the advanced position, in professional terms, of individual tendencies within the artistic activists; Constructivism, Futurism appeared to be an infiltration and stylization of the interests of the workers, not their expression. Lenin and the central committee accused the Proletkult movement as a whole of failing to recognize the primacy of the campaign against illiteracy. But the very reduction of culture to vocational knowledge opened the way for the survival of artistic, scientific, and journalistic professionalism. Thanks to recognition by the centralized party, fashions, cliques, and tendencies among artists were to a certain degree able to assert themselves.

In the Soviet party, the question of the **specific mode of production of cultural revolution** has evidently never been raised. On the contrary, the party insisted, in the same manner as it was used to establishing the political guidelines for state, economy, and war, on also organizing the work that was the object of the Proletkult movement. There was no differentiation between **politics in the sense of the party and the Soviet state** and **cultural revolution**. At the level of politics and of the civil war, the party had to assume the unity of the interests of the peasants and the workers. This level was necessarily abstract. It brought together a consideration of peasant, that is, preindustrial, culture with interests of the workers, who it is true formed a minority but whose cultural mentality was in a position to transcend petty-bourgeois horizons. On an abstract political level, culture, language, and organizational structure of experience must appear as something invariable, as something subject to quantitative transformation—more Soviet citizens with a command of the alphabet—and as something technical—more people capable of industrial discipline and possessing industrial expertise.[5] But this does

5. This approach implicitly favors cultural professionalism. Literacy campaigns are, according to this logic, to be taken up by teachers, art by artists, science by professional scientists. The Proletkult runs counter to precisely this trend. See, for instance, V. Pletnev, "An der ideologischen Front," in

not exhaust the needs for expression of individual classes, in particular not of the workers. Cultural transformation is possible only where the concrete situations, experienced differently by each class, are incorporated. For this reason the cultural-revolutionary movement cannot align itself with the political conception of a united front of workers and peasants; it must concern itself with concrete needs and forces that need to constitute themselves in specific terms before they can enter into alliance.

Cultural-revolutionary transformation consists in the production of alternative cultural conditions. The critique of the old conditions and the criterion for the new take the form of cultural products and a transformed organization of production. The party is, however, not the site for such products or production contexts; it produces, at most, the shaping of political will in the form of professional politics. Members of the politburo or of the central committee who decree cultural revolution from above are thereby not relying on their abilities as politicians or theoreticians, wherein they possess professional knowledge, but on private capacities:[6] whatever literary, scientific, or other general cultural knowledge they happen to

---

*Ästhetik und Kommunikaton 1972.* The creation of Soviet culture by specialized artists and pedagogues, who receive their professional training in ideology production at schools divorced from the production process, results in the masses being cut off from progressive possibilities of self-reliance. In contrast to this, the Proletkult supports the inclusion of all cultural activity in the production process itself—not because the proletarian artist, who regards art as a profession, is alienated from the masses, but because, *being divorced from the production process because of his specialized task, he loses sight of the standards and the object of his work.*

In addition to the party's favoring of cultural professionalism, the only other thing necessary for the development of a rigid "socialist realism" was the system of material incentives and forced demands and prohibitions that followed. This socialist realism no longer has to have a direct link to the masses' needs for expression because it functions on an abstract, harmonious, official political level that overrides any human specificities.

6. Cf., for instance, Trotsky's numerous statements on literature and trends in the fine arts. Even though Trotsky was in favor of a uniform, military-style, disciplined production organization, he was one of the few political functionaries in the Soviet Union who stressed the importance of transforming the relations that characterized proletarian life. See his little-known pamphlet "Problems of Everyday Life" (Hamburg: 1923). In addition, see Gorky's account of a conversation with Lenin in V. I. Lenin, *Über Kultur und Kunst* (Berlin: 1960), p. 632: "I know of nothing more beautiful than the *Appassionata* and could listen to it every day. A marvelous, no longer human music! I always think with pride, maybe naive pride: 'Behold, what works of wonder humans can create!' Then he closed his eyes, smiled, and added in a fit of sadness: 'But all too often, I am unable to listen to music. It affects the nerves, one would like to say nice, silly things and pat people who live in those dirty hellholes and still produce such beauty on the head. But today one cannot pat people on the head without having one's hand bitten off. One must hit people on the head, hit them unmercifully, even though we are theoretically against any type of violence. Hm, hm—what a damned difficult duty to carry out!'" These remarks stem from a conversation, and thus are not situated in a politically formulated context. It is striking that Lenin does not argue in this personal style in any of his political statements on culture and art. On the contrary, he treats the subject very cautiously and precisely does *not* use his private relationship to art and culture as his point of departure. This abstract approach in relation to his own private views does not, however, indicate that he has a coordinated knowledge of production, either of

possess. They have the status of reviewers, because they are themselves to some extent engaged in writing, such as Trotsky or Lenin. That is not to say that they are capable of becoming engineers of cultural revolution, expert producers of a transformed culture for the masses. If they control cultural revolution in this capacity, they import into it—even if in the context of state and party policy they only arrive at correct decisions—an unadulterated bourgeois culture and mentality, which can be eliminated within them only by the transformatory cultural practice of the masses. The party is constructed according to the model of the association and the bourgeois state. It is only when all forms of the bourgeois public sphere have died out that it will no longer be necessary to organize cultural revolution in an autonomous manner.

---

professional artistic expression or of the needs of the masses to have an autonomous form of expression for their way of life (amounting to a cultural-revolutionary transformation of culture). If the production of cultural change is not the object of his revolutionary activities, he cannot claim to be different than other individuals in society when it comes to this matter. Lenin's political interests clearly differ from those of Bogdanov and other Soviet cultural revolutionaries in this respect.

# 15. Frederick Engels on the Party Press and the Public Sphere

Marx's and Engels's attitude to press freedom is governed by the struggle against authoritarian censorship, external censorship of the press, which is directed just as much against the bourgeois as against the proletariat. However—particularly in Germany[1]—the bourgeoisie does not adequately defend itself against such censorship. As with most of the bourgeoisie's revolutionary demands, the task of implementing the demand for freedom from censorship falls to the proletariat.

In 1884 Engels writes in *Der Sozialdemokrat* (no. 11 of 13 March):[2] "The German workers above all had to struggle for those rights that were indispensable to their autonomous organization as a class party: freedom of the press, of association, and of assembly—rights that the bourgeoisie would have had to struggle for in the interests of its own rule but which, in its fear, it now sought to deny the workers. The few hundred isolated members of the federation vanished in the huge mass that had suddenly been hurled into the movement. The German proletariat at the outset thus appeared on the political stage as an extreme democratic party. When we founded a major journal in Germany, the banner thereby was automatically placed into our hands. It could be only that of democracy, but of a

---

1. Formal censorship was less effective in England at this time than in Germany; rather, indirect forms of discipline were—and are still today—efficacious. Whereas in the early nineteenth century, for example, external censorship in Germany in no way reduced the multiplicity of forms of expression in speech and opinions, freedom from censorship in England is accompanied by a conventionalism of ideas and of modes of expression that does not permit deviations from prevailing opinions, the rule of common sense, or, outside of literature, the predominant usage.

2. Reprinted in Karl Marx and Frederick Engels, *Pressefreiheit und Zensur* (Frankfurt: Europäische Verlagsanstalt; Vienna: Europa Verlag, 1969): 146.

democracy that everywhere stressed its specifically proletarian character, which it could not as yet write upon its banner once and for all. If we did not want this, if we did not want to take up the movement at its existing, its most advanced, in fact proletarian end and drive it onward, all that remained for us was to preach communism in a little rag and to found a small sect instead of a large party committed to action."

In a social situation where the experiences of a class have already constituted themselves as a unified whole, externally repressive censorship is just as ineffective as were the antisocialist laws. If, however, such experiences are not yet organized into coherent notions and a unifying will, such censorship fragments the horizon of experience that is taking shape. No doubt Prussian censorship was capable of being an obstacle for the political realization of the interests of the bourgeoisie, too; this was, however, bearable in that this class already had control over the decisive economic instruments of power in society and possessed a coherent experience of production, which in any case tended to take the place of social experience as such. For the proletariat, which still had to develop its mode of production and the organization of its experience, and which was still separated from the means of production, the censorship measures came into play as social experience was taking shape. They handicapped, at crucial points, the organization of this experience.

This is why today, at a time when the Basic Law of the Federal Republic prohibits formal censorship, this question has by no means fundamentally changed. Censorship now appears materialized in the relations of production, particularly in the system of modern public spheres of production. The protection of freedom of opinion for the Bauer publishing house; press freedom as the legitimation for the unhindered expansion of the Springer corporation; the organization of workplaces as a closed society to which even trade unions have free access only in exceptional cases stipulated by law; the right to protect one's personality, which prevents the mass media and the press from publishing the connections of those who own the means of production—all these norms, founded on early bourgeois ideals, operate here as mechanisms of censorship that prevent the creation of a public sphere within which the entire experience of society organizes itself. In light of this, Engels's comment that freedom of the press signifies the relinquishing of the class struggle within the sphere of the press, is true for only quite specific social constellations.[3] For the suppression of a body of social experience, it is sufficient that all the inherited norms and procedures of the bourgeois public

---

3. Engels in *Neue Rheinische Zeitung* (no. 283, from 22 April 1849). Reprinted in Karl Marx and Frederick Engels: *Collected Works*, vol. 9 (New York: International Publishers, 1977), "The Debate on the Law on Posters," pp. 320–29: "Freedom of the press, free competition between opinions means giving freedom to the class struggle in the sphere of the press. And the kind of order that they ardently desire is precisely the stifling of the class struggle, the gagging of the oppressed classes. Hence the party of law and order has to abolish free competition between opinions in the press; by means of press

sphere continue to apply. They themselves carry out the work of destroying experience that censorship hitherto had to accomplish.[4]

Amid the conditions of a communications industry structured on late-capitalist principles, it is important for proponents of a counterpublic sphere to have at their disposal an early bourgeois means of production such as the press or publishing. Having its own journals and printers was vital for the student movement; conversely, the partial exclusion of adequate news about the student movement from the mass media signified a loss of the public sphere. Similarly, the discussion about press freedom cannot be posed solely in terms of the question of producers' charters and the codetermination of journalists and editors in individual press undertakings and media. This determination merely modifies the working conditions in existing press and media production. It does not lead to the autonomous creation of counterproducts, which constitute a counterpublic sphere. For this, at least a minimal control over their own means of production on the part of the direct producers of the communications industry would be necessary.[5] Not criticism alone, but effective counterproduction is required. In this respect, the early bourgeois press offers permanent models of counterproduction to the main trends

laws, bans, etc., it must as far as possible ensure its monopoly of the market; it must, in particular, wherever possible directly suppress the literature provided free of charge in the form of posters and leaflets" (p. 327).

4. The system is supplemented by countless forms of so-called voluntary self-control as they are concretized in the norms for self-policing in the film industry, the bylaws of radio and television organizations, and in the standards of the journalistic profession. This self-policing is ineffectual against abuse by those who produce opinions industrially. In the face of living labor, which attempts to organize social experience for itself, it constitutes an effective barrier.

5. Attempts to organize authors, editors, and directors, to the extent that they remain completely dependent and do not exercise control over means of production of their own, lead to a specific aporia. This becomes apparent today, for example, in the instance of Italian authors' and directors' unions, which combine a high degree of political consciousness and legitimate interest with an equally high degree of practical inability to act. In the confrontations with the owners of the means of production, the lendors, the producers, or the state-owned television, the result is regularly a stalemate in which, at first, neither side wins; capital, however, controls the loopholes and the possibility of redirecting investment. The continuation of this line of organization leads, especially within the European Community in the context of a communications industry that is fusing together, to a final aporia for the emancipatory forces. The problem is repeated in the Federal Republic of Germany in the attempt to unite authors and artists in a media union on the model of the industrial union of print workers (*Industriegewerkschaft Druck und Papier*). If control of the means of production is not included in this organizational project (and this would involve the incorporation of smaller and midsize businesses with emancipatory publishing, printing, and media praxis), then such an organization can always only oppose actual production with ideas, claims of legitimacy, and merely economic social claims. Nothing is changed here in terms of the form or means of production. The living labor contained in the industrial producers who organize themselves in such a fashion is unable to maintain itself with these organizational methods against the interests of capital, especially as these are represented by the media concerns. Projects of this sort have the aura of social and, occasionally, radical struggle; in the long term, however, they by no means represent effective radical or social possibilities for struggle.

of social forces, though it, on the other hand, always remained the expression of the ruling interest.

The importance of such a recourse to early bourgeois modes of production precisely in late capitalism is matched by the degree to which the dead apparatus of the legal positions and procedures attained in the struggle for press freedom can be turned against the creation of an autonomous public sphere. There is therefore no linear way of relating to the historical mixture aggregated under the concept of press freedom: it contains an important opportunity for emancipatory practice, and it represents, in its moribund forms, one of the most important obstacles to the organization of proletarian experience.

Engels writes in an article in the *Neue Rheinische Zeitung* of 27 April 1849: "Posters are a chief means of influencing the proletariat; the proletariat is by its entire position revolutionary; the proletariat, which is equally oppressed under a constitutional or under an absolute regime, is only too willing once again to take up arms; the main danger comes from the side of the proletariat, and so away with everything that could keep revolutionary passions within the proletariat alive! And what is of greater help in keeping revolutionary passions among the workers alive than precisely those posters that transform every street corner into a great newspaper, in which passing workers find the events of the day registered and commented upon, the various opinions set out and debated, when at the same time they come across people of every class and shade of opinion together with whom they can discuss the posters, in other words where they have a journal and a club in one, and all this without it costing them a penny."[6]

What Engels is adumbrating here is essentially a primitive form of what is today encountered in highly organized form—determined by capital interests—in the media cartel. It appeals not to capacities of the senses specialized by forced growth but to totalizing perception. This is the mode of perception of all human characteristics that have not already exhausted themselves in the alienated production process.[7] To move, see, read, listen, inform oneself, be entertained, compare the comments of others, get to know people, gain a concrete picture of the

---

6. Reprinted in Marx and Engels, *Pressefreiheit und Zensur*: 199.

7. Films, comic books, so-called vulgar literature are specific responses to this mode of perception, one that is also expressed for the small educated bourgeois upper class of the 19th century in the synthesis of the arts (*Gesamtkunstwerk*). It is first of all, however, exactly the proletarian—and not the bourgeois-organized—mode of perception. The specialization of the senses outside of the labor process, as it is reflected in the listening necessary for new music, in the reading of great literature, in the highly nuanced seeing of the plastic and visual arts, is, in contrast, a specialization of the aesthetic requirements of those whose powers of perception have not already been absorbed by the labor process. They are specialized senses, which must first be developed in a lengthy process of education as individualized modes of perception permitting concentration. In the absence of this culturally produced one-sidedness, perceptual needs tend rather toward the whole; they resist the essentially tortuous training of individual characteristics at the expense of others, the discontented culture, and insist upon the equal, productive development of all the senses, perceptions, and experiences. The high

whole, join with others, and so on—a living public sphere consists of all these elements. It is because of this that it can be libidinally charged. The fundamental need for communality expresses itself in the collective drive to the relevant places—in the case of events on the political stage, such as the motion of no confidence against the Brandt government, to city centers and public squares; in the case of a strike, to the central points of the factory or the entrances; in the case of the armies of immigrant workers, to the concourses of railway stations. Conversely, the dying out of city centers, the prohibition of assemblies on the factory premises, the clearing of station concourses by the railway police effectively destroy this basic form of the public sphere.[8]

In a letter to Bebel, Engels writes on 1 May 1891 from London:

"And one more thing: since you have been trying to prevent the publication of the article by force, and have issued warnings to *Neue Zeit* that it would, if the occurrence were repeated, possibly also be taken over by the party and placed under censorship, the seizure of your entire press by the party must nevertheless appear to me in a peculiar light. How are you different from Puttkamer if you introduce an antisocialist law within your own ranks? This is more or less a matter of indifference to me personally; no party in whatever country can silence me if I am determined to speak. But I would like you to consider whether it would be better for you to be less sensitive and, in your actions, less—Prussian. You—the party—*have need of* socialist science, and this cannot live without freedom of movement. In which case one must reckon with bother, and the best way is with decency, without flinching. Even mild tension, let alone a rift between the

---

levels of concentration of the individual perceptual parameters, which are the prerequisite for traditional scientific and artistic accomplishments, furnish an analogy on the sensual level to the industrial combinations in heavy-industry socialism; this form of socialism presents, in turn, a complete contrast to the socialistic principle of the equal development of all productive qualities in society, one demanded, for example, by the Chinese Marxists.

8. Similarly, the demolition of cafés, small stores, and so on, of the infrastructure that has grown historically around a university, for the purposes of expansion of this university, leads to the desolation of the university grounds and thereby to a depoliticizing. The same result is produced by a merely functional concern for the necessities of life in the case of the reform universities that are built in the open countryside. Here, for example, neither the organization of protest actions nor the affixing of posters is able to effect change. The precondition for the emergence of public and political communication is the cooperation of various or all parameters of the public sphere.

In this regard, it is interesting to examine the local preconditions by means of which political revolutions become possible in large cities. The public sphere in which the most important impulses of the French Revolution of 1789 arose was, above all, the colonnades around the Palais Royal with their stores and cafés—colonnades built by Henry IV. One should also compare the connection between the demolition of the old market halls with the French Revolution of 1848; the destruction of specific infrastructures of Paris by means of the network of boulevards constructed by Haussmann in the manner of a drainage system that should dry up 'political Paris'; today the superimposition of administrative and banking centers with their skyscrapers upon urban structures has brought about a similar destruction of the public sphere.

German party and German socialist science, would be a misfortune and an embarrassment without precedent. That the leadership and you personally retain and must retain a significant moral influence on *Neue Zeit* and everything else that appears goes without saying. But that must satisfy you, and it can. *Vorwärts* is always bragging about the inalienable freedom of discussion, but there is not a great deal of the latter to be seen. You have no idea how peculiar such an inclination toward coercive measures seem to one here abroad, where one is accustomed to seeing the most senior party leaders called to account as befits them within their own party (for instance, the Tory government by Lord Randolph Churchill). And then you should not forget that discipline within a large party can never be as strict as in a small sect and that the antisocialist law, which fused the Lassalleans and the Eisenacheans together (according to Liebknecht it was his splendid program that achieved this!) and made such close cohesiveness necessary, no longer exists."[9]

Engels insists that neither the proletarian public sphere—the public sphere of the movement as a whole—nor socialist science in the strict sense is to be incorporated into the organizational rules of the party. Both require space for their development; they cannot "live without freedom of movement."[10] This is not a pragmatic or an organizational-technical question. Social-revolutionary change and socialist science are specific forms of production for which the party is not the appropriate site. The party, in its conventional form, is not a site of production at all, but rather it coordinates experiences and political decisions and it belongs, within a politics grasped as a production process of the masses, much more to the sphere of distribution. It is thereby perfectly capable of grasping the initiative for a specific production and organization of interests. But it cannot take the place of this production and organization. Nor would it attempt to do this in the realms of industrial, material production of commodities. However, for the as yet unorganized social experience of the masses or for a production of consciousness, as is the object of a socialist science or a socialist press, there arises, because of the preindustrial, undeveloped structure of these spheres of production, a specific confusion. The party organizers assume that they can—in their spare time, as it

---

9. Reprinted in Marx and Engels, *Pressefreiheit und Zensur*: 232f.

10. Regarding Marx's and Engels's term "proletarian movement," see also *The Communist Manifesto*, in Karl Marx and Frederick Engels, *Collected Works*, vol. 6 (New York: International Publishers, 1976): 477–519: "They [the Communists] do not set up any separate principles of their own, by which to shape and mould the proletarian movement. . . . The Communists are distinguished from the other working-class parties by this only. . . . In the various stages of development which the struggle of the working class against the bourgeoisie has to pass through, they always and everywhere represent the interests of the movement as a whole. . . . theoretically, they have over the great mass of the proletariat the advantage of clearly understanding the line of march, the conditions, and the ultimate general results of the proletarian movement" (p. 497).

were—directly intervene in production. In such a case the party is at odds with the real development of these productive forces.[11]

A socialist party press has, apart from those occasions when a socialist party was not in power and party leaders were also living as writers,. never been successfully established. The only left-wing press concern in Germany, founded by Münzenberg, was organized outside the party, on the basis of a special directive by Lenin, within the framework of International Workers' Aid. The reason for the successive emptying of substance of almost every party press lies in the unresolved dialectic of the actual task of such a press. Within the party and the proletarian movement—contrary to the necessary partisanship that leaves the class enemy libidinally uncharged—it must nevertheless sustain a concrete sense of society as a whole. It must therefore, in anticipation, sublate the partisanship that needs to be upheld at the level of coordination and organization. For this reason it cannot simply take over any of the norms and values of the bourgeois press, such as topicality, entertainment value, emotional support, setting guidelines, and the like. It must furthermore have as its object the proletarian public sphere, which cannot be fashioned by the party but is the task of the working class and of society as a whole, and for this very reason it cannot bind itself to the party line as do official and semiofficial party journals.

In contrast to the proletarian public sphere of a socialist movement, socialist science is not something autonomous. Its manifestation as a sequence of projects, that is, as a mode of production resting on the individual or coordinated labor of people holding salaried posts, is undeveloped. This misleads us as to its true character. In this restricted form its fundamental dependence on the social experiences of the masses is not visible. It is precisely *this* dependence, whereby it organizes quite other experiences than the personal ones of theoreticians or the organizational ones of the party, that necessitates its independence from the party line.

Lenin was aware of the dangers of an identification of philosophical positions with political tendencies. When, during the writing of *Materialism and Empiriocriticism* (1908), he expressed the opinion—in a partly polemical correspondence with Gorky about Bogdanov—that one must "'separate philosophy from party

11. A party that proceeds in such a manner demonstrates that it has not seen through the fetish of the bourgeois mode of production—namely, that the material production of commodities is the social production itself. It loses sight of the most important object of socialist production, that of a relation between human beings and commodities as well as between production and nature. As a consequence, it will ally itself with the apparatus of dead labor rather than with living labor, completely underestimating the most important means of production, the conscious appropriation of the wealth of a society by the producers themselves. From the basic idea of Marxist instruction—that a social production, superior to that of mere commodity production, can be constructed on the basis of socialist science and the potential of the experience of the oppressed masses—all that remains is a hard, dead, self-posited *claim.*

affairs,"[12] he did not, to be sure, want to politically neutralize the level of philosophical debate but rather, in the interest of the more urgent revolutionary class struggle, to prevent the Bolshevik faction from being "dragged into" a philosophical argument, from being compelled "either tomorrow or the next day to make a decision, take a vote, in other words render the argument chronic, boring, and without resolution."[13]

---

12. Lenin, *Briefe*, vol. 2. (Berlin: 1967): 155.
13. Ibid., p. 150.

# 16. Vocabulary and the Proletarian Public Sphere

Lin Piao's instructions on writing recommend that style and vocabulary are to be "toughened and improved by revolutionary practice," "diction close to the people." This denotes two apparently opposing tendencies in the language of the Cultural Revolution, which in reality complement one another:

1. Written language is permanently to be corrected by the "mass line"; that is, it is enriched by words that do not derive from educated language but are newly created by the masses, or are already extant in the historical vocabulary of everyday language without as yet having found their way into educated language.

2. The vocabulary of the mass media and of political work is increasingly based on politicized words taken from neither everyday nor educated language but from theoretical or party jargon (e.g., alienation, system of exploitation, in accordance with the law, oppression, exchange, consciousness, investigation, etc.). These words have not been produced by the people; they are in part wholly alien to the history of the Chinese language. Thus expressions from the Paris Commune of 1871 enter into the linguistic usage of the Chinese provinces. Alongside this are words from the language of the cadres, whose origin can be explained neither from the European nor from the Chinese tradition.

There are two tendencies confronting one another here. The Chinese dialects and local forms, the language of the working masses, are overlaid by the abstract "language of the political circumstances." This is the tendency of standardization: communist formulae repeated millions of times stand in for a social totality that is not yet fleshed out with the practice of the masses. On the other hand, what is also at issue here is the incorporation of the linguistic richness that is expressed least of all in formulae, as well as the language of the production process, which is related not merely to the production of material goods but also to the production of revolutionary struggle, experience, politics, relations between people and parts of the country. This process, a permanent expansion of language, corresponds to a public sphere whose main object is the masses' appropriation of their own prehistory.

There is a similar phenomenon in the linguistic practice of East Germany—under quite different social circumstances. Expressions are used that incorporate elements of the production process but do not correspond to standard language. There are, for instance, countless expressions for the correct way to tighten metal parts and screws. The use of these in politics transfers collective social experience to the solving of political problems. I can say: "Despite long reflection I have not found the tactical political solution to this problem," but I can also express myself as follows: "I've been up and about since five this morning thinking about this problem. I just can't get a lead on it." A pedant would regard this as bad style. Such a way of expressing oneself would be alien to the educated elite of the nineteenth century. Yet in reality it represents an enrichment of language. Such an enrichment is a direct function of the politicization of society. This presupposes a politicization of the forms of expression, which is supplied neither by educated language nor by the colloquial language spontaneously developing alongside standard language, nor by the professional language of science or technical specialists. So long as a society has not chosen between technocratization and politicization, language too will give rise to hybrids that can easily be mistaken for vulgarization.[1]

One aspect of the transformation of the intelligentsia is that its sensitization is directed to the expansion of these linguistic tools. It can accomplish this only if it incorporates its expressive capacities into a "mass line." The form in which this production of communicative tools takes place cannot be controlled, ordered, or promoted by special departments of a political party, not even if the party incorporates ancillary organizations of intellectuals, writers, or composers. The goal is to eliminate such professionalism, not to organize it.

"Diction close to the people" does not mean popularization at any price. It is, rather, precisely the demand that vocabulary should be rationally derived, "sim-

---

1. Here the concept of vulgarization is itself, for the most part, a prejudice of the educated upper classes. The only real deformation of language occurs because of increasing abstraction. Distorted images almost never develop in the popular vernacular, but rather through the transmission of images perversely through different situations. It is thus a deficiency in the sense of the particularity of situations and images that produces the deformation, and not "vulgarity."

ple," that language should consist only of comprehensible elements—a principle that is to be understood in the context of bourgeois exchange society and its specific language. Pestalozzi, for instance, read texts from the French *Encyclopédie* to German-speaking children, texts that these children could not understand. **Precisely by reading texts that subvert listening, he develops in children a notion of otherness, of the alienness of the world. They learn that they do not already know all there is to know, that what the world really is cannot be grasped by immediate understanding. Precisely by doing so, Pestalozzi develops a sense of the richness concealed in reality, something with which the children must come to grips.** Not blind comprehensibility but distance from the other comes before linguistic understanding. Learning something, absorbing it with the senses so as to understand it later, learning to decipher that which is alien after one has made it one's own is an important pedagogic principle that has not been sufficiently absorbed into the value system of bourgeois education.

In an education that merely couples what can be rationally understood with what can be rationally understood, there develops an impatience of comprehension. The practice of the mass media in our countries is obliged to take this impatience into account. A television program, a newspaper report, or a school lesson must contain punch lines, which are short-circuited and which fragment time, in order to keep attention alive. "Dramaturgical incest," the principle that a door in the stage set must be used within the play, that a clothes hook must at some point have an article of clothing hung on it, that a character who appears in the drama must enter into some relationship with other characters—this is the mark of a value abstraction that governs most of the forms of the bourgeois tradition of art and expression. There prevails here a primacy of economy, which drives experience and reality away from the thread of the action. This schematism is alien to language as such. A child will take up words and sentences from its mother that are not geared to the basic message she is trying to get across. However, as soon as this child has undergone the educational process, it will insist on universal comprehensibility. When I quote texts in a foreign language and do not immediately append the translation, there is uneasiness in the auditorium. When a complex topic is elaborated and is not straightaway followed by a popularization, the interest of the listeners diminishes. This creates an almost impenetrable barrier to major philosophical texts, which makes Hegel and much of Marx inaccessible. Language cannot in this way depict the richness of society.

On 27 May 1918 the Council of People's Commissars, under the chairmanship of Lenin, decreed that monuments should be erected to all significant personalities in philosophy, literature, science, and art. So there came into existence in many cities in the Soviet Union plaster depictions of the famous and deceased, of freedom fighters, and so on. Another initiative was the painting of entire streets, in one case even the decoration of an entire town with pictures of historical and revolutionary events.

An opposite tendency was seen in the Chinese Cultural Revolution. Existing monuments of feudal Chinese culture were transferred to new sites; other monuments were replaced, not by new ones, but by works of art, such as the farm, which represents in context the bitter exploitation under feudal rule and the emancipation of the people by the people and which was widely disseminated by modern communications methods (poster, film, book). In contrast, the portrayal of past greatness and significance was combated. Mao engaged in a polemic against the ministry of culture, which, unless it manages to transform itself, should "quite simply be renamed the ministry for emperors, kings, generals, and chancellors, the ministry for young scholars and charming ladies, or the ministry for dead foreigners."

Yet another cultural-revolutionary element underlies the various iconoclastic movements that can be found in the history of Western Europe.[2] Thus the Anabaptist movement in Münster did not arbitrarily destroy monuments; there was, rather, an underlying, expressive intent. Symbols of the past were damaged in such a way that the manifestations of oppression they embodied were brought to light. The monuments were interpreted. A bishop, whose arms were hacked off, was "punished" for his deeds. Disfigurement of the eyes expressed the blindness of a significant personage, and so on.

---

2. Cf. Dieter Metzler, *Bilderstürme und Bilderfeindlichkeit in der Antike* (manuscript, 1971); Horst Bredekamp, *Der vorreformatorische 'Asketische Protestantismus' unter besonderer Berücksichtigung von Savonarolas 'Verbrennung der Eitelkeiten'* (manuscript, 1971); Eberhard Knödler-Bunte, *Bildstürmerische Tendenzen im russischen Proletkult* (manuscript, 1971); Martin Warnke, *Durchgebrochene Geschichte. Die Bilderstürme der Wiedertäufer in Münster 1534–1535* (manuscript, 1972), which derives from the concept of an aesthetics of deformation.

# 17. The Public Sphere of Monuments— the Public Sphere and Historical Consciousness

For all cultures, monuments constitute an attempt to make history symbolically present. The monuments that exist in the Federal Republic are essentially concerned with the commemoration of the dead, the depiction of heroic deeds. They are, however, above all portrayals of rulers or representatives of intellectual or material authority, who represent the past on horseback, as standing figures or portrait heads. If this were history, the present could derive no experience from it. This is because there is no attempt at a differentiation of symbolic depiction. The monument embodies the claims of a man or an event to be remembered. In numerical terms, local founders, industrialists, kings, or princes are preponderant; particularly numerous are monuments commemorating the world wars, Bismarck, and the war of 1870–71.[1] This dearth of historical documentation is also connected with the fact that broad areas of the most recent history of the German people are subject to suppression. There is, for instance, no monument marking Stalingrad. The tendency toward historical impoverishment is, however, as old as the history of the bourgeois public sphere.[2]

The relationship of the proletarian public sphere to historical consciousness is quite different. The proletarian public sphere presupposes making history present, the symbolizing of historical identity, precisely because it cannot paper over breaks in development. Of the many examples from the Proletkult movement

---

1. This proliferation of monuments is perhaps most noticeable in Berlin.
2. Cf. chapter 2, the section titled "The Public Sphere as an Illusory Synthesis of the Totality of Society."

after 1917 we will examine two designs for monuments that give an idea of the themes and expressive potential of monuments.

1. "A temple of machine worshipers. Byzantine cupola. Instead of angels, the figures of communist agitators appear in the pendantives; their heads are replaced by wheels, which are driven from the altar by belts. In the foreground, the mechanized congregation (drawing by S. Krinsky)."[3]

This design for a monument documents a significant error. The problem faced by Soviet Marxists after they had taken power was how to industrialize a country that had hitherto possessed industry only in certain areas. In this context Trotsky and Bukharin spoke of how primitive accumulation had to be made up and industrial discipline implemented under socialist leadership. It was obvious, in this process, that technical productive force as it stands, as manifested in mechanization, should be propagated. An important center for this headlong introduction of scientific work practices and the subsumption of human beings under the law of the machine was, among other examples, Gastev's Central Institute of Labor.[4]

It is evident that communism cannot be serious about understanding human beings as living machines or worshiping machines themselves. It was, however, no less certain that a crucial transitional stage of cultural revolution in the Soviet Union had to be an investment of machines, industrial plants, technical innovations, scientific organization of labor, and discipline with libidinal and optimistic qualities. It is important to see this contradictory phase depicted in a monument precisely because of the distortion connected with it. One could even surmise that monuments depicting such historical moments should be produced in two forms: the one for registering a specific historical situation, one that possibly includes distortions and errors; the other for providing the people an opportunity to deform, change, and improve it along the way. It is necessary to preserve history as well as that which is other than history.[5]

2. "Plan for a Monument to the Third International by Tatlin. The vertically

---

3. Krinsky's illustration is in René Fülöp-Miller, *Geist und Gesicht des Bolschewismus* (Vienna: 1926): 31. The English translation of this book, *The Mind and Face of Bolshevism: An Examination of Cultural Life in Soviet Russia* (New York: Harper Torchbooks, 1965), does not include the illustrations.

4. Cf. Gabriele Lessing, *Der Taylorismus in der Sowjetunion—Ein sozialistisches System zur Schweißauspressung* (manuscript, 1971); V. I. Lenin, *Über wissenschaftliche Arbeitsorganisation* (Berlin: 1971).

5. Cf., for example, Laboe's tower, in which the warships of the First and Second World Wars are honored. Recently, in the immediate vicinity of this monument, a preserved submarine has been displayed. In this instance, it is merely the existence of such warships that is represented, not the relation between the men whose fate is bound up with these ships. There can be no neutral, merely contemplative perspective on such signs of the past. Historical experience must be able to crystallize around them.

layered rooms A, B, and C are made of glass and each have their own mechanisms allowing for movements that are distinct from one another."[6]

"These rooms are arranged vertically and are surrounded by different harmonious support structures. Through a special mechanism, they are kept in constant motion, each at a different speed. The lowest room is cubical in shape and will make one revolution a year. This room is for legislative purposes—in the future, the conferences of the International, as well as sessions of the congress and other governmental bodies, will be held here. The room immediately above this one is shaped like a pyramid, and it will make one revolution a month. Administrative and other executive organs will hold their meetings in this room. The third, the uppermost part of the building, a cylindrical space, will make one revolution a day. This part of the building is in the first place intended to serve information and propaganda purposes, such as the news bureau, newspapers, as well as the publication of pamphlets and manifestos. It will contain telegraph machines, radio apparatus, and projectors for film viewings."[7]

This plan for a building to house the Third International was not carried out. However, it sheds an important light on the translation of historical consciousness into concrete terms. That a whole series of Marxists were overwhelmed by the boldness of the design is shown by Trotsky's question when confronted with Tatlin's design: why does this tower move, why is it transparent, and why isn't it upright?

Tatlin's design translates Marxist conceptual patterns into architectonic and technical possibilities—materiality, the public sphere, complexity of movement, the spiral as the symbol of the rapprochement of party and masses, and so on. From this project alone, it is not possible to gain a picture of the cultural-revolutionary premises underlying the movement to which Tatlin belonged. One must try to imagine what it signifies for the consciousness of the masses when they have absorbed numerous such works as their accustomed public sphere. It is only at this level, at the level of creative impulses of the masses, that works such as this give rise to a differentiated sense of history. One has to imagine that such monuments could harness the mass loyalty that is today bound up with the cigar-box-shaped Lenin mausoleum.

What Tatlin's monument signifies becomes apparent only when it is contrasted with the design of bourgeois monumental architecture. The architecture of the French Revolutionary era too is by and large extant only in the shape of plans.[8] These comprise huge, static monstrosities, which aspire to the cosmos, the landscape, or to vast ideas such as justice; never monuments to which human beings

6. See Fülöp-Miller, *Geist und Gesicht des Bolschewismus,* plates 66–67.

7. Ibid., p. 140.

8. Cf. the catalog for the exhibition: *Revolutionsarchitektur.* Boulée, Ledoux, Lequeu, Staatliche Kunsthalle Baden-Baden, 1970; Akademie der Künste, Berlin, 1.15–2.21, 1971.

can relate. As regards functional buildings, for example, a cowshed, architectonically symbolized by a gigantic cow, human beings are invisible; for cows, too, it is hardly practical. Numerous impulses of this revolutionary bourgeois architecture were taken up by Hitler and Speer. Characteristic of this latter tendency is the purely mechanical connection between public representation, the size of the buildings, "political idea," and purpose. For instance, the tribune structures of the erstwhile Nuremberg rally arena, which look like decorative fortified towers, are in reality pissoirs. The element of mourning in the monument that was to be built in 1950 on the Rhine for all members of the Nazi Party who had lost their lives is expressed simply by gloominess. The reason for this is that the bourgeois public sphere already excluded human use-value from these public buildings before they were even planned or erected.

Tatlin's building, by contrast,[9] where the lowest level, rotating once a year,

---

9. Fülöp-Miller, *The Mind and Face of Bolshevism: An Examination of Cultural Life in Soviet Russia* (New York: Harper Torchbooks, 1965): 100–102: "The whole monument rests on two main axes which are closely connected. In the direction of these axes an upward movement is accomplished on the one hand, but, on the other hand, this is crossed transversely at each of its points by the movement of the spirals. The junction of these two dynamic forces, which are by nature opposed to each other, is intended to express annihilation; but the spirals turning in the opposite direction, by the upward effort of the main structure, produces a dynamic form, which is moved by a system of ever tense, ever agitated axes cutting each other (!). The form will conquer matter, the force of attraction, and seeks a way out with the help of the most elastic and volatile lines existing—with the help of spirals. These are full of movement, elasticity, and speed; stiffly stretched like the muscles of a smith hammering iron. In itself the use of spirals for monumental architecture means an enrichment of the composition. Just as the triangle, as an image of general equilibrium, is the best expression of the Renaissance (!) so the spiral is the most effective symbol of the modern spirit of the age. The countering of gravitation by buttresses is the purest classical form of statics; the classical form of dynamics, on the other hand, is the spiral. While the dynamic line of bourgeois society, aiming at possession of the land and the soil, was the horizontal, the spiral, which, rising from the earth, detaches itself from all animal, earthly, and oppressing interests, forms the purest expression of humanity set free by the Revolution. The bourgeois social order developed an animal life on earth, tilled the soil, and there erected shops, arcades, and banks; the life of the new humanity rises ever higher and higher above the ground. At the same time, the arrangement of the contents of these architectural forms signifies their usefulness. Most of the elements of architecture hitherto in use possessed no practical importance, and remained unorganised. Today the principle of organization must rule and penetrate all art. The monument unites legislative initiative with the executive and with information; to each of these functions a position in space has been assigned corresponding to its nature. In this way, and also by means of the chief building material used, glass, the purity and clearness of initiative and its freedom from all material encumbrance is symbolically indicated.

"Just as the product of the number of oscillations and the wavelength is the spatial measure of sound, so the proportion between glass and iron is the measure of material rhythm. By the union of these two fundamentally important materials, a compact and imposing simplicity and, at the same time, relationship are expressed, since these materials, for both of which fire is the creator of life, form the elements of modern art. By their union, rhythms must be created of mighty power, as though an ocean were being born. By the translation of these forms into reality, dynamics will be embodied in unsurpassable magnificence, just as pyramids once and for all expressed the principle of statics."

actually concretizes a different time scale of decision-making, theorizing, and work from the highest level, which rotates once a day and houses propagandists, journalists, and the authors and disseminators of pamphlets and manifestos, who see their task objectified in the building by its rapid shift of perspective.

In the Federal Republic, we have only one moving monument, the Henninger tower in Frankfurt. Its uppermost level, in which a restaurant is housed, turns on its axis once every hour. There is no central committee situated there; it is filled with beer.

## Appendix: Utopias of Bourgeois, Political Architecture

The designs of bourgeois architecture from the era of the French Revolution (1789–1812) are astonishing products of the imagination. They attempt to express political ideas by architectonic means: the architecture is supposed to "speak," "narrate." In these designs, especially those of Boullée (1728–99), Ledoux (1736–1806), and Lequeu (1757–1825), the utopia of use-values conflicts with the gigantism, the uniform treatment of amassed materials. The tendency to return to nature meets with the retreat from nature as such. Trust in the expressive capacity of technology is matched with the concealment of technical aids, with a facade that appears to be nontechnical. Strict functionalism competes with the inclination to free the materials and the architectonic masses from any purpose: the materials have the tendency to become autonomous and to represent the abstract skill, surpassing all imagination, of the architect and the productive forces that are being set in motion. The contradictions of the bourgeois public sphere, the motives and mental structure that underlie the French Revolution and the Napoleonic Wars, are expressed in this architecture.[10]

Lequeu's design for a "South-Facing Cowshed on a Fresh Pasture" constitutes an allegory for animal husbandry.[11] The cow is covered with cashmere blankets: "As an animal monument it recalls the elephant of the Bastille."[12]

---

10. The massing of Murat's cavalry, that of artillery at Borodino and Leipzig, the tactic of the massed breakthrough of infantry, the setting into motion of vast numbers of soldiers in the direction of the towers of Moscow. Everywhere the idea of beginning a new cycle of life overtaken by the tendency to set in motion the available material, the objective ability, which leaves human interests behind, and to represent it as a giant, merely objective collection of characteristics and energies.

11. See *Revolutionsarchitektur*, published by the Akademie der Künste in cooperation with the Institute for the Arts, Rice University, Houston, Berlin, 1971.

12. On the spot where, in 1789, the Bastille was stormed and demolished, Napoleon wanted to erect a fountain in the shape of an elephant (*Revolutionsarchitektur*, p. 118). The elephant was supposed to carry on its back a tower that one could climb. The hydraulic system, hidden by drapery, was concealed, along with the water pipes, in the tower. Already in 1758 the inventor Ribart had suggested that an immense elephant, arranged inside as a house, be set up on the Place de l'Etoile.

The gigantization of animals, in order to then use them for human purposes—dwellings, observation posts, for example—corresponds to the interest in celebrating the technical omnipotence of the

Another example is the "Cenotaph for a Warrior" by Boullée. A Roman sarcophagus is here enlarged to a gigantic coffin. No individual can lie in such a huge edifice. No one can lift the coffin lid. A frieze consists of larger than life but almost completely identical warriors.

The motif of monumental cemeteries is repeated in numerous variants. They are always so devised that it would scarcely be possible to inter real human beings in these skyscrapers for the dead—the pyramid, the triangle, the regularity on a vast scale, the mastery over material, the lack of windows, the miniaturized entrances and exits, at most a single gigantic doorway. The designs appear to anticipate the buildings' future as ruins, their rediscovery, their eternal aspect.[13]

An example of the return of the repressed is Boullée's "Fort." It consists of a round tower flanked by rectangular towers arranged diagonally. Cannonballs are heaped up between the towers. The entrance is marked by the shield of Achilles: "By means of this collection of weapons and ammunition I wanted to give the building character and at the same time create art." This building immediately recalls the Bastille. Whereas the latter, whose construction began during the era of Henri IV, still contained alterations and sections that had been built over and thereby possessed a historical character, Boullée's Bastille has, even for a prison, too few windows—a naked representation of the available material, an immense accumulation of structural elements, defined by a mass of cannonballs such as cannot be fired in any battle.

Further subjects of these designs consist of palaces of justice, prisons, museums, gigantic book collections,[14] but also lighthouses. There is a design for a lighthouse by Boullée in the shape of a pyramid, a skittle, a column; and one by Lequeu, to guide travelers in the desert, in the shape of a Trajan pillar with spiral staircase.

The expressive capacity of a specific historical consciousness contained in

---

new human over nature, the technical control of nature. For the person of the French Revolution nothing is impossible, nature sets no limits. The same motive constitutes the most important component of the circus, which appears as a popular art form of the French Revolution after 1789. The animals in the circus perform unbelievable and never before seen feats because they must obey man. Lions are tame; they sit up and beg. Elephants stand on one leg, which, given the weight of their bodies, they should not be able to do. In consideration of the revolutionary will of the people, physical laws are subdued; acrobats defy gravity, and so on. The fact that man can fly is constantly varied in the circus and in the cult of ballooning; man masters nature. In the Parisian wit of the period, there is, for example, a representation of how a balloon is being guided by a driver with the help of two eagles, yoked together like horses.

13. Hitler and Speer one day had the model of the buildings planned for the capital of the Reich, Berlin, so arranged as it would appear after 1,000 years as a ruined landscape. This aspect of the ruined landscape is the test of whether the architectural plan was successful or not.

14. What is at issue is the program to anticipate, in buildings, the immense collection of commodities that the commodity world should one day become. *An abundance of justice, of dead museum objects* cannot be represented in a fashion that would be sufficiently colossal.

these examples is imitated by the edifices of the Nazi era, only a tiny number of which were completed and for which plans up to 1950 exist;[15] they attempt to take up this expressive capacity, copy it, or develop it further. By contrast, the bourgeois architecture of other epochs does not have such a need for expression. In line with the indifference of the bourgeois public sphere toward its own representation,[16] the buildings display a leveling, at best a functionalism. Social conditions are expressed in technical buildings, factories, rather than in representative ones. It is possible to trace the incursions of Prussia into southern, western, and central Germany by the virtually "geological" stratum of similar rectangular public buildings in brick in towns such as Mainz, Frankfurt, Magdeburg, Halberstadt, Hannover, Oberhausen. Railway stations differ only in that for practical reasons they generally have round roofs.[17]

15. These plans are to be found in part in the Stadtarchiv in Munich, in part in the Bayerischen Staatsarchiv, where they are preserved unpublished.

16. Cf. chapter 2, the section titled "The Public Sphere as an Illusory Synthesis of the Totality of Society."

17. The National Socialists had also planned monumental public buildings and train stations. The central train station in Munich, which was to have been constructed in the Pasing area, was supposed to have been particularly grand. Avalanches, had they fallen from the immense domed roof, would have destroyed all of the neighboring buildings.

# 18. The Public Sphere of Children

One of the most effective ways of exposing the true nature of any public sphere is when it is interrupted, in a kind of alienation effect, by children. Whether one imagines that troops of them storm the foyer of a luxury hotel, occupy public squares and buildings with a view to getting on with their specific activities, whether they shape the profile of public political assemblies, whether owing to a security lapse they enter a television studio in large numbers during a live broadcast[1]—in every case the reified character of each context, its rigidity, and the fact that the public sphere is always that of adults, immediately become apparent.

Conversely, it is an index of every cultural-revolutionary movement that children's public spheres come into being. The first year after the October Revolution saw not only the founding of Vera Schmidt's children's laboratory in the Soviet Union, but also the establishment of free associations of children, children's republics. The political orientation continued in children's movements, which were an experiment in the self-regulation and self-organization of children in their own specific forms, with posters, children's houses, assembly halls, play areas, and so on. In the initial phase, this was by no means merely a continuation of adult

---

1. A television show planned to include this alienation effect in its program, as children were instructed to spatter emcee Dietman Schönherr's suit with paint. Such a directed action does not constitute, however, a public sphere for children; its effect is one of shock and not of derealization. Rather, the confrontation between the public sphere of children and that of adults presupposes that children are able to pursue their own important affairs and interests, that they can regulate themselves.

structures in the children's sphere, as are children's and young people's organizations, kindergartens, or preschools.[2]

Every authentically proletarian-revolutionary movement embraces all sectors of life, not merely that part of the population defined by capitalism as productive. The protest movements of recent years held fast to this principle. The fact that they did not straightaway focus on the working population derives not only from the difficulty of establishing a link between the intelligentsia and the working class but is also an expression of the structure of such movements. The alternative playgroup movement, the turn toward social work, the interest in the mentally ill (patients' collectives), the campaign of apprentices and the inmates of children's homes, school students' movements—all this is a protest against the reduction of human beings to their productive functions within the capitalist labor process. It corresponds to the axiom—which can, admittedly, only be brought to fruition in alliance with the most powerful productive force in society, the working class— that there is no sense in being concerned only with those people who carry out socially useful work. That this approach is in no way unrealistic is shown by the significance of the education of young children for the training of labor power— something that is being scientifically acknowledged today and that leads to demands for societal control of preschool education. It is not the attitude of the student movement that is unrealistic but the economic restriction of interests to the production process in the narrower sense.[3]

If they are to realize their specific form of sensuality, to "fulfill" themselves, children require a public sphere that is more spatially conceived than do adults. They require more room in which to move, places that represent as flexibly as possible a field of action, where things are not fixed once and for all, defined, furnished with names, laden with prohibitions. They also need quite different time scales from adults in order to grow. As it expands, such a public sphere does come up against substantial material interests. For the activity of children represents, once it begins to develop, a threat to adults' interests in their own lives. Private property has occupied every spot capable of economic exploitation. What a children's public sphere is capable of becoming even in purely spatial form is reduced

---

2. Cf. the significance of the children's movement in the Chinese Cultural Revolution. Here and there—primarily in feudal and semifeudal social structures—children's movements become apparent. It is necessary to distinguish between them and those children's organizations that derive from the ideas of adults, like the Spanish Children's Circus, which recently toured the Federal Republic of Germany and from whose income a children's village (albeit one consisting only of young boys and in which coeducation is strictly avoided) was financed. A similar roll, determined by adults, is played by the conspicuous participation of children in the many Carnival clubs, where the children actively participate with their performances. They speak and act here as precocious adults, dance and dress like stars; they do not act as they do when concerned with their own affairs.

3. Cf. the important study by Gunnar Heinsohn, *Vorschulerziehung heute?* (Frankfurt am Main: 1971), esp. 69ff., 99ff., 169ff.

to children's ghettos. These faithfully mirror the bourgeois public sphere, where everything is strictly defined, the most important things are bracketed out, and everything has its place. For this reason the enclaves within which middle-class children, together with other children, can experience a liberal childhood do not add up to a children's public sphere. The latter, like every proletarian public sphere, has the tendency to incorporate the whole of society; it cannot be organized in small groups. It cannot be the intention of children, if they attempt self-regulation, to pay for this space they have created for themselves with a massive withdrawal from reality and from the adult world, which comprises above all the relations of the parents to one another and to their children. This is why a children's public sphere cannot be created without a material public sphere that unites parents, and without children's public spheres in all layers and classes of society that can establish links with one another. This is precisely what governed the children's republics after 1917 mentioned earlier: that in them children develop outwardly directed activities, take on tasks, and so on. This is not the same as the regimentation of children, the directing of their interests toward the imitation of adult politics, handing over bouquets, keeping children in a constant state of waiting, which is typical of the youth policy of bureaucracies.

The self-organization and self-regulation of children are contested by every type of ruling interest just as vehemently as is the self-organization of the proletariat. Anyone who regards a children's public sphere as a grotesque idea will find it difficult to gain an accurate notion of a proletarian public sphere.

What happens when no autonomous public sphere comes into being? In that case a surrogate is organized from outside, and not indeed in the interests of children but by utilizing their interests and needs for the purpose of control. This occurs, for instance, with children's television. Children sit intently in front of the television screen, and this takes the pressure off adults at certain hours of the day. However, the children remain passive for the duration of the program. They cannot change the program; all they can do is watch it in such a selective way that they can construct their own program. Children, then, to some extent see a completely different program from the one objectively appearing on the screen. This program, which they have put together, holds their interest; but it is not their own.

What concept of reality is, for instance, conveyed in the Pippi Longstocking films? These do not portray human dealings with things; instead, reality is an object of domination: arbitrary, rapid change of scene; arbitrary change of plot, corresponding to the "volatile interests and attention levels of children." This results in wholly unreal accumulations of adventures, concentrations of experience, which the children cannot reproduce in their own activity. Whereas identification with the main character is possible, the pirates, Pippi's enemies and friends, the events and people are like things that drift past and with which the imagination cannot come to grips. Because of the narrative thread, there arises a hierarchy of attention. The guiding idea behind the series is evidently that the desire for omnipotence, which is important for a specific phase of childhood, is satisfied by identification with the powerful figure of Pippi. But omnipotence is the problem of one stage of development, not of all stages. Whereas it would be the goal of a children's public sphere that was active and based on autonomous activity to develop common ego ideals in children, the Pippi Longstocking series feeds children with reinforcements of the superego. The most important mechanism underlying Pippi's aggressiveness and her rapid "victories"—ships, towers, traps, prisons, are generally blown up without further ado—is the identification with the aggressor, that is, the imitation of the behavior of in any case superior adults. This may serve as a psychological safety valve, but it cultivates the behavior patterns in the nuclear family. It is not possible to find a clearer illustration than this series provides of the situation described by Herbert Marcuse and Reimut Reiche as repressive desublimation.

What has been said here about Pippi Longstocking doubtless does not apply to all children's series. The basic scheme—that the series reproduce merely the abstract reverse of total reification—applies to all of them, including "Sesame Street." The passivity of children in front of the television screen therefore selects those qualities that anyway, as reality principle, restrict the autonomy and self-regulation of children. In this context it makes little difference that a series of children's programs with progressive interest tries to inculcate tolerant behavior, understanding toward minorities, and so on. These attempts at indoctrination presuppose that consciousness can be acquired in the same way as professional expertise, although this is not a proven fact. On the contrary, the former entails the development of behavior patterns in children that can be acquired only by involvement with real objects, with a reality that is actively grasped. This is why it is doubtful whether precisely the moral selectiveness in children's series is fulfilling its purpose. In these series children only rarely do any real harm (save to enemies, spies, criminals); they tell lies only in situations where the lie subsequently proves to be morally justified. They help the police and counterintelligence, they perform remarkable feats in the very fields that in reality only adults master (for instance, driving cars in Africa, combating industrial espionage in the desert in the series "Plan Z"). Children do none of these things, not even in their imagination. What they would do if they were allowed to get on with things is not shown. The series that manage to attract children to the television screen subject them to a specific loss of object. This has negative consequences, irrespective of whether the opportunity is taken to learn understanding toward black youths, underdogs, cooperative behavior toward parents, and so on. Such norms are learned by rote. They can be translated into action only when they combine with the components of the child's personality out of which collective ego ideals are constituted. In contrast, a mere inclusion in the catalogue of rigid superego rules has fundamentally nonprogressive consequences, for in the latter, socially useful but stereotypical norms can, in changed circumstances, have wholly repressive effects.[4]

Just as there are specific constellations of needs for a children's public sphere, there are also interests and needs on the part of adolescents for a public sphere that belongs to them.[5] Puberty differs in class terms. Whereas a child from a bourgeois or lower-middle-class home has a psychological moratorium, which, including high school and college, amounts to more than ten years, the working-class child already enters into the disciplined environment of the factory during adolescence. Peter Brückner has rightly pointed out that the working-class child thereby receives a shock that is decisive for its whole subsequent life situation. This means that the working-class child is unable to develop the adolescent phase of reflection, criticism, separation from parents, antiauthoritarian behavior, desire for organization with peers, communication, powerful desire for expression. The destruction of the necessary incubation time for situations in which the pubertal phase could regulate itself also affects, independent of social strata, a large number of isolated individuals. Divorce of a child's parents during puberty, leaving

---

4. As in the case of every form of public space, the point is that it must be possible, in the organization of personal experience, to distinguish between merely fixating repetitions of compulsive situations (the element of control) and the capacity for unmediated experience (the element of autonomy).

5. The impression should not arise from this selection of examples that this principle of a singular, specific public sphere could simply be transferred to all other objects. Rather, the principal object of the category of the proletarian public sphere is to distinguish elementary, organizable interests, which, first of all, pertain to a proper public sphere from those in which nonelementary, globalized contexts of repression (which cannot be excised in the concrete situation) manifest themselves. A public sphere for women, for example, would only repeat the context of repression to which women are subject. Being a woman is not an elementary stage in human or social development; rather, the repression of women, of their specific specialization, is a false construction in that development. The global character of this context of repression must first be dissolved in its single components—and this would not simply be an issue for women.

In contrast, specific situations in the life of women, situations that are subject to social repression, demand a public solution. For example: pregnancy and the most important moments of the mother-child relationship are, in fact, excluded from the public sphere of adults. These situations and phases of life insist upon their own communications network, upon exchange and public sphere.

The singular public spheres of children and youth, the public spheres of women at certain stages of their lives would be components of an encompassing proletarian public sphere, one that would arise out of such concrete single public spheres. It would later, however, be able to absorb these into itself so that none of these public spheres would have the tendency to remain as single; as soon as they arise, they would yield from themselves the connections to all other public spheres and to the totality of society. The proletarian public sphere as the category of the social whole cannot, however, position itself in advance as a political public sphere above the single public spheres that have not yet developed. Above all, it cannot give rise to the public spheres specific to singular life interests from out of its abstract "wholeness." For this reason the catchall tactic in which questions of youth and women—in a manner similar to those of athletes or the faithful—would simply be attached to a cadre organization is wrong. The interests specified here in a proper context of living for each specific stage of life are not something isolated; instead, they bear in themselves an element of the universal.

school, even moving to another town can have the same effect. As far as the overwhelming majority of the population is concerned, the lack of an autonomous public sphere for this important stage of the organization of drives and character leads to the formation of rigid and puritanical impulses. These also affect the few groups who are in a position to express their sexuality, their imagination, and their capacity for criticism more freely.[6]

The object of an adolescent public sphere is above all the formation of ego ideals that embrace the whole of society. Society's dismal attitude toward the "unproductive" period of puberty with its biological time scales, corresponding as it were to convalescence after illness, is shown by the less than adequate offerings of the mass media. These can in any case only be a surrogate for an autonomous public sphere for young people. But in this respect too they are limited to a few series that portray contrived cases of reintegration into society, as well as to the identification models of Western heroes, police officers. It is typical that the major problem of puberty, sexuality, plays no role whatsoever in precisely these programs and films "geared to" young people.[7]

Without an investigation of the real possibilities for specific public spheres of children and young people—as models for public spheres in each and every sector of life—the central question of the public sphere of the factory cannot be correctly posed.

---

6. It would have to be examined whether the direct derivation of the puritanical movements from the worldly asceticism of the early bourgeoisie is a sufficient explanation. It is equally plausible that this impulse, deriving from the upper class, found its raw material in the deterioration of the means for building personalities, especially during puberty. This is a different motivation from that which was effective for the asceticism of the bourgeois.

7. This state of affairs is especially clear in the film industry, where the totality of offerings—consisting of porn movies, action films, mysteries, and art films—stands in an unbearable relationship to the true needs of a youth that is demanding its own public sphere. The strength of the *impulse* toward a public sphere among youth is evidenced by the fact that they represent the only growing part of the moviegoing public. The motivation for this remains almost exclusively the wish to somehow escape from the parental household.

# 19. The Nonpublic Sphere as a Form of Rule—Class "In Itself" and Class "For Itself"

Today actual rule operates—in full accord with the image of it evidently held by workers—in a **nonpublic** manner. This became clear, for instance, in May '68 in France, when the Gaullist regime initially tried to survive by making itself invisible. Thus the army and the police were ordered to show themselves as little as possible; de Gaulle himself disappeared from public view. Plebiscites, television, speeches to the nation, demonstrations by politically amorphous groups of the right and car owners, the threat of the international economic and fiscal consequences of France's breaking out of the ranks of capitalist countries, the **nonpublicly** mooted threat that armored units were advancing on Paris—all these are forms of an illusory public sphere, real linking mechanisms that have nothing to do with the public framework of politics. One element of the unassailability of the Gaullist public sphere lay in its lack of substantiality. Not even a demonstrative public sphere came into being from the right—a car demonstration, a parade, that was all.

To sustain its powers the ruling class requires the abstract linking of the economic context with the repressive tools of public institutions, that is, the control of interconnections that are themselves nonpublic. These comprise, on the one hand, the relationship of the individual country to all other countries with which it is economically linked, and on the other, the linking of the various decentralized and particular spheres of interest in society, where the most varied interests (proletarian, bourgeois, the interests of intermediate social strata, peasant, regional, etc.) have solidified into a provisional equilibrium and a kind of symbiosis. This way of maintaining rule in revolutionary situations (inasmuch as only the control of the abstract links remains) appears to be characteristic of French history. **To the**

**degree that an individual class is not in a position to give politically independent expression to its interests, it feels that it is best represented by the established authorities.**

In contrast to these abstract networks of the ruling bourgeois public sphere, the working class, for its alliances (for instance, with sectors of the intelligentsia) and for the recognition of its own instinctively grasped goals, needs a **public sphere** that organizes those experiences that do not fit into the existing context of society. This proletarian public sphere is a constitutive element of the class itself.

The notion that one can separate class in itself from class for itself is the result of abstraction. It does not describe the concrete circumstances pertaining to the actions of the class. If we take these actions, this practice of social transformation, as our yardstick, the mass that is constituting itself as a class consists precisely in the fact that economic interests, psychological conditions of existence, and consciousness are mediated through one another. In *The Poverty of Philosophy*, Marx spoke of how every class struggle was a political struggle, and in *The Communist Manifesto* the "highest purpose" of the communist is seen in the shaping of the proletariat into a class. From this objective perspective, which takes into account the process of class constitution and not merely its result, it becomes necessary to distinguish social situations in which a class can come into being from those in which this is impossible. Marx viewed the constitution as a class of the nineteenth-century French peasant as impossible.[1]

---

1. Karl Marx, *The Eighteenth Brumaire of Louis Bonaparte*, in Karl Marx and Frederick Engels: *Collected Works*, vol. 11 (New York: International Publishers, 1979): 99–197: "And yet the state power is not suspended in mid air. Bonaparte represents a class, and the most numerous class of French society at that, the *small-holding peasantry*. . . . The small-holding peasants form a vast mass, the members of which live in similar conditions but without entering into manifold relations with one another. Their mode of production isolates them from one another instead of bringing them into mutual intercourse. The isolation is increased by France's bad means of communication and by the poverty of the peasants. Their field of production, the small holding, admits of no division of labour in its cultivation, no application of science and, therefore, no diversity of development, no variety of talent, no wealth of social relationships. Each individual peasant family is almost self-sufficient; it itself directly produces the major part of its consumption and thus acquires its means of life more through exchange with nature than in intercourse with society. A small holding, a peasant and his family; alongside them another small holding, another peasant and another family. A few score of villages make up a department. In this way, the great mass of the French nation is formed by simple addition of homologous magnitudes, much as potatoes in a sack form a sack of potatoes. Insofar as millions of families live under economic conditions of existence that separate their mode of life, their interests and their culture from those of the other classes, and put them in hostile opposition to the latter, they form a class. Insofar as there is merely a local interconnection among these small-holding peasants, and the identity of their interests begets no community, no national bond and no political organisation among them, they do not form a class. They are consequently incapable of enforcing their class interests in their own name, whether through a parliament or through a convention. They cannot represent themselves, they must be represented. Their representative must at the same time appear as their master, as an authority

This has an epistemological-analytical and a practical aspect. From an epistemological point of view, class in itself (it is no accident that the expression refers
back to Kant's "thing-in-itself") denotes the economic interests, the material reason why, for all the importance of subjective elements in actual class struggle,
classes cannot on a matter of principle be founded on consciousness, attitudes,
decisions, and so on. Just as for Kant the thing-in-itself represents the indissoluble
block, the resistance of matter against the transcendental subject's apparatus of
categories, against constitution by the subject, so for Marx nature, the raw material of nature, including the second nature of the objective economic conditions of
existence of human beings, is a natural laboratory, as it says in the *Grundrisse*,
that material substratum that cannot be fully dissolved in society, labor, individual
behavior, and consciousness. In both cases, for Marx and for Kant, what is important for the activity of human beings and what they are capable of knowing is,
however, not this irreducible element but the totality of the forms and circumstances through which it is subjectively and socially mediated.[2]

---

over them, as an unlimited governmental power that protects them against the other classes and sends
them rain and sunshine from above" (pp. 186–88).

2. The spatial horizon of experience of the public sphere belongs also to these forms. Among the
barriers that stand in the way of the constitution of a class in itself (*an sich*) as a class for itself (*für
sich*), the one that can be seen in Marx's analysis of the class struggle in France is not the least significant: the unequal development of the different regions, which are only formally assembled into a
nation. The possibility of a proletarian public sphere as a horizon of experience is here disrupted with
the breakup of the nation into unequally developed zones.

The public sphere of the great French Revolution comprised, in principle, the entirety of humanity;
in reality, however, essential segments of French society were excluded, segments that had nonetheless participated in the Revolution. There is a great deal of evidence to support the assertion that the
most important of the partial successes was gained by the peasants, who, at the decisive moment,
removed the land as a recruiting base for the counterrevolution from feudal control. These peasant
interests, which for hundreds of years had attemped to express themselves in peasant uprisings, were
formally satisfied by the division of the countryside into smallholdings; in the political sphere that the
Revolution engendered, however, they found no expression. While direct democracy was practiced to
a certain extent in Paris, the rest of France—provincial France—was in fact excluded from participation in this sphere. This excluded portion of France avenged itself in that it decided the elections and
responded to every revolution of the nineteenth century up to the Commune by helping the counterrevolution to victory at the decisive moment.

The running forward of the large cities and the move backwards on the part of the entire society of
France are a constitutional, inherent flaw in the French bourgeois public sphere, one from which the
French working class can only receive a false concept of reality, an impracticable form of public space.

Apathy, reforming tendencies, specifically syndicalist forms of the workers' movement, and particu-
larist organization of individual segments of the working class are all attempts to respond to the experience of this impracticable public sphere, which does not permit an "experience" of society as a totality.
With this basic structure are bound up those experiences, described by Marx, of the state and the public
sphere as institutions that serve open class repression and, inasmuch as they are dead, cannot simply be
inverted in the class interests of the workers. Today another level of experience is added to this: that of
the collapse of institutions and of the bourgeois public sphere. In this new, additional experience lies the
key to understanding why the massacres of the nineteenth century were not repeated in May '68.

With respect to the proletarian public sphere, this discussion signifies that the in-itself of society as a whole represents something impenetrable for the individual, something that the senses as presently organized cannot know. The proletarian public sphere exists, however, precisely to the degree that the working class constitutes itself as the subject of revolutionary transformation and thereby represents the interests of society as a whole; this in-itself must be converted into a for-itself.

Antagonistic classes are, in their subjective perspective, not objects to one another. The context whereby this disturbance in perception is mediated is highly complex. It results in the ruling class repeatedly denying that there is any such thing as a proletariat and that, conversely, the workers and their organizations regard a stereotype as the class enemy (whereby it is irrelevant whether this stereotype comprises the obese, brutal, top-hatted factory owner or the employer as "social partner"). This disturbed subject-object relationship of the antagonistic social forces to each other rests only in part on ideological and perceptual distortion: it is at the same time objectively conveyed by the fact that contact between classes is sporadic and partial. In other words, contexts of living are determined via the abstractions of capital relations, but this does not require real contact between them. This determination operates via what are, from the vantage point of the context of living, unreal relations, which recall a bad dream rather than everyday relations between real people. It is precisely this quality that makes it nonpublic, an obstacle to communication, even where this is not intended.

A central question of political conflicts between classes is, accordingly, the specific relationship between the requirements for political constitution, which in the case of bourgeoisie and proletariat are at such different levels that one class no longer even perceives in the other its opposite—not even when they are linked with one another by suppression, resistance actions, struggle, material analysis, calculation, or rage. It has become clear from our analyses thus far that the proletarian class can express itself in neither political nor human terms within the framework of the bourgeois public sphere. This is, however, only one side. It also cannot find itself against this framework, by engaging with an oppositional substance expressed in the bourgeois public sphere: as a negative image of the bourgeois social context the proletariat exists only as a rubblelike accumulation of individual, unconnected qualities.[3] In the process, this bourgeois public sphere is overlaid by the tendencies of capitalism once again to subsume society and the public sphere,[4] to exploit them as raw material, but simultaneously to exclude the social and political content of these efforts from society again. The nonpublic nature of factories, and nonpublic opinion[5] are an expression of the tendency to

---

3. Cf. commentary 20, "The Proletariat—as a Substance and as an Aggregate of Qualities."

4. This subsumption is in part formal, in part real; cf. chapter 6.

5. The concept of nonpublic opinion derives from Franz Böhm; cf. the preliminary remark to *Gruppenexperiment: ein Studienbericht* (Frankfurt am Main: Europäische Verlagsanstalt, 1955).

organize the nerve centers of an apparatus of rule as a point outside of society. Modern capitalism attempts to revoke its social character by the nonpublic sphere, just as under fascism it tried to exaggerate the social character of its activity.[6]

This tendency to adopt a disguise, to distance itself from previous social activity, but at any rate to operate in a nonpublic manner, has a secondary dimension. Should the bourgeois class element prove itself no longer capable of legitimation, the capital nexus frees itself from the latter. The "dictatorship of the bourgeoisie" as it manifests itself, for instance, in the phenomenal force of the bourgeois public sphere, becomes a dictatorship of the *idea* of the bourgeoisie. The bourgeois context of living, which is shaped by private property, dies away if it appears to be an obstacle to further development: one of the "property nexus for itself"[7] with a tendency toward eternalization. This is the experience underlying the sentence "Life does not live."[8] During the golden age of bourgeois life, bourgeois individuals constituted a class in itself and at the same time, in certain restricted spheres (such as music, bourgeois domestic culture), a class for itself. This is the prerequisite for a constitution that is at least in part political. If, by contrast, the capitalist no longer appears in command at all, if he is merely accommodating himself to the functioning of his enterprise and disappears in it, there is no opportunity whatsoever for political constitution and for the constitution of a public sphere. The latter presupposes a minimum of "for-itselfness."[9]

---

6. In both types of reaction in which capitalism separates itself from its own forms, the superstructure is smashed while the base remains as it is. Nothing of these connections, therefore, is altered by the proposition: "Common interest before self-interest."

7. The capacity for labor is a commodity that can speak. The commodity relation, which separates itself from its social consequences, its history, and the class that produced it (that is, from everything that could threaten its existence) is equally a context of objects and relations that can speak—through people who have been made into things. This being-for-itself of the dead apparatus is, however, a complete contradiction to the extent that this process of separation from its own substance, this tendency to live for a thousand years, to live eternally (Karl Marx: "mors immortalis"—eternal death) can only move by means of the always renewed incorporation of contexts of living. This context of repression does not, however, thereby ground itself.

8. Ferdinand Kürnberger, as quoted in Theodor W. Adorno, *Minima Moralia. Reflexionen aus dem beschädigten Leben* (Frankfurt am Main: 1971): 13.

9. It is consistent when, in the course of this line of development, Krupp labels himself a philanthropist, when an industrialist like Flick, with a thermos bottle and a slice of bread and butter, demonstrates a repudiation of consumption in meetings of the executive or supervisory board. Another example is furnished by the preventative health examinations that travel from the managers of European subsidiaries to the parent companies in the United States and in which the physical-material functioning of the former is more carefully considered than, for example, the accounts. As regards the range of this absorption of human qualities into a simply functional context, the provincial character that capitalistic development in most European nations currently has is somewhat deceptive. It is for this reason that the appearance of the continued existence of "personality" can arise again and again, even where it no longer determines the real conditions and where it is no longer presupposed by them.

# 20. The Proletariat—as a Substance and as an Aggregate of Qualities

After a television production of Gerhart Hauptmann's *The Weavers* an employers' organization came forward with the following criticism: under present conditions it is an expression of bias and a distortion of the true situation for such a play from the nineteenth century to be broadcast to two million viewers without a commentary depicting how the condition of the workers and the behavior of the entrepreneurs have changed. They requested that this picture of history be corrected.

Underlying such an intervention is the premise that in the nineteenth century there was indeed a proletariat as a concrete historical phenomenon as described by Marx—in exaggerated terms, in the view of the employers—but that since then the situation of the workers has undergone a fundamental transformation so that today it is only possible to speak of a proletariat in ideological terms. A similar reading underlay the Nazis' assertion that the "Volksgenosse" had taken the place of the proletarian. This procedure is repeated by a series of sociologists who address the question, "Is there still a proletariat?" They set out from the premise that there was originally a tangible proletariat. In these analyses, this conception of a proletariat is generally not broken down into its real elements but is generalized into a concept of subject, stylized into a whole. Then the absence of this substantive whole is empirically established in the real existence of workers, and from this is declared the fact that essential transformation of the working class has taken place. What we have here is first and foremost a confusion of cognitive levels. Whereas the historical proletariat is registered phenomenologically and as an ideal type, the present life conditions of the workers are investigated empirically, in other words, with a view to discovering the specific form in which their existence expresses itself (for instance, their picture of society, the work they do, wage expectations, job satisfaction, etc.).

In complete contrast to this viewpoint is that of dogmatic and revisionist orthodoxies, which emphatically hold fast to the substantive concept of the proletariat, yet at the same time follow a concept of progress according to which the productive focus and technical and scientific development have undergone changes that make it possible today for the masses to transform the functioning of the historically merged productive forces and production techniques in a proletarian sense. Underlying this is the notion that a substantive proletariat can do away with the bourgeois relations of production and take over the legacy, that is, the state of the productive forces, as it is. By this means, technical development, the aggregate of the relations of production, and the proletariat are reified as something substantive and globalized. The bourgeois and proletarian components in "productive forces" and "proletariat," grasped in reified terms as substantive aggregates cannot be separated from one another. The striving toward ever greater "strength" of both these forces, simultaneously with the rational kernel they contain, drags irrational moments with it. The rationality of the party has to turn against the bourgeois relations of rule also conveyed thereby. This results in a division between social theory and empirical reality, political-ideological standpoint and economic practice; it results in a parallelism. The workers' state and workers' culture contain undivided bourgeois and proletarian elements, to which mass loyalty to the socialist fatherland is attached. Work for economic reconstruction embraces, undivided, the proletarian element of work for one's own class, but also the reproduction of the conditions of rule solidified in the industrial labor process. Thereby the hopes, wishes, and illusions that the workers in reality possess can, during leisure, attach themselves to the output of Western television, while at the same time real loyalties have developed toward their own state and its social system in the production process.

Proletarian does not under all social conditions denote a social substance. Thus for instance fascism is "not merely a system of reprisals, of brutal force, and of police terror. Fascism is a particular governmental system based on the uprooting of all elements of proletarian democracy within bourgeois society. The task of fascism lies not only in destroying the Communist vanguard but in holding the entire class in a state of forced disunity. To this end the physical annihilation of the most revolutionary section of the workers does not suffice. It is also necessary to smash all independent and voluntary organizations, to demolish all the defensive bulwarks of the proletariat, and to uproot whatever has been achieved during three-quarters of a century by the Social Democracy and the trade unions. For, in the last analysis, the Communist party also bases itself on these achievements."[1]

It is not, however, only with fascism but earlier that the context of living governed and destroyed by capitalism results in making the workers appendages of

---

1. Leon Trotsky, *Schriften über Deutschland, Gesammelte Werke,* vol. 1 (Frankfurt: 1971): 182.

commodity production, their qualities as human beings unconnected. The proletarian context of living is thus initially defined *negatively*, as a context of blockage wherein experience, needs, wishes, and hopes do concretely come into being but cannot develop in an autonomous fashion. Here the qualities that are taken up by the process of valorization have a different fate from those that are not, and those qualities subject to direct suppression yet another. Those qualities relevant for the process of valorization have the chance to be developed by forced growth; they take part at the highest level of industrial development and technical discipline, but as isolated qualities. A particularly vivid example is the varying development of the qualities of the technical intelligentsia, the specialization of communicative capacities, the development of cooperative qualities. Those human qualities that are not taken up by this valorization interest are subject to only a limited indirect integration. But they do not therefore participate in the highest level of the development of the productive forces; they develop specific atrophied forms and are, in societal terms, linked with one another only in a naturally rooted, random way, at a lower level of production. They are further isolated by the fact that, like the leisure interests, for example, they remain governed by the valorization interest. This includes almost all the cultural and leisure interests of the workers, the qualities that are developed in the family and in the educational institutions but are not directly necessary for employment: hobbies, ideals, and so on.

Whereas these qualities are left to one side, those qualities and needs that are directly exposed to repression are governed by their generally powerless confrontation with the ruling interest. They very likely organize themselves at the highest level of development, precisely on account of the pressure they are subject to. Examples of this are, among other things, sexuality, the activity of the imagination, infringements of the property order. This last set of behavioral modes has the strongest tendency to develop proletarian forms of organization beneath the surface of bourgeois rule. To incorporate them into bourgeois interests is, so long as they are being suppressed, impossible. At the same time, they do not find a form of their own but are in an almost constant pattern of evasion. Within the real proletarian context of living these qualities cannot, as occurs here, be conceptually separated from one another; on the contrary, one and the same quality often takes part in several of these deformations. Under developed capitalist rule, the following holds for proletarian qualities: **from the standpoint of nonemancipation, they are something cohesive; from the standpoint of emancipation, noncohesive.**

Real historical developments do not move on the side of the "complete person" and "whole proletarian" but on the side of their individual qualities.[2] Within these

2. Marx points out a quite similar inversion of subject and predicate in his critique of Hegel's philosophy of the state. According to Marx, Hegel inverts throughout the relationship between the idea and the subject, so that the authentic, real subject of historical movement becomes the predicate. To

individual qualities, in specific fundamental situations, there exist subject-object relations that are not visible to the individual against the background of the totality of the context of oppression. These qualities are aggregated into a subjective capacity for action above all in immediate situations of struggle. In these, however, the danger exists that the otherwise fragmented qualities will be brought together and organized more rapidly than they in fact change, than their own process of development makes necessary.

Class struggles have in this respect their own schematism. For the sake of the identity of those engaged in them, these struggles must anticipate; they must suppose individuals as being whole, whereas the individual proletarian qualities must first transform and organize themselves and separate themselves from the bourgeois components associated with them. In this process, the development of proletarian qualities, the division of individual, historically acquired qualities into their bourgeois and proletarian elements, the freeing of proletarian qualities from distortion, and the connecting of the suppressed as well as the underdeveloped with the highly developed qualities, is, for the moment, brought to a halt—and indeed at precisely those moments where the qualities are set in motion and encounter a situation in which they could organize themselves for themselves.[3]

---

sum up this critique of Hegel: "Development always takes the lead on the side of the predicate" (*Marx-Engels Werke*, vol. 1, p. 209).

3. "Human essence" is thus not a natural substance whose essence has only been inverted by capitalism, to which a return is possible in Rousseau's sense. On the contrary, the human individual first develops as the result of the complete appropriation of his past history. In this context, Marx comments: "The senses therefore directly become theoreticians in their practice. They behave toward the object at hand for the sake of the object; the object itself is a concrete human behavior toward itself and toward human beings, and vice versa. It is only practically possible for me to behave humanely toward the object if the object behaves humanely toward human beings" (*Marx-Engels Werke*, vol. 1, p. 241). It is the individual faculties and individual senses, just as they are produced diffusely by historical development, the proletarian raw material, that make up the content of the proletarian public sphere. Here the proletarian public sphere is the aggregate of situations in which this human sensuality, which has been repressed and which has emerged distorted in relation to capital, comes into its own in a process of subject-object relationships that are linked together. Proletarian public sphere is the name for a process of collective social production whose object is coherent human sensuality.

# Index

Compiled by Hassan Melehy

Koch, Gertrud, xxv n. 28
Koestler, Arthur, 246 n. 9
Kohl, Helmut, xv
Korsch, Karl, 102, 196
Kracauer, Siegfried, xvii, xviii
Krahl, Hans-Jürgen, 85 n. 50
Kraus, Karl, 45 n. 67
Krinsky, S., 277
Krovoza, Alfred, 85 n. 50
Kruger, Loren, xxii n. 23
Kubrick, Stanley, 23 n. 39
Kuda, Rudolf, 197 n. 4
Kunfi, Sigmund, 222
Kürnberger, Ferdinand, 293 n. 8

Labanyi, Peter, ix n. 1
labor: and capital, 20; and commodity, 132–33;
    in England, 187–200, 201–4; and intelli-
    gentsia, 41; and television, 121–24. *See also*
    production; proletariat
Labriola, Arturo, 218
Laclau, Ernesto, xxxii n. 40
Lafayette, Marie Joseph, 245
Landes, Joan, xxviii
language: popular and written, 272–75; and pub-
    lic sphere, 45–49
Larsen, Ernst, xxv n. 28
Larsen, Otto, 99 n. 3
Ledoux, Claude, 278 n. 8, 280
Lengyel, Julius, 222
Lenin, V. I., xlv n. 3, 43, 58, 162, 165, 170, 199
    n. 8, 201–4, 219, 234, 235, 239, 241, 246 n.
    9, 253, 260, 261, 262–63, 270–71, 274, 277
    n. 4, 278
Lequeu, Jean-Jacques, 278 n. 8, 280, 281
Lessing, Gabriele, 277 n. 4
Lethen, H., 49 n. 70
Levin, Thomas, xxxiii n. 44
libidinal economy: and cognitive drive, 23–25
Liebknecht, Karl, 43
Liebman, Stuart, xxv n. 28, xxxv n. 47, xxxv n.
    49, xxxvii n. 51
Liebmann, R., 65 n. 17
Lin Piao, 272
Lippmann, Walter, xi
Litvinov, Maksim, 239
Lloyd George, David, 202
Locke, John, 98
Lorenzer, Alfred, 47 n. 68
Louis XIV, 73

Lukács, Georg, xxii, 36 n. 55, 255–57
Luxemburg, Rosa, 43, 77 n. 36

MacEwen, M., 197 n. 4
Makarenko, Anton, 20 n. 31
Mandel, Ernest, 63–64 n. 15, 66 n. 19
Mao Tse-tung, 27 n. 44, 43, 185, 245, 275
Marcuse, Herbert, xxi, 171, 210 n. 5, 220, 286
Marx, Karl, xxv, xxxiv, xlv-xlvi, xlvii, 2 n. 3, 8
    n. 15, 12 n. 22, 17, 28, 30, 33 n. 53, 38–39,
    45, 56 n. 7, 67, 73 n. 31, 74, 81, 82–84, 88,
    106 n. 12, 130, 132–33, 153–54, 160, 161 n.
    3, 162 n. 5, 164, 175, 177, 178, 180, 183, 184
    n. 33, 186 n. 36, 187, 195, 196, 201 n. 1,
    205–6, 209, 210 n. 4, 222, 225, 243–44,
    250–51, 252 n. 2, 254, 258 n. 1, 264, 265 n.
    3, 267 n. 6, 269 n. 9, 269 n. 10, 274, 290–91,
    293 n. 7, 294, 296–97 n. 2, 297 n. 3
mass media: and capitalism, 133–34; and con-
    sciousness industry, 138–43, 149–51; and
    context of living, 149–59; and film industry,
    152 n. 8; and otherness, 274; and production,
    130–34; and public sphere, xx, xxii, xxiv-
    xxv, xxix-xxx, xliii, xlviii-xlix, 135–37,
    144–48; and Taylorism, 153–54. *See also*
    cinema; culture; television
Mayer, Margit, xv n. 7
McLuhan, Marshall, xl, 115 n. 23
Merleau-Ponty, Maurice, 248–49
Metzler, Dieter, 275 n. 2
Meusel, Alfred, 252 n. 3
Miliband, Ralph, 67
Mills, C. Wright, xi
Morse, Margaret, xxv n. 28
Mouffe, Chantal, xxxii n. 40
Münzenberg, Willi, 270
Musil, Robert, 75 n. 33, 157 n. 17, 167
Mussolini, Benito, 55 n. 3, 215, 221

Napier, Charles J., 192–93
Napoleon III, 55 n. 3
Napoleon, 280
National Socialism, 31, 66, 69, 75–76, 78, 79 n.
    39, 152 n. 10, 166–69, 171–72 n. 16, 186,
    213, 219, 241, 281–82, 294; and societiliza-
    tion, 163. *See also* fascism; Hitler, Adolf
Negrín, Juan López, 42 n. 65
Nelson, Cary, xxx n. 36
Neumann, Franz, 63, 66 n. 20, 68 n. 26, 75–76,
    210 n. 5